State, Economy and Public Policy in Australia

Edited by Stephen Bell and Brian Head

Melbourne
OXFORD UNIVERSITY PRESS
Oxford Auckland New York

OXFORD UNIVERSITY PRESS AUSTRALIA

Oxford New York Toronto
Delhi Bombay Calcutta Madras Karachi
Kuala Lumpur Singapore Hong Kong Tokyo
Nairobi Dar es Salaam Cape Town
Melbourne Auckland Madrid
and associated companies in
Berlin Ibadan

OXFORD is a trade mark of Oxford University Press

© Stephen Bell and Brian Head 1994
First published 1994

This book is copyright. Apart from any fair
dealing for the purposes of private study,
research, criticism or review as permitted under
the Copyright Act, no part may be reproduced,
stored in a retrieval system, or transmitted, in
any form or by any means, electronic, mechanical,
photocopying, recording or otherwise, without
prior written permission. Enquiries to be made to
Oxford University Press.

Copying for educational purposes
Where copies of part or the whole of the book are
made under Section 53B or Section 53D of the Act,
the law requires that records of such copying be
kept. In such cases the copyright owner is
entitled to claim payment.

National Library of Australia
Cataloguing-in-Publication data:

State, economy and public policy in Australia.
ISBN 0 19 553401 8.

1. Australia—Economic conditions—1965– .
2. Australia—Economic policy—1965– . I. Head, Brian, 1948–
II. Bell, Stephen, 1954–

338.994

Edited by Cathryn Game
Indexed by Liz Clark
Typeset by Solo Typesetting
Printed by McPherson's Printing Group
Published by Oxford University Press,
253 Normanby Road, South Melbourne, Australia

Contents

Figures and tables	*ix*
Preface	*xi*

1 AUSTRALIA'S POLITICAL ECONOMY:
    CRITICAL THEMES AND ISSUES
    Stephen Bell and Brian Head   1
    State and economy   2
    Australia's historical pattern of state–economy relations 7
    Australia joins the world economy   11
    The politics of economic adjustment   14
    A receding state?   18
    Notes   21

2 UNDERSTANDING THE MODERN STATE:
    EXPLANATORY APPROACHES
    Brian Head and Stephen Bell   25
    Liberal approaches   26
    Neo-Marxist approaches   41
    Corporatism   55
    Statism   60
    Conclusions   64
    Notes   68

3 AUSTRALIA AND THE GLOBAL ECONOMY
John Ravenhill — 75
The consequences of domestic insulation — 77
Globalisation of the world economy — 81
The Australian response — 87
Australia in a globalised economy — 89
Notes — 93

4 GLOBALISATION, ECONOMIC RESTRUCTURING AND THE STATE
Belinda Probert — 98
Restructuring or post-Fordism? — 99
Australia and the internationalisation of capitalism — 104
Globalisation, social structure and inequality — 108
Post-Fordist politics — 110
What role for the Australian state? — 113
Notes — 116

5 THE POWER OF ECONOMIC IDEAS? KEYNESIAN ECONOMIC POLICIES IN POST-WAR AUSTRALIA
Greg Whitwell — 119
What is Keynesianism? — 120
From balanced budgets to discretionary fiscal policy — 121
'The political power of economic ideas' — 123
Hall's three criteria and the Australian experience — 125
Conclusion — 139
Notes — 140

6 THE ARBITRATION SYSTEM SINCE 1967
Braham Dabscheck — 142
Institutional setting: Australia's three-tiered system of wage determination — 144
1967–74: The total wage — 147
1975–82: From wage indexation to a wages freeze — 150

1983–93: The Accord(s) to enterprise bargaining	*154*
Summary and conclusion: Can lightning strike in the same place thrice?	*161*
Notes	*163*

7 THE POLITICAL ECONOMY OF FEDERALISM SINCE 1970

Peter Groenewegen	*169*
A statistical overview of fiscal federalism 1972–93	*170*
Three new federalism policies: Whitlam, Fraser and Hawke	*175*
Vertical fiscal imbalance	*178*
Alternative revenue-sharing possibilities	*180*
Tied grants for specific purposes	*182*
Fiscal equalisation: What role for the Grants Commission?	*184*
The Loan Council and public investment	*187*
Policy coordination for national microeconomic reform	*187*
Is there a federalism agenda for the 1990s?	*189*
Notes	*190*

8 EMPLOYERS' ASSOCIATIONS, CORPORATISM AND THE ACCORD: THE POLITICS OF INDUSTRIAL RELATIONS

Trevor Matthews	*194*
Australian employers and the problem of collective action	*195*
The structures of business representation	*202*
The Accord: Corporatism without business	*207*
Employers take the initiative: Enterprise bargaining	*210*
Conclusion	*216*
Notes	*218*

9 CAN THE STATE 'MANAGE' THE MACROECONOMY?

John Wanna	*225*
State–economy relations	*226*
Economic management before 1980	*228*

Macroeconomic problems and policy responses of the
1980s and early 1990s   229
Limits of policy: Having impact but not
necessarily managing   234
Winners and losers: Sectoral impacts of economic policy   236
Can the state manage the 'economy'?   238
Conclusions   242
Notes   244

10 STATE STRENGTH AND STATE WEAKNESS: MANUFACTURING INDUSTRY AND THE POST-WAR AUSTRALIAN STATE
Stephen Bell   250

Reactive and anticipatory industry policy, weak states
and strong states   252
Australia's pattern?   256
Conclusion   265
Notes   266

11 MICROECONOMIC REFORM
Rolf Gerritsen   269

The Australian political economy and
microeconomic reform   270
Modelling microeconomic reform   273
Why did microeconomic reform issues arise in the 1980s?   277
The conditions for success or failure?   279
Three sets of microeconomic reform case studies   282
The future 'politics' of microeconomic reform?   285
Conclusion   287
Notes   288

12 THE WELFARE STATE AND ECONOMIC ADJUSTMENT
Lois Bryson   291

Increasing demands on the welfare state   292

Demands on the Australian social security system	295
Responses to increasing demands in a time of economic adjustment	296
The overtaking of the 'wage-earners' welfare state'	306
Notes	311

13 THE GREENHOUSE EFFECT AND THE POLITICS OF LONG-TERM ISSUES

Ian Lowe	315
The greenhouse effect	316
A short history of Australian responses	317
Greenhouse: The political debate	319
Formulation of public policy	322
Features of Australian public policy	323
Business constraints on policy change	325
Prospects for a long-term view	328
Conclusion	330
Notes	330

14 ENVIRONMENT, ECONOMY AND STATE

Elim Papadakis and Anya Moore	334
Competing paradigms	336
Transforming the institutional order	337
Transforming the ALP regime	340
Controlling the agenda	342
The developers	346
The environmentalists	348
Conclusion	350
Notes	351

15 WOMEN, THE STATE AND PUBLIC POLICY

Marian Simms	354
Femocrats	356

The women's movement and the state	*359*
Women and the electoral arena	*363*
Feminist theory and the state	*366*
Notes	*372*

CONTRIBUTORS — *375*

INDEX — *378*

Figures and tables

Figure 3.1	Australia's terms of trade, 1950–92	*76*
Table 3.1	The Australian economy in comparative perspective	*80*
Figure 3.2	Current account balance as a percentage of GDP	*81*
Figure 3.3	Trade-weighted exchange rate of the Australian dollar	*82*
Figure 3.4	Australia's principal export markets, 1990	*82*
Figure 3.5	Australia's net overseas debt	*91*
Table 6.1	National wage case increases as a percentage of changes in male average minimum wages, 1967–68 to 1974–75	*148*
Table 6.2	Wage indexation increases as a percentage of change in total wage, 1975–81	*151*
Appendix 6.1	Australian economic indicators, 1967–68 to 1991–92	*162*
Appendix 6.2	Industrial disputes in Australia, 1967 to 1991	*163*
Table 7.1	Funds available to state and local government sectors from Commonwealth payments to and borrowing by states and territories, selected years 1971–72 to 1992–93	*171*
Table 7.2	Commonwealth payments to state and local government sectors by function (net basis), selected years 1971–72 to 1992–93	*172*
Table 7.3	Sources of revenue for each level of government 1989–90 (%)	*179*

Preface

The problems of Australia's economic performance have seen economic policy take centre stage in public life in recent years. Yet if much of politics has been dominated by economics, it is also true that economic life is strongly influenced by politics. This book seeks to contribute to the growing literature in political economy by analysing the relationships between the state and economy in Australia. In particular, the book is designed to explore the political, institutional, ideological and historical dimensions of critical public policy issues, especially those linked to economic policy.

The book can be read as a series of essays exploring the role and capacities of the state in Australian economic life, both in historical and in more contemporary terms. It can also be read as an analysis of the politics of economic, environmental and social policy, with particular emphasis on the state's role in shaping policy outcomes. The book should prove useful to both undergraduate and post-graduate students in a range of disciplines, particularly politics, economics, sociology and history.

Given the wide practical and theoretical scope of the field of state–economy relations, there are inevitable gaps in a collection such as this. Nevertheless many arenas of state activity and state–economy interaction are explored. Moreover, one of the unifying themes of many chapters is an effort to understand the policy complexities of recent efforts to confront the challenge of structural economic adjustment.

No attempt was made to impose a uniform or overarching theoretical framework. The first two chapters in the volume provide broad contextual and theoretical treatments of state–economy relations. Subsequent chapters deploy a wide range of analytical strategies to analyse specific issues and policy arenas.

We would like to thank Liz Clark and Rosemary Smuts at the University of Tasmania for research and computing assistance. We also thank Jill Lane of OUP for her encouragement and patience.

1

Australia's political economy: Critical themes and issues

Stephen Bell and Brian Head

In the economic debates of the 1960s the leading economist Peter Karmel emphasised what he saw as the market-oriented character of Australia's capitalist economy. 'The Australian economy', he wrote, 'is predominantly a private enterprise market economy ... the allocation of resources ... is determined by the forces of supply and demand.'[1] The following year the federal Treasury espoused a similar view, seeing Australia as a 'predominantly free enterprise' economy, a view also traditionally shared by business.[2] Yet such market-oriented notions did not go unchallenged. Writers such as Max Newton, for example, saw the need to debunk what he saw as the prevailing free enterprise 'myths' in Australia and argued instead that the history of the state's economic role in this country amounted to a form of 'de facto economic planning'.[3] Sol Encel made much the same point when he argued that 'government enterprise, intervention, regulation and protection have for more than a century been the dominant factors in the growth of industry'.[4] Although at first appearing contradictory, both of these competing depictions from the 1960s were in fact reasonably accurate. The apparent contradiction stems only from conflating different aspects or different levels of Australia's historic pattern of state–economy relations. Australia's peculiar mixture of market forces and state intervention in the economy and the changing complexion of this mixture through time are the focus of this chapter, which is designed to introduce critical themes and issues in Australia's changing pattern of state–economy relations.

The chapter begins by discussing various generic aspects of the state's role in capitalist economic systems as a prelude to looking more specifically at the historical dimensions of the state's economic role in the Australian context. The chapter then looks at the way in which Australia's changing role in the world economy has challenged, in recent decades, Australia's historic pattern of state–economy relations. This leads to a discussion of some of the key political variables that have shaped recent efforts to restructure state–economy relationships. The chapter closes by considering the issue of whether such efforts are producing a substantial reduction of the state's economic role in this country. Overall, the purpose of this chapter is to provide an overview of the critical dimensions of Australia's political economy, especially in relation to the analyses that follow in subsequent chapters.

State and economy

The boundaries between the state and other spheres (such as economy or society) are usually drawn simply by listing the specific institutions in each sphere. For example, social institutions include family/household structures, religious and cultural institutions, the organisation of gender and ethnic relations, and voluntary associations. However, the overlap and mutual interdependence of social, economic and governmental/ administrative activities and resources is much greater than is implied by mainstream economic theory.[5] The latter, as developed from the 'classical political economy' of Adam Smith through to twentieth-century marginalist and neo-classical approaches, has explained economic activity in terms of individuals seeking to optimise benefits through rational exchange of goods and services. According to Friedman, and other champions of this *individualistic* market conception, the role of the state is ideally limited to a few 'core' functions such as providing defence, law and order, and general rules of fair dealing. The state is seen as an external body, parasitic on a free society, but a necessary evil to avoid the greater evils of coercion and insecurity.[6]

In response to the naivety and historical amnesia of market individualism, diverse groups of economists (including Keynesian and neo-Marxist writers) have developed alternative frameworks that recognise the significant *institutional* basis of economic and governmental activities, the role of non-market economic transactions and the importance of constraints and hierarchies affecting economic choices.[7] The realities of oligopoly and barriers against new players entering a market are well recognised by most economists. The extent of competition clearly varies considerably in different product markets, both in the private and public sectors. As Rolf Gerritsen argues in chapter 11, removing impediments to competition became the underlying rationale for 'microeconomic reform' in the 1980s and 1990s.

The role of government in modern economies vastly exceeds the narrow role recommended by Friedman, who detects unnecessary and wasteful interventionism in every policy area. Governmental economic policy spans several key dimensions, including fiscal, monetary, industrial, infrastructure, innovation, training, trade and welfare policies. Economic stabilisation and external trade balance are core objectives, but most governments have sought, for electoral reasons, to induce economic growth preferably at a rate higher than that of comparable nations. Economic policy is highly politicised owing to several factors, including divergent policy approaches in political party platforms, mobilisation of interests around specific programs and the inevitability of winners and losers from economic restructuring and policy changes. Much of the debate on economic policy consists of hard-nosed debate about sectional interests overlaid by the rhetoric of efficiency and the national interest.

In the economy, then, politics matters, and in formal Westminster terms it is elected governments (through control over parliament) that hold power in liberal democracies such as Australia. Yet it is important in analysing state–economy relations to focus on more than the policy actions of particular governments. Indeed, although it is commonplace to speak of 'government' intervention in the economy, in reality a wide range of public institutions have an impact on the economy, many of which have a good deal of operational autonomy from the government of the day. It is often more appropriate, then, to speak of 'state'–economy relations because the concept of the state is better able to incorporate the fact that a wide range of public agencies, departments and statutory authorities, not just governments, interact with the economy.[8] *The state* is a collective institutional term, useful in forms of analysis that see public policy outputs as resulting not just from the actions of government but also from wider patterns of activity and institutional dynamics within the state, particularly the role of key departments and independent statutory authorities. The concept of the state is also useful because it focuses attention on the way in which relatively embedded practices of public institutions and past patterns of policy often have enduring effects well beyond the tenure of specific governments.

Definitions vary but *the state* is essentially the entire apparatus of formal roles and public institutions that exercise political authority over populations within a given territory. Modern Western states began to emerge in Europe from the sixteenth century, and large historical shifts involving the transition from feudalism to capitalism, the breakdown of absolutist rule, as well as industrialisation and warfare, have since forged the modern system of nation states.[9] Under democratic regimes, the legitimacy of the state and its authority to make and enforce laws is seen to rest on popular consent or on some kind of democratic mandate. Authoritarian states, on the other hand, often rule on the basis of force and repression and seek to suppress the organisations and expressions of critical dissent typical of a liberal–democratic regime.

Modern liberal–democratic states may be characterised and analysed in a wide range of ways.[10] As a first step, however, it is useful to see the state as consisting of a complex set of interacting institutions and, in this regard, it is traditional to distinguish between the executive, legislative and judicial branches of the state apparatus.[11] The legislature is the law-making arm of the state but also has a crucial role in determining the composition of government, which requires majority control of votes within parliament. The executive arm of the state has expanded considerably in historical terms and consists of the governing élite (in Australia the cabinet or ministry is drawn from the ruling party/s in parliament), together with the bureaucratic apparatus of administration, implementation, enforcement and repression (e.g. public service departments, regulatory agencies, military and police forces, public utilities and state trading enterprises, diplomatic and intelligence personnel, etc.). The judicial apparatus of the state interprets law and passes authoritative judgement in the settlement of legal disputes. This role typically encompasses areas of criminal or commercial law, but in federal political systems, such as Australia, the High Court also plays a key role in interpreting the constitution and in settling disputes between Federal and State Governments.

In institutional terms, then, *the state* is a more expansive term than *government*. The government is but one component of the wider state apparatus and is the ruling party or coalition within parliament, which (under Westminster-style systems) forms the ministry and controls the operations and decisions of cabinet. Nor is the state the same as the 'public sector'. The latter term is generally used to refer to the part of the economy that comes under public ownership and control. Normally, the 'public' world of state institutions is contrasted with the nominally 'private' realm of civil society and the 'private' capitalist economy. In reality, however, such sharp notional boundaries are often blurred. Defence contractors in the US, for example, are intimately connected to the major defence bureaucracies. In other contexts, the state organises private interests and, in some cases, nominally private-interest associations are granted a role as 'private-interest governments' in order to administer aspects of public policy.[12] Even more elaborately, in corporatist policy arrangements, associations representing labour and capital may attain a quasi-public status acting in tandem with the state as co-developers and implementers of public policy.[13]

In liberal–democratic countries such as Australia, the power and authority of the state is often fragmented, and the formal authority that governments have in determining public policy is often not the same as real control. An elected government might be frustrated in implementing key areas of its policy program, not only because of opposition from organised economic and social interests or because of unfavourable economic or international conditions, but also because of ineffective control over its 'own' state apparatus. The degree of such control depends on constitutional constraints and administrative complexities. Far from being a monolithic entity, the state might be torn by internal conflict and find it difficult to orchestrate coherent policies. In some cases governments have little administrative control over key, formally 'independent' statutory authorities. In other cases the government's policy and administrative capacities are constrained by bureaucratic routines, the priorities of bureaucratic élites, traditions of civil/political control over the military and police forces, judicial independence, and the state's ability to raise revenue through taxation or borrowing.[14]

In federal political systems the autonomy and policy capacities of national and regional governments are further circumscribed by constitutional mandate. In Australia, for example, there has existed a formal division of powers between State and Commonwealth Governments since Federation in 1901. On the one hand, the states are responsible for service provision in education, welfare, transport, health and public housing, and they also provide or regulate energy supply, prices, courts, prisons, police, mineral exploration, land use, environment, consumer affairs, ports, roads, water resources, some forms of taxation and most aspects of criminal, civil and commercial law. The Commonwealth, on the other hand, has national responsibilities for defence and external affairs; powers that include overseas trade and investment, immigration, customs and excise. The Commonwealth controls the issuing of currency, the regulation of interstate trade and industrial arbitration, posts and telecommunications, and corporations and banking. Over time the Commonwealth has also gained power over Aboriginal affairs, income taxation, social security, public sector borrowing and civil aviation, and it has exercised influence over the states through tied grants for areas of state responsibility such as education, transport and health services.

The political economy of federalism is discussed more fully by Peter Groenewegen in chapter 7, but for now it is useful to note that Australian federalism has tended to produce a complex and often contradictory set of structures, in many cases fragmenting 'national' policy-making and opening many points of influence for economic interests. The result has often produced a tussle between State and Commonwealth Governments over a range of economic policy issues.[15] The subcentral structures of public authority in Australia were dominant at the time of Federation in 1901, and although there has been a steady growth in the scope and importance of central (federal) responsibilities, these subcentral levels of public authority have not yet lost their significance in Australian public policy.

Such conflicts often reflect bureaucratic rivalries, jurisdictional disputes, partisan differences between governing parties and buck-passing between State and Commonwealth Governments as well as the alignment of State Governments with particular regional economic interests. Interstate economic conflicts are often translated into policy conflicts within the federal arena. This is because the Federal Government controls exports, tariffs, imports, foreign capital inflows, company income tax, export incentives and other policy areas which have a differential impact on the various clusters of industries located in different states. In the tariff arena, for example, there have historically been conflicts between the resource-rich states of Queensland and Western Australia (which have favoured tariff cuts) and the manufacturing states, particularly South Australia and Victoria (which resisted tariff reductions).

Yet it is important not to exaggerate the argument that federalism equals policy conflict and fragmentation. Nor is it correct to see the concerns of State Governments as a simple reflection of regional economic pressures. Indeed, since the late 1980s, there has been a good deal of cooperation between the states and the Commonwealth over pressing issues of economic restructuring, particularly in key areas of microeconomic reform (transport, the waterfront, etc.) and in establishing a more coherent approach to national regulatory standards.[16]

In general terms, there are many ways to describe the role of the state within capitalist economic systems and within liberal–democratic regimes. One relatively eclectic approach is simply to list broad areas of functional activity. For example, Davis, Wanna, Warhurst and Weller describe the state as an economic developer and producer (promoting economic development through subsidising private investment, producing various goods and services, providing infrastructure or acting as a joint venturer); as a protector and upholder (general welfare state provisions, law and order and the defence of property rights, as well as military defence and security operations); as a regulator (control or prohibition of activities in relation to business or the labour market, as well as immigration controls); as an arbitrator (adjudication of disputes); and as an organiser (influencing or sponsoring the organisation of societal interests and groups and favouring some groups over others).[17]

Other writers, particularly Marxists and radicals, have analysed state action as a process of serving the interests of the capitalist class and, more broadly, the needs of capitalism as a system. From such a perspective, the actions of states within capitalist democracies are seen in terms of a number of key functions or principles. Marxists such as Claus Offe, for example, have posited four operational principles that are imposed on the state in any liberal–capitalist system.[18] The first principle is exclusion: there is a formal separation between the state and economy under capitalism, and the state is barred from directly controlling key parameters of the economy, particularly investment and production decisions. These are left largely to private enterprise. The second principle, which follows from the first, is dependence: this principle holds that the state is dependent on capital and the capitalist-dominated accumulation process, not only for state revenues (through taxation) but also for the economic prosperity and electoral viability on which governments depend. The third principle is maintenance: this follows from the dependence principle and involves maintaining and servicing the needs of the capital accumulation process in terms of a range of state actions and inputs, such as corporate tax relief, industry subsidies and public infrastructure support. The fourth principle is legitimation: this particularly involves policies such as welfare provision, education and the maintenance of law and order aimed at reducing class conflict and enhancing societal acceptance of the capitalist system. Theories of the state in capitalist societies are discussed in more detail in chapter 2.

Australia's historical pattern of state–economy relations

Offe's conceptualisation of state–economy relations within capitalist democracies could be a useful starting point for analysis of a particular system such as Australia. Nevertheless, it is a highly generalised account, and it assumes a pervasive capitalistic logic which is often unable to explain more detailed state–economy interactions in specific contexts. Moreover, Offe's account has little capacity to explain the often marked differences in patterns of state–economy relations found in different capitalist economies or the changes in such patterns in the same economy over time. In this sense, Offe's account is essentially generic and ahistorical.

The limits of such an approach become obvious when examining the historically pervasive role of the state in promoting and structuring capitalist economic development in the Australian context. The character of economic development in the nineteenth century in this country was marked not by a private enterprise capitalist juggernaut served by a dependent state. In many respects, the opposite was the case. As Pusey puts it, the state 'was *not excluded* from the private economy but rather joined it in a relationship of strong partnership'.[19] Indeed, it was not until the 1930s that private investment outstripped public investment in the economy.[20] Such a pattern is hardly consistent with Offe's exclusion principle; a principle that only really held in the classic laissez-faire developmental contexts of early industrialising societies such as Britain and the US. In Australia the problems of infrastructure provision (roads, railways, ports, urban services, communications) in a vast and sparsely settled continent saw colonial governments, not private enterprise, play a leading role in underpinning the process of economic development. According to Butlin:

> *Traditionally, Australian colonial governments during the second half of the nineteenth century performed what was, in effect, a general management role in their economies. In its essence 'colonial socialism' entailed direct action by governments to attract foreign (British) resources of labour and capital, through public borrowing overseas and large-scale programmes of publicly-assisted migration; the investment of British capital in publicly-owned fixed assets in Australia; the concentration of this investment in public business undertakings, primarily in transport and communications; and the delivery of market services by these public enterprises.*[21]

Nor was the state a simple defender or legitimator of untrammelled capitalist interests during this period. In a classic encounter between what writers such as Polanyi would see as the confrontation between the forces of social amelioration versus the untamed market,[22] coalitions of urban social liberals and labour movement reformers forced through a range of measures that centred on democratic rights, wages, working conditions and welfare legislation. By the depression of the 1890s working-class mobilisation had forged the first labour party in the world, and colonial governments enacted measures including compulsory arbitration of industrial disputes, wages boards, old age pensions, unemployment relief work, labour bureaux and women's enfranchisement. By the turn of the century Australia was widely seen as one of the world's 'laboratories of social reform and democracy'.[23]

Moreover, the impact of the gold rushes and the strength of Australia's export staples economy, particularly the wool economy, had produced a level of economic prosperity that saw Australia's per capita income level the highest in the world at the turn of the century. In relative terms, Australians were rich, and they wanted to stay that way. In the context of Australia's tradition of active state involvement in economic development and social reform, the first decade of the twentieth century saw the new Federal Government forge a protectionist blanket around Australia's economy and society. Protectionist urban industrial interests and the labour movement combined to defeat rural free traders in what had been a long-running conflict in the former colonies over trade protectionism. The other key elements in this historic 'class compromise' included the extension of arbitration to the federal arena and the imposition of rigid 'white Australia' immigration controls. The minimum wage determination contained within the famous Harvester judgement emanating from the federal arbitration system in 1907 was yet another indicator that labour and key segments of urban capital were willing to forge an alliance of convenience under the auspices of state protection.[24] In essence, the protection of a high-wage labour market (characterised by centralised wage fixing, minimum wages and immigration controls) was to be sustained by an increasingly expansive system of trade protectionism. In Australia's first major tariff enquiry in 1929, the Brigden Report warned that it saw 'no influence' within the Australian tariff system 'to counteract the indiscriminate and indefinite extension of the tariff'.[25] The warning was prophetic in what became an increasingly politicised and politically expedient protectionist regime. Although decreasingly committed in the 1950s and 1960s to the 'social protection' afforded by welfare state programs, by the late 1960s Australia had become one of the most (tariff) protected countries in the OECD.[26]

Francis Castles' model of 'domestic defence' provides a very useful analysis of Australia's historical attempts to shield itself from the rigours of the international market.[27] Drawing on the work of Katzenstein,[28] Castles contrasts Australia's wide-ranging protectionism with the elaborate policies of economic adjustment and 'domestic compensation' (such as social welfare, regional and industry policies, labour market and training programs) which have been used in a range of other small, open trading economies in northern Europe (e.g. Sweden, Norway, Austria and Switzerland). Such policies and programs have been used, particularly in the post-war era, to help adjust these economies to the competitive pressures of the international marketplace. Clearly, the Australian pattern of domestic insulation from external pressures was very different from the competitiveness strategy adopted in northern Europe. Yet Australia did well for much of the twentieth century by selling farm and mineral commodities to world markets. In contrast, the small European economies started out poor and have prospered in the twentieth century only by developing internationally competitive manufacturing and service industries. Over time, these economies became relatively dynamic while Australia, by contrast, remained relatively static in its approach to wealth creation. Indeed, Australia largely sought to prevent change rather than adapt to it.

Despite these differences, however, both Australia and the small European economies developed political processes to work out explicit compromises between domestic political interests and, in turn, these were geared to a relatively interventionist state role in the economy. Indeed, in both settings, domestic political coalitions working in tandem with the state actively steered the pattern of economic development. In post-war Australia, for example, protectionist policies, active immigration programs and open-door foreign investment policies were used to drive a process of rapid industrialisation. Greg Whitwell argues in chapter 5 that during World War II and the immediate post-war era, Australia also proved to be relatively receptive to the new Keynesian policies of macroeconomic management whereby the Commonwealth used fiscal and monetary policies to regulate the macroeconomic cycle. In the wake of the social dislocation of the 1930s depression and the war, the activist federal Labor Governments of the 1940s also expanded Australia's welfare state system.[29]

The size of the state and the scope of state activity continued to expand during the post-war era at both state and federal levels and, overall, the developments sketched above suggest something like a relatively 'statist' historical pattern of state–economy relations in this country. Although post-war political scientists largely neglected the role of the state,[30] some scholars have depicted the Australian state as something of a prime mover that has shaped the economy and, through policies of 'domestic defence', has shielded both capital and labour from market perturbations for much of the twentieth century. Accordingly, Michael Pusey argues that:

> *Australia was 'born modern' ... Through its controls over tariffs and industrial relations, and a direct control over wages and thus over the distribution of national income, the state held and used its power both to resist private capital interests and, within that large measure of 'relative autonomy', to form or at least protect the social structure. Consequently, it was a state that ... looks rather like a very 'strong' state or even a 'dominant' state.*[31]

However, Pusey and others have argued that there was a sea-change in the 1980s that saw a turn to market liberalism in this country, a historic departure from earlier statist traditions. The problem with this interpretation, however, is that it is historically misleading. As suggested at the beginning of this chapter, and as argued more fully in chapter 10, statism has been only one historical facet of Australian political economy. Equally important has been the fact that Australia has always embraced relatively liberal notions of market freedom and management prerogative, particularly at the level of firms and industries. In this sense, the rhetoric of free enterprise has always been taken seriously by business and by conservative political élites.[32] But how can free enterprise be reconciled with Australia's statist traditions? The answer is to recognise that market freedom and statism have historically operated at different levels of the state–economy relationship in Australia. In particular, and with the major exception of industrial arbitration where the state has historically intervened at the level of specific workplace relationships,[33] the state has been reluctant to intervene in the detailed workings of the economy. Thus, there has been a pattern of macro-structuring and micro-freedoms with respect to the state's role in the Australian economy; a kind of statist laissez-faire has operated.

A good example of how this worked can be seen in industry protectionism. Tariff and quota protection has historically shielded domestic manufacturing industries from international competition and has had a profound effect on the structure of the economy. This macro-structuring role, however, was not accompanied by any attempt to impose conditions (such as efficiency criteria) on the industry recipients. In this sense,

Australian protection came without accountability, without strings. As early as 1929 the Brigden Report had warned that such a state of affairs was likely to produce a situation in which industry became lazy and dependent. As the report argued,

> *The most disquieting feature of the tariff has been the stimulus it has given to the demands for government assistance of all kinds with the consequent demoralising effect upon self-reliant efficiency throughout all forms of production.*[34]

The contrast here with successful Asian economies is instructive. In Japan and in a number of other East Asian economies, for example, post-war protectionism went hand in hand with policies to ensure fierce domestic competition and to orient domestic firms towards international competitiveness.[35] Australian protectionism came without such microeconomic oversight.[36] In fact, in a range of areas from foreign investment and trade practices to the operation of key utilities and service industries, there was a pattern of neglect in microeconomic policy and very little state scrutiny of the detailed workings of the economy. As Hughes puts it, manufacturing industry 'was left largely to its own devices'.[37] Indeed, in many sectors, the impact of generalised protection meant that even the constraints normally imposed by market competition had been suspended. The ruling assumption throughout twentieth-century Australia has been that market actors, not government officials, knew best how to run their firms and industries. Rarely has the Australian state challenged the concept of the autonomous firm or the concept of private management prerogative. For these reasons, writers such as Pusey are wrong to see market liberalism as a novel twist to Australia's political economy.

Australia joins the world economy

Australia's policies of domestic insulation and its pattern of inattention to competition policy and microeconomic reform were only sustainable so long as the economy's wealth-creating sectors remained internationally viable. The key industries in question were the rural and mineral exporting industries which had historically paid Australia's way in the world and which for decades had provided the economic resources to support our inefficient manufacturing base as well as inefficient practices in key utility and service industries. When the economic strength of these key rural and commodities industries was challenged, so also was Australia's traditional pattern of state–economy relations. Economic change ultimately forced political change.

Of course, economic and political causes and effects are rarely straightforward. Yet in explaining this important shift in policy outlook, the constraints and opportunities arising from the economic context (and how this is interpreted) is a key dimension. This is particularly so in a small trading economy such as Australia's, which bobs about like a cork in a much larger economic ocean. John Ravenhill discusses Australia's changing role in the international economy in chapter 3, but for now it is worth briefly discussing some of the recent changes in Australia's place in world trade and how it has affected domestic political arrangements.

A key issue here is the nature of Australia's exposure to the world economy, particularly our traditional dependence on rural and mineral exports. In 1990–91, 51 per cent of Australia's exports were from the rural and resources sectors, and a further 8 per cent of exports consisted mainly of processed or refined commodities. Only 13 per cent of Australia's exports were classed as 'elaborately transformed manufactures', and much of our 'services' exports (20 per cent of total exports) are in fact generated by tourism.[38] This kind of export profile is more like that of a third world staples/resort economy than that of an advanced industrial economy, whose export profile is typically weighted much more towards high value-added manufactures exports (which, in recent decades, has been the fastest growing area of world trade).

The problem with Australia's trade pattern is that for most of the post-war era the prices received for rural and mineral products have fallen relative to the prices paid for the bulk of our (largely manufactured) imports. This secular decline in our terms of trade (in part reflecting the increased availability of rural and mineral products in world markets) has made it much harder in recent decades for Australia to pay its way in world trade. For example, by 1985 Australia had to export 75 per cent more by volume than it did in 1955 just to fund a given level of imports.[39] This pattern of relative trade decline has seen a ballooning of Australia's current account deficit since the early 1970s. Yet as long ago as the early 1960s there were those who warned of the dangers of Australia's reliance on commodities exports. As James Vernon (later to chair the Vernon committee of enquiry) wrote in 1962:

> *It does not seem realistic to think that our Australian aspirations are going to be satisfied if we rely heavily on primary exports for their achievement. Everything in world trade points the other way.*[40]

Subsequent efforts at structural economic adjustment (winding back inefficient, uncompetitive industries, together with attempts to diversify the economy towards higher value-added products and services and manufactured exports) have proceeded slowly. Even in the early 1980s there was a widespread view that Australia could still do well on the back of rural exports and resources booms. Only during the mid to late 1980s did Australian policy-makers really face up to the imperative of structural economic adjustment. As Treasurer Keating stated in an interview in 1986:

> We must let Australians know truthfully, honestly, earnestly, just what sort of an international hole Australia is in. It's the price of our commodities—they are as bad in real terms as since the depression. That's a fact of life now—it's got nothing to do with the government. It's the price of our commodities on world markets, but it means an internal economic adjustment ... If this government cannot get the adjustment, get manufacturing going again ... then Australia is basically done for. We will just end up being a third-rate economy ... a banana republic.[41]

Structural adjustment of the Australian economy in recent decades has focused mainly on efforts to reduce national protectionism, to expose the economy more to the competitive pressures of the international economy and to increase the efficiency of government utilities. These efforts, starting with the protection reductions, began in the late 1960s. Subsequent landmarks on the path to trade liberalisation have been the Whitlam Government's 25 per cent tariff reduction in 1973 and the major subsequent program of tariff cuts by the Hawke and Keating Governments in the late 1980s and the early 1990s. Overall the changes, though protracted and difficult, have been nothing short of a watershed. Australia has moved from being one of the most protected economies in the western world in the late 1960s to what could well be one of the least protected by the end of the century.[42]

This shift points to a key dimension in Australian political economy in the 1980s and 1990s: namely, the increasing integration of Australia into the international economy. Traditionally, Australia's exposure to the world economy has involved not only trading relationships but also a high degree of reliance on capital inflow. Foreign capital and overseas borrowing have played a major role in Australia's economic development and in funding balance of payments deficits. With trade liberalisation, together with moves in the 1980s to deregulate Australia's financial system and to remove exchange controls and float the dollar, Australia's integration with the world economy has become almost complete; a move that increasingly challenges the very concept of a national economy in a world increasingly dominated by massive transnational flows of investment and trade. To survive or prosper in such a context Australia, in competition with other countries, must be able to provide an investment environment attractive to footloose transnational investment capital. Australia is also highly dependent on capital inflow to service mounting debt and on global financial markets not to let the value of the Australian dollar slip too far. Accordingly, the expectations of the market (particularly overseas investors, lenders and currency traders) are increasingly influential in shaping domestic economic policy decisions, especially in relation to government debt, interest rates, inflation and wage levels.

The politics of economic adjustment

In a major economic statement in 1991, Labor Treasurer Keating announced that the program of tariff reductions contained within the statement 'ends forever Australia's sorry association with the tariff as a device for industrial development'.[43] Leaving aside the question of whether the tariff device itself was faulty or whether the real problem was the way tariffs were used, it is nevertheless the case that domestic trade liberalisation has spearheaded attempts to change the structure of the economy in recent decades. In this sense, the process of tariff reform has led and other policy instruments have followed. Much of the heat generated by the politics of economic adjustment has come from attempts to either speed up, slow down or block protection reductions.[44] A good deal of conflict has also attended the issue of what kinds of policies should accompany or support the process of tariff reductions. By themselves, such reductions will expose the economy to greater competitive pressures, a process explicitly designed to kill off or scale down weaker uncompetitive industries.

Greater competition, however, does little in a positive sense to help build new industries. Accordingly, there has been considerable pressure on Federal and State Governments to 'do something' to assist economic adjustment positively. At the national level, interventionists, particularly in manufacturing industry, in sectors of the union movement and in the Labor left, have pushed for positive forms of industry policy (research and development assistance, export incentives, etc.), and Federal Governments have responded since the late 1970s by pushing such assistance to levels which are high by historical standards in Australia.

In more recent years, there has been an attempt to make up for decades of neglect in the microeconomic arena. Attempts are underway to reduce inefficiencies in areas such as the waterfront and other areas of the transport system, as well as in areas such as communications and a range of public utilities. Rolf Gerritsen discusses the political realities and constraints on microeconomic reform in chapter 11, but here it is useful to note that policies in this area have again followed in the wake of trade liberalisation measures. Many commentators (particularly in industry) have argued that there has been insufficient integration between positive industry assistance measures, microeconomic reform and the push to reduce protection.[45]

There have also been attempts to bring other arms of policy to bear on the problems of economic adjustment. The long post-war economic boom ended in the mid-1970s, and the onset of stagflation saw challenges to the earlier Keynesian certainties relating to macroeconomic management. Since 1975 macroeconomic management has involved various attempts to impose restrictive fiscal and monetary policies to scale back state expenditure and the public sector (to 'make room' for the private sector), or to recess the economy deliberately in order to impose wage discipline on the unions (a strategy of the Fraser Government), or to help stabilise the current account in the face of Australia's declining trade performance (the Labor Government's response of the late 1980s).

John Wanna discusses the dynamics of macroeconomic policy in more detail in chapter 9, but it is worth noting here that the intensity of the inflationary conflicts between labour and capital over profits and wages in the 1970s and early 1980s has been eclipsed somewhat by the challenges of structural economic adjustment in the 1980s. Indeed, in broad terms, direct confrontation between labour and capital in the 1980s has been substantially moderated. Under the post-1983 policies of the Accord, the union movement under the ACTU has bargained with successive federal Labor Governments in a process that Trevor Matthews in chapter 8 refers to as 'corporatism without business'. The aim has been to moderate wage claims in return for various policy concessions by governments in order to increase business profitability and thus, hopefully, to induce new investment and a rebuilding of the economy.

Policy agreements under the Accord have also focused on shifting the basis of wage bargaining to give greater emphasis to issues of workplace reform, award restructuring and productivity. In chapter 6 Braham Dabscheck discusses changes to the arbitration system in recent decades and explains trends towards softening the centralised character of Australian wage bargaining with moves towards more flexible enterprise bargaining arrangements.

The important shift in union stance during the 1980s, away from an earlier preoccupation with distributive and wage issues towards what some would see as a more economically responsible approach, is typical of the direction of public policy as a whole in Australia. Except for some notable environmental policy decisions which have blocked major resource development projects,[46] the broad direction of public policy and of state–economy relations since the early 1980s has become much more focused on key issues of economic competitiveness and Australia's trading prospects. Thus, Ian Lowe argues in chapter 13 on the greenhouse issue that Australia's responses have been constrained by short-term concerns about the economy. Similarly, chapter 14 by Papadakis and Moore traces attempts by federal Labor to reconcile tensions between economic development and the environment. Many other policy areas, from education to intergovernmental relations within the Australian federation, have also been altered in an attempt to restructure and promote the economy. Moreover, as Lois Bryson argues in chapter 12, various trimming and targeting practices in social policy have been adopted to make the Australian welfare state more economically efficient.

In attempting to explain changes in state–economy relations in Australia, it is important, as suggested above, to give due consideration to the pressures that changes in the economy impose on prior policy arrangements. It is also important to emphasise the impact that previous patterns of policy have on current policy deliberations and on the ideas which inform contemporary policy debates. For example, there is an influential view in Australia that protectionism has not worked[47] and that state efforts to intervene selectively in the economy are likely to be inept or poorly managed. Clearly, such historically formed notions have a potentially powerful impact on policy choice.

It is also important to stress that constitutional rules and traditions and the institutional character of the state are important in shaping public policy and the broader pattern of state–economy relations. As argued above, Australia's federal political structure is one aspect of this relationship. Many recent statist writers have also emphasised that the institutional architecture of the state, particularly the policy mandates and relative authority or pecking order of various state agencies and departments, can be an important influence in shaping public policy.[48] The organisational attributes of key economic players such as labour and capital are also important in shaping the policy choices and options open to the state.[49] For example, the Labor Government's Accord with the trade unions in the 1980s would have been impossible without effective centralised union organisation under the auspices of the ACTU. Similarly, the capacity of business interests to engage in centralised public policy forums or Accord-style corporatist policy networks has been severely limited because of the chronic fragmentation and disunity of the peak business associations.[50]

One of the most common explanations for the broad trends of policy change described above, particularly the stress on economic performance, is that mounting pressure from business on the state is largely responsible. It is wrong, however, to see public policy as a simple reflection of business power, and there are important reasons why capital does not always have its interests fully protected and why individual businesses and sectors of capital are not always successful in influencing state policies.[51] Indeed, in many cases the general interests of business are impossible to assess because different sectors of business have conflicting interests. There are relative winners and losers within business as a whole on such issues as tariffs, the level of government spending, monetary policy, the level of the currency, regulation of export prices, regional development and capital inflow. Even on some issues such as holding down wage levels, where the common class interests of business might seem obvious, some sectors of industry (especially monopolies and highly profitable industries in the resource sector) have been willing and able to break ranks and pay above-average labour costs in order to reduce disruptions in production. It follows, from this recognition of the diversity of capitalist interests, that some businesses will be adversely affected—even to the point of bankruptcy or to absorption by competitors—by particular policy decisions and by general trends in business activity. In the long term, some sections of business must become unprofitable, and the state is usually more concerned with encouraging industries seen as the motor of investment and capital accumulation (and employment generation) than with constantly bailing out weak or marginal firms. Certainly, the major push to reduce protectionism in recent years should be seen in this light.

Rarely, then, does the state confront a unified business community, and this lack of unity often provides the state with a degree of latitude and autonomy in dealing with what are often quite particularistic business concerns. Moreover, it is essential to recognise that state agencies have their own institutional power base (resources, information, organisation, legality, discretion over policy implementation, etc.), which can allow them to develop a policy perspective independently of the particular views or policy demands of business.[52] Of course, the degree of independence actually exhibited is variable and must be established empirically in each case. In some cases, particular agencies of the state may be virtually captured by certain sectors of capital. In other cases, the capacity of the state to push ahead with particular policy strategies in the face of business opposition might be quite pronounced.[53]

A further reason why (particular) business interests might not be fully protected is that state policies might be inconsistent, mistaken, ill-considered, politically opportunistic or otherwise inadequate from the viewpoint of capital. The state's economic policies might fail to cure inflation, promote growth, dampen wage costs, stabilise the currency, secure a steady capital inflow or whatever else might be necessary for business confidence in the various sectors of industry. Moreover, the interests of capital might be partly displaced by countervailing pressures, not only within the state apparatus but also in the general arena of political conflict with welfare groups, environmentalists or trade unions.

Historically, it has been the political power of the organised labour movement, through its electoral and industrial influence, that has successfully imposed constraints on capital, particularly in relation to wages, workplace conditions and industrial awards under the arbitration system. Since 1983, under Labor's various Accord strategies, the labour movement has broadened its policy focus and linked wage bargaining to other policy issues such as taxation, superannuation, health insurance, industry policy and the reform of work practices and award restructuring. Many in business have resented this institutionalisation of union influence within the framework of the Accord, and it is likely that under a future conservative Federal Government there would be a considerable reduction in all forms of institutionalised contact between government and the union movement.

At the height of the Accord in the 1980s business became concerned at what it saw as the growth of union influence and power under the Accord. Yet at a general level of analysis, the power of the labour movement is insufficient to balance that of capital. As Offe suggests, in terms of the exclusion and dependence principles, the state in Western societies has little direct control over the process of capital accumulation and thus remains dependent on capital for this vital function. The ability to withhold investment, to decide on the location and timing of investment or to displace labour, gives business a good deal of leverage in bargaining over the terms of economic development. In this sense business, in general terms, has a good deal of structural power because of its strategic position in the functioning of a capitalist economy.[54]

Increasingly, with Australia's growing integration in the international economy, such dependence occurs at both national and international levels as governments are forced to maintain the confidence not only of the local business community but also of overseas investors, lenders and currency traders. In a context of mounting national debt, dependence on foreign capital inflow and heavy trading of the Australian dollar on global currency markets, governments have become increasingly anxious not to pursue policies likely to generate adverse 'market' reaction. It is for this reason that business, as a whole, cannot be analysed as just another interest group. Although the power of particular firms and sectors might be variable, Marsh and Locksley are correct to argue, at a more aggregate level, that 'capital is not just the first amongst equals, its power is qualitatively and quantitatively different'.[55]

A good example of this form of structural power at work can be seen in the policy dynamics of the Accord in the 1980s. Despite business concerns about the closeness of the government–union relationship, it was the unions, not business, that made the key concessions. In particular, the dynamics of the Accord involved wage moderation in an attempt to spur much-needed business reinvestment in the economy. Over the 1980s real wages were reduced by about 10 per cent while the share of national income going to profits climbed significantly. The politics of the Accord, then, provides important insights into the operation of the structural power of business. It is a form of power rooted in all economic sectors on which governments and wage-earners depend. Moreover, the most decisive aspects of the politics of the Accord did not stem from overt political activity but instead were constituted by the heavily structured context in which political behaviour occurred: a context, in this case, where government and unions were dependent on but unable to control business investment.[56]

Business enterprises are themselves often ambivalent concerning the actual (and ideal) relationships of state and capital. Although accepting the inevitability—if not desirability—of a wide range of supportive or regulatory measures, business leaders have always contested the scope and directions of state intervention in economic affairs. Business attitudes might be summed up in the proposition that state intervention is double-edged: a powerful ally or partner, but simultaneously a competitor for generalised control, whose supportive activities rapidly turn into excessive interference and costly red tape. According to the ideology of most business organisations, the ideal relationship between state and capital is that of a complementary partnership. This, of course, is only possible to the extent that business and the state share a consensus about national economic, social and political goals, and to the extent that this consensus is not effectively challenged by other interests, such as the labour or environmental movements. Business demands for—and objections to—state intervention are therefore selective and ad hoc, but there is an ultimate principle that the control by capital over investment decisions should be absolute. As suggested above, the rhetorical defence of market forces and private enterprise has always been taken seriously by business and is largely directed against forms of state intervention that appear to jeopardise business control over profitability, investment and, ultimately, over the economy.

A receding state?

In the last two decades, particularly since the end of the long post-war boom in the mid-1970s, the economic–liberal and business critique of state intervention has become much more sustained. Indeed, the post-war Keynesian/protectionist consensus has been abandoned, and in its place economic liberalism and the rhetoric of market forces and state minimalism has exerted a powerful influence on public policy and state–economy relations.[57] Even key parts of the labour movement, including State and Federal ALP Governments and even some parts of the union movement, have subscribed to certain elements of economic liberalism.[58] Moreover, state and federal bureaucratic élites have also adopted or strengthened earlier commitments to aspects of economic liberalism.[59] The general aim has been to reduce the state's influence over the economy in favour of market forces, to scale back the public sector and to make business and society generally less reliant on state assistance. Such a program stems from a belief that the post-war growth of the state excessively politicised the economy and overloaded the state and in turn the economy with excessive political demands by interest groups, unions and business. Too much attention, it is argued, was paid to wealth distribution, not wealth creation. Excessive demands generated too much regulation of business and too much taxation and government spending. Critics also pointed to examples of failed state intervention, picking losers instead of winners and mismanagement of state-owned enterprises.

Despite past activism, the size of the state in Australia (measured by taxation levels, size of public sector as a proportion of GDP, welfare state measures, etc.) remains relatively small in comparative terms. In 1988, for example, social security transfer payments as a proportion of GDP averaged 14 per cent for OECD countries as a whole, yet the figure in Australia was only 9.3 per cent, the lowest of eleven major OECD countries including well-known 'small' welfare states such as the US and Japan.[60] There is a degree of irony in the fact that, in comparative terms, it has been the smaller and in some cases the least interventionist states that have produced the biggest economic–liberal reactions. This is true of Britain, the US, New Zealand and Australia. Clearly, then, the strength of such a reaction has as much to do with a country's political traditions and domestic politics as with the actual size of its state.

Given the anti-statist mood in Australia in recent times it is useful to ask, by way of concluding this chapter, whether economic liberalism has wound back the state's economic role in recent years and what the shape of future developments is likely to be. Posing such questions, however, is easier than answering them, largely because there are so many facets of the state's economic role. The size of the state in fiscal terms, for example, appears to have diminished in recent years; a trend that might well continue or even accelerate under future conservative Federal and State Governments. Thus, total public sector outlays as a proportion of GDP declined from a peak of 42.5 per cent in 1985–86 to 36.5 per cent in 1988–89; this trend has been partly reversed in more recent times in response to economic recession.[61] The size of the state in these fiscal terms, however, often tells us little about the authority of the state or its overall impact on the economy. Indeed, relatively small fiscal states, such as Japan's, might wield considerable public authority. It is important, therefore, to look at the public authority or public power dimension of the state's role, particularly at state interventions which directly regulate or shape economic activity.

Here the Australian pattern is mixed. There has been an increase in state regulation in some areas in recent years, particularly in relation to companies and securities regulation, consumer protection and in some areas of environmental protection. In other areas of the economy, however, the opposite has occurred, particularly in relation to deregulating the banking system in the 1980s, floating the Australian dollar, and harmonising or deregulating aspects of interstate commerce. When these changes are added to the winding down of national border protection, the abolition of most of the former controls over capital movements and the commercialisation of government corporations, it is clear that the extent of public authority or control over the economy has been considerably reduced. Yet this apparent drift towards state minimalism is not as straightforward as it seems. State action and new forms of state intervention, at least in the short to medium term, might be required to facilitate longer-term state withdrawal from the economy. New forms of positive assistance to industry have accompanied the process of protection reductions, for example. A good deal of effort and resources have also been expended in recent microeconomic reform initiatives and competition policy by both State and Federal Governments.

Wyn Grant sees this process of state-assisted marketisation of the economy as a process of 'partisan state-led adjustment'.

> *Unlike company-led adjustment where the task of change is left in the hands of companies operating in an approximation of a market economy, partisan state-led adjustment involves interventions by government in order to create the conditions in which, ultimately, such company-led adjustment can occur. State intervention is necessary because companies lack the political will and capacity, and the management determination, to see adjustment through on their own. Conditions must be created in which free enterprise can flourish, but business cannot do this by itself, partly because of what is seen as spinelessness, partly because the obstacles are so great that they can only be tackled through the determined use of state power.*[62]

This is a model of state intervention in the name of market forces. Although it often offends hard-line economic liberals, it is what is typically required if democratic states are to implement market-oriented strategies. Although there is mounting criticism of economic rationalism in Australia, it is too early to tell whether it will amount to a concerted reaction or to a return towards earlier statist traditions. What is certain, however, is that earlier statist efforts to shape the economy according to a broad policy design or structural plan have been successfully challenged by economic liberalism and economic internationalism. Although many currents of state activism continue, Australia is now more of a market economy than at any time in its history and, increasingly, the key markets in which Australia participates are organised on a global scale. Compared to earlier historical capacities, the Australian state has lost a great deal of economic sovereignty and management capacity as significant parts of the economy become absorbed into the wider global system of capital flows and economic exchange.

Notes

1 P. Karmel (1961), 'The role of government in the Australian economy', *Public Administration*, 10:2, 165.
2 Treasury (1962), *The Australian Economy*, AGPS, Canberra.

3 M. Newton (1965), 'The economy', in A. F. Davies and S. Encel (eds), *Australian Society*, Cheshire, Melbourne.
4 S. Encel (1970), *Equality and Authority: A Study of Class, Status and Power in Australia*, Cheshire, Melbourne, p. 319.
5 F. Block (1990), *Post-Industrial Possibilities: A Critique of Economic Discourse*, University of California Press, Berkeley.
6 M. Friedman (1962), *Capitalism and Freedom*, University of Chicago Press, Chicago; M. and R. Friedman (1980), *Free to Choose*, Macmillan, Melbourne.
7 The profoundly unhistorical character of the market–liberal approach was thoroughly exposed many years ago by K. Polanyi (1957), *The Great Transformation*, Beacon Press, Boston. For recent developments in institutional economics and economic policy, see J. E. Alt and K. A. Crystal (1983), *Political Economics*, Wheatsheaf, Brighton, UK.
8 B. Galligan (1984), 'The state in Australian political thought', *Politics*, 19:2, 82–92.
9 G. Poggi (1978), *The Development of the Modern State*, Hutchinson, London.
10 S. D. Krasner (1984), 'Approaches to the state: Alternative conceptions and historical dynamics', *Comparative Politics*, 16, 223–46; P. Dunleavy and B. O'Leary (1987), *Theories of the State*, Macmillan, London.
11 See G. Davis, J. Wanna, J. Warhurst and P. Weller (1988), *Public Policy in Australia*, Allen & Unwin, Sydney, chapter 2.
12 W. Streeck and P. C. Schmitter (1985), 'Community, market, state—and associations: The prospective contribution of interest governance to social order', in W. Streeck and P. C. Schmitter (eds), *Private Interest Government: Beyond Market and State*, Sage, London.
13 B. W. Head (1990), 'Corporatism', in J. Summers et al. (eds), *Government, Politics and Power in Australia*, 4th ed., Longman Cheshire, Melbourne.
14 For a discussion of 'state capacity' in these terms see T. Skocpol (1985), 'Bringing the state back in: Strategies of analysis in current research', in P. B. Evans et al. (eds), *Bringing the State Back In*, Cambridge University Press, Cambridge, especially pp. 11–25.
15 B. W. Head (1986) (ed.), *The Politics of Development in Australia*, Allen & Unwin, Sydney, chapter 1.
16 B. W. Head (1993), 'State governments and Australian business', in R. Stewart (ed.), *Government and Business in Australia*, Allen & Unwin, Sydney.
17 G. Davis et al. (1988), *Public Policy in Australia*, pp. 33–4.
18 C. Offe (1975), 'The theory of the capitalist state and the problem of policy formation', in L. N. Linberg et al. (eds), *Stress and Contradiction in Modern Capitalism*, Lexington Books, Mass; see also J. O'Connor (1973), *The Fiscal Crisis of the State*, St Martins Press, New York.
19 M. Pusey (1988), 'State and polity', in J. M. Najman and J. S. Western (eds), *A Sociology of Australian Society*, University of Queensland Press, St Lucia, p. 30 (original emphasis).
20 N. G. Butlin (1983), 'Trends in public/private relations 1901–75', in B. W. Head (ed.), *State and Economy in Australia*, Oxford University Press, Melbourne, pp. 83–4.
21 N. G. Butlin (1983), p. 82.
22 K. Polanyi (1957), *The Great Transformation*, Beacon Press, Boston.
23 This concept is described in F. G. Castles (1985), *The Working Class and*

Welfare, Allen & Unwin, Sydney; and F. Farrell (1987), 'Australia: A laboratory of social reform', in Australian Labor Party (NSW Branch), *Traditions of Reform in New South Wales*, Pluto Press, Sydney.
24 'Broadly speaking, these were the employers in the manufacturing or construction and service industries who could not afford protracted and expensive industrial disputes, and who sought protection from foreign or sweated domestic competition.' See S. F. Macintyre (1983), 'Labour, capital and arbitration 1890–1920', in B. W. Head (ed.), *State and Economy in Australia*, Oxford University Press, Melbourne, p. 105.
25 Brigden Report (1929), *The Australian Tariff: An Economic Enquiry*, Melbourne University Press, Melbourne, p. 7.
26 L. Glezer (1982), *Tariff Politics*, Melbourne University Press, Melbourne; G. A. Rattigan (1986), *Industry Assistance: The Inside Story*, Melbourne University Press, Melbourne; M. A. Capling and B. Galligan (1992), *Beyond the Protective State: The Political Economy of Australia's Manufacturing Industry Policy*, Cambridge University Press, Melbourne; S. Bell (1993), *Australian Manufacturing and the State: The Politics of Industry Policy in the Post-War Era*, Cambridge University Press, Melbourne.
27 F. G. Castles (1988), *Australian Public Policy and Economic Vulnerability*, Allen & Unwin, Sydney.
28 P. Katzenstein (1985), *Small States in World Markets*, Cornell University Press, Ithaca, NY.
29 R. Watts (1987), *The Foundations of the National Welfare State*, Allen & Unwin, Sydney.
30 B. Galligan (1984).
31 M. Pusey (1991), *Economic Rationalism in Canberra: A Nation Building State Changes its Mind*, Cambridge University Press, Melbourne, p. 213.
32 S. Bell (1992), 'Business–government relations: The ideological context,' in S. Bell and J. Wanna (eds), *Business–Government Relations in Australia*, Harcourt Brace Jovanovich, Sydney.
33 Another exception is the detailed regulation of production, pricing and marketing of certain agricultural commodities by state boards, especially in the period 1920–60. See N. G. Butlin, A. Barnard and J. J. Pincus (1982), *Government and Capitalism*, Allen & Unwin, Sydney, pp. 81–7.
34 Brigden Report (1929), p. 6.
35 R. Wade (1990), *Governing the Market: Economic Theory and the Role of Government in East Asian Industrialisation*, Princeton University Press, Princeton, NJ.
36 S. Bell (1993), chapter 1; J. Stewart (1991), 'Traditional Australian industry policy: What went wrong', *Prometheus*, 9:2, 249–64.
37 H. Hughes (1964), 'Federalism and industrial development in Australia', *Australian Journal of Politics and History*, 10, p. 337.
38 Commonwealth of Australia (1991), *One Nation*, AGPS, Canberra, p. 28.
39 Australian Manufacturing Council (1986), *Future Directions for Australian Manufacturing Industry*, AGPS, Canberra, p. 4.
40 J. Vernon (1962), 'Problems of industrial growth', *Manufacturer's Monthly*, 15 June, p. 15.
41 Quoted in F. G. Castles (1989), 'Social protection by other means: Australia's strategy of coping with external vulnerability', in F. G. Castles (ed.), *The Comparative History of Public Policy*, Polity Press, Cambridge, p. 16.

42 M. A. Capling and B. Galligan (1992); S. R. Bell (1993); J. Stanford (1992), 'Industry policy in Australia', in J. Stanford (ed.), *Industry Policy in Australia and Europe*, Sir Robert Menzies Centre for Australian Studies, Institute of Commonwealth Studies, University of London, AGPS, Canberra; R. Castle (1991), 'The protection of Australian industry: Intervention or laissez-faire?' *Current Affairs Bulletin*, October.

43 Commonwealth of Australia (1991), *Building a Competitive Australia*, AGPS, Canberra, p. 2.1.

44 M. A. Capling and B. Galligan (1992); S. Bell (1993).

45 See, for example, L. Tingle (1990), 'Employers call for faster reforms', *Australian*, 11 April.

46 N. Economou (1992), 'Problems in environmental policy creation: Tasmania's Wesley Vale pulp mill dispute,' in K. J. Walker (ed.), *Australian Environmental Policy*, University of New South Wales Press, Kensington.

47 For a contrary view see J. Carroll and R. Manne (1992) (eds), *Shutdown: The Failure of Economic Rationalism and How to Rescue Australia*, Text Publishing, Melbourne.

48 S. Bell (1993), 'Statist theory', in A. Parkin et al. (eds), *Government, Politics, Power and Policy in Australia*, Longman Cheshire, Melbourne.

49 P. Hall (1986), *Governing the Economy*, Polity Press, Cambridge.

50 S. Bell and J. Wanna (1992) 'Power interaction and restructuring: Concluding comments', in S. Bell and J. Wanna (eds), *Business–Government Relations in Australia*.

51 See J. Ravenhill (1989), 'Business and politics', in R. Smith and L. Watson (eds), *Politics in Australia*, Allen & Unwin, Sydney; and S. Bell (1992), 'The political power of business', in S. Bell and J. Wanna (eds), *Business–Government Relations in Australia*.

52 P. B. Evans et al. (1985), *Bringing the State Back In*, Cambridge University Press, Cambridge. See also the discussion in chapter 2 below, pp. 60–3.

53 S. Bell (1989), 'State strength and capitalist weakness: Manufacturing capital and the Tariff Board's attack on McEwenism', *Politics*, 24:2, 23–38.

54 J. Ravenhill (1989); S. Bell (1992).

55 D. Marsh and G. Locksley (1983), 'Capital in Britain: Its structural power and its influence over policy', in D. Marsh (ed.), *Capital and Politics in Europe*, Frank Cass, London, p. 59.

56 D. McEachern (1991), *Business Mates: The Power and Politics of the Hawke Era*, Prentice Hall, Sydney.

57 See N. Blewett (1982), 'The challenge of the new conservatism', in G. Evans and J. Reeves (eds), *Labor Essays*, Drummond, Melbourne; M. Sawer (ed.) (1982), *Australia and the New Right*, Allen & Unwin, Sydney.

58 B. W. Head (1988), 'The Labor Government and economic rationalism', *Australian Quarterly*, 60:4, 466–77.

59 M. Pusey (1991).

60 H. V. Emy and O. E. Hughes (1991), *Australian Politics: Realities in Conflict*, Macmillan, Melbourne, table 10.2, p. 397.

61 Commonwealth of Australia (1992), *Budget Paper No. 1, 1992–93*, AGPS, Canberra, table 1, p. 6·5.

62 W. Grant (with J. Sargent) (1987), *Business and Politics in Britain*, Macmillan, London, p. 246.

2
Understanding the modern state: Explanatory approaches

Brian Head and Stephen Bell

Understanding the relations between the state and the economy is one of the central issues in the social sciences. This chapter provides an introduction to some of the main conceptual problems involved in analysing state–economy relations in advanced capitalist societies, such as Australia.[1] There is particular emphasis in this chapter on analysing and evaluating the explanatory capabilities of existing theories of the state. Accordingly, there is less emphasis on the normative/prescriptive elements of recent state theory. Nor is there any special focus in this chapter on Australian conceptions of the state,[2] or the specific features of the Australian political economy discussed elsewhere in this volume.

Most approaches in state theory assume a significant degree of separation between the economic and the political/governmental spheres — an assumption that emerged in its distinctively modern form in late eighteenth-century Europe and America. Institutional developments centring on limited government, representation and administrative efficiency dominated the subsequent debates through to the mid twentieth century. However, the focus of this chapter is on contemporary perspectives and issues (rather than the historical development of institutions, theories and problems).[3] Special attention is given to the most important varieties of liberal and neo-Marxist theorising on the state and political economy, as well as two recent hybrid accounts, corporatism and statism, which, in part, can be seen as responses to the liberal and Marxist traditions. The theories discussed below have been chosen with two aims in mind: to introduce major authors and approaches to those readers unfamiliar with literature on the state and political economy; and to provide a general guide to the theoretical issues underlying the following chapters on substantive aspects of the Australian political economy.

It should also be noted that the theoretical categories used below are far from watertight. There have been internal disputes and divergent analytical approaches taken by theorists within both liberalism and Marxism, and the coherence of each group is often illusory. At the most basic explanatory level, however, it can be said that liberal theorists tend to rely on an individualistic/action frame of reference, whereas Marxists tend to apply more systemic explanatory factors, including class analysis and the impact of economic/productive forces in shaping social and political relations. The new hybrid theories such as corporatism draw on elements of both liberalism and Marxism, and in recent statist theory there have been some interesting attempts to build bridges between the liberal–Weberian and Marxist analytical traditions.[4] In an important sense, then, there has been a broadening of analytical perspectives on the modern state. In the 1980s in particular, this pattern of theoretical development has increasingly challenged the earlier certainties and comprehensive theoretical claims of both liberalism and Marxism.

Liberal approaches

The approaches considered in this section tend to assume that individuals or groups (including formal organisations) are the proper units of analysis and that public policy is a result of the competition for power and influence among such individual and group interests. However, there is a range of views about how democratic the system is (or should be) and about the nature of the state and its ability to influence (and to be influenced by) economic processes. Discussion will focus on the following approaches: classical pluralism; revisions to this including so-called corporate pluralism, as well as Lindblom's radical pluralism;[5] and public choice theory and economic liberalism. The contribution of public policy and public administration literature in relation to recent theories of the state will also be briefly discussed.

One of the most obvious features of everyday political life in liberal–democratic societies is the importance of organised groups that mobilise and articulate a wide range of interests and values. Among these groups, political parties have a special status, insofar as they are the key actors in the electoral system, seeking to form a government and thereby gain a general capacity to determine the shape of public policies. A multitude of more specialised groups espouses the interests and beliefs of particular sections of the economy and society. These include manufacturers, miners, farmers, graziers, retailers, banks, government employees, metal-workers, churches, students, pensioners, women, ethnic minorities, moral campaigners and so on.

Pluralism, with its view of government policy being shaped by the push and pull of pressure groups, provided a very influential account of politics in liberal capitalist societies (particularly in the US, Britain and Australia) for much of the post-war era. It is a relatively broad and diverse theoretical approach, and over the years various attempts at revision have occurred. These revisions will be discussed later, but for the moment we deal with conventional or so-called 'classical' pluralism.

Classical pluralism

In this account, much like the competitive marketplace in liberal economic imagery, group competition within the political marketplace is seen as a relatively open and democratic process. Inequalities of power between groups are acknowledged, but classical pluralists maintain that the open and fluid nature of power and the wide array of political issues ensures that no one group systematically dominates political outcomes. Thus the overall impression, summed up in pluralist theory, is that the political system is open to a wide range of influences, that no single group's interest prevails across a spectrum of significant issues and that the system is therefore democratic and responsive to shifts in public opinion. This impression is reinforced by the mechanisms of representative government, whereby the party or coalition in office may be removed in periodic elections.[6]

The policy implications of such a pattern of government–interest group interaction have been well described in the literature dealing with 'disjointed incrementalism' as a policy-making style. As described in the early works of Charles Lindblom, multiple power centres in the interest group struggle produce a process of 'partisan mutual adjustment' and policy 'incrementalism': a pattern whereby constant cross-cutting conflicts and compromises between interests, together with a cautious 'steady as she goes' approach to policy-making, produces small incremental policy steps following established routines. Lindblom described this as a reasoned process of 'muddling through'.[7]

The activities of interest groups and political parties should clearly be recognised in any theory of the relations between the state and economy; the important question, however, is whether such a focus can provide a sufficient explanation of the structures and processes at work. Pluralist theory, especially in its post-1950 American version, has been subjected to severe criticism on empirical, methodological and normative grounds; this debate has been summarised by other writers and will not be repeated here at length.[8] The main criticisms are as follows. Electoral competition and group bargaining do not guarantee that the political system will be open or responsive to all groups, to poorly organised groups or to ordinary citizens. There is little probability that the interests of the most powerful economic groups can be successfully challenged. Nor is there any guarantee that general interests (e.g. conservation of natural resources) will be adequately articulated and protected.

Moreover, as Lukes has argued, pluralism's view of power is 'one-dimensional'.[9] The exercise of power is seen in voluntarist, person-centred terms within a behaviourist analytical framework which examines only overt or observable political activity focused on particular policy decisions; the so-called 'decisional' analysis of power. A range of critics, stressing the importance of less observable forms of power, have pointed to the inadequacies of this approach. Part of the power of dominant interests might consist in keeping some issues or policy options from being seriously considered. This covert form of power can be variously described as the politics of non-decisions, controlling the agenda of public discussion or successfully defining the consensus in a way which de-legitimates more radical proposals.[10] Finally, there is not much evidence to show that political parties are themselves highly democratic organisations sensitive to the views of their own members and of the wider community. Thus, pluralist theories of liberal democracy — insofar as they offer an empirical description/explanation of power relations and of the process of public policy formation in advanced capitalist societies — must be judged deficient, however attractive pluralism might be as one criterion of a truly democratic system.

In the pluralist perspective, the economic activity of the state itself remains ambiguous. In one version, state policy represents the outcome of the balance of economic forces in the group struggle; the state passively registers the views of the dominant group (or coalition of interests) on particular issues. The state is thus available as an instrument for carrying out the policies of the majority of voters or a majority coalition of interests; or it simply reflects the compromises arising from the conflict of group forces in the economy and society.[11] This account of state economic activities is naive and misleading. It suffers, on one hand, from its equation of policy with majority rule and the general will, as if the formal procedures of elections and debate ensure that public policy always reflects a majority viewpoint. On the other hand, this account makes no allowance for the institutional interests of the state apparatuses, the state's capacity to resist or transform demands from private interests and the inability of the political executive to control policy implementation.

A second (and more sophisticated) version of pluralist analysis attributes to the state an active and independent role: policing the rules of fair play in the group struggle, attempting to uphold the general or public interest against the inevitably narrow and selfish interests of organised groups, and defending the basic institutions and values of the system (and thereby its own autonomy). However, this analysis begs the question of why the state undertakes such roles and, more particularly, neglects the problem of how the general interest is determined, how the consensual values are defined and which interests benefit from a given conception of the rules of the game. In a third version of pluralism, the state itself is dissolved into its multiple constituent groups, each pursuing its own interests or its own conceptions of the public interest.

This serves to demonstrate that the conception of the state, and of state–economy relations, is both elusive and contradictory in mainstream pluralist writings. Apart from a recognition of the complexity and importance of group interests and electoral politics in the policy-making process, there is little to recommend the classical pluralist analysis of political economy. There is insufficient appreciation of the systemic or structural constraints under which a government and its policy advisers operate in an advanced capitalist society, no account of the state apparatus as a set of structures distanced from both the government and from the economic groups, no explanation of historical change in state–economy relations and no linkage to the international context of public policy formation and implementation.

Corporate pluralism and policy communities

Since the 1960s there have been some significant revisions of pluralist theory. One such revision is so-called corporate pluralism.[12] Early pluralist writers such as Truman had pointed to 'institutionalised relationships' between interest groups,[13] governments and organisations of the state. The essence of corporate pluralism as developed by Lowi is the notion of unequal or privileged group access to government policy-making arenas.[14] Unlike classical pluralism, with its emphasis on an open, fluid, ad hoc, lobbying style of relationship between interest groups and the state, corporate pluralism depicts a more structured and formal relationship between certain insider interest groups and the state. As Streeck notes, classical pluralism tends to see 'interest groups as neatly separate from the state',[15] but corporate pluralism sees a more integrated pattern of relationships between the state and certain key interests.

The work of Richardson and Jordan (among others) has been important in the further development of the corporate pluralist model of group–governmental relations. For Jordan and Richardson, public policy-making occurs not so much in parliament or indeed even in cabinet, but in a more decentralised pattern of policy communities involving institutionalised interaction between key departments, relevant statutory authorities, advisory committees and a range of select, client interest groups. As Jordan and Richardson argue: 'there is a natural tendency for the political system ... to encourage the formation of stable policy communities, one of the primary purposes of which is to achieve a negotiated and stable policy environment'.[16] According to this model, policy-making occurs in discrete sectors corresponding to broad functional areas of administrative activity such as health, agriculture, manufacturing or education, with each sector possibly divided further into smaller policy communities dealing with more specific policy areas. Relationships within policy communities can be characterised as having 'preferred operating procedures', particularly in terms of consultation, compromise and the search for consensus. Like previous (i.e. classical) models of pluralism, this pattern of group–government relationship also tends to produce a conservative, risk-averse, incremental policy-making style. Relevant ministers and departments play a co-ordinating role in dealing with relevant policy communities and then push for resources and favourable policy decisions at the centre of government, typically within cabinet.

It is clear that corporate pluralism reveals important dimensions of policy-making not explored by more traditional pluralist models. One of the strengths of seeing policy-making and state–economy relations in corporate pluralist terms involves the stress on how the dynamics of policy-making can vary between policy sectors, each with their own particular participants and structured patterns of relations between organised interests and the state. Another advantage is that corporate pluralism stresses that access to policy-making forums might be limited to those groups with sufficient power or with relevant functional interests in a particular policy arena. This stands in stark contrast to the notions of relatively open access to government stressed by classical versions of pluralism.

Yet problems with such an approach also need to be pointed out. For example, the constant reference by writers such as Jordan and Richardson to relationships involving negotiation and bargaining within policy communities suggests an assumption of relatively even power between members of a policy community. But how realistic or helpful is this assumption? As in virtually all variants of pluralism, the role of the state remains ambiguous. Moreover, the assumption about relatively equal power among policy community participants is extended to cover internal dynamics as different as government-led policy initiatives, agency capture by interest groups, cooption or bargaining. Clearly, the notion of a policy community covers a range of quite different possible interactions between groups and government, yet these remain insufficiently specified within the work of policy community writers such as Jordon and Richardson. A related question is whether members of a policy community always operate according to consensual rules of the game. Indeed, for a model of political interaction, the policy communities approach says surprisingly little about power, conflict or hierarchy.[17] Moreover, how widespread are such policy communities, and do they occur in some policy arenas but not in others? Such questions are part of a larger set of questions about government or state autonomy and about the degree to which state leaders have their own policy agendas independent of pressure or business groups. Finally, we need to return to questions about the exact nature of the political relationships within policy communities. In particular, do interest groups play an advisory role in policy-making (as Richardson and Jordan appear to suggest), or do they play a more active and direct role in policy formulation or, indeed, in policy implementation?

Radical pluralism

A common problem identified above with classical and corporate pluralism is their restricted conceptions of power. In response to these problems, two strands of revisionist pluralism have been elaborated by writers such as Charles Lindblom and David Vogel.

Although once a major classical pluralist writer, Charles Lindblom was prepared in his later work to recognise the central importance of major capitalist interests in a capitalist economy, or what he calls the 'privileged position of business in policy making'.[18] As noted above, Lindblom was previously best known for his theory that the policy-making process, including the budgeting process, could be largely understood as incrementalism, whereby minor adjustments were made to existing programs and policies.[19] This notion has been widely debated and has been indirectly adopted by some of the theorists of overloaded government; Richard Rose has argued, for example, that creeping incrementalism in state spending is a juggernaut because small changes eventually add up to patterns of expansion in programs, fuelled by rising community expectations, which are very difficult to reverse.[20]

Lindblom's later writings focus more clearly on the power and influence of large corporations. Indeed, he finds an incompatibility between their enormous power and the principles of representative government embodied in liberal democratic theory. He argues that the economic arena is dominated by the large corporations and that the governmental and parliamentary arena is obliged to regard corporate interests as of paramount importance. His argument about the political influence of business is of special relevance to our discussion and is summarised below.

Lindblom provides a straightforward account of why governments (and administrators) pay special attention to looking after business interests. Capital occupies a privileged position because the major decisions on investment, output, employment and so on in a capitalist economy are taken by large private corporations. Given that all the citizens have a common interest in a sustained level of economic activity as the foundation of their material standard of living, voters tend to reward governments that preside over a period of economic stability and growth and punish governments associated with a period of economic decline. Thus, public policy-makers are bound to protect business interests and to bolster the confidence of investors in order to enhance economic performance and hence the government's prospects of re-election. Lindblom also draws attention to the empirical evidence of the extensive activities of business lobbies in the formal and informal processes of policy formation and implementation, and emphasises the capacities of business interests to influence public opinion.

Thus, Lindblom, in an argument that wholly rejects the conclusions of classical pluralism, presents a critical−liberal account of why the state and capital share a fundamental interest in the profitability of large corporations; an interest that he believes would exist even without the reinforcement stemming from a high level of personal interaction, common social background and values and the effects of business propaganda. To ignore the basic interests of big business is to court electoral disaster for a government, although there remains plenty of room for disagreement on secondary issues and on modes of implementation. The force of this quasi-structural argument about business influence (i.e. that power resides in the structural arrangements of the political economy) applies equally to reformist and conservative parties; regardless of program and ideology, governments must protect the profitability and long-term interests of capital. What is more, Lindblom claims that corporations tend to operate cautiously in the absence of state assistance; they generally require positive inducements to perform at full capacity. Once established, these forms of assistance are not easily withdrawn; they are part of the expectations of business. Lindblom also claims that most forms of state regulation of business are really forms of business protection, rather than threats to profitability.[21]

One of the problems with Lindblom's arguments about business power, however, is that they are essentially ahistorical. The image conveyed is one of overarching business dominance, yet such a model tells us little about the changing dynamics of business power over time. One pluralist writer who has attempted to overcome this problem is David Vogel, whose explanation of the changing dynamics of group influence in American public policy provides at least a partial corrective to the problems found in Lindblom's account.[22]

In a research program explicitly designed to challenge 'static' conceptions of business power and of business−state relationships, Vogel sets out to explain the political ascendancy of American social reformism in the late 1960s and early 1970s in the face of business opposition, as well as the subsequent reassertion of business power later in the decade. A key explanation, Vogel argues, involves the changing level of business political power during the period under study. Vogel agrees with Lindblom that business, by virtue of its control over the economy, can enjoy great power and a privileged position in politics. But Vogel then introduces various caveats, arguing that factors such as the state of the economy and the level of business mobilisation in politics also determine business power and that these factors vary through time. As he says:

> *Seen from this perspective, Lindblom is partially correct; business is in a uniquely privileged position to persuade the public that the satisfaction of its demands is essential if high growth rates are to be restored. But there is nothing automatic about this business confidence weapon; indeed like the effects of investment itself, it may work only after a considerable time lag. It is also apt to have limited political significance in a relatively prosperous period.*[25]

This notion of the historical variability of capitalist power, and the way it is linked to the autonomy and interventionist capacities of the state, is also reflected in the work of Marxist writers, such as Fred Block (see below).

It is important, however, to recognise that writers such as Lindblom, Vogel and Block operate at an aggregated level of analysis utilising general analytical categories, such as 'business' or 'capital'. While analysis at this level is important in highlighting the state's broad dependence on the aggregate results of capitalist economic activity, such analysis is likely to miss important elements of capital–state relationships at a more disaggregated, sectoral level where the state (or parts of the state) interact with specific businesses, industries or fractions of capital. At this level of analysis, abstract theories of the state's structural dependence on capital accumulation (even those which accept the historical variability of such dependence), can be a poor guide to how the state relates to particular fractions of capital in different conjunctures.[24] In the 1980s the Thatcher Government, for example, sought to restructure the British economy and promote capital accumulation on a new footing, but this entailed a confrontation with established manufacturing industry. Much the same has also happened in Australia in the 1970s and 1980s. In both cases, the state has displayed a significant degree of autonomy and has acted against particular fractions of capital in the name of wider economic goals. Following Lindblom, then, business can occupy a privileged position in politics, but it is clear that some sectors of business will be more privileged than others. The power of sectors of capital in these terms will vary historically in relation to changes in the economy and strategies for capital accumulation.[25]

Public choice

Unlike the liberalism of Lindblom or Vogel, which, at least in part, utilises higher system-level concepts, such as the structural power of business, public choice theorists and economic liberals generally adopt a stark action-oriented, individualistic frame of reference. Accordingly, the role of the state and the dynamics of state–economy relations are explained largely in terms of the self-interested actions and motives of rational individual actors.

Public choice theory begins from a market metaphor: the political and governmental arenas operate as a system of self-interested exchanges in a manner akin to product markets. Individuals are all assumed to be engaged in attempts to maximise benefits for themselves, whether as voters, interest group members, politicians, regulators and bureaucrats (in the public sphere) or as consumers, producers and investors (in the private market economy). Individual action is seen primarily as the articulation and pursuit of individual preferences. However, it is recognised that some areas of life are inherently collective; diverse preferences have to be accommodated under social rules, practices and policies, and some interests are shared to a degree that accommodates collective action. Public choice theory seeks to analyse various arrangements for making collective decisions and their relation to particular patterns of economic outcomes.[26] And in the version of public choice represented by James Buchanan, there is a strong advocacy of checks and balances and constitutional devices to limit the power of legislatures and political executives in order to guard against excessive public expenditures, unnecessary interventionism and threats to economic and political liberties.[27]

Public choice provides a series of arguments to undermine the notion that governments, politicians and bureaucrats essentially pursue the public interest. This somewhat cynical interpretation of the political market has a certain plausibility in the modern age of media marketing of political leaders, open inducements for political support and scepticism about whether welfare spending is of more benefit to the poor or the program administrators. However, the public choice approach should be judged on its analytical accuracy and explanatory power, not just its ability to tap into public sentiments critical of politicians and bureaucrats. Public choice makes important claims about a number of aspects of public policy formation and the state. These are forcefully outlined by Charles Rowley:

> *Public policies are viewed as the outcome of the forces of demand and supply as they impinge on the political market-place. Individual citizens are assumed to make known the profile of their individual preferences ... And they attempt to influence government to satisfy those preferences by resort to the instruments available, notably by voting, by pressure-group and social movement activities, by private provision, by migration or even by revolution. Political parties are viewed as coalitions which 'log-roll' on electoral platforms designed to satisfy a variety of objectives, such as power, patronage, ideology,*

private income and probability of election. The government is viewed as maximising such objectives during its period of office subject to some constraint defined on the probability-of-election variable. A further important influence in the supply of public policies is seen to stem from bureaucracy, with senior bureaucrats viewed as maximising their utility in terms of the specific reward-cost structure which confronts them.[28]

Some of these points are sketched briefly below, beginning with the electoral arena. *Voters* are essentially political consumers, choosing between electoral products on the basis of rational self-interest. *Political parties* are regarded in public choice theory as organisations primarily aimed at winning office. Politicians and party organisers are basically interested in power. Where the electoral system allows a two-party system to emerge, as in most of the Anglo-American democracies, there will be a tendency for party policy frameworks to converge near a median point rather than polarise towards ideological extremes; this is linked to the logic of gaining an electoral majority.[29] Thus, policies are offered to the public as short-term strategies to achieve popular support. According to some writers, state economic policies are adjusted in a cyclical fashion to maximise electoral support in the months leading up to an election: a process often called the 'political business cycle'.[30]

However, these assumptions about party politics have not been consistently borne out by recent experience, e.g., the ideological polarisation of the Thatcher years in Britain (1979–91) and the sharply contrasting programs offered by the major parties in several federal elections in Australia since the late 1970s. There is considerable evidence of greater volatility in voters' support for major centre parties and opportunities for minor parties to make significant—if temporary—impacts on public debate and policy formation. Moreover, election platforms of some major parties have involved promises to cut the public sector rather than increase spending to buy votes, and the correlation between electoral timing and economic upswings is by no means a close relationship.

In regard to bureaucracy, public choice theory proposes that bureaucrats will seek to expand the budgets and staffing of their agencies, motivated by a desire for the personal status and material benefits which generally flow from controlling larger resources. They might also seek to reshape the role or mandate of their agencies to promote their career paths or to steer clear of awkward problem arenas. The obvious conclusion is that bureaucracies are self-serving, overresourced and inefficient; that is, they expand beyond the level necessary to provide a specified service in the most cost-effective way. This tendency is also caused by the lack of competition (between public agencies and private organisations) for the most efficient delivery of services.[31] The modern debates about privatisation and contracting-out of government services are directly related to the public choice assumption that public provision is likely to be more expensive than a privately provided alternative. Empirical studies are required to test all of these propositions. Moreover, it is clear that the current trend in public bureaucracies is for power to move towards senior managers adept at cost-cutting, improving productivity and generating a greater focus on results/outcomes, rather than those managers who spend more or employ more staff. All governments are examining contracting-out as an alternative to direct provision of services by the public sector. More attention is being paid to approaches that optimise value for money. Deregulation and privatisation are being pursued even by Labor governments.[32]

Public choice theory has also developed an interesting analysis of 'rent seeking'; that is, an analysis of the ways in which resources or profits flowing only to particular interests can be established and protected by state action. The public choice literature is very critical of state incentives, licences, subsidies and quotas that privilege some groups at the expense of taxpayers, consumers or business in general. This criticism leads to a broader analysis of economic and social regulation. The assumption of public choice writers is that economic regulation generally operates in the interest of the regulated firms (e.g. by excluding potential competitors) or that social regulation generally operates in the interests of the regulatory bureaucracy (rather than in the public interest). These are very contentious areas of research and debate and have been discussed in detail elsewhere.[33] As before, the need for detailed study of particular cases is paramount.

An interesting application of the public choice approach to explaining levels of national economic performance in different Western nations has been undertaken by Mancur Olson.[34] His basic argument is that the pattern of interest group pressures that are at the heart of economic policy might eventually tend to produce rigidity or sclerosis and thus become a brake on innovation and economic growth. The variations in economic growth rates in different nations is partly caused by the variations in the way lobby groups attach themselves to key policy domains. Narrowly based special-interest organisations and their collusive practices (including barriers to entry by new players) are especially likely to reduce overall national efficiency.

> *The growth of coalitions with an incentive to try to capture a larger share of the national income, the increase in regulatory complexity and governmental action that lobbying coalitions encourage, and the increasing bargaining and complexity of understanding that cartels create, alter the pattern of incentives and the direction of evolution in society. The incentive to produce is diminished; the incentive to seek a larger share of what is produced increases. The reward for pleasing*

those to whom we sell our goods or labor declines, while the reward for evading or exploiting regulations, politics and bureaucracy and for asserting our rights through bargaining ... becomes greater.[35]

Olson argues, for example, that Britain by the 1970s had 'acquired so many strong organisations and collusions' that it suffered from 'an institutional sclerosis that slows its adaptation to changing circumstances and technologies'.[36] Applying his framework to Australia, Olson claims that the post-war history of protectionism and domestic-oriented manufacturing is a good illustration of special-interest rigidities leading to a decline in the international competitiveness of the Australian economy.[37] This argument is certainly compatible with many recent Australian analyses of the need for deregulation and a free trade approach to expose the economy to effective competition and thereby stimulate greater productivity, efficiency and an export orientation.

The public choice approach encompasses a diverse range of authors and themes. Many of the questions raised about the supply of 'public goods', government services and regulatory frameworks are very important. However, the rational self-interest psychology that underlies most of the public choice approach is questionable, and the normative assumptions in favour of the private sector at the expense of public authority are sometimes an obstacle to reasoned debate.[38] It is also important to recognise that many of the criticisms that apply to classical pluralism also apply to public choice theory; mainly that it has a narrow conception of political power, that its analysis at the level of individual choice and action tends to ignore or downplay wider institutional and structural influences on the state and that it has a limited conception of the complex linkages between state and economy.

Economic liberalism

Economic liberalism—as a prescriptive theory of state–economy relations—relies heavily on public choice analysis and on the strictures and assumptions of neo-classical economics. Also referred to as economic rationalism or market liberalism, this body of theory and prescription argues that a restoration of a free market in economic and political life would solve most of the serious problems besetting governments in modern capitalist societies.[39] For a time during the late 1970s and 1980s economic liberals united with so-called neo-conservatives to criticise the excessive role of the state in economic and social life. The term *New Right* was coined to describe what in fact became a successful electoral coalition in a number of Western countries, particularly in Britain and the United States. In recent years, especially since the early 1990s, conservatives have become sceptical of untamed market systems and of untrammelled liberal freedoms, and there is evidence of mounting conflict between economic liberals and conservatives on these issues.[40]

The primary concern of economic liberals involves a reassertion of certain laissez-faire assumptions of eighteenth-century 'classical' political economy (Smith and Hume) and a sustained polemic against the inflationary expectations and state-dependency attitudes aroused in the community in the wake of post-war Keynesian economic management, protectionism, welfarism and public sector expansion. The first assumption of economic liberalism is that productive activity (and thus the creation of national wealth) is confined to the private sector of the economy, whose goods and services are marketed in competition with other producers. Secondly, growth in the public sector's share of gross domestic product (GDP), raised through the taxes and charges which pay for state expenditures, is incompatible with the growth of a healthy private (productive) sector. Thirdly, it is claimed that high levels of state spending and borrowing contribute greatly to inflation and to higher interest rates through competition for loan funds between the public and private sectors. Fourthly, individual liberty (and the liberty of private corporations) is held to be jeopardised by the growth of state bureaucracies, regulations, planning and controls over a wider range of economic and social activities. Fifthly, a symmetry is typically perceived between the existence of a free market economy and a free market in political ideas and organisations; in other words, the market economy is believed to be a necessary (although not a sufficient) precondition for a liberal-democratic political system.[41]

A set of policy recommendations follow from the above assumptions. If most forms of state expenditures are wasteful and unproductive, then there should be severe but selective cuts. If the profitability and expansion of the private sector is being undermined by high taxes and charges and inadequate incentives for investment, then the state should reduce corporate taxes and charges and increase incentives. The state should balance its budget and minimise its borrowings in order to cease competing with business for loan monies and in order to halt the upward spiral in politicians' electoral promises; this would reduce inflation and interest rates and release funds for private sector expansion. Given the assumption that the free market is the most efficient allocator of resources, it follows that the level of state regulation should be cut; the state's interference in the availability and pricing of inputs for production (e.g. finance, energy, transport, labour, manufactured commodities) should be diminished, while state enterprises should be sold to the private sector as far as possible. The provision of public goods by the state (e.g. heavily subsidised services in public health care, higher education and public transport) should be replaced to a large degree by the user-pays principle. The latter is only feasible if citizen-consumers have more discretionary control over the disposal of their income. This implies the need for a reduction in personal income tax rates, giving individuals more choice in where they spend their money. At the same time, incentives should be provided to encourage individuals to join voluntary insurance schemes (e.g. for health services), although this could remain compulsory in some fields (e.g. third-party motor vehicle insurance, contributory national superannuation and pension schemes). Any shortfall in state revenues would be made up through rises in indirect taxes, such as a consumption tax or a value-added tax.

In short, the economic role of the state, according to this view, is essentially that of enhancing the profitability of the private sector through reducing public-sector constraints on profits and incomes and through deregulating market forces. The primary economic objectives are efficiency and ultimately growth; the primary political objectives are to dampen electoral pressures for Keynesian deficit budgeting and reduce the perceived overload on the scope of state activities.[42] Recent economic liberalism represents an attempt to purify liberal doctrines which, since the Great Depression of the 1930s, had become overlaid by welfarism, meliorism and interventionism — part of the legacy of Keynes and his rejection of laissez-faire. To some extent, this revival of pure liberalism also represents a rejection of the pork-barrel group bargaining approach to public policy, which has been so influential in liberal–democratic systems and especially in the United States.

There is no space for detailed criticism here; this has been undertaken elsewhere.[43] Suffice to note that this market-based theory shares the defects of all social philosophies that understand economic and political processes as resulting from the sum of individual actions or that idealise the economy as an autonomous system.[44] Criticism has become more intense in recent years as experiments in free market economics in a number of countries have been seen to fail. There is little real understanding in economic liberalism of the complex linkages and dependencies between society and economy. Distributive justice, or social equity, is given a low priority. Liberty is identified with a lack of restraints over individual and corporate action, but the source of constraints is seen as the state rather than the actions of domestic monopolies and multinational corporations. The call for a reduced public sector overlooks the importance of public investment in training and infrastructure for economic growth. The preoccupation with the public sector's share of GDP overlooks the difference between transfer payments and final expenditure on goods and services by governments. Finally, it is noticeable that the state is expected to increase its activities in some areas (such as defence, law and order, tax incentives, efforts to cut real wage levels and policing of welfare claimants) while cutting expenditure in 'unproductive' areas (state employment, public housing, health, welfare, etc.). This points not so much to a policy of severely cutting the size of the public sector as to a rearrangement of the economic priorities of the state in response to the political agenda of economic liberalism.[45]

Public administration and public policy studies

Institutional analyses of the operations and structures of the state apparatus have developed a very large body of writing under the broad heading of public administration and public policy literature. The main weakness of this approach to the understanding of state–economy relations has been a general neglect of the economic forces acting on and through the state. In other words, the institutional perspective of public administration and the process focus of much of the public policy literature, lacking an adequate social theory, resorted to pluralist, public choice or other theories whenever it became necessary to explain linkages between the state and the economy.

Despite this, and despite continual criticism that the literature of public administration and public policy has been theoretically weak, there is much to be learned from descriptions and analyses of the structures, routines and problems (e.g. policy development or implementation) of the departments, agencies, boards, commissions and so on that comprise the state's administrative institutions. Much light has been shed on the organisational resources available to governments and on some of the constraints on the efficiency and adaptability of public bureaucracies.[46] Relationships between parliament, the executive and the bureaucracy, including relations between ministers and senior administrators, have been closely studied, with special emphasis on the themes of accountability, responsibility and efficiency. Research on such areas as organisational change, public finance and budgeting, administrative history, policy coordination, economic and social planning, and problems of implementation and evaluation in a federal system of government, have provided valuable insights into the operations of the state; but they are insights that can be appropriated by other approaches and would have to be integrated into any theoretically informed or comprehensive account of state–economy relations in Australia.[47]

One of the questions arising from this literature concerns the so-called relative autonomy of the state, a notion that is further discussed in other sections. The public administration and public policy literature supports those who argue that each section of the state apparatus tends to develop an institutional self-interest that helps to define its collective responses to demands from other bureaucratic and governmental agencies and from economic interest groups. This is partly a matter of maintaining control over certain resources (personnel, expenditures, information, etc.), and partly a matter of established modes of operations (routines, priorities, status, etc.). There is also evidence concerning the ways in which different business interests (sectors of capital) can develop harmonious relations with particular sections of the state apparatus which may have been established to regulate such sectors of economic activity; this in turn has posed problems for achieving a consistent or integrated approach to economic policy.

But the theories under discussion in this section do not—with one or two exceptions—attempt to offer a complete picture of the relations between public authorities and other spheres of organisation. Having no social theory linking organisational analysis to economic and political change, these theories tend to focus on demonstrating how certain policies and procedures are internally determined and implemented, rather than explaining why some types of policies are dominant and others excluded, or why the state is unable to control the economy effectively. Change is seen as coming from outside the arena of the state apparatus, which then responds in various ways to these external stimuli. The economy is simply 'out there', an untamed and often demoralising ocean of forces, tendencies, capacities and demands that the bureaucracy monitors on behalf of the political executive. Some reformist bureaucrats and ministers traditionally believed in the possibility of rational manipulation of these economic forces in accordance with certain political priorities and economic objectives; certainly, this was the spirit of the Keynesian era of post-war macroeconomic management. However, the difficulties in attaining a satisfactory degree of political control over economic processes (short of directive planning) are ascribed by traditional reformers to a deficiency in information or a lack of political willpower, instead of an inadequate understanding of economic power and of state–economy relations.

Neo-Marxist approaches

Contemporary neo-Marxist theorists have found much to agree with in Lindblom's quasi-structural account of business power, although they have criticised many aspects of the liberal perspective on state and economy typified by pluralist theory. The neo-Marxist writers selected for discussion in this section have all rejected the vulgar or orthodox Marxist assumption that the state is simply an instrument serving the interests of the capitalist (ruling) class.

As the prospects of socialist revolution disappeared in the advanced capitalist nations, there arose a number of more empirical varieties of neo-Marxist theory seeking to explain the actual links between class interests and public policy; the implications of welfare benefits and social–democratic governments; the cultural/ideological processes of social integration; and the limited reformism of the labour movement. There is no space here to describe the evolution of European neo-Marxism through Gramsci, the Frankfurt School of critical theory, the Austro-Marxists and others through to the Euro-communist theories of the 1970s and post-Soviet market socialism of the 1990s. The focus is rather on modern Western theorists who have arguably made some contribution to the understanding of power relations and policy formation in liberal democratic systems under conditions of advanced capitalism. Particular attention is paid to the following theorists: Miliband, Poulantzas, Block, O'Connor and Offe.[48]

Attention is also given to more recent movements within Marxist theory that have sought to move beyond narrowly class-based forms of analysis in order to develop wider explanatory frames of reference. The discussion here will focus on recent contributions by Miliband, Block and Jessop. The concepts and explanations that they advance should not be applied uncritically to Australia or any other society; this requires careful case studies and historical research. What they do provide, however, are some useful critiques of liberal approaches and some stimulating suggestions for alternative explanations of structures and processes in particular societies.

Miliband: Critique of liberal democracy

Ralph Miliband in the 1970s attempted to develop an empirically based alternative both to the liberal–pluralist analysis of power (which had emphasised the diffusion of economic and political power and the responsiveness of government to public opinion) and to the orthodox Marxist view of the state as the instrument of the capitalist ruling class.[49] In *The State in Capitalist Society*, his critique of pluralist economic and political theory consisted primarily in demonstrating, through comparative data on Western Europe and the United States, that economic power is highly concentrated rather than fragmented; that managers and property owners have similar interests and values; that there are important interchanges and linkages, and similarities in social backgrounds and beliefs, between state élites and corporate élites; that the advent of labour governments[50] has done little to alter the basic power structure of capitalist societies, although the system has certainly been humanised; that state economic policies consist largely both of protecting certain industries/corporations and of promoting the general interests of capital; and finally that the agencies of mass communication and consensus formation tend to sustain the existing arrangements, that is, to reproduce the social relations and values of capitalism.

Miliband's critique of one key strand of the orthodox Marxist account of the state, which sees the state as simply serving the interests of monopoly capital, stems from his view that the specific relations between state and economy should be empirically determined instead of deduced from a priori assumptions about the necessary or instrinsic structures of capitalism. According to Miliband, the very term *capitalist state* begs the question of how a particular state and economy are related, for that term suggests an invariable type of relation in which the state must always act in predetermined ways.[51] Orthodox Marxism, or at least those strands which downplay the possibilities of state autonomy, thus obscures the important historical variations in the institutional forms of the state apparatus and policy-making processes and the changes in state—economy relations. It lapses into abstract functionalism at the very point where concrete analysis should begin. There is, therefore, a crucial conceptual difference between the 'capitalist state' and 'the specific and changing forms of state—economy relations in a particular capitalist society'. According to Miliband, the existence of a capitalist class with a dominant influence on public policy has to be empirically demonstrated, and the exact nature of its links with state agencies and policy-making has to be specified for each society. Moreover, the possibilities for (and constraints on) radical reform need to be carefully considered.

Miliband's work has sometimes been seen (e.g. by Poulantzas) as typifying an instrumentalist theory of why the state tends to act in the interests of capital rather than in the interests of labour. Instrumentalist explanations, in this sense, are those that explain policy outcomes as the result of the activities (lobbying, debating, persuading, bargaining, etc.) and of the values (ideologies, motives, expectations, etc.) of the participants in the processes of policy formation. An instrumentalist explanation would focus on the values and activities of the state and corporate élites (seen as the most powerful participants) and would demonstrate their common outlooks, the interchange of personnel between them and their extensive channels of communication. Critics of this conceptual and explanatory framework point out that similar policy outcomes might still result even if the state personnel (e.g. the party in government, the senior bureaucrats) had a working-class social background and reformist values. Moreover, the instrumentalist framework does not really transcend the conceptual orientations of pluralism.

Miliband in fact readily agreed with this critique of instrumentalist explanations. He avoided explanations relying solely on the subjective outlooks of élite leaders and the outcomes of group pressures. In subsequent work, Miliband has given a threefold explanation of why the state tends to further the class interest of capital.[52] Firstly, the state élite and corporate élite tend to have similar outlooks and class origins. Secondly, the economic power of capital is mobilised effectively to promote its objectives at all points in the formation and implementation of public policy. Thirdly—and herein lies the major concession to his critics—Miliband noted the importance of the general 'structural constraints' of the capitalist system that narrow the 'practical options' for the state élite. In particular, Miliband acknowledged that capital's systematic control over the economy in capitalist societies gave capital a powerful 'investment veto' weapon that could be used to influence state policies. He claimed that none of these three types of explanation, in isolation, can adequately account for the state's tendency to identify the public interest with that of capital. This last remark indicates that, for Miliband, neither pluralism nor the so-called structuralist version of

Marxist theory, represented by Poulantzas, offers a satisfactory explanation of the state and of state–economy relations.

Poulantzas: Class fractions and relative autonomy

In his early work Nicos Poulantzas was concerned above all to establish a theoretical account of the relations between the political and economic spheres in advanced capitalist societies.[53] He rejected the vulgar economic–determinist theory in which the political level (superstructure) is an ideological reflection of the pattern of capitalist class domination in the economic level (base). Poulantzas instead adopted Althusser's notion of the relative autonomy of the political, economic and ideological instances or levels of a social formation. The social formation (the concrete historical society, as distinct from the abstract model of the capitalist mode of production) was understood as a complex articulation of levels, proceeding at uneven rates of change, in which the economic level nevertheless remained 'determinant in the last instance'. Thus, while the political level was given more prominence by Poulantzas than by orthodox Marxism, the economic level (and thus the domination of capital) remained the theoretical core of the explanatory framework.

The state, in this perspective, could not be understood simply as the tool of the capitalist class or of monopoly capital; neither could it be understood as independent of such forces. In the long run, however, the capitalist state 'can only correspond to the political interests of the dominant class or classes'.[54] This notion of a necessary correspondence between state and capital severely qualifies the relative autonomy of politics. Poulantzas' functionalist position is reinforced by his refusal to define the state in terms of specific institutions (e.g. parliament, bureaucracy, police, etc.), and his insistence on conceiving the state in terms of its functional role in the reproduction of class domination: it is 'the factor of cohesion of a social formation'.[55] Such an approach to understanding the state's relations with the economy and social institutions retains a doctrinaire element inconsistent with his critique of orthodox Marxism.

The basis for a more historical analysis of class interests and the state is provided, however, in Poulantzas' insistence that the class structure of a social formation in advanced capitalism is fragmented and complex and that the political interests of classes may be expressed in changing patterns of class alliances. Capital is not monolithic, and the 'common interests of capital' are difficult to determine. It is necessary to recognise the existence of class fractions whose conflicting interests cannot readily be settled and whose common interests cannot be determined without the mediation of the state.[56]

The major fractions of capital can be divided in terms of economic sector—e.g. financial, industrial, commercial or agricultural—or in terms of the size and power of enterprises—e.g. local, monopoly or transnational capital. According to Poulantzas, developing a perspective elaborated by Gramsci in the 1920s, the politically organised capitalist fractions constitute a power bloc, centred on a hegemonic fraction of capital. Political alliances between various classes (or between class fractions) further suggest that there might be a complex series of class struggles over the formation of public policy. The extent to which the state gains a relative autonomy from the dominant classes in a particular social formation will depend on

the precise conjuncture of the corresponding class struggle (the specific configuration of the power bloc, the degree of hegemony within this bloc, the relations between the bourgeoisie and its different fractions on the one hand and the working classes and supporting classes on the other, etc.).[57]

In his last major work Poulantzas developed the theme of class conflict over the directions of public policy, but he continued to have difficulties in finding a satisfactory conception of the state itself. He rejects two traditional characterisations of the state: that it be conceived as a thing or instrument, available for capture by a class to carry out class policies, in which case the state would have no autonomy; alternatively, conceived as a subject, the state would have autonomy in pursuing the policies formulated by those who wield its bureaucratic power, and it might resist the demands of the dominant class (or other classes) in order to implement rational general interests. Poulantzas, by contrast, claims that class conflicts and contradictions are inherent in the very organisations of the state and in the determination of state policies. The state, so to speak, is the site of class struggle. In his own words, the state is the 'specific material condensation of a relationship of forces among classes and class fractions'. Class contradictions, he continues, 'are the very stuff of the state: they are present in its material framework and pattern its organisation; while the state's policy is the result of their functioning within the state'.[58]

Poulantzas claims that the organisational role of the state is to constitute the 'political unity of the dominant classes, thereby establishing them as dominant'. It can perform this task more effectively 'insofar as it enjoys relative autonomy of given fractions and components' and of particular interests.[59] However, the plausibility of this claim turns largely on whether the state can accurately identify the general interest of capital and can implement effective strategies for securing this interest. But if the various apparatuses of the state may be controlled, as Poulantzas notes, by different class fractions,[60] and if state policies register the shifting patterns of class alliances and conflict over hegemonic leadership of the power bloc, then it would seem that the state is not able to discern the so-called general interest of capital nor to maintain any real distance from the dominant fraction of capital. Poulantzas' theory lacks an adequate account of the institutional specificity of the state, including an appreciation of the organisational and other resources which state apparatuses can use to further their institutional self-interest and relative autonomy from classes.

Having implanted the notions of class domination and class conflict at the heart of the state, Poulantzas subsequently oscillates between ascribing a key explanatory role to the political level (the conjuncture of class alliances and class political organisation) and appealing to a residual economic determinism (the structure of economic forces is ultimately decisive). Poulantzas seldom examines in detail the actual impacts of state intervention in advanced capitalist economies. Sometimes, however, he makes a remark that could form the basis for a fruitful line of inquiry into the contradictory effects of state economic policy: 'At one and the same time, it is driven to do both too much (crisis-inducing intervention) and too little (being unable to affect the deep causes of crises)'.[61] For more detailed insights into the causes and consequences of state intervention, it is necessary to consider some of the writings of Block, O'Connor and Offe.

Block: Relative autonomy reconsidered

Writing in the late 1970s and early 1980s, Fred Block attempted to avoid some of the pitfalls of previous neo-Marxist approaches by focusing more attention on the activities of political leaders and senior bureaucrats (whom he calls 'state managers'). Given that the dominant economic class does not rule in any direct sense in a liberal–democratic system, it is necessary to specify the processes by which the interests of capital tend to be promoted and defended in state policies.[62] Block argues that the pressure group activities of capital, and the existence of 'bourgeois cultural hegemony', would not suffice to explain the content of public policy. The problem, he claims, is to find an explanation not only of why the state avoids clearly anti-capitalist policies, but also of why the state has historically sought to rationalise and restructure capitalism. Assuming that there can be no such thing as a coherent and unambiguous capitalist class-consciousness which could guide or instruct state managers, it is necessary to seek alternative lines of inquiry.

Block's initial solution is to emphasise—as did Lindblom—the importance for state managers of maintaining a high level of economic activity. This has two aspects. The first is the familiar argument that governments face electoral defeat unless they can assure economic prosperity. Secondly, the state's ability to raise revenues through taxation and borrowing depends on a high level of economic activity. Much depends, therefore, on the state's capacity to sustain a general climate of business confidence. State interventions might arise in response to working-class demands and class conflict, but are shaped by the state managers' institutional self-interest in buttressing their own power and in promoting economic efficiency and accumulation. Unlike public choice theory, which assumes that bureaucrats always seek to spend ever-increasing amounts of public funds, for Block state managers can engage in rational restructuring and cost containment.

Some of these themes are developed further by Block in his analysis of the structural position of state managers in advanced capitalist societies.[63] He attempts to reconcile Marxist forms of class analysis with Weber's conception of the state as an independent form of power. Block suggests that state power (and thus public policy) will be constrained by class power in specific ways and in different degrees in particular systems. State managers seek to expand their institutional power subject to the political rules of the game and to the (changing) limitations imposed by class power. The modus vivendi established between state and capital in most circumstances has been highly favourable, in Block's view, to the interests of capital. This is because state managers are obliged to protect national economic and political interests in international relations, promote social harmony, maintain the conditions for accumulation and profitability, and stabilise the business cycle. Politicians and bureaucrats pursue these policies to enhance their own political advantage and institutional self-interest and not simply because of the lobbying activities and media influence of businesses.

Block notes that in addition to class (capital/labour) conflicts over policy, there are important government/business conflicts because some social policies require increased taxes and wider spheres of state regulation and because some industrial policies have a differential impact on various sectors of capital. However, Block argues that social reforms, once institutionalised, can often become methods of social control. In temporary periods of national crisis the 'investment veto' power of business over state policy might be partly suspended, allowing state managers to extend their economic controls, potentially against the interests of (at least some sections of) business. In periods of severe economic depression, during war and during periods of post-war reconstruction, Block argues, the state might have a greater degree of autonomy from capital and is able to restructure state–economy or state–society relations.

Like revisionist pluralists such as Vogel, Block's account introduces a historically dynamic account of state–economy relations. From the 1970s, Block noted, there has been a capitalist backlash against the 'drift towards more dirigiste economic policies', including forms of corporatist planning.[64] Block claims that this pro-market offensive has been a strategy by capital to avoid the imposition of further economic controls by the state in a period of uncertain economic growth and restructuring.

This style of neo-Marxist argument is not as doctrinally pure as the economic determinist and functionalist theories that dominated radical accounts of state–capital relations until the 1960s. In taking the state seriously as a set of institutions and decision-makers having their own resources and interests alongside those of capital, Block's analysis offers a more complex and realistic explanation of the tensions and accommodations between state and capital. Unlike the deductive theories, this blend of Weber and Marx leads directly to historical case studies that recognise the specific patterns of political and economic relations in different societies and at different times. As argued below, it is an approach that also allows a fruitful dialogue with the critical liberalism of Lindblom and with the neo-Weberian state-centred approach of Skocpol and others.

O'Connor: Accumulation, legitimacy, fiscal crisis

Another influential neo-Marxist theorist of contemporary state–economy relations is James O'Connor. Although his major work, *The Fiscal Crisis of the State*, was published in 1973, his arguments about fiscal politics and state budgeting in advanced capitalist societies have reflected major themes in state–economy relations in later decades, particularly in the relatively market-oriented societies dominated by the doctrines of economic liberalism.

O'Connor noted that, although there is no 'iron law' that state expenditures must rise more rapidly than revenue collections, there has nevertheless been widespread evidence of a 'fiscal crisis' of the state in advanced capitalism. This crisis arises from the 'structural gap' between outlays and revenue, which is caused by (a) increasing pressures for social expenditures and the socialisation of costs of economic development and restructuring, and (b) the political constraints on raising taxation levels. O'Connor argues that state spending generally helps to increase private profitability and to maintain social harmony; much of this spending is necessary to complement private investment and absorb the costs of social and technical infrastructure, welfare services and so on. The fiscal crisis can be tackled by attempts either to cut state spending or to raise higher revenues through taxation, public enterprises or borrowing. The economic–liberal backlash of the 1970s and 1980s against welfarism and 'big government', with attendant attempts to wind back or restructure state expenditure, has been a key response to fiscal crisis.[65] The other main response has seen states attempt to fend off fiscal shortfalls through mounting debt levels (the US) and/or massive sales of state assets through privatisation (the UK). The political problem for the left, in O'Connor's view, was to challenge the 'near-monopoly on the question of taxation' enjoyed by the right and to point out the class interests underlying important issues such as the 'distribution of the tax burden, the volume of state expenditures and budgetary priorities'.[66]

O'Connor identifies two basic, and often contradictory, functions of the capitalist state: firstly, maintaining or creating the conditions for profitable private accumulation, and secondly, maintaining or creating the conditions for social harmony or legitimisation. A capitalist state that openly uses its coercive power to help one class accumulate resources at the expense of other classes runs the risk of losing its legitimacy and might undermine the basis of its democratic support; although it must be said that the experience of the 1980s reveals that democratic states seem able to marginalise the poor and unemployed while still maintaining broad support. On the other hand, a state that ignores the necessity of assisting the process of capital accumulation risks drying up the source of its own power, the economy's surplus production capacity and the taxes drawn from this surplus (and other forms of capital).[67] O'Connor divides state expenditures into two main categories: social capital and social expenses. Social capital spending facilitates profitable private accumulation and can be seen as (indirectly) productive because it raises productivity or lowers the costs of the reproduction of labour. On the other hand, social expenses are unproductive but are necessary for the legitimacy of the system. O'Connor notes that because of the 'dual and contradictory' character of the state's functions, most items of expenditure and most state agencies are involved in both the accumulation and legitimacy functions simultaneously. Despite this complexity, O'Connor claims that in principle it is possible to determine the 'political–economic forces served by any budgetary decision'.[68]

The fiscal crisis of the state is worsened, according to O'Connor, by the growth in the wages bill for state employees (unrelated to productivity and inflated by the higher-wage tendency in the private monopoly sector). Moreover, there is an increasing number of welfare dependants or 'state clients' (who, from the viewpoint of capital, are 'surplus population'). Pressures on the state budget also arise from the political claims of special interests: businesses seeking social investment, labour seeking welfare expenditures, etc. Such claims, determined by political struggle, are not subject to rational coordination and can lead to considerable 'waste, duplication and overlapping of state projects and services'.[69] The plurality of interests and state agencies appears to place an overload of demands on state expenditures.

However, O'Connor regards the system as far from pluralist; in his view, it is dominated by the interests of monopoly capital. This orientation is reinforced by the state's institutional self-interest in promoting the expansion of large private corporations. However, like most exponents of this position, O'Connor is unable to provide a satisfactory account of how the class interests of the monopoly sector are identified and relevant incentives implemented by the state. Coordination by a 'class-conscious political directorate' is necessary, in his opinion, to transcend the level of disparate interests.[70] O'Connor claims that the class interests of monopoly capital emerge 'unintentionally' through the administrative mediation of the 'political directorate'—a view that bears some resemblance to Poulantzas' theory. However, this form of structural theory remains inadequate unless the specific processes of administrative mediation of monopoly sector interests can be shown in empirical case studies.

The issue of capitalist class-consciousness is an unresolved difficulty. The question of how class interests are translated into state policy has been at the core of Marxist approaches to state/capital relations; some recent theorists, however, have adopted a somewhat different approach by focusing more directly on the state's attempts to find administrative solutions to the economic, political and cultural crises of advanced capitalism. This alternative perspective is most evident in the work of Offe.

Offe: The state as crisis manager

Like O'Connor, Claus Offe makes it clear that the state's activities, far from being simply 'functional for capital', can involve contradictory policies and important concessions to the working class. Capital is obliged to contest many of the state's proposals and might not always succeed in defending its interests. Offe concedes that capital constitutes the dominant economic force in capitalist societies. But the power of economic classes cannot be understood, in advanced capitalism, without examining the structures and operations of state institutions and the ways in which they shape the resolution of class conflict and are themselves objects of class conflict.

One of the key aspects of contemporary state intervention is welfare spending and the provision of community services: the so-called welfare state. In an early functionalist critique of welfare provision under capitalism, Offe stressed the limited objectives and notable inefficiency of welfare policies, their inability to modify the structures of economic and political power, and the parallel system of subsidies for industry, which entail 'capitalism for the poor and socialism for the rich'.[71] Offe even conceded several points to economic liberals like Milton Friedman who had argued that welfarism was inflationary, ineffective and wasteful. However, Offe significantly revised this critique of the welfare state in response to the economic–liberal and neo-conservative offensive of the 1970s and 1980s. The welfare state and its objectives, scope and financing became one of the major themes of theoretical and political debate. Offe came to argue that the key challenge was to defend and extend the welfare state in more democratic and egalitarian directions, taking account of the positive program of the 'new social movements' based on ecology and feminism.[72]

In his analysis of political authority and class structures, Offe poses the question of how, in a parliamentary system, the interests of capital can gain the degree of state protection they require. His initial answer is that the political institutions themselves tend to ensure that democratic demands are articulated through narrow consensual channels.[73] Major political parties tend to exclude radical demands and work within the consensual rules of the game, and are internally undemocratic in their operations, thus allowing narrow leadership groups to steer the political machine. Interest groups are effective only if they represent important economic groups (with real bargaining power) and are prepared to compromise. Parliament is essentially controlled by the executive and is not a forum for serious debate on priorities. In other words, the political institutions act as filters that screen out radical programs and assign special status to élite leaders who work within the continuing framework of procedures and policies.

Offe's critique of the political system as an arena of system integration and legitimation can be contrasted with his more complex analysis of state interventionism in advanced capitalism. Offe's later writings are rather less functionalist; he is more inclined to detect tensions and contradictions in the policy process. With the growing role of state regulation of economic activities, it becomes clearer that the state is essentially engaged in 'cautious crisis management and long-term avoidance strategy'.[74] Primary attention has to be given to problems of economic stability, international trade and ensuring the (passive) support of the citizens. The class character of the state's activities arises not only from external pressures or social constraints but also from the selective internal structuring processes of the state itself. These processes both dampen anti-capitalist policies and avoid adopting every short-term sectional interest of particular business lobbies.[75] The relationship between the state and the accumulation process in a capitalist economy thus has four main elements: (a) the state does not directly control private decisions on production and investment; (b) it is, however, expected to create or maintain the conditions needed for capital accumulation; (c) the state's existence and power depend on the revenues derived from the private accumulation process; and (d) the state performs a legitimation function for the capitalist system by equating the general interest with that of business while denying the class content of this equation.[76]

Offe argues that the main forms of intervention have changed historically, according to different perceptions of the threats to the economic system. Allocative forms of intervention—where the state assists accumulation by distributing resources (land, revenue, coercion, etc.) already under state control—have more recently been joined by productive forms of intervention, where the state makes contributions (e.g. economic, social and technical infrastructure) necessary for the accumulation process. In this second mode of intervention, the state cannot merely react to group demands but must formulate rational strategies which protect the general conditions of accumulation.[77]

Traditional bureaucratic–administrative types of decision-making are adequate for allocative problems, but not for the new forms of productive intervention. Planning is ineffective if opposed by sections of capital. So there remain major problems and potential crises of authority and legitimation.[78]

This politicisation of economic relations under advanced capitalism is also a major theme with other neo-Marxists, particularly Jurgen Habermas.[79] Economic politicisation has undermined the fatalistic acceptance of the nature-like outcomes of market processes typical of earlier phases of capitalist development. In the current phase, politicisation of economic activity is reflected in bouts of inflation, industry rent-seeking, a crisis in public finances (hence a deterioration in community services) and uneven sectoral and regional policies. In addition to the conventional views of state planning/intervention as either ineffective or as hamstrung by competing interests, we also find in Offe and in Habermas the view that certain forms of state economic activity actually undermine the core principle of capitalism (exchange values as determined by the market). The state itself becomes involved in producing use values (collective goods, public services) and facilitates the development of use-value orientations among public sector workers and marginalised groups, e.g. welfare dependants.[80] Thus, the state's market-replacing activities might also pose a threat to the central tenet of capitalism: the universal character of exchange-value commodity relations.

This process of decommodification within an increasingly politicised economy not only contradicts the state's efforts to sustain the commodity form (such as worker retraining to improve labour saleability) but also erodes the polity/economy distinction so central to laissez-faire market ideology. In this way the visible hand of the state becomes increasingly pervasive and carries with it all sorts of political and ideological ramifications. Traditional capitalist tenets regarding private enterprise and corporate autonomy are threatened and, increasingly, the welfare state is forced to move beyond market valuations into increasingly conflict-ridden areas where agreement over substantive ends is lacking. Offe argues that all this represents the 'structural weakening of the normative and moral fibres of a capitalist commodity society'. He suggests that this does not necessarily imply 'any automatic tendency towards crisis or the breakdown of capitalism'.[81] However, he does suggest that the dilution of the centrality of 'property rights' by 'citizen rights' opens up new areas of conflict and political struggle within the state. It also increases the means available for resisting capitalism's commodity-based determinations.

Offe accepts much of the economic liberal and neo-conservative analysis of structural tensions within advanced capitalism and argues that: 'Much of the neo-conservative literature reads like a series of case studies confirming the Marxist thesis that bourgeois democracy and the capitalist mode of production stand in a precarious and imminently indissoluble relation of tension'.[82] Offe stresses the intractable nature of these crises and contradictions. At one point he states that 'capitalism cannot coexist with, neither can it exist without, the welfare state'.[83] Yet he argues that solutions based on a revival of the market—on depoliticising economic relations and recommodifying the functions of the state—are unlikely to succeed. This is because he sees the modern state as too central to the continuous functioning of the capitalist economy and to the life chances of a large range of (dependent) social groups. Moreover, Offe argues that neo-conservatism will find it impossible to recreate the norms and traditions that would underpin moderation of demands and belt-tightening.

Although Offe's work is rich and suggestive, it suffers from a number of limitations. Firstly, his work is pitched at the level of the single nation state, which ignores the international dimensions of contemporary capitalism. In particular, Offe ignores the global dimensions of capital mobility, especially in terms of major flights of capital away from the regulatory and fiscal burdens of first-world welfare states. Secondly, while Offe makes a number of telling points in his critiques of economic liberalism, he also tends systematically to underrate the ideological and political capacities of recent crisis management. In his way, he fails to give due weight to recent success in revitalising market-based ideologies and in curtailing working-class power in a range of Western countries. This blind spot in Offe's analysis points to a more general problem in his work: namely, his excessively generic, schematic approach to the state. Offe's analysis sets up an ideal-typical model of the state in crisis, which is insufficiently sensitive to national variations of history, cultural traditions, labour movements, parties, business structures and political institutions.

Marxist revisions

The Marxist theories discussed above all present a class analysis of the state in advanced capitalist societies. In extreme formulations, as in the work of Poulantzas, only classes have power and all politics is rooted in the dynamics of class relations. Yet since the late 1970s Marxist theorising and research has tended to soften this class emphasis. As noted above, Block's work amounted to an attempt to combine insights from Marxist and Weberian accounts of the state; the latter emphasising administrative, legal and coercive sources of state power separate from the dynamics of class politics. Not long before his death, Poulantzas insisted that the integrity of Marxist analysis could only be maintained if analytical primacy was granted to underlying economic determinacy and class analysis.[84] And yet the period since the early 1980s has seen a number of

Marxist writers search for a somewhat more eclectic position with an emphasis on historical contingency and the potential for a plurality of class and non-class influences on state action, including state power itself. For example, in a 1983 essay on state power and class interests, Miliband supported the basis of Block's claims that 'state power is *sui generis*, not reducible to class power'[85] and argued that:

> *The dynamic of state action is explained by Marxism in terms of the imperative requirements of capital or the inexorable pressure of capitalists; and these are indeed of very great importance. But to focus exclusively on them is to leave out of account other very powerful impulses to state action generated from within the state by people who are in charge of decision-making power. These impulses undoubtedly exist; and they cannot be taken to be synonymous with the purposes of dominant classes.*[86]

Other Marxists such as Bob Jessop have continued this line of argument by stating that neither societal forces nor the state 'should be privileged as an automatic starting point for explanation'.[87] What these Marxist revisionists seem to be saying, then, is that there is no such thing as a distinctively 'Marxist' analysis of state action; one that is simply reducible to class politics or to the economic imperatives of capital. Indeed, as Block has recently argued:

> *The key concepts that promised to provide coherence to a Marxist analysis did so at the cost of an unjustifiable narrowing of the array of causal factors. The Marxist concept of class, for example, tends to exclude the possibility that non-class social actors could play a significant role in determining historical outcomes. However, attempts to incorporate these non-class actors into the theoretical framework result in reduced coherence and a position that is no longer recognisably Marxist ... In sum, it becomes apparent that Marxism's effort to explain phenomena is incomplete ...*[88]

If such departures are becoming less recognisably Marxist, they nevertheless open up possibilities for synthesis with other theoretical approaches that recognise that states have power and a degree of autonomy with respect to societal or class pressures and with respect to the specific details of policy-making and implementation. Two such approaches are discussed below: corporatism and statism.

The common thread that revisionist Marxism shares with most versions of corporatism and with the milder versions of statism is that within a broad terrain of action (whose outer limits are defined by what in most circumstances is the practical need to preserve the basics of existing relationships of production) there is potential leeway for state autonomy and discretion; the exact amount in any given arena being an empirical/historical question. Contrary to some of the stronger statist claims, however, such state autonomy should not be seen in monolithic terms wherein a state can stand above or aloof from society. States are often divided politically and institutionally, and the boundaries between state and society are often not very clear.

Corporatism: The state, organised interests and policy networks

This blurring of public and private boundaries has been a central feature of corporatist literature. Corporatism, as a policy-making system, gives state recognition to major economic interest organisations (or other powerful interests in other discrete policy arenas), granting them a major voice in policy formation and implementation in return for their cooperation. Cawson describes corporatism as a policy-making system in which private organisations representing key functional interests (usually in the economy) 'engage in political exchange with state agencies over public policy outputs which involves those organisations in a role which combines interest representation and policy implementation through delegated self-enforcement'.[89] Hence, key interest associations become quasi-public in their role, an arm of the state's policy-making and implementation apparatus.[90] In such a system, crucial areas of policy can be removed from the day-to-day cut and thrust of politics and thus depoliticised; decisions rest on agreements formed by the leadership of peak interest associations and state élites, outside the conventional framework of parliamentary and bureaucratic policy-making. Common sites of corporatist policy-making include arenas where coordination between key economic or social interests and the state are considered imperative for effective policy-making. Typically, these include wages or incomes policies and industry adjustment policies. Corporatist decision-making is intended to be more or less binding on all the participants, but, at least within democratic systems, there remains a good deal of reliance on voluntary compliance.[91]

In the arena of incomes policy, there was very little Australian interest in such an approach until the advent of the federal Labor Government in 1983. Until the early 1980s the corporatist approaches common in Western Europe had found only a limited response in some sections of the Australian Labor Party, while non-Labor parties had generally been content to exclude the labour movement from key decision-making processes. The Australian experience of corporatist arrangements has been confined to a number of specific industry restructuring plans under Labor in the 1980s[92] and to the Accord-based wages system, described by Trevor Matthews in chapter 8 as 'corporatism without business'.

In general terms, the main implications of corporatist forms of policy-making in Western societies may be summarised in six points. Firstly, there is a shift in the locus of decision-making from parliament towards bargained outcomes in administrative and quasi-legal forums, thus strengthening a trend which had already become quite pronounced independently of corporatism.

Secondly, 'social contract' restraint on incomes, 'social wage' benefits negotiated with the state and productivity agreements may be seen as the incorporation of union leadership into the national consensus and a step away from a class-conflict perspective. Debate continues about whether this implies a strengthening or weakening of the labour movement, although in recent Australian experience there appears to be more evidence for the latter conclusion.

Thirdly, there is typically no corresponding guarantee by private corporations that investment or employment levels will be maintained, and the control exercised by firms over their workforce is not normally undermined by the obligations their industry association leaders might incur through a corporatist agreement. In this regard, corporatist arrangements typically involve asymmetrical obligations on labour and capital.

Fourthly, contrary to Winkler's claim[93] that corporatism anticipates a new mode of production (with public control over privately owned corporations), corporatist arrangements can instead be understood as one of several possible strategies available in an advanced capitalist system for attempting to manage economic crisis (inflation, recession, restructuring), to boost economic productivity, to curb industrial militancy and to promote consensus formation (in which the general interest is held to rest on the profitability of business).

Fifthly, corporatism in liberal democracies has most often been associated with social democratic or labour governments, seeking a deal with the union movement which would assist economic stability and higher productivity, and hence provide a more secure base for redistributive policies.

Sixthly, conservatives and market liberals, however, have been suspicious of corporatism because of its implicit economic planning, 'artificial' distortion of market price mechanisms, enhancement of union influence, possible restrictions on investment decisions and further displacement of parliamentary sovereignty in the political arena.

The radical left, of course, has always been suspicious of any 'social contract' or wages accord; its members fear that corporatism might simply increase business profits, incorporate union leaders without substantial benefits for the working class and effectively exclude other kinds of (often more militant) demands from the industrial and political agenda.[94]

In recent years it has been suggested that the explanatory insights of corporatist literature had already been anticipated by corporate pluralists, and for this reason it has been claimed that corporate pluralism is 'difficult to disentangle from corporatism'.[95] It is true that corporatist literature synthesises elements from the established theoretical traditions, both pluralist and Marxist. Yet it is also true that corporatist literature provides a stronger account of linkages between the dynamics of interest group politics and wider economic forces and state-based economic management issues. Firstly, corporatist literature has been better able to explain the occurrence of an assertive and activist state, a critical ingredient in any successful corporatist policy arrangement. Although corporatist literature has been criticised from time to time for being ambiguous about the precise role of the state, it is nevertheless clear that corporatism is most likely to emerge when the state is sufficiently autonomous for it not to be the captive of interest groups but not sufficiently strong or authoritative for it to rule by decree and hence avoid the need for cooperation from affected groups. The existence of this functional requirement means that, compared to any straightforward pluralist account, corporatism is better able to explain the privileged access of key economic groups within the state, as well as the imperatives driving the need for coordination and collaborative efforts between interest groups and the state in the face of problems ranging from inflation to industry restructuring.

Secondly, in relation to the imperatives for collaboration, a defining element of successful corporatist structures 'is the high degree of collaboration *among* the groups themselves'; a factor often overlooked in pluralist accounts, which tend to focus on discrete group/state relationships.[96]

Thirdly, there is a stress on representational monopoly in corporatist structures, a factor that stands in contrast to the representational heterogeneity and diversity emphasised in pluralist accounts.

Fourthly, again in contrast to pluralist accounts, corporatists emphasise the internal discipline and control functions of group élites.[97]

Fifthly, such a function stems from the requirement in corporatist structures for group élites to be able to deliver the cooperation and compliance of group members, which, in turn, is necessary since groups are required to play an active role in implementing centrally agreed policies. These last elements stand in direct contrast to pluralism's more voluntary, bottom-up view of group interactions with the state.

The demanding ideological and organisational requirements of corporatist arrangements, however, reduce its applicability and increase its fragility as a public policy strategy. Contrary to some earlier predictions,[98] there is no broad-based drift towards corporatist policy solutions in advanced capitalist states, and it is this kind of limited relevance that defines the empirical limits of corporatist explanations of group/state dynamics.

It is useful to see corporatism as only one type of 'policy network', meaning a distinct and structured pattern of interaction between organised interests and the state. Atkinson and Coleman have analysed a range of policy network interactions between the state and organised business interests and have identified some important structural underpinnings of policy networks. These involve, on one hand, the level of state centralisation, coordination and autonomy from societal interests and, on the other, the level of 'business mobilisation'; that is, the level to which business interest associations are politically active, are coordinated and able to participate in centralised policy forums within the state. The specific combination of these variables, according to Atkinson and Coleman, produce tendencies towards certain patterns of business–state interaction — or policy networks. Atkinson and Coleman discuss a variety of such policy networks, ranging from the more traditional models of pluralism to models with an increasingly directive state role. These include (among others): clientele pluralism, corporatism, parentela pluralism and state-directed policy networks.[99]

If, as suggested above, the corporatist policy network involves the fusion of policy formulation and policy implementation, Atkinson and Coleman suggest that certain other types of policy networks disaggregate such a coupling. For example, the 'clientele pluralist' network mainly involves delegated implementation, particularly for functions such as industry self-regulation. Atkinson and Coleman describe clientele pluralism as a system involving delegated government authority to private business groups, typically to the leading trade, business or professional association/s in an industry, sector or profession. The central dynamic here involves business support for (or at least acceptance of the need for) the state to offload certain responsibilities on to business. This is but one aspect of wider practices of concerted associative behaviour that Streeck and Schmitter have referred to as 'private interest government'.[100] Such a pattern of interaction between business and the state requires that the relevant business associations be mobilised to have sufficient information about industry or professional practices, as well as mechanisms for control over members or the means for effective self-policing.

'Parentela pluralism' involves both a low level of business political activity and a fragmented yet responsive state. Typically, the state enjoys only limited autonomy from sectional interests and depends on their support. In this network, the absence of a strong and centralised state, together with limited business organisation, produces a pattern of business–state interaction wherein fragmented business interests or a few leading firms in a given sector forge close links with leading politicians or the ruling political party. As Atkinson and Coleman explain:

The party in power dominates the state and the members of the government are willing, indeed, eager, to intervene, employing a partisan calculus in the administrative process ... When it comes to the bureaucracy, decision making authority is dispersed, technical expertise is weak, and a professional, bureaucratic ethos is scarcely developed. Accordingly, individual politicians have freedom to exert pressure ...[101]

The advantage of these policy network typologies is that they allow for a more fine-grained analysis of interaction between organised interests and the state than can be achieved with the less precise notions of 'policy community' (discussed above in the section on corporate pluralism). 'Policy community' implies formalised group interaction with the state but reveals little else. In contrast, the key dimensions of policy network analysis, such as the degree of centralisation and the autonomy of the state bureaucracy from party élites or external interests, allow us to establish models that explain how 'weak' states can be captured by partisan political interests, whether inside or outside the state or both, as in the case of parentela pluralism.

Importantly, policy network analysis also points to the way in which group–state interaction and public policy-making are often not just the outcome of one-way pressure from groups to government. Governments and state agencies often place heavy demands on interest groups.[102] Business associations in Australia report a constant stream of governmental or bureaucratic requests for information on industry trends or for opinions on policy options. Moreover, state leaders can play a very active role in shaping patterns of interaction between groups and the state and in acting as power brokers among competing interests. Governments and their administrative agencies can also block the access of certain groups to forums of policy-making or resort to creating, enhancing or activating interest groups where effective representation of certain interests does not materialise. As Streeck points out, in Germany:

Ministerial departments tend to discourage individual firms from contacting them directly on matters that can be dealt with by their associations ... By urging firms to go through established associational channels, state officials increase the functional importance and the prestige of associations in relation to their members [and] they help interest groups speak with one voice.[103]

Government and the bureaucracy should not be seen, then, as the passive recipient of external group demands.

In cases where the state has a high degree of independence from sectional interests and where there is only a limited degree of business mobilisation, it might be possible for government or key state agencies to distance themselves from group pressures and adopt a more directive role. Atkinson and Coleman refer to this type of policy network as a 'state-directed' network. When, for example, protectionist policy networks began to unravel in the late 1960s in Australia, this type of state-directed policy network gradually emerged (for a time) in its place.

Different policy networks tend to be associated with different types or styles of policy-making. As noted above, more traditional models of interest group pluralism are typically associated with a reactive and incrementalist style of policy-making. In such a system the sheer welter of competing interests, the difficulties of defining a coherent policy direction, the limited independence of the state from sectional interests and fragmentation of political authority make for an uncertain, reactive, short-term policy approach. Such a pattern might be well suited to a relatively stable policy context but, as critics of incrementalism pointed out long ago,[104] such contexts are probably rare. Moreover, the policy drift and reactive nature of incrementalism is unable to cope if major, planned changes or significant new departures in policy are required.

Atkinson and Coleman apply their typology of policy networks to the area of industry policy and argue that ad hoc, pluralist networks are unable to deal with the policy demands of industry sectors requiring proactive change or significant restructuring. (The same conclusion would apply to attempts to mount concerted incomes policies, which typically require close cooperation and agreement between key functional economic interests.) For policies requiring such a concerted, planned and anticipatory policy style, Atkinson and Coleman argue that state-directed, corporatist, clientele pluralist or 'concertation' policy networks would be the most appropriate. In the latter network, a highly mobilised business sector works hand-in-hand with an active and autonomous state; a form of interaction not uncommon in business–state policy networks in Japan.[105]

Instances of strong state coordination or centralisation are rare in Australian experience. The fragmentation of the Australian state further limits the degree of state autonomy from important economic interests and limits the capacity to implement state-led policy initiatives. Moreover, business interests are often fragmented, and business associations are often unable to provide effective leadership. None of this facilitates anticipatory, proactive or coherent policy-making.

Statism: State autonomy and institutions

Statist literature emerged in the late 1970s and has been critical of pluralism and Marxism, both of which are seen as 'society-centred' explanatory methods; pluralism because it sees societal (including commercial) interests as largely determining state action, and Marxism because class forces are seen as driving the state. In contrast, statists propose a 'state-centred' explanatory account that gives analytical primacy to state autonomy and state structures and argues that state action is not wholly reducible to or determined by wider social forces.[106] As Skocpol, a leading statist, argues, the state is an entity

> *with a logic and interests of its own not necessarily equivalent to, or fused with, the interests of the dominant class in society or the full set of member groups in the polity ... In contrast to most (especially recent) Marxist theories, this view refuses to treat states as if they were mere analytical aspects of abstractly conceived modes of production, or even political aspects of concrete class relations and struggles. Rather it insists that states are actual organisations controlling (or attempting to control) territories and peoples.*[107]

In 1985 Skocpol and her associates brought together the work of a number of statist writers in a collection of essays entitled *Bringing the State Back In*. In her introduction to the book, Skocpol boldly announced that a 'paradigmatic shift seems to be underway in the macroscopic social sciences, a shift that involves a fundamental rethinking of the role of states in relation to economies and societies'.[108] While insisting that 'the state certainly does not become everything', the central argument of this neo-Weberian approach is that the role of the state needs to be re-evaluated and seen much more as a 'weighty actor' both in domestic and international political environments. According to statists such as Stephen Krasner, 'the defining feature of a political system is the power of the state in relation to its own society'.[109] Hence, state autonomy emerges as a major theme in statist literature. As Skocpol explains:

> *States conceived as organisations claiming control over territories and people may formulate and pursue goals that are not simply reflective of the demands or interests of social groups, classes, or society. This is what is usually meant by 'state autonomy'. Unless such independent goal formation occurs, there is little need to talk about states as important actors.*[110]

Beyond the emphasis on state power and autonomy, statist writers stress the importance of institutional analysis.[111] In tandem with questions about state autonomy, this focus on institutional analysis is often framed within wider sets of questions about what particular states are likely to be able to achieve in policy terms. Here the focus is on questions about so-called state capacity. Statists adopt a typically state-centric account in arguing that the most important determinants are the particular resources which state élites have at their disposal and the nature of the institutions they work within. For a number of writers (not all of them avowedly statist) notions of state autonomy and state capacity have led to the concepts of 'state strength' and 'state weakness'. According to Atkinson and Coleman, for example, 'strong states are able to realise goals in the face of opposition from society's strongest elements; weak states are more easily penetrated by societal groups and find it difficult to resist their demands'. Beyond this, 'state strength is a function of bureaucratic centralisation, the quality of bureaucratic élites, and the degree of control exercised by the state over financial resources'.[112] Skocpol refers to these as the 'universal sinews of state power'[113] while Atkinson and Coleman consider that bureaucratic centralisation is probably the most important attribute of a strong or capable state. 'The emergence of multiple centres of authority is the quintessence of state weakness', they argue.[114] Although there has been some questioning of whether it is helpful to attempt to characterise whole states as either weak or strong,[115] so-called strong states such as France and Japan, with strong centralising tendencies and élite bureaucratic traditions, are typically contrasted with what are seen as less autonomous and more fragmented weak states such as the US, Britain or Canada.

Statist theory has been a useful counterpoint to forms of analysis that have focused narrowly on society-centred explanatory factors. Yet criticisms of the statist approach have focused on its often excessively state-centred character. As Mitchell argues, 'the statist approach always begins from the assumption that the state is a separate entity, opposed to and set apart from a larger entity called society'.[116] The statist formulation, building on the Weberian focus on state power and authority, is an attempt to address the long-standing problem of how to define the boundaries of the state but, as Mitchell argues, this solution comes with significant conceptual cost. The main problem, of course, is that the boundaries of the state can rarely be tightly defined; on the whole, they are fuzzy, not sharp. The statist response is to define the state narrowly and to focus on the preferences and actions of key or central state élites. Rather than seeing the state as a self-contained entity, however, Mitchell and other critics have suggested an alternative approach that analytically incorporates the state's uncertain and porous boundaries and brings in a wider array of explanatory factors, many of them society-centred.

Accordingly, Jessop warns against reifying and absolutising any notion of a defined state–society boundary and instead talks of an 'emergent, partial, unstable and variable social distinction'.[117] Block argues that the attempted 'sorting out of state and society-centred variables is ultimately arbitrary ... state and society are interdependent and interpenetrate in a number of ways ... arguments about which of these factors are more important tend to divert us from the more important issue of understanding the complex and changing interaction between state and society'.[118] Finally, Mitchell argues that 'the state–society divide is not a simple border between two free-standing objects or domains, but a complex distinction *internal* to these realms of practice'.[119] In this alternative approach, what we call state action is typically the product of common effort and shared power involving state *and* societal actors. Even in cases of so-called strong states such as Japan, most of the recent political research broadly confirms a model of 'negotiated consent' between public and private sector actors in forging state policy or in underpinning state capacity.[120] In this view, even in cases where the state or parts of the state act against powerful societal pressures, this is normally the result of particular state élites forging alliances with given factions in society. This 'coalition' model can account for apparent instances of authoritative state action but does not rely on seeing the state as a unitary or free-standing entity distanced from social forces. In this view, then, the state is as much or more about social relations than it is about formally authoritative institutions or actors. Moreover, state power in this view becomes something of a network or relational concept, suggesting that a proper understanding of state power is impossible without reference to wider societal clusters of power that lie beyond it.

It is clear, then, that at the frontiers of contemporary research on state action and state–economy relations, there is a wide range of explanatory variables at hand. The earlier and more constricted analytical frameworks and the grander theoretical pretensions of both pluralism and Marxism have, in part, been superseded by more open-ended approaches featuring a complex array of explanatory variables. The sterile debate between society vs state-centred modes of analysis has also been challenged by an approach that sees state action as a relational aspect of state–society interaction.[121] Moreover, unlike Marxism, which has traditionally posited a high degree of commonality between capitalist states in response to what are seen as the universalist imperatives of capital, the more recent approaches discussed here tend to stress critical differences in the form and detailed operations of such states. In this sense the state becomes a variable whose structure, role and capacities are shaped historically by a complex array of historical, institutional, ideological and economic pressures.

Elite theory: A note

Elite theories generally begin from the assumption that rule by élites is evident in all advanced societies, that élite rule is inevitable (given the apathy and passivity of the mass of citizens) and even desirable (given the dangers to social order which might result from mass participation in politics).[122] Some élite theories, more sensitive to the socioeconomic and organisational factors underlying the entrenchment of power élites, have focused their attention on the processes of centralisation of corporate economic power, the sociology of bureaucratic organisation (in both the state and private sector) and the growing demand for technically trained managers and researchers in advanced industrial economies. Building on the Weberian tradition of bureaucratic analysis, with its theme of the triumph of technical rationality, technocratic theories have provided useful insights into the growing power of corporate managers in major firms, the relative power of the executive over the legislative branch of the state, the transformation of substantive political questions into matters of technique and administration, and the minimal role of the citizen-voter in choosing between alternative political élites through the electoral process.

According to writers like C. Wright Mills and G. W. Domhoff, the concentration of power in the hands of a few élites, which are largely unaccountable for their actions, is the antithesis of democracy.[123] Mills argued that—at least in the United States—three levels of power were identifiable: the ordinary citizen-voters had virtually no power; the organised groups and medium-sized corporations formed a competitive and pluralistic middle level; while the most crucial decisions for the nation were taken in the light of the common interests of the 'power élite' (the leaders of the big corporations, central government and the military). The most powerful leaders were those who commanded the most powerful institutions: the corporations and the state.

Theories of elitism and technocracy range from relative complacency about the necessity of expert leadership (Schumpeter), to stern criticisms of irresponsible and unaccountable élites (Mills and Domhoff) and pleas for participatory democracy.[124] Elite theories, emphasising the importance of élites in the policy-making process, are one type of realist response to the democratic wishful thinking of classical pluralist analysis. The clash between pluralist and élite perspectives dominated a great deal of the debates on political power in the 1950s and 1960s.

The problem with élite theory, however, is that beyond pointing to the existence of public and private élites, it contributes little to contemporary analysis of the state. In particular, élite theory lacks an adequate theory of economic power and of the relationship between state and economic institutions. To a large extent, élite analysis of the state and public policy fails to go beyond the insights of corporate pluralist analysis. The combined resources of Marxist and statist literature provide much richer analytical concepts and approaches.

Conclusions

Both general theoretical remarks and more specific comments on Australian political economy in the 1990s emerge from this chapter. The theoretical conclusions may be summarised in six points.

Understanding the Modern State 65

1 It is not possible to develop a satisfactory general theory of 'the state' or of 'the economy' or of the relations between such general categories. An adequate theory of such phenomena would have to be historically grounded, explaining the sets of relations (structures, processes, tendencies) of a particular system in a particular period (e.g. economic interests and the state in Australia in the 1990s) and establishing contrasts and continuities with other societies.
2 It is mistaken to assume a priori that the activities of the state in a particular capitalist society will always be functional for capital, as implied by orthodox Marxists critics of capitalism and liberal democracy. It is also mistaken to assume an inherent incompatibility between the interests of the various sectors of capital and the expansion of the state's economic activities, as asserted by the economic liberal critics of big government. Both the assumption of a necessary functional harmony and the assumption of a necessary antagonism between the state and capital are philosophical starting points rather than the conclusions of comparative historical research.
3 The economic activities of the state cannot be explained entirely in terms of the demands or needs of economic interest groups, whether capital or labour or a broader range of organised interests. The structures and operations of the state have an important degree of institutional autonomy from economic forces, largely because the state commands key resources of its own — coercive, legal, administrative, programmatic, informational and ideological — that allow it to transcend a purely passive relationship to the economic interests in its own society. Moreover, the policies of political parties (which form the government in a liberal–democratic system) cannot be explained simply as the political expression of certain economic class interests.
4 However, the economically relevant activities of the state are at the same time constrained by the major concentrations of economic power and by the logic of profitable investment in a capitalist system. It is important to understand the historical process by which the economic structure of a particular society becomes established and modified; a process that takes place both through and despite the political and legal powers of the state. The strongest sectors of business are typically the most important broad influences on public policy, but the extent to which their interests are accurately perceived and actively promoted by the state is a matter for empirical investigation, not deduction from a theory of the capitalist mode of production.
5 The political economy of a capitalist nation state such as Australia operates in the context of both a political network of nation states and an economic network of international trade and investment. These global patterns have a major impact on domestic patterns of

economic growth, industrial specialisation, regional development or decline, national economic policy and the structure of state agencies dealing with defence and economic regulation. In particular, the globalisation of capital markets and business information have introduced new constraints on national governments.

6 In summary, the adequacy of a theory purporting to explain the actual roles of a liberal–democratic state in a capitalist economy should be judged in terms of the following criteria:

- ability to explain the specific institutional patterns of state and economy and policy frameworks at a given phase of development (e.g. Australia in the 1990s);
- avoidance of reductionist and functionalist modes of explanation, thus allowing a full account of political and social change, incoherence and inconsistency in economic and social policies, and forms of conflict in which the results are unpredictable;
- explanation of trends in the domestic economy and state policies within the context of international relationships.

These criteria make it clear that the theories outlined above, taken singly, do not offer a satisfactory account of the processes and structures of the liberal–democratic state and the capitalist economy, whether in Australia or other similar Western societies. Theoretical approaches need to go beyond earlier preoccupations with interest groups, class analysis or a narrow focus on state institutions or élites. All these factors need to be addressed when analysing and explaining state action. A richer and more complex approach that satisfies the criteria above would allow for different policy dynamics in various sectors of both the state and the economy, explain changes over time in these policy dynamics and facilitate comparative studies of policy frameworks in other periods and in other societies and nation states. Establishing how Australian patterns of social, economic and political life differ from those in other Western nations can provide significant insights into the nature of contemporary Australia, as evidenced by the major works of Francis Castles.[125]

Theoretical and conceptual analysis does not occur in a vacuum, of course, and changing fashions in state theory are linked to substantive changes in the political economy of advanced societies. The revival of theorising about the state in advanced capitalist societies in recent decades is due partly to the expanding and changing forms of state intervention in the economy, partly to the inadequacies of traditional theories (constitutionalism, pluralism, orthodox Marxism) in explaining these changes and partly to the failure of state regulation to produce economic stability and growth in most of the capitalist world since the end of the long post-war boom in the early 1970s. In Australia a revived interest in state theory arose at a time when sectoral conflict between industries seeking more assistance and those seeking deregulation of domestic and overseas markets came to the forefront, minerals and energy resource industries were becoming the main focus of new investment, tariff protection was being reduced and manufacturing industries were losing considerable ground to cheaper imported goods. Moreover, at this time the expansion of the public sector itself became a subject of critical analysis and debate. The size of the public sector, which had gradually increased in the 1960s and expanded rapidly in the early 1970s, was strongly criticised by market liberals and neo-conservatives who pointed to the implications of a large public sector for high taxation, public debt, workplace productivity, problems with inflation and interest rates, and reduction in choice for citizens and corporate investors.

The state in Australia has always been interventionist, as noted in chapter 1. In explaining the nature of this interventionism, the important historical and organisational issues for investigation include the types of interaction between state, business, labour and community interest groups, the ways in which political parties and state institutions have mediated and shaped the organisational forms of interest representation and the effects of such mediation on public policy. Changes in policy frameworks cannot be explained simply as a result either of political opportunism and electoral politics, on the one hand, or the interplay of class conflict on the other hand. The relations between the Australian state, the national economy and international economic and political structures are crucially important. In an increasingly globalised financial network, the evaluations of credit security made by international credit rating agencies are an effective discipline on both the public sector and corporate business. Competition for funds entails, moreover, that low overseas transaction costs for share-trading leads to pressure on governments in Australia to cut costs for business on local stock exchanges.

Following the decline of the Cold War, there has been a revival of trade competition and continued protectionist measures in the 1990s by the major capitalist trading blocs—the USA, Japan and the European Community. These developments will have enormous impacts on Australian trade. The effects of the international division of labour and new trading alignments are being felt in many sectors, and the range of state responses to these problems (industry restructuring, export incentives, tariff reform, technological change, pressures for exchange rate adjustment, etc.) throw considerable light on the nature of contemporary state–economy relations.

Establishing what is new about Australian policy responses to these problems (e.g. the dominance of economic rationalism) is an important part of understanding the changing modes of state intervention in Australia. The following chapters provide concrete analysis of the intersections between the political and economic spheres, integrating the study of the micro level of group and institutional decision-making processes and the macro level of public policy in the context of national and global economic development.

Notes

1 The range of theories discussed in this chapter is necessarily very limited. Thus, little indication can be given of the vast modern literature on the liberal–democratic state and on the nature of contemporary capitalism.
2 See B. Galligan (1984), 'The state in Australian political thought', *Politics*, 19:2, 82–92.
3 For historical accounts of modern nation states, see for example: B. Moore Jr. (1967), *Social Origins of Dictatorship and Democracy*, Beacon Press, Boston; G. Poggi (1978), *The Development of the Modern State*, Hutchinson, London; T. Skocpol (1979), *States and Social Revolutions*, Cambridge University Press, Cambridge; K. Dyson (1980), *The State Tradition in Western Europe*, Martin Robertson, Oxford; J. A. Hall (ed.) (1986), *The State in History*, Blackwell, Oxford.
4 B. W. Head (1984), 'Recent theories of the state', *Politics*, 19:1, 36–45. For extensive overviews of modern approaches to state theory, see D. Held (1989), *Political Theory and the Modern State*, Polity Press, Cambridge; P. Dunleavy and B. O'Leary (1987), *Theories of the State*, Macmillan, London; R. Alford and R. Friedland (1985), *Powers of Theory: Capitalism, the State and Democracy*, Cambridge University Press, New York; M. Carnoy (1984), *The State and Political Theory*, Princeton University Press, Princeton; B. Frankel (1983), *Beyond the State?*, Macmillan, Melbourne.
5 This categorisation of pluralist theory relies on M. J. Smith (1990), 'Pluralism, reformed pluralism and neo-pluralism: The role of pressure groups in policy-making', *Political Studies*, 38: 2, 302–22.
6 The best-known (United States) theorists of pluralism in the late 1950s and early 1960s were Robert Dahl, Nelson Polsby and Arnold Rose. The standard British accounts of parliamentary or representative government at that time also tended to convey a similar picture of democratic processes and group competition.
7 See, for example, C. E. Lindblom (1959), 'The science of "muddling through"', *Public Administration Review*, 19:6, 79–88.
8 All the élite theories and Marxist theories involve substantial empirical criticisms of pluralism. Important methodological issues are also raised in W. E. Connolly (ed.) (1969), *The Bias of Pluralism*, Atherton, New York; P. Bachrach and M. Baratz (1970), *Power and Poverty*, Oxford University Press, New York; S. Lukes (1974), *Power: A Radical View*, Macmillan, London; J. Schwarzmantel (1987), *Structures of Power*, Wheatsheaf, Brighton, UK, ch. 1; M. J. Smith (1990).
9 S. Lukes (1974), ch. 2.
10 S. Lukes (1974), chs 3, 4 and 7.
11 See E. Latham (1952), 'The group basis of politics', *American Political Science Review*, 46:2, 376–97; D. B. Truman (1951), *The Governmental Process*, A. Knopf, New York; K. Loewenstein (1965), *Political Power and*

the *Governmental Process*, University of Chicago Press, Chicago; N. Polsby (1964), *Congress and the Presidency*, Prentice-Hall, Englewood Cliffs; D. R. Mayhew (1974), *Congress: The Electoral Connection*, Yale University Press, New Haven; J. M. Berry (1984), *The Interest Group Society*, Little Brown, Boston.
12 See A. G. Jordan (1990), 'The pluralism of pluralism: An anti-theory', *Political Studies*, 38:2, 286–301.
13 D. Truman (1951), p. 10.
14 T. J. Lowi (1969), *The End of Liberalism*, Norton, New York.
15 W. Streeck (1983), 'Between pluralism and corporatism: German business associations and the state', *Journal of Public Policy*, 3:3, 265.
16 A. G. Jordan and J. J. Richardson (1987), *Government and Pressure Groups in Britain*, Clarendon Press, Oxford, p. 181; J. J. Richardson and A. G. Jordan (1979), *Governing Under Pressure*, Martin Robertson, Oxford; W. A. Kelso (1978), *American Democratic Theory*, Greenwood Press, Westport; T. J. Lowi (1969), *The End of Liberalism*, Norton, New York.
17 T. Matthews (1988), 'Vitally important allies?: The role of interest groups in government decision making', *Australian Journal of Public Administration*, 47:2, 156.
18 C. E. Lindblom (1980), *The Policy-Making Process*, 2nd edition, Prentice-Hall, Englewood Cliffs, p. 71. See also Lindblom (1977), *Politics and Markets*, Basic Books, New York.
19 C. E. Lindblom (1959).
20 R. Rose (1978), *The Juggernaut of Incrementalism*, Centre for the Study of Public Policy, monograph series, University of Strathclyde, Glasgow.
21 Lindblom (1977), ch. 13; Lindblom (1980), ch. 9. For a critical appreciation of Lindblom's writings see B. W. Head (1993), 'Charles Lindblom: Democracy, power and policy analysis', *Canberra Bulletin of Public Administration*, No. 71; S. Bell (1992), 'The political power of business', in S. Bell and J. Wanna (eds), *Business–Government Relations in Australia*, Harcourt Brace Jovanovich, Sydney; and J. Ravenhill (1989), 'Politics and business', in R. Smith and L. Watson (eds), *Politics in Australia*, Allen & Unwin, Sydney.
22 D. Vogel (1983), 'The power of business in America: A reappraisal', *British Journal of Political Science*, 13:1, 19–43; D. Vogel (1987), 'Political science and the study of corporate power', *British Journal of Political Science*, 17:4, 385–408; D. Vogel (1989), *Fluctuating Fortunes: The Political Power of Business in America*, Basic Books, New York.
23 D. Vogel (1983), p. 42.
24 See S. Bell (1989), 'State strength and capitalist weakness: Manufacturing capital and the Tariff Board's attack on McEwenism,' *Politics*, 24:2, 23–39.
25 For an elaboration, see S. Bell (1992).
26 See, for example: W. J. Baumol (1965), *Welfare Economics and the Theory of the State*, Bell, London; A. Breton (1974), *An Economic Theory of Representative Government*, Aldine, Chicago; D. Mueller (1979), *Public Choice*, Cambridge University Press, Cambridge; D. Whynes and R. Bowles (1981), *The Economic Theory of the State*, Martin Robertson, Oxford.
27 J. M. Buchanan (1978), 'From private preferences to public philosophy: The development of public choice', in Institute of Economic Affairs, *The*

Economics of Politics, Institute of Economic Affairs, London, pp. 1–20; J. M. Buchanan (1975), *The Limits of Liberty*, University of Chicago Press, Chicago; G. Brennan and J. M. Buchanan (1985), *The Reason of Rules*, Cambridge University Press, Cambridge.

28 C. K. Rowley (1978), 'Market failure and government failure', in Institute of Economic Affairs, *The Economics of Politics*, p. 37.
29 A. Downs (1975), *An Economic Theory of Democracy*, Harper & Row, New York.
30 See, for example, the summary and critique by P. Whiteley (1986), *Political Control of the Macro-economy*, Sage, Beverley Hills and London, ch. 3.
31 G. Tullock (1965), *The Politics of Bureaucracy*, Public Affairs Press, Washington; W. A. Niskanen (1971), *Bureaucracy and Representative Government*, Aldine-Atherton, Chicago.
32 See the arguments in M. James (ed.) (1987), *Restraining Leviathan: Small Government in Practice*, Centre for Independent Studies, Sydney.
33 See, for example, B. W. Head and E. McCoy (eds) (1991), *Deregulation or Better Regulation?* Macmillan, Melbourne, esp. chs 1, 2, 12 and 13; and J. J. Pincus and G. Withers (1983), 'Economics of regulation', in F. Gruen (ed.), *Surveys of Australian Economics*, Vol. 3, Allen & Unwin, Sydney.
34 M. Olson (1982), *The Rise and Decline of Nations*, Yale University Press, New Haven; M. Olson (1984), 'Australia in the perspective of the rise and decline of nations', Centre for Economic Policy Research, ANU, Canberra, Discussion Paper 109.
35 M. Olson (1982), p. 72.
36 M. Olson (1982), p. 82.
37 M. Olson (1984), pp. 26–33.
38 For critical reviews of public choice theory, see P. Dunleavy (1991), *Democracy, Bureaucracy and Public Choice*, Harvester Wheatsheaf, London; and P. Self (1985), *Political Theories of Modern Government*, Allen & Unwin, London, ch. 3.
39 For major statements, see the many works of Milton Friedman, such as (1962) *Capitalism and Freedom*, Chicago University Press, Chicago, as well as recent Australian works on economic policy such as J. Freebairn, M. Porter and C. Walsh (eds) (1989), *Savings and Productivity*, Allen & Unwin, Sydney.
40 See, for example, the conservative criticisms in J. Carroll and R. Manne (eds) (1992), *Shutdown: The Failure of Economic Rationalism*, Text Publishing, Melbourne; see also conservative critiques of economic liberalism in *Quadrant* magazine, for example, R. Manne (1992), 'The future of conservatism', *Quadrant*, January–February.
41 See M. Friedman (1962), *Capitalism and Freedom*.
42 On the concept of 'overload', see A. King (1975), 'Overload: Problems of governing in the 1970s', *Political Studies*, 23:2 and 3, 283–96; S. Brittan (1975), 'The economic contradictions of democracy', *British Journal of Political Science* 5:2, 129–59; C. Offe (1984), *Contradictions of the Welfare State*, Hutchinson, London.
43 M. Sawer (ed.) (1982), *The New Right in Australia*, Allen & Unwin, Sydney; K. Coghill (ed.) (1987), *The New Right's Australian Fantasy*, McPhee Gribble/Penguin, Melbourne; M. Pusey (1991), *Economic Rationalism in Australia*, Cambridge University Press, Melbourne; D. Horne (ed.) (1992),

The Trouble with Economic Rationalism, Scribe, Melbourne; S. Rees et al. (1993), *Beyond the Market: Alternatives to Economic Rationalism*, Pluto Press, Sydney.
44 See F. Block (1990), *Post-Industrial Possibilities: A Critique of Economic Discourse*, University of California Press, Berkeley.
45 See A. Gamble (1988), *The Free Economy and the Strong State: The Politics of Thatcherism*, Macmillan, London; and B. W. Head (1983), 'Fraser's liberalism', in E. L. Wheelwright and K. Buckley (eds), *Essays in the Political Economy of Australian Capitalism*, Vol. 5, ANZ Book Co., Sydney.
46 The major international literature is surveyed in B. G. Peters (1984), *The Politics of Bureaucracy*, 2nd edition, Longman, New York; N. B. Lynn and A. Wildavsky (eds) (1990), *Public Administration: The State of the Discipline*, Chatham House, Chatham, NJ; J. W. Fester and D. F. Kettl (1991), *The Politics of the Administrative Process*, Chatham House, Chatham, NJ.
47 The Australian literature is surveyed in D. Corbett (1992), *Australian Public Sector Management*, Allen & Unwin, Sydney; J. Wanna et al. (1992), *Public Sector Management in Australia*, Macmillan, Melbourne; G. Davis et al. (1993), *Public Policy in Australia*, 2nd edition, Allen & Unwin, Sydney; J. Halligan and J. Power (1992), *Political Management in the 1990s*, Oxford University Press, Melbourne; and B. Galligan, O. Hughes and C. Walsh (eds) (1991), *Intergovernmental Relations and Public Policy*, Allen & Unwin, Sydney.
48 Among the more important neo-Marxist writers excluded from consideration, we might mention I. Gough, A. Wolfe, E. O. Wright, E. Mandel, G. Therborn, B. Fine and L. Harris; and the German 'capital logic' theorists in J. Holloway & S. Picciotto (eds) (1978), *State and Capital*, Edward Arnold, London.
49 R. Miliband (1973), *The State in Capitalist Society*, Quartet, London (first published 1969).
50 See also R. Miliband (1972), *Parliamentary Socialism*, Merlin Press, London and R. Miliband (1982), *Capitalist Democracy in Britain*, Oxford University Press, Oxford.
51 R. Miliband (1973), p. 51.
52 R. Miliband (1977), *Marxism and Politics*, Oxford University Press, Oxford, pp. 68-74.
53 N. Poulantzas (1973), *Political Power and Social Classes*, New Left Books, London.
54 N. Poulantzas (1976), 'The capitalist state', *New Left Review*, 95, 72.
55 N. Poulantzas (1972), 'The problem of the capitalist state', in R. Blackburn (ed.), *Ideology and Social Science*, Fontana, London, p. 246.
56 N. Poulantzas (1973) and N. Poulantzas (1975), *Classes in Contemporary Capitalism*, New Left Books, London, part 2.
57 N. Poulantzas (1976), p. 72.
58 N. Poulantzas (1978), *State, Power, Socialism*, New Left Books, London, pp. 129, 132.
59 N. Poulantzas (1978), p. 127
60 N. Poulantzas (1976), p. 75; N. Poulantzas (1978), pp. 133, 155.
61 N. Poulantzas (1978), p. 191. For an extended exposition and critique, see B. Jessop (1985), *Nicos Poulantzas: Marxist Theory and Political Strategy*, Macmillan, London.

62 F. Block (1977), 'The ruling class does not rule', *Socialist Revolution*, 7, 6–28.
63 F. Block (1980), 'Beyond relative autonomy: State managers as historical subjects', in R. Miliband & J. Saville (eds), *Socialist Register 1980*, Merlin Press, London, pp. 227–42.
64 F. Block (1980), p. 237.
65 J. O'Connor (1973), *The Fiscal Crisis of the State*, St Martin's Press, New York, pp. 2, 9, 221.
66 J. O'Connor (1973), pp. 235, 246.
67 J. O'Connor (1973), p. 6.
68 J. O'Connor (1973), p. 7.
69 J. O'Connor (1973), pp. 40, 9.
70 J. O'Connor (1973), pp. 67, 69.
71 C. Offe (1972), 'Advanced capitalism and the welfare state', *Politics and Society*, 2, 482.
72 C. Offe (1984), *Contradictions of the Welfare State*, Hutchinson, London, chapter 6 and pp. 292–9.
73 C. Offe (1976), 'Political authority and class structures', in P. Connerton (ed.), *Critical Sociology*, Penguin, Harmondsworth, pp. 388–421.
74 C. Offe (1976), p. 415.
75 C. Offe (1974), 'Structural problems of the capitalist state', in K. von Beyme (ed.), *German Political Studies*, Vol. I, Sage, Beverly Hills and London, p. 37.
76 C. Offe (1975), 'The theory of the capitalist state and the problem of policy formation', in L. Lindberg et al. (eds), *Stress and Contradiction in Modern Capitalism*, Heath, Lexington, pp. 126–7.
77 C. Offe (1975), pp. 128–34.
78 C. Offe (1975), pp. 136 ff. For a critique of Offe, see J. Keane (1984), *Public Life and Late Capitalism*, Cambridge University Press, Cambridge, chapter 3.
79 J. Habermas (1975), *Legitimation Crisis*, Beacon Press, Boston.
80 J. Habermas (1975), pp. 60–6.
81 C. Offe (1984), p. 129.
82 C. Offe (1984), p. 66.
83 C. Offe (1984), p. 153.
84 N. Poulantzas (1979), interviewed by Stuart Hall and Alan Hunt, *Marxism Today*, July, p. 67.
85 F. Block (1980), p. 229.
86 R. Miliband (1983), *Class Power and State Power*, Verso, London, pp. 68–9.
87 B. Jessop (1990), 'Putting states back in their place: State systems and state theory', in A. Leftwich (ed.), *New Directions in Political Science*, Edward Elgar, London, p. 53.
88 F. Block (1987), *Revising State Theory*, Temple University Press, Philadelphia, p. 34.
89 A. Cawson (1986), *Corporatism and Political Theory*, Blackwell, Oxford, p. 38.
90 C. Offe (1981), 'The attribution of public status to interest groups', in S. Berger (ed.), *Organising Interests in Western Europe*, Cambridge University Press, Cambridge.
91 The best discussions of contemporary corporatism may be found in P. C.

Schmitter and G. Lehmbruch (eds) (1979), *Trends Towards Corporatist Intermediation*, Sage, Beverly Hills and London; G. Lehmbruch and P. C. Schmitter (eds) (1982), *Patterns of Corporatist Policymaking*, Sage, Beverly Hills and London; J. H. Goldthorpe (ed.) (1984), *Order and Conflict in Contemporary Capitalism*, Oxford University Press, Oxford; W. Grant (ed.) (1985), *The Political Economy of Corporatism*, Macmillan, London; A. Cawson (ed.) (1985), *Organised Interests and the State*, Sage, Beverly Hills and London; and A. Cawson (1986), *Corporatism and Political Theory*, Blackwell, Oxford. See also B. W. Head (1990), 'Corporatism', in J. Summers et al. (eds), *Government, Politics and Power in Australia*, 4th ed, Longman Cheshire, Melbourne.

92 See, for example, M. A. Capling and B. Galligan (1991), 'Corporatism with a difference: The textile, clothing and footwear plan', *Australian Journal of Public Administration*, 50:1, 47–60.

93 J. T. Winkler (1976), 'Corporatism', *European Journal of Sociology*, 17:1, 100–36.

94 For neo-Marxist critiques, see J. Westergaard (1977), 'Class, inequality and corporatism', in A. Hunt (ed.), *Class and Class Structure*, Lawrence & Wishart, London, pp. 165–86; L. Panitch (1980), 'Recent theorisations of corporatism', *British Journal of Sociology*, 31:2, 159–87; and B. Jessop (1990), *State Theory*, Polity Press, Cambridge, ch. 4.

95 A. G. Jordan (1990), 'The pluralism of pluralism: An anti-theory', p. 229 (note 12 above).

96 G. Lehmbruch (1977), 'Liberal corporatism and party government', reprinted in Schmitter and Lembruch (eds) (1979), p. 150.

97 Crouch considers this 'stress on discipline and control of membership... to be fundamental to establishing the value of corporatism as a concept contrasting with pluralism'. See C. Crouch (1983), 'Pluralism and the new corporatism: A rejoinder', *Political Studies*, Vol. 31, 454.

98 P. C. Schmitter (1974), 'Still the century of corporatism?', *Review of Politics*, Vol. 36, 85–131.

99 M. M. Atkinson and W. D. Coleman (1989), *The State, Business and Industrial Change in Canada*, Toronto University Press, Toronto.

100 W. Streeck and P. C. Schmitter (eds) (1985), *Private Interest Government: Beyond Market and the State*, Sage, London.

101 M. M. Atkinson and W. D. Coleman (1989), p. 84.

102 W. Streeck (1983), 'Between pluralism and corporatism' (note 15 above).

103 W. Streeck (1983), p. 270.

104 Y. Dror (1964), 'Muddling through: "Science" or inertia?', *Public Administration Review*, 24:3, 154–7.

105 R. J. Samuels (1987), *The Business of the Japanese State*, Cornell University Press, Ithaca.

106 For a review of this approach see S. Bell (1993), 'The new statist theory: A critical assessment', in A. Parkin et al. (eds), *Government, Politics, Power and Policy in Australia*, 5th edn, Longman, Melbourne.

107 T. Skocpol (1979), *States and Social Revolutions*, Cambridge University Press, New York, pp. 27 and 31. See also J. A. Hall (ed.) (1986), *The State in History*, Blackwell, Oxford and M. Mann (1986), *The Sources of Social Power*, Cambridge University Press, Cambridge.

108 T. Skocpol (1985), 'Bringing the state back in: Strategies of analysis in

current research', in P. B. Evans, D. Rueschemeyer and T. Skocpol (eds), *Bringing the State Back In*, Cambridge University Press, Cambridge, p. 7.
109 S. Krasner (1978), 'United States commercial and monetary policy', in P. Katzenstein (ed.), *Between Power and Plenty: Foreign Economic Policies of Advanced Industrial States*, Harvard University Press, Cambridge, p. 57.
110 T. Skocpol (1985), p. 9.
111 J. G. Marsh and J. P. Olsen (1989), *Rediscovering Institutions*, Free Press, New York.
112 M. M. Atkinson and W. D. Coleman (1989), p. 54.
113 T. Skocpol (1985), p. 16.
114 M. M. Atkinson and W. D. Coleman (1989), p. 54.
115 S. Wilks and M. Wright (1987), 'Conclusion: Comparing government–industry relations: States, sectors and networks', in S. Wilks and M. Wright (eds), *Comparative Government Industry Relations*, Clarendon Press, Oxford, p. 284.
116 T. Mitchell (1991), 'The limits of the state: Beyond statist approaches and their critics', *American Political Science Review*, 85:1, 89.
117 B. Jessop (1990), *State Theory*, Polity Press, Cambridge, p. 287.
118 F. Block (1987), p. 21.
119 T. Mitchell (1991), p. 290 (emphasis in original).
120 R. J. Samuels (1987).
121 Interestingly, Skocpol (1985: 20) advocates the use of such a 'relational' approach; this is not a well-developed aspect of statist literature.
122 On the inevitability of élites, the classical works are those by Pareto and Mosca. For a defence of élites and a critique of participatory democracy, see J. Schumpeter (1954), *Capitalism, Socialism and Democracy*, Allen & Unwin, London, Part IV; also G. L. Field & J. Higley (1980), *Elitism*, Routledge & Kegan Paul, London. For a study of multiple élites in Australia see J. Higley, D. Deacon and D. Smart (1979), *Elites in Australia*, Routledge, London.
123 C. W. Mills (1956), *The Power Elite*, Oxford University Press, New York. The work of Mills has been elaborated in a number of publications by William Domhoff. For example, G. W. Domhoff (1983), *Who Rules America Now?* Simon & Schuster, New York.
124 Among critics of élitism, see P. Bachrach (1967), *The Theory of Democratic Elitism*, Little, Brown, Boston; J. Meynaud, *Technocracy* (1968), Faber, London; K. Prewitt and A. Stone (1973), *The Ruling Elites*, Harper & Row, New York.
125 F. G. Castles (ed.) (1991), *Australia Compared*, Allen & Unwin, Sydney; Castles (ed.) (1989), *The Comparative History of Public Policy*, Polity Press, Cambridge; Castles (1988), *Australian Public Policy and Economic Vulnerability*, Allen & Unwin, Sydney; Castles (1985), *The Working Class and Welfare*, Allen & Unwin, Sydney; Castles (ed.) (1982), *The Impact of Parties*, Sage, Beverly Hills and London. The major work on comparative public policy drawing on American, European and Japanese examples is A. J. Heidenheimer et al. (1990), *Comparative Public Policy*, 3rd edition, St Martin's Press, New York.

3

Australia and the global economy

John Ravenhill[1]

Australia is a small, peripheral economy, heavily dependent on the export of primary commodities, and has always been vulnerable to shocks transmitted by the global economy. Earnings from primary product exports are notoriously unreliable; agricultural commodities are subject to supply-induced variations while the demand for and price of minerals depends heavily on the rate of economic growth in world manufacturing. The variability of Australian export prices in the years 1960–89 was among the highest of all OECD countries.[2] Such variability makes economic management particularly difficult for governments, almost invariably leading to 'stop–go' or 'boom–bust' cycles and, through its effects on the exchange rate, hinders export-oriented and import-substituting manufacturing.[3]

When the anticipated resources boom at the end of the 1970s failed to materialise, governments finally came to appreciate that the principal economic problem facing Australia was that its export specialisation was in commodities of decreasing importance both in international trade and to the world economy generally. The rate of growth of trade in primary commodities in the post-war period fell far below that of trade in manufactures. In the 1970s two factors exacerbated this trend. The first was that the success of OPEC in 1973–74 in dramatically raising oil prices prompted a move towards manufacturing techniques which used energy and raw materials less intensively. Synthetics, such as fibre optics, were increasingly substituted for minerals. The manufacturing economy, in Drucker's words, was becoming decoupled from the raw materials economy.[4] The second unfavourable trend, reviewed in more detail below, was the growth in agricultural protectionism and, in particular, the dumping of subsidised exports in third-country markets.

The consequence of these trends was that the prices of primary commodities tended to fall relative to those of manufactured goods. Primary producers had to sell more of their exports to pay for the same volume of manufactured imports — in other words, their terms of trade deteriorated. Australia was no exception (see figure 3.1). The trend of

Figure 3.1 Australia's terms of trade, 1950–92

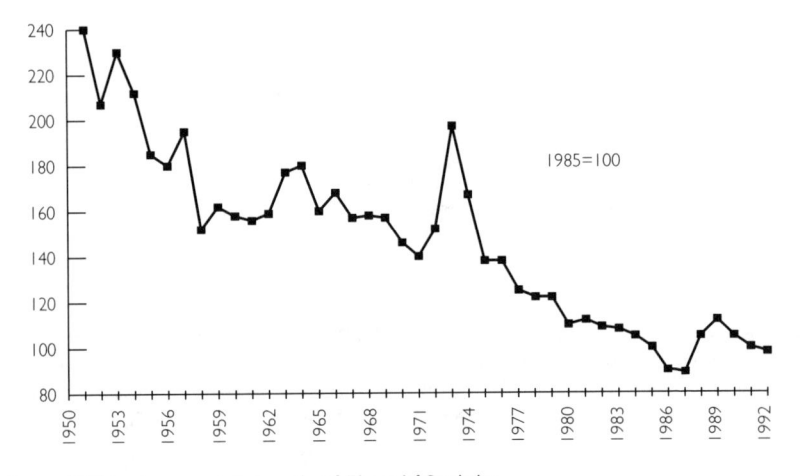

Source: IMF (various years), *International Financial Statistics*.

Australia's terms of trade has been steadily downward since the Korean War boom, although the trend has been interrupted periodically by sharp reversals. In the mid 1980s Gruen estimated that on average over the previous thirty years Australia had to increase exports by 2 per cent each year to pay for the same volume in imports. After 1970 the terms of trade declined more rapidly so that exports had to be expanded by 3 per cent annually to pay for the same volume of imports. Close to half of the productivity increase in Australia in the 1970s was offset by the declining terms of trade.[5]

Australia's international competitiveness paradoxically has suffered in the long term from the very factors that sustained the country's high standard of living through the last hundred and fifty years: its comparative advantage first in the production of rural commodities and then in minerals. The very success of the primary product sector inevitably hindered diversification of production and exports. A booming primary sector generated inflation at home and exerted pressure for a revaluation of the Australian currency (the 'Dutch disease' problem). Beside these structural constraints, the public policy choices made by successive Australian governments in the period since Federation have in themselves made a significant contribution to Australia's inability to compete effectively in the global economy at the end of the twentieth century.

This chapter reviews the reasons why Australian public policy choices that were intended to reduce the vulnerability of domestic sectors to external fluctuations left the country poorly prepared for competition in an increasingly integrated global economy. It then examines the creative foreign economic diplomacy that has been undertaken by Labor governments since 1983 in response to fears of growing protectionism. The chapter concludes by considering the adequacy of measures to promote domestic economic restructuring in the context of the rapidly changing nature of world manufacturing.

The consequences of domestic insulation

Governments are inevitably constrained in their policy choices by the characteristics of the domestic economy. The existence of such constraints does not, however, imply that there is no latitude at all for creative problem-solving. There are choices to be made, alternative paths that might be pursued. The decisions made by governments and their social partners in turn weigh heavily on the possibilities open to their successors. Australia's current economic problems owe as much to the policy choices made in the first eighty years of Federation as to the constraints imposed by the country's 'natural' comparative advantage in the production of primary products.

Unlike the governments of other small economies, Australia decided to pursue a path, in the terminology used by Castles, of 'social protection' rather than 'domestic compensation'.[6] In other words, Australian governments until the 1980s sought to insulate social sectors as much as possible from the negative consequences of the economy's vulnerability to externally induced shocks. A dual economy emerged in which inefficient manufacturing and service sectors rode on the back of the rents generated initially by the largely very efficient (by world standards) rural sector and subsequently by this sector in conjunction with the mining industry. 'Organs of syndical satisfaction', in Miller's terms,[7] were established for each of the major social sectors: arbitration commissions to guarantee a 'living wage' to labour; the Tariff Board to provide compensatory protection to manufacturing industry for the high wages that it was forced to pay; and marketing boards to stabilise the prices received by rural producers.

The post-war decision to provide 'protection all round', which governments saw as necessary to promote a sufficient manufacturing base to sustain the desired increase in population, was the most important factor in shaping Australia's contemporary economic difficulties. Protection of infant industries in itself was not necessarily undesirable; the problem in Australia was that governments never forced the infants to mature. Indeed, the belief, widespread not only among union leaders and manufacturers but also in government circles, was that Australian manufacturing, given the high wage structure, would never be able to compete effectively in world markets—a belief not shaken until the 1970s when the wage rates of successful manufactures exporting countries, first European and then Japan, soared beyond those of Australia. Unlike the pattern in Japan and the East Asian newly industrialising economies, protection in Australia was not made conditional on economic performance. Instead, the further some industries, most notably textiles, clothing, footwear and automobiles, fell behind international standards of productivity, the more their protection was increased. Australian governments, complaining with some justification that successive rounds of tariff reductions under the GATT (General Agreement on Tariffs and Trade) had ignored Australia's principal exports—agricultural products—failed to join other industrialised countries in lowering protection on manufacturing industries in the 1960s.

The lack of export orientation of manufacturing industry was reinforced by several factors. Not only did tariffs and/or quotas protect companies from international competition but also there was frequently little effective domestic competition. Manufacturing production in Australia is among the most highly concentrated in the world. And, where there were domestic rivals within an industry, their positions were frequently buttressed by 'all the restrictive practices known to man'.[8] Collusive price-fixing was largely untouched by the law until 1974; anti-monopoly laws and their enforcement, although tightened in the 1970s, remain weak by international standards today.[9] Such regulatory failures are particularly important in that the presence of vigorous domestic competition was identified by Michael Porter as among the most important factors in causing firms to acquire an international competitive advantage.[10]

Second, the desire of post-war governments to build a manufacturing base quickly, together with the aversion of Prime Minister Menzies to any form of government interference with the private sector, led governments to offer a virtual open slather to transnational corporations. Again, the contrast with Japan and the Asian newly industrialising economies is instructive. These countries sought to build strong domestic manufacturing corporations; the access of transnational corporations was strictly limited; governments attempted to unbundle the package of finance, technology and management expertise that the corporations offered, concentrating on the acquisition of technology; where corporations were given access their operations were often conditional on the transfer of technology to local companies and on their engaging in joint ventures with these companies.[11]

In Australia, in contrast, subsidiaries of TNCs were seldom subject to local content or other performance criteria, not required to undertake exporting and until the 1970s were given a free rein to purchase any Australian competitors. Indeed, rather than compelling the local subsidiaries of TNCs to engage in exporting in return for access to the domestic market, Australian governments allowed a situation in which many TNC subsidiaries were subject to restrictions on their export activities imposed by the parent company. A survey at the end of the 1950s found, for instance, that 55 per cent of British subsidiaries surveyed were subject to restrictions on their right to export to Asian markets; the figure for American subsidiaries was 40 per cent.[12]

The share of TNC subsidiaries in Australian manufacturing is second among industrialised countries only to Canada. Although the subsidiaries of TNCs undoubtedly contributed to Australia's post-war growth through the technology they introduced and the management expertise they provided, Australian governments might have driven a far more effective bargain on technology transfer, on local content and on exporting requirements. Another frequently observed disadvantage of dependence on TNC subsidiaries is that research and development activities are usually located in the country where the TNC has its home base. The low level of corporate research and development in Australia is often identified as one of the principal factors behind Australia's poor international economic performance.[13] This might be as much a reflection of the lack of an export culture, however, as of the dominance of TNCs. Caves notes that independently owned firms in Australia undertook even less basic research than the subsidiaries of TNCs.[14]

Finally, made-to-measure protection, designed to compensate local manufacturers for relatively high wages compared to those paid in Britain, gave the highest levels of protection to the most labour-intensive activities, such as clothing manufacture; in other words, those where Australia was least likely to have a comparative advantage and thus those least suited to domestic promotion.[15] Other factors also impeded those few firms interested in exporting: the local currency was overvalued in the 1950s and 1960s owing to the government's desire to maintain the link with sterling; work practices on the railways and at the ports were significantly below international best practice; competition among the states led to the fragmentation of markets; and insufficient investment was made in human resource development, particularly technical training.

The cumulative effect of all these factors left Australian industry ill-equipped for the increasingly competitive global economy of the 1970s.

With very few exceptions such as metals, virtually all of the highly tradable sectors of the economy were dominated by subsidiaries of transnational corporations domiciled elsewhere.[16] The value of exports of elaborately transformed manufactures—the fastest growing segment of international trade—in the early 1980s was less than $3 billion, or only 10 per cent of the country's total exports. More than a quarter of these manufactured exports were sold to New Zealand and Papua New Guinea. Australia had only one domestic corporation that was a major exporter of manufactures, BHP Steel. In contrast, Canada had thirty times more exports of non-resource-based products from large export firms.[17] The production of most Australian companies was concentrated in non-tradable goods and was therefore unlikely to contribute to Australia's exports. In the words of a recent report to the Australian Manufacturing Council, 'the Australian-domiciled firms which are large enough to be MNEs [multinational enterprises] are concentrated in products and sectors where technology and transport costs favour overseas production as the path of international expansion'.[18]

By the mid 1980s the proportion of Australia's exports that consisted of unprocessed raw materials was higher than it had been in 1973–74.[19] Australia's policies of domestic insulation ensured that the country failed to participate in the expansion of trade in manufactured goods, except as a consumer. As a consequence, the Australian economy was more closed (measured by the ratio of exports to GDP) than any other in the OECD at the end of the 1980s with the exceptions of Japan and the United States, both of which had domestic markets many times the size of Australia's (see table 3.1).

Table 3.1 The Australian economy in comparative perspective

	Primary commodities (% of exports)		Exports of goods and services (% of GDP)	
	1965	1990	1965	1990
Australia	86	63	15	17
New Zealand	93	75	22	28
Canada	63	37	19	25
Germany	12	10	19	32
France	29	23	13	23
Italy	22	10	13	21
Argentina	94	65	8	14
Spain	60	24	10	17
Austria	25	12	25	41
Turkey	98	32	6	19
Japan	9	2	11	11
USA	35	22	5	10

Source: World Bank (1992), *World Development Report 1992*, Oxford University Press, New York.

The combination of specialisation in the export of commodities that have become less important in world trade, and a domestic manufacturing sector that not only has been uncompetitive in the export of elaborately transformed manufactures but has also been unable to satisfy domestic demand for these goods, led to a widening current account deficit from the early 1970s onwards (see figure 3.2). In turn,

Figure 3.2 Current account balance as a percentage of GDP

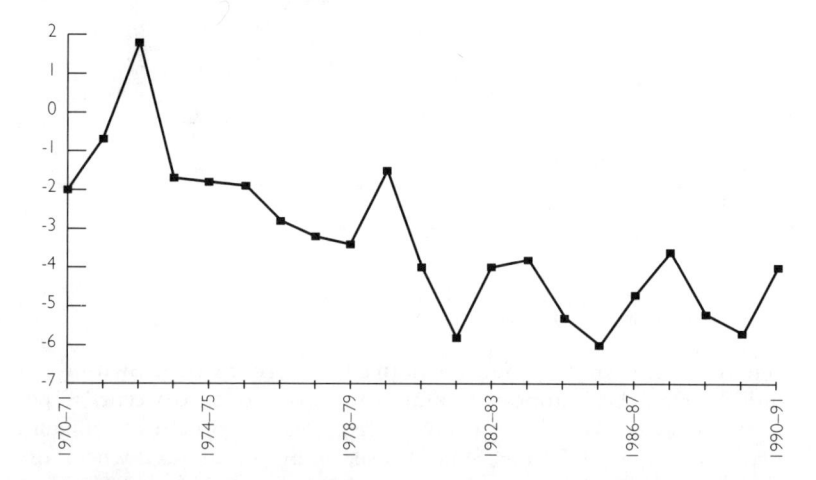

Source: R. A. Foster and S. E. Stewart (1991), *Australian Economic Statistics, 1949–50 to 1989–90*, Reserve Bank of Australia, Occasional Paper No. 8, Sydney.

this has caused a secular depreciation of the Australian dollar against the currencies of major trading partners (see figure 3.3). Of course, this made not only Australian exports and but also Australian assets, such as real estate and local companies, less expensive for foreigners to purchase. And it automatically provided the equivalent of additional tariff protection to the domestic manufacturing sector. Meanwhile, as the old social contract based on the politics of domestic insulation broke down, Australia was left without socially protective measures designed to promote and cope with the costs of economic restructuring.

Globalisation of the world economy

More than most industrialised countries, Australia has a major interest in the preservation of a stable and open world economy. The distance that separates Australia from its major markets makes the country an unlikely member of any regional trading bloc. In addition, Australia's trading pattern is much more diverse than that of other small high-income economies; its largest market, Japan, accounts for only 26 per

Figure 3.3 Trade-weighted exchange rate of the Australian dollar

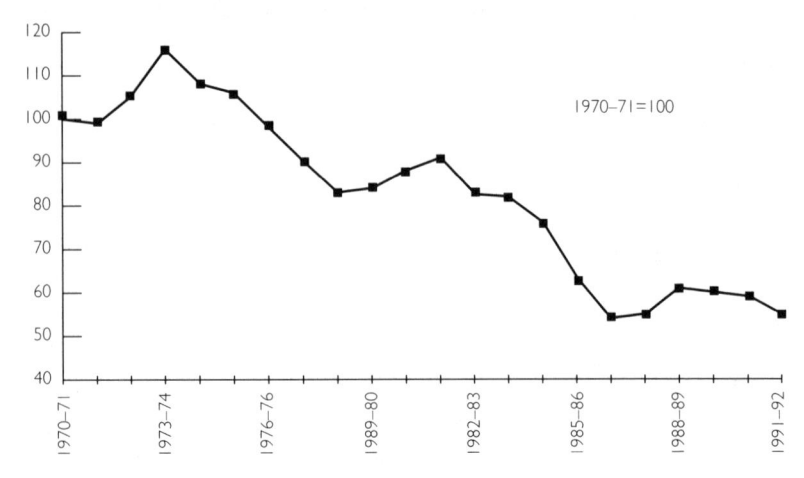

Source: R. A. Foster and S. E. Stewart (1991), *Australian Economic Statistics, 1949–50 to 1989–90*, Reserve Bank of Australia, Occasional Paper No. 8, Sydney.

cent of total exports (see figure 3.4). In contrast, for Sweden, Switzerland and Austria, the European Community consumes 54 per cent, 58 per cent and 65 per cent respectively of their total exports. And Canada's dependence on the United States is even more pronounced with more than 72 per cent of exports going to its southern neighbour.[20] The 'new mercantilism' — the growth of protectionist measures — that has characterised the world economy since the early 1970s is thus of particular concern to Australian governments.

Figure 3.4 Australia's principal export markets, 1990

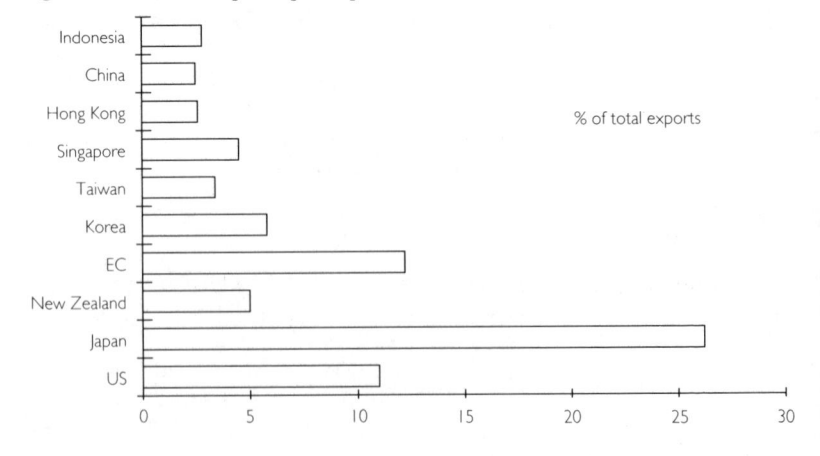

Source: IMF (1991), *Direction of Trade Statistics Yearbook*.

Paradoxically, the current problems of the world economy can be attributed to the very success of the post-war liberal economic order in promoting world trade and economic growth through the globalisation of production. The liberalisation of international trade through successive rounds of GATT negotiations in the 1960s and 1970s, and the restoration of currency convertibility by European countries in the 1950s, laid the foundations for a post-war order in which international trade increased far more rapidly than world production. The principal instrument for this was the globalisation of world production in which transnational corporations played a major role.

In the Australian literature, discussion of the globalisation of production has focused predominantly on the role of TNCs in transferring labour-intensive stage of production to low-wage countries. The literature that examined this 'new international division of labour' is particularly unsophisticated; states are reduced to passive actors in a process that is allegedly masterminded in corporate headquarters.[21] And to a considerable extent this literature missed some of the more important trends in globalisation: the diffusion of technology to Western Europe in the 1950s and 1960s and, more recently, to East Asia, and the important role played by the state in shaping comparative advantage in many economies.

With the globalisation of production, first Western Europe and then Japan rapidly closed the gap between their incomes and that of the United States. And, in the 1980s, the newly industrialising countries of East Asia were particularly effective in positioning themselves to take advantage of the accelerated process of globalisation. The dominant position that the United States held in the world economy in the immediate post-war years has inevitably been undermined. The US increasingly has been less able and less willing to underwrite the collective good of a liberal international economy.

The relationship between the relative decline of the US and the maintenance of a liberal international economic order has been one of the principal debates in the literature of international political economy since the mid 1970s. In its simplest form, the 'theory of hegemonic stability' suggests that a liberal international economic order is associated with a hegemonic power that has both the capacity and the incentive to finance this collective good.[22] In periods of transition from one hegemon to another, or when there are a number of powers of roughly equal standing, the theory predicts that there is a greater likelihood that an open economy will break down. A number of objections to these hypotheses have been raised; in particular, it is now generally agreed that a simple structural explanation is inadequate and must be accompanied by an examination of the forces that motivate states to engage in cooperative and leadership activities.[23] But the theory does appear to provide a plausible explanation for US behaviour in the trade field in recent years.

In the first quarter of a century after the war, the US permitted its principal trading partners to discriminate against its exports. Largely for security reasons—its concern to rebuild the economies of its new allies as a bulwark against the perceived threat of Soviet expansionism—it tolerated German and Japanese undervaluation of their currencies and Japanese protectionism, and actively encouraged the formation of the European Community. But as these economies rapidly closed the gap with its own, the US was increasingly unwilling to underwrite the costs of a liberal economic order. Three factors have encouraged this behaviour.

First, the pace of globalisation has accelerated particularly with the growth of the Eurodollar market in the 1970s and the subsequent liberalisation of the international financial system. Competitive advantage in the increasingly integrated world economy is changing more rapidly as the product cycle shortens. Accordingly, countries are increasingly competing to attract the industries that will be the technological leaders of the future.

Second, the most rapid increase in trade has occurred in intra-industry trade; that is, in products which are differentiated primarily by brand name. Such trade cannot be explained by traditional theories of international trade alone. It is based less on natural endowments and comparative advantage than on competitive advantage gained from being the pioneer in a particular field ('first mover advantages') and from experience that leads to more efficient production ('learning by doing' effects). In an increasingly oligopolistic global economy where enormous investments are required in research and development, competition is far from perfect. Companies can earn above-normal profits even in the long run—contrary to conventional economic theory. And the new trade theory shows that it is possible for governments to intervene to give advantage to their domestic producers.[24] On the other hand, the new trade theory predicts that governments that play by the rules of the old free trade game are liable to end up with, in the terminology of game theory, the 'sucker's payoff'. There is considerable scepticism in the United States among economists and politicians alike that its government is capable of fashioning an industry policy that could exploit the insights of the new trade theory.[25] But there is a widespread belief that other countries have gained an unfair advantage by engaging in the predatory trade policies that the new trade theory appears to justify. This applies most obviously to Japan, but also to such heavily subsidised European projects as the Airbus consortium.[26] The allegedly unfair trade practices of other countries are seen by some as legitimising 'justifiable disobedience' towards US obligations under the GATT; that is, unilateral action by the US to attempt to persuade trading partners to abandon unfair practices.[27]

Third, the rate of growth of most national economies has slowed markedly since the first of the oil price shocks in 1973. Industrialised countries deflated their economies in reaction to the strain that the oil price rises of that year and 1979 imposed on their balance of payments. Growth has been slower, unemployment has risen; the costs of adjusting to changes in the world economy accordingly have also increased.

The US response to its relative economic decline has been to engage increasingly in protectionist measures. Although a convincing argument can be made that the growth of the new protectionism has been necessary in order to sustain domestic commitment to an economic order that still remains relatively open,[28] it is nevertheless the case that the new protectionism causes immediate damage to the trading partners of the US. As Australia has traditionally exported few manufactured goods, the major impact on Australia of US protectionism of this sector occurs through the damage it does to other Australian trading partners whose consequent slower rates of growth reduce their demand for Australian raw materials. The one exception to this has been the 'voluntary' export restraint that Australia has been forced to enter into on steel exports to the US.[29]

The major deleterious impact on the Australian economy of the growth in US protectionism has been felt by agricultural producers. The US has lost patience with the protectionist agricultural policies practised by the European Community and, in particular, its dumping of subsidised surpluses in third-country markets. In 1985 the US Government introduced the Export Enhancement Program, which was designed to enable American agricultural exporters compete with the EC by providing similar export subsidies. In a 1989 report the Bureau of Agricultural Economics calculated that the subsidies, which amounted to more than $US23 billion in the first four years, had cost Australian wheat farmers more than $200 million per year.[30]

The US, of course, is by no means the only or the worst offender on agricultural subsidies: Australia also loses from European subsidies to wheat, dairy, beef and sugar farmers, and from Japanese and Korean protection of their domestic rice and beef farmers. The ludicrous state of global agricultural trade was nowhere better illustrated than by the proposed New Zealand purchase in 1991 of heavily subsidised Saudi Arabian wheat (which would have displaced Australian exports). In aggregate, agricultural protectionism is estimated to cost Australia more than $3 billion annually in lost exports.

Two other attributes of the new US trade policy have also had a negative impact on Australia. The first is the increased bilateralism in US trade policy, again reflecting US frustration with the protectionism practised by its trading partners. The principal manifestation of this has been the increasing resort to section 301 of the Trade Act of 1974 and the so-called 'Super 301' provisions set out in section 310 of the 1988 Trade Act.[31] Under the latter Brazil, India and Japan were named as 'priority countries' against which retaliatory action could be taken if trade practices found to be unfair were not terminated; Japan eventually agreed to participate in the Structural Impediments Initiative which, from the US perspective, was intended to apply pressure for improved access to Japanese markets. To what extent such measures will have an adverse impact on Australia depends on the agreements that the US reaches with the other parties. If they provide for liberalisation of market access on a most-favoured-nation basis then Australian exporters might well benefit—as has been the case with the agreement reached between the US and Japan on reducing protectionism of the Japanese beef market. On the other hand, there is always the danger that countries will attempt to head off American pressure by making concessions that are of benefit only to US exporters. Japan appeared to be pursuing this course with a number of agricultural products in the 1970s; fears have been expressed that the January 1992 Japanese 'commitment' during President Bush's visit to Tokyo to increase imports of US automobile parts would come at the expense of third-country suppliers including Australia.[32] The general danger in bilateralism is that it heralds a move away from a rules-based to a power-based trading system with obvious negative repercussions for small economies like Australia.

The second dimension of recent US trade policy that has particularly concerned the Australian Government is its new-found enthusiasm for negotiating trading agreements with its neighbours on the American continent. Again, the US administration has argued that the intention of such agreements—initially with Canada and subsequently with Mexico through the North American Free Trade Agreement, with the possibility of extension to selected Latin American countries—is to promote general trade liberalisation. US negotiators perceived such moves as providing additional leverage in the Uruguay Round of GATT negotiations. But the danger for Australia is that the consolidation of a North American Free Trade Area will further reinforce tendencies towards the fragmentation of the world economy into regional trading blocs. Twenty per cent of world trade already takes place within the European Community; this percentage is likely to increase with the completion of the Single Integrated Market in 1992 and the accession of new members in subsequent years. As noted at the beginning of this section, Australia with its small domestic market is particularly vulnerable to any further restrictive moves by its principal trading partners that impede access for its exports.

This discussion of the new mercantilism has focused on the US—not because it is the worst offender but because until recently it has been the most enthusiastic proponent of a liberal trading order and has substantially underwritten its costs. The US remains the single most important player in the global economy. Its recent move towards protectionism is symptomatic of the behaviour of most other industrialised countries.

The Australian response

Australia's international response to the challenges posed by the reactions of the leading economic powers to the increasing globalisation of the world economy has been far more innovative than its domestic response. The Labor Government has pursued an active strategy of trade diplomacy in an effort to promote trade liberalisation, particularly a reduction in agricultural protectionism, and to prevent the fragmentation of the global economy into closed trading blocs. These moves have also served a secondary purpose: the frequently stated requirement for consistency between the government's international advocacy of trade liberalisation and its domestic economic policies served as a means of symbolically tying its hands and a signal to local interest groups that the government had no intention of deviating from its efforts to reduce levels of protection at home.[33]

Australia's trade diplomacy has used two principal instruments. The first has been attempts to convince the public in its principal trading partners, particularly the European Community, of the virtues of liberalised trade by publicising the costs to them of their governments' agricultural protectionism. In a similar vein, the government has engaged in efforts to 'export the Industry Commission' by attempting to persuade other countries of the virtue of having a politically impartial body to review the costs to their own economies of their protectionist measures. So far there has been no rush to duplicate the IC. To estimate the impact of the efforts to publicise the costs of other countries' protectionist policies is more difficult. The Bureau of Agricultural Economics' Red Book on the European Community's Common Agricultural Policy certainly attracted attention when it was published and provided further ammunition to the policy's critics within the EC.[34] Whether it succeeded in changing any opinions is another matter.

The more important instrument of the Labor Government's trade diplomacy has been coalition-building. The two principal examples are the Cairns Group of 'fair' agricultural traders and the Asia–Pacific Economic Cooperation (APEC) grouping. GATT talks have always been dominated by the large trading states as negotiations are based on the trading of concessions, the major players being concerned to ensure that concessions on market access be extracted from their trading partners equivalent to those that they themselves have given. Small economies by definition have small domestic markets; the concessions that they can offer individually are of little value to large economies. Trade in products of particular interest only to small economies therefore has often not figured highly on GATT's agenda. The most glaring example is agricultural trade, which was initially excluded from GATT deliberations at the insistence of the United States.

The Cairns Group links Australia with thirteen other agricultural producers whose aim has been to ensure that a reduction in the levels of agricultural subsidies is achieved through the Uruguay Round of GATT negotiations.[35] The group has succeeded in keeping agriculture to the forefront of the GATT agenda, although how successful it would have been without the determination of the Bush administration to push the European Community towards reform of the CAP is questionable. And, as the Group of 77 discovered during the debate over the New International Economic Order in the 1970s, influence over agendas certainly does not translate into control over outcomes. How the Uruguay Round will be resolved was still uncertain in mid 1993; the Cairns Group is vulnerable to a bilateral deal between the US and the EC that meets these countries' individual concerns while ignoring some of the other issues of central interest to the group. The solidarity of the group has also yet to be severely tested: it remains to be seen whether the coalition is united enough to be able to use its joint bargaining leverage by, for example, refusing to sign new GATT codes on services if it fails to extract significant concessions on agricultural policy reform.

The establishment of APEC in 1989 was another landmark for Australian trade diplomacy in engineering what had been impossible before: an economic grouping that formally links Australia with the dynamic economies of East Asia.[36] The initiative again reflected Australian concern to avoid any movement towards a fragmented global economy based on closed trading blocs. It was also a response to the fear that the government's preferred strategy of relying on multilateral talks for the freeing of trade was in danger of foundering on the rocks of the Uruguay Round. Interestingly, the United States and Canada were not included in the original proposal made by Prime Minister Hawke on a visit to South Korea in January 1989. Not only did the US and Canada press their claims for membership but also Japan insisted that APEC should not be confined to countries of the western and southern Pacific.[37]

Much has been written about APEC by Australian academics. Many of them are people who have been closely associated with the initiative and/or with the Department of Foreign Affairs and Trade. As a consequence there has been little attempt at critical assessment of what APEC might be able to accomplish.[38] As far as Australia is concerned, the underlying objective of APEC is to ensure that any economic grouping to emerge in the region be consistent with GATT principles and not discriminate against the interests of non-member states. The Australian Government is obviously also determined to prevent proposals such as that of Malaysia's prime minister, Dr Mahathir, for an East Asian economic grouping, which excludes not only North America but also Australia, from becoming reality. But beyond these negatives, it is unclear what APEC—variously described as a 'process', an 'idea' and a 'framework'—can realistically accomplish.

The implicit assumption appears to be that APEC will be able to work to change protectionist government policies through publicising the costs of these policies and through the 'education' and socialisation of government officials into the liberal norms to be promoted by the grouping. Transnational coalitions of officials committed to liberal trade and able to change the policies of their home governments where they conflict with the principles of liberal trade, seem to be expected to emerge from the process. These are heroic assumptions. Little credence is given to the powerful role in the policy-making process of domestic groups with vested interests in maintaining protection.

As the current Minister for Foreign Affairs and Trade, Gareth Evans, acknowledges, APEC's 'achievements are not yet spectacular'.[39] To be sure, these are early days and APEC might play a useful, albeit modest, role in reducing the transactions costs of regional trade through improving information exchange and through other measures to enhance trade transparency. But there is little sign that APEC has had any influence on sensitive policy issues, for example, on the stance of the Japanese and Korean Governments on rice imports in the Uruguay Round negotiations or on US protection of its textiles industry.

The initiatives in trade diplomacy taken by the Labor Government since 1983 in response to worrying trends in the global economy illustrate both what can be done by a middle-sized power such as Australia and the limits to its influence. The building of a coalition of small countries dependent on agricultural exports displayed considerable initiative and was an effective means of enhancing their potential bargaining influence. Without the general support of the US for its objectives, however, there must be doubt as to what the Cairns Group could accomplish. A similar qualified assessment must be applied to APEC: a worthy initiative in itself, the exchange of information might help to avoid unnecessary minor frictions. But there are few grounds for believing that it will be any more successful than other diplomatic forums for resolving the fundamental trade tensions within the Pacific.

Merely being active in its diplomacy in constructing coalitions is, however, increasingly important for a country like Australia. Since the early 1980s the management of the world economy has occurred increasingly through summitry—particularly the Group of Seven major industrial powers from which Australia, unlike Canada, is excluded. Active trade diplomacy and coalition building has enabled Australia to have its voice heard, even if there is no guarantee that the major economic powers will listen to what it is saying.

Australia in a globalised economy

By the end of the 1970s Australia's policy of domestic insulation was no longer tenable. The domestic coalition that sustained it fractured as agricultural exporters became increasingly disenchanted with the costs of protection of the manufacturing sector, and the instruments that enforced insulation were becoming increasingly ineffective.

Nowhere was this more obvious than in the financial sector where efforts to insulate the domestic economy rested on the fixed exchange rate, restrictions on capital movements and controls over interest rates. The globalisation of international finance in the 1970s and early 1980s undermined the effectiveness of such measures. Indeed, they were increasingly counterproductive in that they disadvantaged the Australian banking system compared to non-banking intermediaries, which were able to exploit global financial markets to circumvent government controls. The deregulation of the financial system was, therefore, inevitable. But for a government committed to domestic liberalisation it also had the advantage of facilitating economic restructuring (as currency depreciation offset some of the costs of tariff reductions) and of exerting pressure on unions and the Arbitration Commission to heed the possible effects of wage increases on the dollar.[40]

Deregulation, particularly of the financial sector, which was where liberalisation was most quickly achieved and most complete, increased Australia's exposure to the global economy. This reduced the effectiveness of some domestic policy measures, especially monetary policy[41] and made every government policy subject to the scrutiny of the foreign exchange 'jocks'. Their importance was magnified by the Australian dollar quickly becoming a plaything of international speculators; since the float the Australian dollar has become the sixth most traded currency in the world (after the US dollar, the yen, the Deutschmark, sterling and the Swiss franc) despite Australia's not being in the top twenty exporting countries.

Financial market deregulation also paved the way for a massive increase in Australia's overseas debt in the 1980s. Net foreign debt rose from $16.5 billion on the eve of deregulation in 1982 to $144.8 billion at the end of 1991 (see figure 3.5). Debt at the end of this period was equivalent to 38 per cent of GDP, the highest level ever recorded, up from a mere 6.2 per cent in 1981–82. Australia's debt to GDP ratio was second only to New Zealand's among OECD countries. Debt service (the share of export earnings devoted to interest payments on debt) was close to 20 per cent. The link with financial market deregulation is that the bulk of the debt was owed by the private sector, which went on an orgy of overseas borrowing once capital controls were removed.

Some economists, notably John Pitchford,[42] have argued that because more than 90 per cent of Australia's net foreign debt is held by the private sector, it should not be perceived as a political or economic problem for Australian governments. His argument rests, first, on the belief that Australia's floating exchange rate will ensure that trade deficits are reduced by causing resources to be switched from domestic production into exports. Second, he asserts that if private companies are

Figure 3.5 Australia's net overseas debt

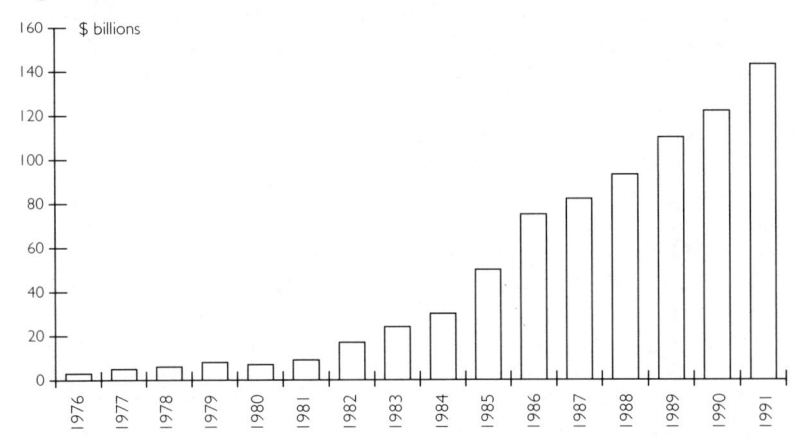

Source: R. A. Foster and S. E. Stewart (1991), *Australian Economic Statistics, 1949–50 to 1989–90*, Reserve Bank of Australia, Occasional Paper No. 8, Sydney.

unable to service their foreign debts they will go bankrupt, causing a loss to the foreign investor rather than a burden to the domestic economy. Other economists believe that the first argument overstates the capacity of the Australian economy to switch from domestic to export production because most of the country's export industries do not produce on a significant scale for the domestic market. Increased exports will therefore depend on additional, capital-intensive, long-term investments. And Pitchford's second argument ignores the costs through, for example, higher charges for overseas borrowing, that are imposed on all Australians by private companies' defaulting on their foreign debts (and, indeed, through the damage done to the country's credit rating by the overall level of debt).

The debt burden has placed constraints on government policy. As 56 per cent of the debt is denominated in foreign currencies, depreciation of the Australian dollar leads to an increase in the value of the debt and in debt-servicing costs. In the December quarter of 1991, for instance, 40 per cent of the $6 billion increase in net debt was caused by currency depreciation.[43] As the government's 'One Nation' statement noted:

> High levels of external debt leave us more exposed to external developments, such as slowing world growth and falls in commodity prices, that could set in train processes leading to sharp reductions in national wealth and living standards.[44]

As worrying as the volume of debt was the failure of the private sector to use the borrowed funds productively. Much of the borrowing appeared to have been frittered away on asset stripping, greenmail attempts and real estate speculation. The surge in business investment from 1985–86 to 1988–89 was the largest boom in thirty years. But a study by Reserve Bank economists showed that real estate operators and developers alone were responsible for 27.5 per cent of total new investment. Close to half of the total was accounted for by the finance sector; only 27 per cent of the new investment occurred in the manufacturing sector and this was devoted almost exclusively to import replacement capacity. The proportion of manufacturing investment in export-creating capacity remained fairly constant over the period.[45]

The failure of business to invest in new capacity for export manufacturing demonstrated a lack of response to the improved investment environment created under the Labor Government's Accord with the union movement. The profitability of the manufacturing sector nearly doubled during the eight years of the Accord; at the end of the 1980s it stood at its highest level for twenty-five years.[46] The Labor Government's faith that business could be trusted to respond positively to the creation of a favourable investment environment appeared misplaced by the end of its third term of office. To be sure, there was some growth in the exports of elaborately transformed manufactures after 1989, but with the absence of new investment in capacity for export manufacturing, this might have been what the AMC terms 'opportunist' exporting in response to the downturn in the local market. The surge in exporting was trumpeted by proponents of the level playing-field approach as success for their policies but, ironically, a significant percentage of the surge in manufactured exports came from offset arrangements under the automobile industry plan, much maligned by economic rationalists. Many of the other sources of increased manufactured exports had similarly benefited from government assistance whether in the form of industry plans (e.g., BHP steel) or 'partnership arrangements' whereby agreements were negotiated with the subsidiaries of TNCs for increased local expenditure on research and development (e.g., the telecommunications sector).

To dismiss the recent increase in manufactured exports as totally lacking in significance would be premature. The crucial test will be whether these exports are maintained once the local economy picks up. The low level of new investment in capacity for export manufacturing gives little ground for optimism.

The Australian economy at the end of the first decade of liberalisation, given its lack of large-scale exporters of sophisticated manufactures, appears poorly placed to compete in a world economy characterised increasingly by processes that Ostry has labelled 'techno-globalism'.[47] This term refers to the growth of corporate alliances between large TNCs in response to the increased research and development costs of developing new projects in leading-edge sectors. The gestation period for products is lengthening but the product lifecycle is shortening. Techno-globalism further emphasises the importance of intra-industry trade but in this instance in technologically sophisticated products. Ostry estimates that in the twenty years between 1966 and 1986 the percentage of high-technology goods in world exports climbed from 14 to 22 per cent.

In a world in which capital, technology and skilled labour are increasingly mobile, competition between governments is intensifying to ensure that their countries are selected as the site for the development and production of new high-technology products. Traditional conceptions of comparative advantage have little relevance to this new competition. As a report to the Australian Manufacturing Council noted:

> *The central shift required by this alternative logic is that we no longer see government as primarily an arbitrator or umpire (implicit in the level playing field vision). Governments are competing—sometimes in collaboration with industry—against other governments to attract investment and the tax streams on employment that follow ... Australia is a small and peripheral economy. Our task is not to pick winners but rather to create an environment in which (enough) winners pick Australia.*[48]

As the 1991 OECD report *Strategic Industries in a Global Economy* makes clear, in attempting to create an investment climate attractive to winners, Australia will be competing with countries that not only have reduced domestic impediments to business activity but also offer a range of government supports that embrace the application of non-tariff barriers, such as stringent rules of origin requirements, the imposition of high local content requirements, the selective provision of industrial sites, the strategic support of private R & D, discriminatory procurement practices and selective measures lowering the cost of capital.[49] To date neither of the major Australian political parties have displayed much understanding of the changing nature of the global economy and the measures necessary to compete within it. The economics profession in Australia, meanwhile, appears to be fixated with nineteenth-century concepts of comparative advantage.[50] Not only does manufacturing industry in Australia lag well behind international best practice but so too does the debate on industry policy.

Notes

1 I am grateful to J. L. Richardson for comments on an earlier draft.
2 It was exceeded only by those of Finland and Sweden, and was more than twice those of Japan and Switzerland. S. Harris (1992), 'The international

economy and domestic politics', in I. Marsh (ed.), *Governing in the Nineties*, Longman Cheshire, Melbourne.
3 R. Gregory (1976), 'Some implications of the growth of the mineral sector', *Australian Journal of Agricultural Economics* 20:2, 71–91.
4 P. Drucker, 'The changed world economy', *Foreign Affairs* 64:4, 768–91.
5 F. H. Gruen (1985), 'How bad is Australia's economic performance and why?', Centre for Economic Policy Research, Discussion Paper No. 127, Australian National University, Canberra, September.
6 F. G. Castles (1985), *Australian Public Policy and Economic Vulnerability*, Allen & Unwin, Sydney. The concept of 'domestic compensation' is derived from P. Katzenstein (1985), *Small States in World Markets*, Cornell University Press, Ithaca.
7 J. D. B. Miller (1959), *Australian Government and Politics*, Gerald Duckworth, London.
8 N. G. Butlin, A. Barnard and J. J. Pincus (1982), *Government and Capitalism: Public and Private Choice in Twentieth Century Australia*, Allen & Unwin, Sydney, chapter 5.
9 J. Ravenhill (1993), 'Business and politics', in R. Smith (ed.), *Politics in Australia*, 2nd ed., Allen & Unwin, Sydney.
10 M. E. Porter (1990), *The Competitive Advantage of Nations*, Free Press, NY.
11 On Korea see R. Mardon (1990), 'The state and the effective control of foreign capital: The case of South Korea', *World Politics* 43:1, 111–37.
12 H. W. Arndt and D. R. Sherk (1959), 'Export franchises of Australian companies with overseas affiliations', *Economic Record* 35, 239–42.
13 Australia ranks sixteenth of the twenty-four-member OECD in its expenditure on research and development as a percentage of GDP: Australia is ahead only of Ireland, New Zealand, Yugoslavia, Iceland, Spain, Portugal, Greece and Turkey. Unlike most other OECD countries, business contributes only a minority (40 per cent) of all R & D expenditure in Australia.
14 R. E. Caves (1984), 'Scale, openness and productivity in manufacturing industries', in R. E. Caves and L. B. Krause (eds), *The Australian Economy: A View from the North*, Allen & Unwin, Sydney, p. 326.
15 See, for instance, K. Anderson (1987), 'Tariffs and the manufacturing sector', in R. Maddock and I. W. McLean (eds), *The Australian Economy in the Long Run*, Cambridge University Press, Cambridge, p. 168.
16 P. Yetton, J. Davis and P. Swan (1992), *Going International: Export Myths and Strategic Realities*, Australian Manufacturing Council, Melbourne, p. 17.
17 AMC (1990), *The Global Challenge: Australian Manufacturing in the 1990s. Final Report of the Study by Pappas Carter Evans & Koop/Telesis*, Australian Manufacturing Council, Melbourne. A useful summary of some of the main findings of the report is presented in R. Evans (1991), 'The Global Challenge Report and the clash of paradigms', in M. Costa and M. Easson (eds), *Australian Industry: What Policy?* Pluto Press, Leichhardt, pp. 15–46.
18 Yetton, Davis and Swan (1992), p. 18.
19 P. J. Lloyd (1991), 'Domestic processing, value added and globalisation', in C. Hamilton (ed.), *The Economic Dynamics of Australian Industry*, Allen & Unwin, Sydney.
20 Calculated from data in International Monetary Fund (1991), *Direction of Trade Statistics Yearbook 1991*, IMF, Washington, DC.

21 For a discussion of how the new international division of labour has been treated by Australian authors see J. Ravenhill (1991), 'International political economy: An Australian perspective', in R. A. Higgott and J. L. Richardson (eds), *International Relations: Global and Australian Perspectives on an Evolving Discipline*, Department of International Relations, Research School of Pacific Studies, Australian National University, Canberra, pp. 209–27.

22 C. P. Kindleberger (1973), *The World in Depression 1929–39*, University of California Press, Berkeley; S. D. Krasner (1976), 'State power and the structure of international trade', *World Politics* 28, 317–47.

23 For discussion of the theory of hegemonic stability see, for instance, R. O. Keohane (1980), 'The theory of hegemonic stability and changes in international economic regimes', in O. R. Holsti, R. M. Siverson and A. L. George (eds), *Change in the International System*, Westview Press, Boulder; R. O. Keohane (1984), *After Hegemony: Cooperation and Discord in the World Political Economy*, Princeton University Press, Princeton; and D. Snidal (1985), 'The limits of hegemonic stability theory', *International Organization* 39, 579–614.

24 The literature on the new trade theory is immense. For an excellent summary of findings to date see J. D. Richardson (1993), '"New" trade theory and policy a decade old: Assessment in a Pacific context', in R. A. Higgott, R. Leaver and J. Ravenhill (eds), *Pacific Economic Relations in the 1990s: Conflict or Cooperation?* Allen & Unwin, Sydney. A useful introduction is P. R. Krugman (ed.) (1986), *Strategic Trade Policy and the New International Economics*, MIT Press, Cambridge, MA. For the implications for Australia of the new trade theory see T. Matthews and J. Ravenhill (1992), 'Strategic trade theory and its implications', in J. Wanna and S. Bell (eds), *Business-Government Relations in Australia*, Harcourt Brace Jovanovich, Sydney, pp. 178–88; and C. Hamilton (1991), 'Strategic trade policy and its relevance to Australia', in C. Hamilton (ed.), *The Economic Dynamics of Australian Industry*, Allen & Unwin, North Sydney, pp. 272–88.

25 One collection of articles by economists that, with a few exceptions, is sceptical of the desirability of the US Government attempting to pursue any form of strategic trade policy is R. Z. Lawrence and C. L. Schultze (eds) (1990), *An American Trade Strategy: Options for the 1990s*, Brookings Institution, Washington, DC.

26 P. F. Drucker (1987), 'Japan's choices', *Foreign Affairs* 65: 5, 923–41. S. D. Krasner (1987), *Asymmetries in Japanese-American Trade: The Case for Specific Reciprocity*, Institute of International Studies, University of California, Berkeley.

27 R. E. Hudec (1990), 'Thinking about the new section 301: Beyond good and evil', in J. Bhagwati and H. T. Patrick (eds), *Aggressive Unilateralism: America's 301 Trade Policy and the World Trading System*, University of Michigan Press, Ann Arbor, pp. 113–59.

28 J. G. Ruggie (1993), 'Unravelling trade: Global institutional change and the Pacific economy', in R. Higgott, R. Leaver and J. Ravenhill (eds), *Pacific Economic Relations in the 1990s: Conflict or Cooperation?* Allen & Unwin, Sydney.

29 It should be recorded, however, that BHP has failed to fill the quota that it was allocated in the years since the VER was imposed.

30 *Australian Financial Review* (14 November 1989). See also G. Miller (1987), *The Political Economy of International Agricultural Policy Reform*, Australian Government Publishing Service, Canberra.
31 See J. Bhagwati and H. T. Patrick (eds) (1990), *Aggressive Unilateralism: America's 301 Trade Policy and the World Trading System*, University of Michigan Press, Ann Arbor.
32 On agricultural products see A. George (1983), 'The changing patterns of Japan's agricultural import trade: Implications for Australia', Pacific Economic Papers, Australia-Japan Research Centre, Australian National University, Canberra, January; on the automobile parts issue see *Australian Financial Review*, 19 February 1992.
33 R. Higgott (1991), 'The politics of Australia's international economic relations: Adjustment and two-level games', *Australian Journal of Political Science* 26:1, 2–28.
34 Australian Bureau of Agricultural Economics (1985), *Agricultural Policies in the European Community: Their Origins, Nature and Effects on Production and Trade*, Australian Government Publishing Service, Canberra.
35 The other members of the group are Argentina, Brazil, Canada, Chile, Colombia, Fiji, Hungary, Indonesia, Malaysia, New Zealand, Philippines, Thailand and Uruguay.
36 APEC builds on the Pacific Economic Cooperation Council (PECC), a tripartite (government, industry and academia) body established in 1980, which was designed to promote consultation on economic policy issues. Beside Australia, APEC's original membership included the six ASEAN states (Brunei, Indonesia, Malaysia, Philippines, Singapore and Thailand), Canada, Japan, Korea, New Zealand and the US. In 1991 the 'three Chinas'— the People's Republic, Hong Kong and Taiwan—joined. For the history of economic cooperation efforts in the region see P. Drysdale (1988), *International Economic Pluralism: Economic Policy in Easy Asia and the Pacific*, Allen & Unwin, Sydney.
37 G. Evans and B. Grant (1991), *Australia's Foreign Relations in the World of the 1990s*, Melbourne University Press, Melbourne, p. 230.
38 An exception is a typically iconoclastic article by Helen Hughes (1991): 'Does APEC make sense?', *ASEAN Economic Bulletin* 8:2, 125–36, which concludes that 'the APEC work programme is unlikely to stimulate trade or any other economic activity'. For an earlier sceptical assessment of the benefits of economic regionalism in the Asia Pacific area see M. Kahler (1988), 'Organising the Pacific', in R. Scalapino (ed.), *Pacific-Asian Economic Policies and Regional Interdependence*, Institute of East Asian Studies, University of California, Berkeley, pp. 329–50.
39 G. Evans and B. Grant (1991), p. 126.
40 J. O. N. Perkins (1989), *The Deregulation of the Australian Financial System: The Experience of the 1980s*, Melbourne University Press, Melbourne.
41 Raising interest rates to deflate the domestic economy, for instance, could prove counterproductive in the deregulated financial environment by attracting large flows of foreign capital. These had the potential not only to increase the domestic money supply but also, by driving up the exchange rate, to make it more difficult for Australian firms to export and easier for consumers to buy foreign goods.

42 J. Pitchford (1990), *Foreign Debt: Myths and Realities*, Allen & Unwin, Sydney.
43 *Australian Financial Review*, 4 March 1992.
44 Quoted in Ross Gittins (1992), 'Debt: Out of sight and out of mind', *Sydney Morning Herald*, 2 March, p. 21.
45 C. Kent and P. Scott (1991), *The Direction of Australian Investment from 1985/86 to 1988/89*, Reserve Bank of Australia, Economic Research Department Research Discussion Paper No. 9106.
46 R. G. Gregory (1991), 'The current account and economic policy in the 1980s', in C. Hamilton (ed.), *The Economic Dynamics of Australian Industry*, p. 20.
47 S. Ostry (1991), 'Beyond the border: The new international policy arena', in *Strategic Industries in a Global Economy: Policy Issues for the 1990s*, OECD, Paris, pp. 81–96.
48 Yetton, Davis and Swan (1992), p. 72.
49 The principal findings of the report are summarised in W. Michalski (1991), 'Support policies for strategic industries: An introduction to the main issues' in *Strategic Industries in a Global Economy: Policy Issues for the 1990s*, OECD, Paris, pp. 7–14.
50 R. Garnaut (1989), *Australia and the Northeast Asian Ascendancy*, Australian Government Publishing Service, Canberra.

4

Globalisation, economic restructuring and the state

Belinda Probert

Almost every unpleasant dose of medicine that Australians have been asked to swallow since the early 1980s has been prescribed to promote something called 'restructuring'—a historic process which is held out as the only cure for our economic and social ills. It is not only our domestic institutions and practices that must be restructured but also our links to and place in a rapidly changing world—a process often referred to as 'globalisation'. Key elements of the restructuring process, such as the reduction of the public sector, deregulation and privatisation of industry and even welfare, together with the decentralisation of the wages system, have long been characterised as desirable by the political right. Given the impact of such policies on traditional social democratic objectives, it is not surprising that their implementation by the ALP in government has been controversial. The process of restructuring has none the less been remorselessly promoted as vital to our survival as anything more than a 'banana republic'.

This is not to suggest an absence of political conflict over the transformations required. Political debates about restructuring and globalisation have been heated in Australia, as elsewhere, but they have been conducted within a very narrow frame of reference. Both major parties have essentially been engaged in promising that they are the party that can bring about restructuring and globalisation most effectively. Microeconomic reform, the restructuring of outdated industrial awards, tariff reduction, flexibility, flexibility and yet more flexibility have become the icons of both major parties. Sceptics and critics have, since the early 1980s, been confined to the margins of political debate (although there are signs of renewed intervention from both the right and the left[1]).

The narrowing of our local political agenda itself needs to be seen in a global context. As Manuel Castells points out:

> *In the 1980s, restructuring clearly took place in the US under Reagan and in the UK under Thatcher; but it also took place in France under a socialist government, with communist participation ... Restructuring took place in most of Western Europe: in the Pacific Rim, given impetus by the internationalization of the economy; and in the Third World, as a result of austerity policies often dictated by international financial institutions. Each restructuring process followed a specific path, depending on the economic, social and political conditions of the various countries; but in all cases it had to deal with similar policy questions and went through similar political debates, converging on a restricted set of economic policies.*[2]

Given the scope and scale of the political and economic changes being ascribed to the imperatives of globalisation and restructuring, it is surprising that these concepts have been subjected to relatively little critical scrutiny in Australia. In particular, a sense of historical specificity seems to be missing. There is nothing particularly new about the processes of restructuring and globalisation as integral features of the dynamic of capitalism. Is it simply that now we can no longer resist them or control them? Before we abandon politics to economics we need to consider these concepts more carefully.

Restructuring or post-Fordism?

Restructuring is endemic and ubiquitous. The term is used to emphasise the radical nature of the economic transformation under way, but it does not carry any particular theoretical weight and is generally used in a descriptive sense. At its most basic it is used in the context of a particular industry or even a firm to describe changes in the organisation of production aimed at improving profitability.

One of the earliest accounts of this process in the 1980s is to be found in Julianne Schultz's book about the restructuring of BHP's steel division in Wollongong.[3] The book is a damning indictment of the human costs incurred in that neutral-sounding process. Schultz insists that 're-structuring is a code word' that hides the reality of the job loss involved in 'manufacturing industry's transition from labour-intensive to capital-intensive'.[4] In 1982 BHP lost $144.2 million, but by 1984 it was able to announce its largest-ever profit of $638.7 million, of which $72 million came from its steel division. The restructuring that made this turnaround possible cost 15 000 people their jobs.[5] The benefits and costs of restructuring BHP steel are shown by Schultz to have been distributed in a profoundly inequitable manner, yet she has no doubt of the need for such restructuring. Indeed, it could be argued that the process of labour-displacing technological innovation is as old as capitalism itself and that what happened in Wollongong was merely a particularly painful example because of the high dependency of that town on one industry. It is interesting to note that the steel industry is often cited to illustrate the shift from mass production of a standard product to flexible, small-scale production of differentiated products (of 'boutique' steels)—as the exemplar of the possibilities created by new forms of work organisation and technological innovation.[6]

The danger, however, of relying on the manufacturing case study as an exemplar of the process of contemporary restructuring is that it is easy to ignore the transformations occurring in other sectors and to miss the scale of social and political transformation that appears to be part of the process on a larger scale. It is these issues that define the specificity of restructuring in the 1980s and 1990s.

This is not to say that the idea of looking at the process of restructuring in a particular town is misguided. On the contrary, one of the most impressive attempts to develop a 'restructuring' approach is a close study by Bagguley et al. of an even smaller town, that of Lancaster in England's north-west.[7] This study describes many familiar economic changes, including the decline of traditional manufacturing industry (lino, textiles and chemicals) and the rise of service sector employment. But what is distinctive is the authors' concern to avoid any simple reductionism in their analysis and to recognise the full range of different strategies that can be used in restructuring. Thus, in their analysis of industrial restructuring they note that it can involve technical change or production reorganisation or spatial relocation.[8] Industrial restructuring might involve workforce flexibility based on multiskilling and enlarged job functions, but it might equally well involve—as in the case of textile firms—more night shifts around expensive new technology. Bagguley et al. are aware of the range of restructuring strategies that may be adopted partly because they appreciate the role that gender and ethnicity play in shaping employers' strategies and in providing strong forms of resistance to certain kinds of flexibility.

Rather than simply confining its analysis to the restructuring of Lancaster's struggling manufacturing sector, this study gives equal weight to the restructuring of the service sector. The authors argue that an even broader range of strategies is available for restructuring service industries, including public services.[9] They link the massive pressures on public service restructuring directly to pressures to restructure manufacturing, arguing that both are the result of declining profitability in the private sector which translates into growing pressure on public budgets. The outcome of struggles over public sector restructuring is, of course, political, with some countries better able to preserve public sector employment and service delivery than others.

Restructuring theory—a term used by radical geographers such as Scott & Storper and Massey[10]—is concerned with both the geographical and social evolution of the labour process and capitalist production. For Bagguley et al. the core of restructuring theory is 'an analysis of the processes and strategies through which capital seeks expanded accumulation'.[11] Yet for these authors the complexity of these processes is overwhelming. The particular places observed as locality studies seem to be even more particular when studied closely. Bagguley et al. recognise that the current wave of restructuring is a response to a general economic crisis, but they are unwilling to see this crisis in the totalising frameworks offered by, for example, those who analyse these changes in terms of a transition from Fordism to post-Fordism, or from mass production to flexible specialisation. However, given the ubiquity of the crisis, and of pressures to restructure not just factory work but also almost every social institution, these totalising frameworks offer important challenges.

Within Australia, as elsewhere, there has been a vigorous debate about whether some of the changes we are witnessing can usefully be located in what has been called the decline of Fordism and its replacement with something called, somewhat unhelpfully, post-Fordism. These debates about Fordism have, however, been confined largely to the pages of journals such as *Labour and Industry*, where industrial relations specialists argue over what is actually happening in individual factories.[12] In this context *Fordism* refers primarily to a system of mass production of standardised goods employing semiskilled workers in Taylorist forms of work organisation, using specialised equipment, while post-Fordism (or flexible specialisation) refers to small-batch production of a variety of products, the use of flexible machinery and micro-electronics, and the employment of a skilled and flexible workforce. In their original North American or European formulations these terms referred not merely to different production systems but to associated modes of social and political regulation. Thus Fordism, for example, was not simply a method of organising factory work but a regime of mass production and mass consumption that was established because of a particular political compact between capital and labour.

The analytic appeal of the debate over Fordism lies precisely in its totalising ambitions and in its ability to suggest the historical specificity of the current round of restructuring. For many writers, particularly those influenced by the French 'regulation' school, the current crisis arose out of the insoluble contradictions developed within the regime of accumulation which was established after the economic disaster of the 1930s.[13] In order to appreciate the profound links between the economic, social and political transformations occurring today, it is important to recognise the essential features of that regime, including its 'modes of social and political regulation'. The version I am using here owes much to Manuel Castells, not because his characterisation is unique, but because I think he has something distinctive to say about the mode of development being constructed out of this crisis.

For Castells and many others three central features account for the post-World War II years of economic growth and political and social stability in the advanced capitalist countries. The first was the establishment of a social pact between capital and labour after the class war of the depression; second was a general acceptance of the need for (Keynesian) state regulation and intervention into the economic sphere; and third was the setting up of mechanisms to control the increasingly international economic order.[14] In particular, the success of mass production (Fordism) required the simultaneous transformation and regulation of consumption to ensure stabilised mass markets. As Castells remarks, 'post-war Fordism has to be seen, therefore, less as a mere system of mass production and more as a total way of life'.[15]

The Fordist regime of accumulation was founded more particularly on a labour process based on Taylorist principles of work organisation and Henry Ford's emphasis on mechanisation. The system of mass production, as it became popularly known, involved a growing polarisation between skilled mental labourers and unskilled factory operatives, and increasing mechanisation leading to a sharp rise in productivity. Such a dynamic regime of accumulation could survive without economic crises because of the particular mode of regulation established after the war on the basis of the compact between capital and labour. Despite differences between countries the following ingredients were present: social legislation covering minimum wage levels and ensuring wage rises in line with increased national productivity; social welfare measures which guaranteed that almost everyone remained consumers even when they were excluded from paid work; and the provision of credit as the economy demanded. As Alain Lipietz concludes, the 'ground rules' of this system

> *conferred on the state an active responsibility for controlling the economy; through budget deficits, or government spending, it could stimulate growth. As overseer of the banking system, it could ease or restrict credit and thereby boost or slow down investment by firms and individuals. The use of these 'levers' was dubbed 'Keynesian policy'.*[16]

These elements have in turn created growing contradictions, leading eventually to a crisis of accumulation. Within each Fordist state, Taylorist work organisation finally provoked widespread backlashes, with militant strike action becoming commonplace. In many countries workers successfully increased their share of profits.[17] At the same time Taylorism, with its emphasis on depriving the majority of workers of autonomy and skill, prevented further increases in worker productivity except by means of costly new technologies. Meanwhile, the increasing internationalisation of markets and production compromised the ability of individual states to regulate their affairs. Increased domestic purchasing power now led to increased imports. These imports needed to be matched by increasing exports, but successful exporting required lower costs and lower wages in particular. As one French economist concluded:

> *For imports as well as exports, to achieve the right trade balance, each country was obliged to damp down its domestic demand and look to others to absorb its surplus production. Unfortunately, trading partners were doing exactly the same, leading to the kind of demand-side crisis which post-war Fordist regulation had eliminated in the national context.*[18]

Among the writers who have been working within the framework of a crisis of Fordism there is less agreement about what has been established on the wreckage of Fordism. Australian writers about post-Fordism have tended to focus only on the extent to which significant enterprises have adopted policies of flexible specialisation. However, while such firms might well succeed in restoring their own profitability, this tells us little about how the global economy is to be managed to avoid crises. For some writers who have adopted the 'regulation' framework, the stability of any post-Fordist regime is still in doubt.[19]

Castells, on the other hand, suggests that a new model of capitalist development 'with national variations and diverse fortunes' has in fact now emerged, which has altered the three key elements of the Fordist model. First, capital has succeeded in appropriating a significantly higher share of profits by using a number of different strategies, all of which weaken labour.[20] At its most stark this has involved a head-on confrontation with the trade union movement, as in Reagan's attack on the air-traffic controllers and Thatcher's attack on the miners. But it has also been achieved by workplace restructuring, as well as the employment of weakly organised workers such as women and immigrants. In some countries, such as Australia, a similar effect has been achieved with the active assistance of the trade union movement, hoping to set declining living standards against long-term union survival.

The second element in this new model is that state intervention has shifted away from political legitimation and social redistribution towards what Castells calls 'political domination' and capital accumulation. Whatever the ideological claims of new right governments, Castells insists that this shift is not one that can be understood as the withdrawal of the state from the economic scene. He characterises it as 'a new form of intervention, whereby new means and new areas are penetrated by the state, while others are deregulated and transferred to the market'.[21] Deregulation, privatisation, regressive tax reform, state support for high-technology R & D and for the key industrial sectors required by the new informational economy and other familiar measures illustrate the 'simultaneous engagement and disengagement of the state in the economy and society'.[22]

The third element, and for Castells the most critical to the success of this model of capitalist accumulation, has been the 'accelerated internationalisation of all economic processes to increase profitability and open up markets through the expansion of the system'.[23] It is in this area that communication and information technologies have dramatically shaped the form of the restructuring of capitalism. The contemporary internationalisation of capitalism increases profitability in several ways, and it 'connects segments of markets across borders, increasingly differentiating societies vertically while homogenizing markets horizontally'.[24]

Australia and the internationalisation of capitalism

The process of internationalisation is, perhaps, the most complex element of post-Fordist models. It is also of particular importance for Australia, which has always been so dependent on international trade. How adequate are the frameworks used to analyse Australia's position in the global economy, given the changes of the 1980s?

During the 1960s Ted Wheelwright developed a powerful critique of Australia's dependence on foreign capital. In it he pointed out that Australia was in the process of exchanging its historic imperial dependency on Britain for a new economic (and military) dependency on the US. Attention was focused very much on the issue of foreign ownership and control of Australian firms. Under the Whitlam Government this line of thinking culminated in plans to 'buy back the farm'. '"Connorism" was a form of economic nationalism intended to reduce the plundering of Australian resources by transnationals.'[25] Behind this thinking lay continued confidence in the value of Australia's natural resources (the mining boom) on world markets. Nationalist aspirations focused on the importance of regulating ownership and preserving the benefits of Australia's natural resources for Australians while at the same time seeking to reduce the country's economic reliance on these commodities.

By the early 1980s attention had shifted to the crisis of manufacturing and to what was seen as the 'deindustrialisation' of Australia. As Humphrey McQueen put it, 'huge problems persist because Australia's entire economy is being de-labourised under overseas control and during a protracted world recession'.[26] A new international division of labour was appearing in which large quantities of mass production work were being relocated to low-wage countries, posing a dramatic threat to manufacturing employment in the US as well as Australia. Australia's role in this new international division of labour was to supply vital raw materials (coal, iron, etc) to the successful industrial nations and, increasingly, to provide opportunities for rest and recreation to Japanese citizens, who were managing to avoid deindustrialisation through the sheer genius of 'the Japanese model'. Countries that had rejected the Taylorist basis of work organisation and substituted systems that mobilised the skills of line workers at the actual point of production (such as Japan, West Germany and Sweden) were noticeably more successful as the crisis of Fordism took hold in the 1970s and 1980s and gained from the trade war.[27]

Focusing primarily on labour costs as the factor influencing investment decisions, David and Wheelwright present an international league table for the mid 1980s that vividly illustrates the shift of Fordist manufacturing to low-wage countries.[28] By 1985 manufacturing accounted for only 17 per cent of Australian GDP, ranking it below not only the newly industrialised countries of South Korea, Taiwan, Hong Kong and Singapore but even Malaysia and Thailand, and on a par with India.[29] In this framework deindustrialisation is clearly to be taken as an indicator of economic decline.

Such an approach is, it seems to me, unable to grasp the complexity of what has been going on. The process of globalisation to which Castells refers is extremely difficult to accommodate within this traditional framework for analysing Australia's position in the world economy. First, the boundary between manufacturing and other service activities has become very hard to draw, and increasingly such boundaries do not coincide with national ones. Second, this model fails to engage with the post-Fordist thesis, which argues that there are ways in which the corporate dinosaurs of the Fordist period can respond to a crisis of profitability without simply relocating as much work as possible to low-wage countries (see, for example the debate on 'lean production'[30]). And at a more empirical level it does not help to explain the growth of certain service industries, which account for the growth of a relatively wealthy section of the population in Australia.

The specific characteristics of the new global economy are addressed more usefully by writers such as Saskia Sassen, and although the focus of her latest book is the global cities of New York, London and Tokyo, her identification of key new elements in the global capitalist system are critical to any appreciation of Australia's place within it. Like Castells, Sassen starts by assuming the demise of the post-World War II model of economic growth, which was 'characterized by the vast expansion of a middle class and formal labour markets' and which promoted mass consumption.[31] And, like Castells, she argues that the new, emerging order hinges centrally on what she calls the globalisation of the economy. The continued relocation of industrial production to low-wage countries is part of this globalisation, not only reducing costs but also helping to break the power of organised labour in the advanced countries. In this way the social compact that underpinned Fordism is dismantled, even though assembly lines and mass production are retained at a transnational level.

According to Sassen, however, this increased geographical decentralisation of production (and of services) has not been accompanied by any parallel decentralisation of ownership. As a result it leads to a massive increase in the need for centralised control functions. The key actors in these new global control systems are not simply multinationals (the traditional focus of nationalist critique) or big banks but a whole range of specialist producer services. These control functions are concentrated in what Sassen calls global cities. The increasingly global system requires far greater numbers of specialist experts in banking, accounting, law and other financial and business services, and these activities are concentrated in 'agglomerations'. These cities are both nodal points for the coordination of processes and particular sites of production where the specialised services that enable complex organisations to manage a dispersed network of factories, offices and services outlets are produced. These cities are also the places for financial innovations and the making of markets, both of which are essential to the internationalisation and expansion of the financial industry.

> *To understand the structure of a global city, we have to understand it as a place where certain kinds of work can get done, which is to say that we have to get beyond the dichotomy between manufacturing and services. The 'things' a global city makes are services and financial goods.*[32]

Information and communication technologies play a critical role here, promoting and enabling the centralisation of control over global production.[33] Far from promoting decentralisation, these technologies are what make possible the growth of global systems of production under centralised control. And in themselves, as massive investments in infrastructure, they promote further agglomeration. 'Such facilities demand major investments in fixed capital and continuous incorporation of innovations ... Established telecommunications centers have what amounts to an almost absolute advantage.'[34]

Castells gives communication and information technologies an even more prominent role in shaping the new capitalist system. He argues that the present context is 'characterised simultaneously by the emergence of a new mode of socio-technical organization (which we call the *informational mode of development*) and by the restructuring of capitalism'.[35] Indeed, 'restructuring could never have been accomplished, even in a contradictory manner, without the unleashing of the technological and organizational potential of informationalism'.[36]

Like Sassen, Castells suggests that information technologies promote the centralisation of knowledge, and he argues that

> *the informational world is made up of a very hierarchical functional structure in which increasingly secluded centers take to its extreme the historical division between intellectual and manual labour. Given the strategic role of knowledge and information control in productivity and profitability, these core centers of corporate organizations are the only truly indispensable components of the system, with most other work, and thus most other workers, being potential candidates for automation from the strictly functional point of view.*[37]

From the Australian perspective it is important to note Castells' further claim that the central role now played by technology transfer means that 'effective accomplishment of the internationalisation process requires access to these knowledge centers, ruling out the adoption of an isolationist stance, which would lead only to the technological obsolescence of those economies and firms holding it'.[38] New knowledge is now the key to increased productivity because of its impact on the other elements of the production process. The revolutionary impact of technological change in the 1980s stems from the fact that the core new technologies are focused on information processing, with their main impact on processes (found everywhere) rather than products.[39]

What authors such as Castells and Sassen have to offer is a framework within which to reconceptualise the notion of the decline of manufacturing and the rise of services in countries such as Australia. First, it is clear that there is no such thing as a service sector but a vast range of service industries. Second, the key to the new economic order is not consumer services but producer services, which need to be near each other and which constitute the fastest-growing sector. Third, it is not helpful to think of manufacturing and services as separate or as service employment replacing manufacturing in some sort of evolutionary process. On the contrary, the growth of services is intimately connected to the reshaping of manufacturing on a global level. As Robert Reich puts it, 'in fact all manufacturing businesses are coming to entail services, and all large businesses are spinning into webs of smaller businesses'.[40] For Reich, the image we need is that of an enterprise web. The centre of this web 'provides strategic insight and binds the threads together'.[41] 'The threads of the global web are computers, facsimile machines, satellites, high-resolution monitors and modems—all of them linking designers, engineers, contractors, licensees and dealers worldwide.'[42] Nations try to regulate the flows across their borders, but this is an increasingly futile exercise.

The question for Australia, from this perspective, is not simply how much manufacturing work has been lost overseas but the extent to which any Australian city has become a significant site for the production of producer services and financial goods, whether for national, regional or international networks. It has, for example, been argued that Sydney has consolidated its role as an international finance centre and host to the regional headquarters of major foreign firms. Producer services provided the fastest-growing source of employment in Australia in the 1980s, stimulated by the deregulation of the financial system, and these jobs have been strongly concentrated in Sydney.[43]

The characterisation of the new global system developed by authors such as Castells and Sassen provides a far better sense of the sheer dynamism involved in the process of globalisation than those perspectives trying to adjust the 'new international division of labour' of the late 1970s and early 1980s to current complexities.[44]

Globalisation, social structure and inequality

The state's role in controlling the economy under Fordism was not devised for the purpose of making Fordism work, even if that was its effect. Much of the state's activities, in regulating wage increases and providing welfare, for example, was the outcome of organised struggle by workers and social democratic or labour parties. The collapse of Fordism and the restructuring of capitalism is having profound effects on the social structure of almost every nation state—effects that need to be considered in analysing the nature of demands made on the state.

The new phase of economic globalisation has set in motion rapid social changes, particularly in the newly industrialising nations. The relocation of substantial productive activity from high-wage to low-wage countries has seen the growth of a significant middle class in countries that Australia has been wont to define as third world. Perhaps more disturbing from Australia's point of view is the suggestion that economic and social conditions for significant numbers of workers within the most successful global cities are coming increasingly to resemble those of workers in the third world. Many observers have pointed to the growing polarisation of the social structure in cities like New York, London and Los Angeles.[45] Clearly, constraints on welfare spending and a reduced public sector are factors behind any increased polarisation, as is the decline of increasingly uncompetitive manufacturing.[46] More controversially, however, Sassen has suggested that the success of 'global cities' is linked to the adoption of policies that are in fact detrimental to manufacturing.[47]

For Sassen, earlier phases of capitalist restructuring, including Fordism, meant that substantial growth in one centre translated into overall national growth. She suggests that the centrality of mass production and mass consumption created 'a balanced urban system and national integration' in the developed nations.[48] What is distinctive about post-Fordist economic restructuring is that growth centres are increasingly divorced from their local and national economies. Major cities, for example, 'tend to have overrepresentation of the main producer services industries: advertising, banking and finance, legal services'. Other cities, which were once industrial centres, are meanwhile in decline, with 'underrepresentation of these services'.[49] Sassen's argument is that growth built on a global market orientation induces discontinuity in the urban hierarchy and that these problems will be exacerbated in as much as telecommunications are likely to reinforce existing tendencies towards the concentration of global producer services in some cities. In Australia, differentiation between Sydney and Melbourne has increased with the concentration of producer services in the former and manufacturing in the latter. This is 'one part of a re-alignment of the geography of economic activity which is taking place within the nation, with significant consequences for the urban system'.[50]

Evidence of an increasingly polarised wage structure in the US was provided in the late 1980s by the political economists Bennet Harrison and Barry Bluestone.[51] Despite the very different industrial relations framework, similar trends have now been confirmed in Australia.[52] Bennet and Harrison argued that a key factor was the loss of manufacturing employment, which traditionally provided a relatively flat wage structure, partly because of strong unionisation. The growth of employment in producer services is itself characterised by an extremely polarised wage structure. That is, producer services involve significant numbers of high-wage professional and technical employees but even greater numbers of low-wage clerical workers, usually women, and nothing much in between.

The process is, however, more complex than this suggests. There is, for example, some evidence that the distribution of wages is becoming more unequal within all social strata and within a wide range of industries. Several factors help to explain this, apart from the sectoral shift from manufacturing to services. Castells, for example, argues that high technology itself appears to contribute to an occupational structure characterised by polarisation and segmentation of the labour force.[53] And pressure to restructure labour markets, wages and working hours is occurring in all areas as part of capital's strategy to reduce labour's share of profits.

On top of these changes, it is also necessary to recognise the effect of the broader institutional changes associated with the demise of the Fordist regime and particularly the demise of the post-war compact between labour and capital. In the US the virtual destruction of unions in the private sector is a key factor in wage polarisation, with low wages a characteristic of non-union areas.[54]

It is Sassen who argues most strongly that the increase in low-wage jobs and casual employment is articulated with the growth of the knowledge industries, the growth of high-income professional jobs and the resulting gentrification of global cities. In part, it is the new wealthy class with its distinctive consumption patterns that creates a large pool of low-wage work.[55] The old, Fordist middle class spent their incomes on buying new houses in the suburbs, on cars and white goods, which created a demand for mass-produced goods — goods made in factories by a largely unionised workforce. The new post-Fordist middle class spends its large disposable income on rather different goods and services — on renovating inner-city housing, eating in restaurants, entertainment, personal services and avoiding mass-produced consumer items in favour of individualised and preferably craft-produced ones. These demands translate into industries that rely to a far greater extent on sweated work and outwork. In London, for example, 20 per cent of workers in hotels and catering are on temporary contracts, and hiring halls are in use again. In the garment trade in both London and New York there has been a major revival of sweating and outwork. Indeed, Sassen argues that wages in these cities are now low enough to allow these workers to compete with some cheap Asian imports.[56]

The idea that the richest parts of the first world are now creating the conditions for the development of a new 'third world' in their midst is a shocking one. Yet Sassen claims that in New York most of the poor are now children, in contrast to the situation during the years of the long boom, when it was the elderly who were poor. In London, too, there has been a massive increase in the numbers living in poverty, reaching 1.8 million in 1985–86.[57] For Sassen, these trends represent a rupture with the past on several dimensions. First, there is a new ideology of consumption, based on the consumption of style; second is a new degree of poverty; third is a new type of city-centre development that represents a massive appropriation of public resources and urban space; and fourth, the institutionalisation of casual labour markets.[58] For David Harvey, the vast increase in part-time and casual employment is the single most convincing indicator of the demise of Fordism and its replacement with what he calls 'flexible accumulation'.[59]

Post-Fordist politics

There are several different levels at which one might begin to think about the political impact of the changes described here. Perhaps the most familiar is that which tries to analyse how the changing occupational structure affects class relations. Both Sassen and Castells argue strongly that the new global production arrangements have a profoundly fragmenting impact on the social structure of the advanced capitalist countries. The strength of organised labour has been undermined by a variety of strategies, of which the direct onslaught by new right governments is only one. Labour has been perhaps more permanently weakened by changes in work organisation and work relocation. As suggested above, restructuring around new information technologies allows part-time work, temporary and contract work on an unheard-of scale. Subcontracting and networking are on the increase, with the effect of segmenting labour, while management maintains its unity via networking.[60] Manufacturing itself has a more polarised occupational structure characterised by gender and ethnic divisions. And at a global level there is a greater spatial differentiation, with higher-level functions concentrated in certain privileged locations and assembly functions scattered over more and more varied locations.

These changes reveal the extent to which the 'mode of regulation' associated with the years of Fordism has been undermined. Michael Burawoy, in his study of the ways different 'factory regimes' affect class consciousness and forms of politics in the wider arena of the state, suggests that the globalisation of capital has contributed a new form of control over factory workers. The 'new despotism' differs from the earlier arbitrary tyranny of the supervisor over *individual* workers.

> *The new despotism is the 'rational' tyranny of capital mobility over the* collective *worker... The fear of being fired is replaced by the fear of capital flight, plant closure, transfer of operations, and plant disinvestment.*[61]

From a slightly different perspective Lipietz emphasises similar effects in the transition to post-Fordism, pointing to the 'fragmentation of social existence, with firms playing the role previously performed by the mother country (we must stand together against competitors), and the world market becoming the operating environment'.[62] Lipietz compares this to the feudal social order under which feudal lords offered their peasants 'protection against attack by other lords, and also land in return for work'.

> *A particular social order was justified by the existence of generalized conflict, and the overall system remained stable for a long time. Naturally it was continually disturbed by wars and incursions and gratuitous revolts, but it was precisely this fact which made a feudal hierarchy acceptable as protection against the harsh conditions of the period.*[63]

The political impact of the collapse of Fordism is most apparent in the rise of new right politics, which appear to take on the cause of restructuring most transparently. However, it could be argued that it is traditional social democracy that has suffered the greater crisis. This is particularly true of the Australian Labor Party, which was in power at the federal level for most of the 1980s. The ALP has been trying to manage the transition to a new globally restructured economic order and to ensure a share of the new global control functions for Australia (via, for example, the deregulation of banking and telecommunications, tariff reductions and so on), while at the same time trying to maintain the loyalty of its traditional working-class supporters whose livelihoods are being devastated by the very same policies. It could be argued that the ALP (and many other social democratic and labour parties) has accepted the inevitability of post-Fordism, with its emphasis on the techno-economic imperative, and the dilution of any sense that there are choices to be derived from a democratic political system.

The notion that global restructuring has placed severe strains on the political culture and institutions of the advanced industrial countries is taken even further by Robert Reich in his book, *The Work of Nations* (1991). In a passage as relevant to Australia as the US he writes:

> *The usual discussion about the future of the American economy focuses on topics like the competitiveness of General Motors, or of the American automobile industry, or, more broadly, of American manufacturing, or, more broadly still, of the American economy. But, as has been observed, these categories are becoming irrelevant. They assume the continued existence of an American economy in which jobs associated with a particular firm, industry or sector are somehow connected within the borders of the nation, so that American workers face a common fate; and a common enemy as well: The battle fields of world trade pit our corporations and our workers unambiguously against theirs.*[64]

However, as Reich points out, this is no longer the case. What is good for General Motors is no longer good for auto workers in Detroit because there are hardly any left in Detroit. Those who do work on US assembly lines are probably getting their pay from a company based in Tokyo. The economic well-being of Americans in the global market no longer depends on any particular American corporation or industry but on the functions those particular workers perform—the value they add. 'No longer are Americans rising or falling together, as if in one large national boat. We are, increasingly, in different, smaller boats.'[65]

Reich identifies three broad categories of work for Americans in the future, defined by the competitive positions available in the global economy: routine production services, in-person services and symbolic–analytical services. It is those with the symbolic–analytic skills who hold the dominant position in the new world order, and in these occupations America has a major advantage because of the quality of its education system. But for the other two categories of workers 'the law of supply and demand does not bode well'.[66] Routine producers are confronted with an immense and rapidly growing world-wide pool of competing labour. In-person service providers suffer, if more indirectly, because of local low-wage competition from, for example, immigrants and from rapid technological change.

A similarly pessimistic view of the difficulties confronting the American political system is expressed by Castells, who sees a 'growing social schizophrenia' resulting from

> on the one hand, regional societies and local institutions and, on the other hand, the rules and operations of the economic system at the international level. The more the economy becomes interdependent on a global scale, the less can regional and local governments, as they exist today, act upon the basic mechanisms that condition the daily existence of their citizens. The traditional structures of social and political control over development, work and distribution have been subverted by the placeless logic of an internationalized economy enacted by means of information flows.[67]

What role for the Australian state?

The emphasis in this chapter on the new global political economy is not intended to be an exercise in economic reductionism with the political relations waiting to be read off from the economic. On the contrary, it could be argued that the political relations of post-Fordism are extremely unsettled. Manuel Castells argues that a 'new model of capitalism' has now emerged in which the state has been successfully captured by capital so that its activities are primarily directed towards promoting accumulation rather than legitimation. Yet, in the 1990s, the accompanying doctrine of economic rationalism is beginning to look less secure politically. In Australia, in particular, fully fledged economic rationalism has remained remarkably unpopular. It is, of course, the case that powerful elements of the ALP and the trade union movement have come to the view that certain elements of economic liberalism— deregulation and tariff reductions, for example—are necessary and desirable. On the other hand, debate over public health care, public education and access to unemployment benefits remains vigorous. The growing polarisation in the distribution of wages and in access to employment are significant pressures. Moreover, the relatively low levels of taxation in Australia, and the relatively small size of the public sector as a whole, suggests that there is plenty of room for argument still. Thus, political traditions and the political system of representation remain important.

Looking at the economic inequality and political challenges created by the collapse of Fordism in the United States, Robert Reich sees the central issue as one of how to nurture sentiments of what he calls 'positive economic nationalism', a creed he distinguishes from zero-sum nationalism and impassive cosmopolitanism.[68] In this way each nation must attempt to 'cope with the centrifugal forces of the global economy which tear at the ties binding citizens together—bestowing ever greater wealth on the most skilled and insightful, while consigning the less skilled to a declining standard of living'.[69]

A variety of proposals for reconstructing the public provision of social welfare on a new basis have been developed. They are yet to be seriously considered by social democratic and labour parties but are already promoted by the 'alternative parties' of Western Europe. These proposals include policies for a guaranteed minimum income or universal basic allowance.[70] More radically, Alain Lipietz (who was elected as a Green regional councillor in 1992 in France) proposes the establishment of a 'new sector of activity' limited to some 10 per cent of the labour force. In this sector workers would be employed by 'agencies for socially useful schemes', subsidised from public revenue but untaxed.[71]

Leaving aside the effectiveness of such appeals to the values of community, citizenship and social justice, there remains the question of the constraints on state action imposed by the globalisation of the economy. Within Australia the revival of interest in industry policy that has occurred with the waning influence of hard-line economic rationalism reflects a belated recognition of the role the state has played in almost every recent national economic success story. If the objective is to participate more successfully in the new global economy, states also have a major role to play in areas such as the development of telecommunications and other kinds of communications infrastructure. Looking at the problems from a different angle, it would seem premature to abandon the debate on protection, with renewed pressure to reverse the trend towards zero tariffs in the face of persistently high levels of unemployment. Using the examples of the textile, steel and semiconductor industries, the US economist Robert Kuttner argues that 'in an imperfect world, national policies can and do capture or create advantages'.[72]

Yet the limitations of these approaches to competing in the global economy are apparent when we consider the immense instability of the new post-Fordist world. The problems Australia faces have their own distinctive historical origins, but they are common to many other countries and are a predictable outcome of international economic and trade relationships. Any country that expands too quickly for its own internal productive capacity will end up with a trade deficit. In this situation there are two alternatives: either to engineer a recession (Keating's recession that we had to have) or to borrow. Countries that go into recession reduce the market for other countries' exports yet further. Countries that borrow to pay for them cause interest rates to rise, which then discourages productive investment in favour of financial speculation.

For some observers, therefore, it is the process of globalisation itself that must be controlled, with growing demands from many different quarters for the political 'management' of free trade. Robert Kuttner insists that 'if nations wish to retain domestic production capacity, and not to cede their entire market to foreign suppliers, it is possible to design relatively liberal and balanced managed trade regimes'.[73] Countries might begin with those products in which nations are already restraining trade and establish explicit managed trade agreements based on 'balance of benefits'.[74] At the global level managed trade could address the problem of maintaining overall balance in the trading system, with penalties for those nations running chronic trade surpluses.

Along similar lines, but from a more radical and specifically ecological perspective, Herman Daly and John Cobb have developed a challenging critique of the benefits of international trade.[75] Much of the radical nature of their proposals hinges on the role they define for 'community' in control over economic and political life, but they argue that it is at the national level that communities must currently be mobilised. 'Nation-states are today extremely important societies. They are in many instances the only loci of power capable of asserting themselves effectively against those forces that erode all community.'[76] This is not to preclude the possibility of a genuinely European community emerging, or a common-market-based community in Central America. 'The main formal point is that a political community cannot be healthy if it cannot exercise a significant measure of control over its economic life.'[77] Daly and Cobb go on to recommend the establishment of 'balanced' international trade through such measures as import quotas and capital immobility.

In so schematically summarising these arguments for a new and historically even more important role for the state it must be emphasised that this 'state' is not simply the Fordist state revived, with new international links. On the contrary, the Fordist welfare state was seriously weakened by popular resentment about its bureaucratic and authoritarian aspects. Radical proposals for renewing the dynamic of national political institutions hinge on a range of recommendations for democratisation and participation that are essential to their popular espousal. Such proposals are clearly marginal to most contemporary political debate. Their significance, however, lies in the fact that globalisation and restructuring have created a highly unstable and crisis-ridden environment in which alternatives will continue to be needed.

Notes

1 See, for example, J. Carroll and R. Manne (eds) (1992), *Shutdown: The Failure of Economic Rationalism and How to Rescue Australia*, Text Publishing, Melbourne, and P. Vintila et al. (eds) (1992), *Markets, Morals and Manifestos*, Institute for Science and Technology Policy, Murdoch University, Perth.
2 M. Castells (1991), *The Informational City*, Basil Blackwell, Oxford, pp. 3–4.
3 J. Schultz (1985), *Steel City Blues*, Penguin, Ringwood.
4 J. Schultz (1985), p. vii.
5 J. Schultz (1985), p. ix.
6 See M. Piore and C. Sabel (1984), *The Second Industrial Divide*, Basic Books, New York, pp. 208–10 and R. Reich (1992), *The Work of Nations*, Vintage Books, New York, p. 82.
7 P. Bagguley et al. (1990), *Restructuring: Place, Class and Gender*, Sage, London.
8 P. Bagguley et al. (1990), p. 33.
9 P. Bagguley et al. (1990), pp. 63–7.
10 M. Scott and M. Storper (eds) (1986), *Production, Work, Territory*, Allen & Unwin, Boston; D. Massey (1984), *Spatial Divisions of Labour*, Methuen, London.
11 P. Bagguley et al. (1990), p. 9.
12 For two contrasting views see J. Mathews (1989), *Tools of Change*, Pluto Press, Sydney and T. Bramble (1988), 'The flexibility debate: Industrial relations and new management production practices', *Labour and Industry*, 1:2, 187–209.
13 M. Aglietta (1979), *Theory of Capitalist Regulation*, New Left Books, London; M. Piore and C. Sabel (1984); D. Harvey (1989), *The Condition of Postmodernity*, Basil Blackwell, Oxford.
14 M. Castells (1991), p. 21.
15 M. Castells (1991), p. 135.
16 A. Lipietz (1992), *Towards a New Economic Order: Postfordism, Ecology and Democracy*, Polity Press, Cambridge, p. 7.
17 A. Glyn and R. Sutcliffe (1972), *British Capitalism, Workers and the Profit Squeeze*, Penguin, London.
18 A. Lipietz (1992), p. 18.
19 David Harvey (1989), for example, remains unsure whether 'there is to be any medium-term stability to the present regime of accumulation', p. 196; Alain Lipietz (1992), p. 146, in a more politically motivated vein, characterises the present moment as 'a cross-roads'.
20 M. Castells (1991), p. 23.
21 M. Castells (1991), p. 25.
22 M. Castells (1991), pp. 25–6.
23 M. Castells (1991), pp. 26–7.
24 M. Castells (1991), pp. 26–7.
25 G. Crough and T. Wheelwright (1982), *Australia: A Client State*, Penguin, Ringwood, p. 6.
26 H. McQueen (1982), *Gone Tomorrow: Australia in the 80s*, Angus & Robertson, Sydney, p. 218.

27 A. Lipietz (1992), p. 39.
28 A. David and T. Wheelwright (1989), *The Third Wave: Australia and Asian Capitalism*, Left Book Club, Sydney.
29 A. David and T. Wheelwright (1989), p. 7.
30 P. Womack et al. (1990), *The Machine that Changed the World*, Macmillan, New York.
31 S. Sassen (1991), *The Global City*, Princeton University Press, Princeton, p. 249.
32 S. Sassen (1991), p. 5.
33 S. Sassen (1991), pp. 165–6.
34 S. Sassen (1991), p. 19.
35 M. Castells (1991), p. 2. For further elaboration of the concept of 'the informational mode of development' see pp. 28–32.
36 M. Castells (1991), p. 29.
37 M. Castells (1991), p. 30.
38 M. Castells (1991), p. 31.
39 See also D. Harvey (1989) on this question.
40 R. Reich (1992), *The Work of Nations*, Vintage, New York, p. 94.
41 R. Reich (1992), p. 96.
42 R. Reich (1992), p. 111.
43 K. O'Connor and D. Edgington (1991), 'Producer services and metropolitan development in Australia' in P. Daniels (ed.), *Services and Metropolitan Development: International Perspectives*, Routledge, London and New York.
44 A. Lipietz (1987), *Mirages and Miracles: The Crisis of Global Fordism*, Verso, London.
45 See in particular M. Davies (1990), *City of Quartz*, Verso, London.
46 See M. Davies (1993), 'Who killed LA? A political autopsy', *New Left Review*, No. 197, for a damning indictment of public spending cutbacks.
47 S. Sassen (1991), pp. 12–13.
48 S. Sassen (1991), p. 165.
49 S. Sassen (1991), p. 166.
50 K. O'Connor and D. Edgington (1991), p. 213.
51 B. Harrison and B. Bluestone (1988), *The Great U-Turn: Corporate Restructuring and the Polarizing of America*, Basic Books, New York.
52 B. Gregory (1992), 'Aspects of Australian labour force living standards: The disappointing decades 1970–1990', Copland Oration, 21st Conference of Economists, Melbourne.
53 M. Castells (1991), pp. 188, 190.
54 M. Castells (1991), p. 202.
55 S. Sassen-Koob (1982), 'Recomposition and peripheralization at the core', *Contemporary Marxism*, 5, 88–100.
56 S. Sassen (1991), p. 281.
57 S. Sassen (1991), p. 271.
58 S. Sassen (1991), p. 317.
59 D. Harvey (1989), p. 191.
60 M. Castells (1991), p. 190.
61 M. Burawoy (1985), *The Politics of Production*, Verso, London, p. 150 (emphasis in the original).
62 A. Lipietz (1992), p. 33.

63 A. Lipietz (1992), p. 34.
64 R. Reich (1992), p. 171.
65 R. Reich (1992), p. 173.
66 R. Reich (1992), p. 245.
67 M. Castells (1991), p. 347.
68 R. Reich (1992), chapter 25.
69 R. Reich (1992), p. 3.
70 P. Van Parijs (ed.) (1992), *Arguing for Basic Income*, Verso, London.
71 A. Lipietz (1992), pp. 99–106.
72 R. Kuttner (1989), *Managed Trade and Economic Sovereignty*, Economic Policy Institute, Washington DC, p. 23.
73 R. Kuttner (1989), p. 36.
74 R. Kuttner (1989), pp. 36–7.
75 H. Daly and J. Cobb (1989), *For the Common Good*, Beacon Press, Boston.
76 H. Daly and J. Cobb (1989), p. 173.
77 H. Daly and C. Cobb (1989), p. 174.

5

The power of economic ideas? Keynesian economic policies in post-war Australia

Greg Whitwell

Keynesianism had a profound influence on macroeconomic policy in Australia during the first three post-war decades. Eventually it was to fall out of favour, jeered by economic rationalists as misguided and harmful. Yet the point remains that, from a comparative perspective, the Australian experience is noteworthy in that Keynesianism was adopted early, enthusiastically, with apparent ease and then subsequently endured, more or less unchallenged, for a remarkably long time. One of the aims of this chapter is to explain why this was the case. In addition, and more broadly, the chapter aims to use the adoption of Keynesianism in Australia to explore the relationship between economic ideas and economic policy.

Many commentators, discussing the political economy of the post-war period, pin the labels 'Keynesian revolution' or 'Keynesian era' on the first thirty post-war years. Such labels are inappropriate because they suggest a commonality of experience, which was in fact absent. In some countries Keynesian ideas never gained a foothold; in others they remained relatively unimportant in comparison to other techniques, such as indicative planning; in still others they were adopted in the early post-war years only then to be abandoned; and in some they were embraced only belatedly. The diverse reaction to Keynesianism raises many questions of a more general nature. How is it that some economic ideas acquire political influence while others do not? What conditions are necessary for ideas to become the basis for new policy approaches? Through what mechanisms do economic ideas become accepted and implemented by governments? These are challenging questions. In exploring the adoption of Keynesianism in Australia we can begin to provide answers to them.[1]

What is Keynesianism?

Definitions of Keynesianism vary greatly. One needs to turn to Keynes' masterwork, *The General Theory of Employment, Interest and Money*, published in 1936, and to his subsequent writings on wartime policy to find the essence of Keynesianism.

Three things seem especially important. First, Keynes' economics focused on the determination of output and employment and the role therein of effective demand. Production levels and the extent, more generally, to which potential resources were utilised were seen to be limited by effective demand. Second, Keynes had a particular view of the inherent tendencies of the unregulated capitalist system. Keynes insisted that the economic system did not tend towards full employment equilibrium but tended instead towards an 'underemployment' equilibrium. Furthermore, Keynes emphasised the volatility of the economic system. He considered the unregulated system prone to cyclical fluctuations (booms and depressions), which arose partly because of the perverse effect of uncertainty on the expectations of investors. Shifts in mood from optimisim to pessimism affected aggregate demand principally through their influence on investment expenditure. Third, Keynes regarded governmental activities in a largely positive light; for it was only by governments purposefully directing the system that full employment could be achieved and maintained and that inflation could be minimised. With the exception of some vague and often misrepresented comments on the 'socialisation of investment', Keynes' preference was the use of indirect methods to manage the economy, notably budgetary and monetary policy, rather than the imposition of direct methods such as prices and wages controls.

Perhaps Keynes' most significant contribution to the notion of economic management was his re-evaluation of the role of budgetary policy. Indeed, the term *Keynesian Revolution* is most commonly associated with the abandonment of balanced-budget principles (the idea that expenditure should not exceed expected revenue) and the acceptance instead of budget deficits or surpluses to regulate the level of economic activity. Keynes is attributed with having transformed the conception of the budget as a basic accounting exercise to an effective instrument for exercising economic management. He provided a new perspective: his argument was in effect that what was at issue was not the balancing of the budget itself but the balancing of the economy as a whole.

While Keynes was anxious to avoid any direct interference with the exercise of individual initiative and choice, he believed that the growth of the public sector, or at least an increase in the relative importance of public sector investment, would provide an important stabilising force in the system. This is what he had in mind in calling for the 'socialisation of investment'. The assumption was that the public sector was somehow less prone to the degree of volatility that characterised the behaviour of investors in the private sector.

From balanced budgets to discretionary fiscal policy

The adoption of Keynesianism in Australia can be seen most readily in the Federal Government's approach to budgetary policy. Throughout the 1930s the annual budget continued to be seen by most parliamentarians and certainly by the Treasury as a mere financial statement rather than as an instrument of stabilisation. This view was linked in turn with the belief that governments were essentially impotent in their ability to deal with unemployment. The budget was seen by the Treasury in terms of 'mere money', governed by accounting—balance-sheet— principles. Budgeting was simply a matter of estimating expenditure and then determining the ways in which the revenue to cover this expenditure could be raised. Balanced budgets were the inviolable ideal.

By the end of World War II, however, there had been a marked change in attitude. The war saw the Commonwealth explicitly accept the notion of economic control or management. The 1945 white paper, *Full Employment in Australia*, was the great symbol of this change in attitude. The white paper opened with the declaration that the government considered full employment a 'fundamental aim'. Unemployment was branded an evil. The provision of 'the general framework of a full employment economy, within which the operation of individuals and businesses could be carried on', was deemed a responsibility and an obligation of Federal and State Governments. The white paper represented a fundamental break with the past. It involved looking at the economy differently. Output levels, rather than cost and price levels, were now the main source of attention. Linked with this, the importance of aggregate demand was recognised and emphasised. Despite a certain haziness about just how the budget would be used, it was now appreciated that the budget affected, and was affected by, the rest of the economy. More importantly, the government was now proposing a form of intervention in the economy previously considered unwise and improper. Expenditure levels were to be regulated by offsetting variations in public capital expenditure so as to maintain balance in total expenditure. As a result, fluctuations in the economy were to be controlled, the instability to which the economy seemed inevitably prone was to be excised, and employment was to be maintained at continuously high levels.

Apart from the white paper, the extent to which official thinking had changed by the end of World War II can perhaps be best seen in the Treasury's comment in a 1946 memorandum that:

> *It is now fully accepted government policy that in framing the Budget, in scrutinising expenditure proposals and preparing revenue measures, the Treasury must be guided not only by narrow financial considerations but also by its assessment of the existing and prospective level of employment and National Income after taking into account the effect of the financial proposals under consideration. Banking and monetary policy must also be directed towards the same end by the Treasury. The Budget and monetary policy have become vital instruments of Government policy in relation to employment, the cost of living, wages and social justice.*[2]

Here was evidence that the economists in the Treasury's General Financial and Economic Policy branch (established in 1943) had come to grips with the need to regard the budget differently. The viewpoint was distinctly Keynesian.

The most famous (and notorious) example of the Treasury's determination to convert Keynesian budgetary theory into practice was the so-called 'Horror Budget' of 1951. The budget represented the first explicit use of fiscal policy for anti-cyclical purposes. The budget was openly Keynesian in practice, principle and spirit, despite the fact that it was introduced to fight not unemployment but inflation. Furthermore, it was an attempt to meet persistent criticisms that governments had failed in their attempts to educate the public in the principles of the 'new economics'.

The Treasurer, Arthur Fadden, began his budget speech by explaining the inflationary process and did so by employing Keynesian 'gap' analysis (a concept introduced in Keynes' *How to Pay for the War*, published in 1940). The Treasurer explained that budgetary policy was crucially important in regulating economic activity. He outlined, in straightforwardly Keynesian terms, the principles that he believed such policy should follow:

> *The Government believes firmly that under the present highly inflationary conditions total receipts should do more than cover total expenditure—they should be sufficient also to provide a substantial surplus. Modern thought on the relation of public finance to economic stability is quite clear on the point that in times of depressed trade and employment, governments may justifiably run*

> *into deficit and even finance some part of the needs with central bank credit, so raising the level of community spending power. It is a vital corollary of this view, however, that in times of excessive demand and scarcity of labour, governments should draw away from the public in taxation and loans more than they spend for current purposes ... If ever there was such a situation which called for such a measure, it is surely the situation we now face in Australia.*

Accordingly, increases were announced for a range of taxes, including income tax, company tax, sales tax and customs and excise duties. The nominal budget surplus was $229 million.

An essentially Keynesian approach to budgetary policy remained the norm for the 1950s and 1960s. Gough Whitlam, prime minister from 1972 to 1975, recalls that:

> *During the years of the post-war economic boom, questions of economic management were scarcely deemed to require original answers. The broad principles, and indeed objectives, of Keynesian economics held sway over the major parties. If prices rose and the supply of labour grew short, then expenditure was tightened, taxes increased and credit squeezed to produce a decrease in inflation and employment. If prices fell and employment grew scarce then expenditure was expanded, taxation decreased and credit relaxed to produce an increase in prices and employment. The apparent clarity and certainty of economic management opened up new prospects and induced high hopes for social reform.*[3]

'The political power of economic ideas'

In a stimulating recent analysis of the spread of Keynesian ideas among nations, Peter Hall distinguishes between three broad approaches to the question of how and why Keynesian ideas and policies were accepted.

The economist-centred approach

The first is the *economist-centred approach*. The implicit assumption here is that the adoption of Keynesian policies occurred as a result of the expert advice provided to politicians by economists. The task, then, is to explain two things: Why did professional economists become so enamoured of Keynesian modes of analysis? Why was it, if you like, that they were persuaded to accept the theoretical characteristics of Keynes' ideas? It might be, Hall says, that a Kuhnian-type analysis of paradigm shifts will provide some of the clues to these questions. The other thing to be explained is by what means, and through what institutional arrangements, do professional economists communicate with and influence policy-makers? More precisely, how do institutional arrangements structure the nature of that communication?[4]

Hall argues that the economist-centred approach has one great virtue and one weakness as an explanation of the impact of Keynesian ideas. The virtue is that it draws 'attention to the qualities of Keynesian ideas themselves. It suggests that ideas may have a persuasiveness, and hence a political dynamism, of their own; and it forces us to ask which ideational qualities make for persuasiveness and which detract from it'.[5] The defect is that it probably exaggerates the influence of economists over policy.

The state-centred approach

Another approach to the adoption of Keynesianism is the *state-centred approach*. The argument here is that 'the reception accorded new economic ideas will be influenced by the institutional configuration of the state and its prior experience with related policies'.[6]

On the first point—the institutional configuration of the state— analysts who adopt the state-centred approach focus their attention on the capacity of bureaucracies to implement new ideas and programs. The capacity of bureaucracies to do so will be influenced by 'the relative openness of policy-making institutions to advice from outside economists ... and the administrative biases implicit in the institutional division of responsibility within the state'.[7] For example, in Britain in the 1930s the Treasury was both extremely powerful and biased against higher spending whereas in Sweden the bureaucracy had a tradition of close collaboration with academic economists. It was perhaps not surprising, then, that the Swedish bureaucracy gave considerable weight to the reflationary program of public works advocated by the Stockholm school of economists.

On the second point—the importance of prior experience with related policies—one could again contrast Sweden and Britain. Prior experience with public works projects as a means of ameliorating unemployment made the Swedish state more receptive to Keynesian ideas, whereas in Britain, where its prior experience was with unemployment insurance, the Labour Party and a great many policy-makers fixed their attention on it rather than on proposals to boost public works expenditure.

Hall suggests that the state-centred approach has certain merits:

> *It draws our attention to the role that administrative, as opposed to purely economic, problems play in the process of economic policy-making. It reminds us that the officials responsible for economic policy during the interwar period were usually not economists, and that even in the postwar period, they have had many concerns besides developments in economic theory. Most important, the state-centred approach provides us with a set of tools for explaining cross-national variation in the reception given Keynesian ideas.*[8]

Its weakness is the overriding importance it attaches to the state apparatus and to officials. The implied suggestion is that politics and political leaders play a minor role in the determination of policy and the adoption or rejection of new approaches.

The coalition-centred approach

This criticism cannot be levelled against the third approach, the *coalition-centred approach*. Here politics is of central importance. As Hall explains, this approach

> *emphasises that politics must mobilise support among broad coalitions of economic groups on whose votes and goodwill elected politicans ultimately depend. Hence, a nation's readiness to implement Keynesian policies may be said to turn on the ability of its politicians to forge a coalition of social groups that is large enough to sustain them in office and inclined to regard Keynesian measures as something that is in their interest. The feasibility of such a coalition, in turn, rests on the ingenuity of politicians and the constellation of preferences expressed by the relevant economic groups.*[9]

What is valuable about this approach, Hall says, is the 'renewed emphasis' given 'to the broader political context in which Keynesianism figures'. Also, 'it reminds us that politics is ultimately about the conflict among groups with divergent interests for claims on scarce resources'. Its main weakness is that 'it leaves somewhat open the question of how these groups come to define their interests in a particular way'.[10]

In explaining the influence of Keynesian ideas, each of the three approaches outlined above tends to see different actors as occupying centre stage: economists in the first, public servants and officials in the second, and politicians (and social groups) in the third. Hall's own view, to which I now turn, seems to be that the spotlight should be pointed at all three actors.

Hall's three criteria and the Australian experience

Hall does a brave job of trying to weld together the three approaches in putting forward his own schema for explaining the reception given to Keynesianism in different nations. What I want to do here is to describe Hall's framework and apply it to the Australian experience in an attempt to understand why Keynesian ideas were embraced so readily by both professional economists and policy-makers.

Hall's argument is that the adoption of Keynesian ideas as a basis of economic policy required that these ideas be (seen to be) viable in economic, political and administrative terms. Each of these criteria had to be satisfied for Keynesianism to be adopted readily. Conversely, failure to satisfy one or more of the criteria slowed the acceptance of Keynesianism and, in some cases, prevented it altogether. What is noteworthy about Australia is that all three criteria were satisfied by the end of World War II.

Hall further embellishes his arguments by suggesting a variety of additional considerations—the orientation of the governing party, the structure of state and state–society relations, the structure of political discourse and the impact of World War II—that need to be understood to achieve a comprehensive explanation of the adoption of Keynesianism. For convenience, and to avoid unnecessary overlap, these 'additional considerations' will be merged within Hall's three criteria.

Economic viability

The 'economic viability' of economic ideas refers to their ability to provide a solution to current economic problems. Keynesian proposals focused on the problem of unemployment and hence tended to be taken more seriously in countries in which it was the pressing economic problem of the day. In those countries in which inflation was the main problem, Keynesianism could be dismissed as being of little relevance.[11]

In this respect the acceptance of Keynesian ideas in Australia has to be seen against the fact that during the 1930s the unemployment rate was, as far as one can tell from the available statistics, among the highest in the world. One has to appreciate, too, that at the end of World War II it was widely assumed in Australia that there would soon be a slump after an intense but short-lived boom. The return of mass unemployment, eradicated during the war, was considered the major economic problem. The publication of the 1945 white paper was testimony to the seriousness with which this possibility was viewed. It was acknowledged that the imbalance between aggregate demand and supply would cause problems of inflation in the early post-war years, but this was expected to be only a transient difficulty. Without purposive action the hopeless insecurity of the 1930s would re-emerge.

Presenting the *Full Employment* white paper, the Minister for Post-War Reconstruction, J. J. Dedman, declared:

> *To the individual thrown into idleness by the failure of the economic system to provide employment, this failure meant poverty, frustration, disillusionment and bitterness. Even those fortunate enough to remain in their jobs were threatened by a sense of insecurity.*[12]

Reflecting this insecurity, pressure for a government commitment to high employment became intense. Australians wanted living standards raised and, above all, unemployment banished.

Changing historical conjunctures can play a pivotal role in the development of new policy terrains by opening up or closing down policy choices. The importance of World War II in stimulating debate on, and in some countries aiding the acceptance of, Keynesianism can hardly be overestimated. In the first place, the war was significant in that it provided such a stark contrast to the preceding decade of depression and mass unemployment. The return of full employment during the war years gave great potency to the demands for a commitment to high employment. The argument in essence was that if government expenditure could be used to remove unemployment during wartime, surely it should be possible to continue to do so in peacetime.

This in turn leads to the point that the war experience was important in that it confirmed for most Australian economists the veracity of Keynes' message. The war was associated with a remarkable increase in the relative size of the public sector. It was associated, too, with the centralisation of financial strength in the Federal Government following the introduction of uniform taxation in 1942, by which the Federal Government became for the remainder of the war and after it, through legislation passed in 1946, the sole levier of income and company taxes in Australia. Here at last were the necessary structural characteristics for Keynesianism to be tested. Robert Skidelsky, referring to wartime Britain, argues that

> *the problems of war finance provided the first opportunity to test out the new Keynesian techniques of measuring and regulating the levels of aggregate income and output. Keynes himself had doubted whether it would be politically possible 'for a capitalist democracy to organise expenditure on the scale necessary to make the grand experiment to prove my case—except in war conditions'. The Second World War provided the necessary laboratory.*[13]

This point is equally applicable to Australia. For most Australian economists, Keynes' theory seemed to have been vindicated. To repeat: the war was associated with unprecedented leaps in the level of government expenditure as well as a substantial decline in the level of unemployment. For those with economics training the causal connection between spending and employment was now clearly established, and the notion of economic management became a distinct possibility.

Another relevant consideration, as Skidelsky points out, is that periods of war can stimulate a willingness to experiment because they are associated with 'the large-scale replacement of official personnel' and/or 'an influx of "new men" whose ideas, personalities and interests have previously disqualified them from "normal" politics'. Certainly in Australia, major personnel changes occurred in the federal public service during the war. Because of the exigencies of war and because of a shortage of able administrators, many young graduates who joined the public service were able to bypass the established channels of promotion and assume relatively senior positions. What happened was not so much a case of official personnel being replaced as their simply being swamped by a large number of (at first) temporary recruitments. What stands out about so many of these recruits is that they had been trained as economists. In fact, many of Australia's leading economists—Douglas Copland, L. F. Giblin, Roland Wilson, 'Nugget' Coombs, J. B. Brigden, R. C. Mills, Ronald Walker—were placed in positions of major administrative responsibility.

The power of these senior economists was further enhanced by the fact that they were brought together into a single committee formally entitled the 'Financial and Economic Advisory Committee' but usually referred to simply as 'F & E'. Roland Wilson had suggested that F & E should be 'a small central "thinking committee" to which all sorts of problems could be submitted for general advice'. In the event it did rather more than this, for its main task was 'to co-ordinate the basic economic policies of the various executive arms of the government'.[14]

Hall points out that, in addition to its ability to deal with pressing economic problems, several other factors will determine a new theory's economic viability:

> *These include the qualities of the new doctrine* qua *economic theory. Any doctrine is more likely to be accepted by professional economists if it is theoretically appealing, and that will turn on its relationship to existing theory.*

He notes that Keynes went out of his way to couch the *General Theory*

> *in terms that would force his readers to forsake their traditional concepts and learn a new language in order to appreciate his insights. Therefore, The General Theory was likely to meet initial resistance until younger scholars seeking a new research program could take it up and eventually press the new view on the economics profession as a whole. That is precisely what happened.*[15]

Certainly the younger Australian economists seemed to be the most enthusiastic about the *General Theory*. H. C. ('Nugget') Coombs recalls:

> *The publication in 1936 of John Maynard Keynes'* General Theory of Employment, Interest and Money *was for me and for many of my generation the most seminal intellectual event of our time. It was not an easy book. Many of the ideas on which it was based were then unfamiliar, and the book itself showed evidence of haste in composition so that its structure did not emerge sharply from initial reading. Nevertheless, it did not fail to generate excitement from first*

> contact, and soon I had become convinced that in the Keynesian analysis lay the key to comprehension of the economic system.[16]

Yet it was not just the younger economists who became Keynesian converts. Senior economists, like Giblin and Copland, accepted the essence of Keynes' message. Despite some reservations, they too became enmeshed in the excitement generated by the *General Theory*.

A number of reasons can be put forward to explain why so many members of Australia's rather small economics profession were willing to accept Keynes' arguments. In the first place, there was something of a Cambridge connection. Giblin, Professor of Economics at the University of Melbourne, was an old Kingsman like Keynes, having joined the college in 1893. His acquaintance with Keynes dated from 1918 and was renewed not long after the publication of the *General Theory* when Giblin spent several months during 1937–38 in residence at Kings. Ronald Walker, of the University of Sydney, had studied at Cambridge, too, in the days of ferment, 1931–33, when Keynes began drafting the *General Theory*. Another Cambridge connection was W. B. Reddaway, a former supervision pupil of Keynes and, in 1936–37, research fellow in economics at the University of Melbourne. Reddaway reviewed the *General Theory* for the Australian economic journal, the *Economic Record*. Fully appreciative of the significance of Keynes' insights, Reddaway expressed his strong support for the arguments presented. Yet another Cambridge connection was Colin Clark, who first worked with Keynes in 1930 on the Economic Advisory Council. On the recommendation of Keynes, who held his statistical work in high regard, Clark was appointed to a university lectureship in statistics at Cambridge, a post held from 1932 to 1937. Clark soon established a reputation as one of the leading authorities on the calculation of national income. He returned to Australia in 1937 and set to work, with J. G. Crawford, on a statistical analysis of Australia's national income.[17]

Clark's work on national income points to another factor that contributed to the acceptance of Keynes' framework among Australian economists: an interest in the aggregative approach. Referring to the nature of economic study in Australia in the 1920s, Copland could point in 1951 to 'the habit which Australian economists seemed to develop of seeing the economy as a whole, and of realising the possibility of initiating centrally planned policy to counteract maladjustments within the economy'.[18] This might well be an exaggerated claim, influenced by hindsight. It is true, however, to quote Copland, that during the 1920s 'the national income was the focal point of discussion'. Copland observed that

> whereas today we are mainly concerned with movements in some of the Keynesian variables which make up the national income and

> expenditure, the emphasis in the earlier period was on the national income itself, this being quite properly regarded as an index of economic welfare and thus a good starting point for economic enquiry.[19]

What is also important, Hall says, in determining the economic viability of a new theory are the structure of a country's national economy and the kind of international constraints which it faces. Keynesian policies might well have been resisted by small open economies, such as Australia, where any stimulus to demand was likely to worsen balance-of-payments problems by increasing imports. Certainly the Australian experience in the early 1930s, when it faced the spectre of massive overseas debt, a collapse in the volume and value of exports and consequent balance-of-payments problems, consolidated a pre-existing bias towards the virtues of conservative fiscal policies. In addition, the high level of debt owed by Australian governments to London financiers would have made it difficult to depart from the canons of sound finance insisted on by Sir Otto Niemeyer and his colleagues even if the idea of an expansionary public works program had gained domestic political support. (Niemeyer visited Australia in 1930 as the representative of the Bank of England. His mission was to investigate Australia's financial difficulties and determine a solution to them. He impressed on the Federal Government that any discussion of obtaining relief from London would necessarily involve the question of government financial policy more generally.) The view also prevailed in Australia that economic recovery depended much less on official policy than on the movement of commodity export prices. It was taken for granted that there was little that anyone could do about the latter. It was simply a matter of waiting and praying until prices and profits improved.

During the 1950s and 1960s, by contrast, Australia's overseas debt as a percentage of GDP remained relatively low. Although balance-of-payments problems emerged frequently, the problem was seen to arise less from a failure of exports and more from a tendency for aggregate demand to exceed aggregate domestic supply. The major aim of budgetary policy was not to provide a stimulus to a flagging economy but rather to dampen what appeared to be a tendency towards excess demand.

Administrative viability
Discussing the next criterion, administrative viability, Hall says that

> Keynesianism was more likely to be accepted if it accorded with the long-standing administrative biases of the officials responsible for approving it and seemed feasible in light of the existing implementational capacities of the state.[20]

He also argues that

> the official reception given to a new economic theory can be conditioned by the way in which power over economic policy making inside the state itself is distributed among agencies with different biases, and by prevailing perceptions of the capacity of the state to implement the new policy.[21]

An outstanding feature of economic policy-making in Australia in the 1930s was that regulation was exercised by a plethora of competing institutions, including the Federal Government, the states, the Tariff Board, the Commonwealth Bank, the Commonwealth Arbitration Court, wages boards and the Loan Council. A variety of marketing schemes also operated. No mechanism existed to coordinate the approach of these institutions. Indeed, one of the tragedies of the Great Depression was that the Federal Government was both unable and unwilling to exercise leadership in economic affairs. Even if the Federal Government had wanted to do so, the fact is that there was a totally inadequate administrative support system in the 1930s. The federal Treasury was weak and ineffectual, and the Commonwealth Bank, whose powers were highly circumscribed, could not be said to be even remotely a truly central bank. While both of these institutions had certainly become more powerful and more influential by the end of the decade, serious problems remained of inadequate coordination and an unwillingness to accept common economic criteria.[22] It follows that this was not a propitious situation in which Keynesian ideas could have gained a foothold and become the basis for new policy initiatives.

By 1945, however, the power of the Federal Government relative to the states had increased dramatically, the federal bureaucracy had been greatly strengthened and the Treasury had emerged as the premier institution advising on economic policy. In fact the Treasury had a virtual monopoly on budgetary and monetary matters through the 1950s and 1960s. It also had a close working relationship with the central bank, the Reserve Bank, which was created in 1959 as the successor to the Commonwealth Bank. Together with the Treasury, which tended to overshadow it, the Reserve Bank shared the role of providing advice on monetary policy. Some problems, it is true, still remained. The Conciliation and Arbitration Commission could frustrate the Federal Government by granting what the latter deemed inappropriate wage rises. The economic activities of State Governments might sometimes be inconsistent with the Federal Government's wishes. But a great many of the administrative problems of the 1930s had been solved.

Hall underlines the importance of what he refers to as the permeability of the civil service. This has to do with such things as whether an administration is willing to use public commissions and outside experts or whether it relies heavily on a group of senior and permanent civil servants who have a near monopoly on economic information and the provision of advice. Such structural issues were important in determining the speed with which Keynesian ideas were initially accepted and then the subsequent durability of the attachment to them. It might be that in a country with a relatively permeable civil service, and here the United States is the prime example, Keynesianism was accepted early and with apparent ease but never became firmly entrenched because pro- and anti-Keynesian economists moved in and out of different administrations. In Britain, as noted earlier, the Treasury's power and predisposition contributed to the slow adoption of Keynesian policies. Nevertheless, once the Treasury did eventually accept them, 'its hierarchical administrative structure rendered them an entrenched component of the policy process for over thirty years'.[23] Likewise, in Australia in the post-war period, the Federal Government's heavy reliance on the Treasury meant that Keynesian ideas, which were eventually accepted by the Treasury by the end of World War II, became as in Britain 'an entrenched component of the policy process'.

Another factor that conditioned the state's receptiveness to Keynesianism was 'the degree to which power over macroeconomic management was concentrated'.[24] The more concentrated was this power, the more feasible, it would seem, was Keynesian demand management. Here Australia was something of an exception. While it was by no means as fragmented as the United States, and while the Commonwealth's relative financial power increased more or less continuously from World War II onwards, the Federal Government's attempts at anticyclical demand management were made difficult by the existence of Australia's federalist structure. Economists complained repeatedly about irresponsible and spendthrift State Governments thwarting the Federal Government's attempts at expenditure control in situations of excess demand. However, it should be said that this did not lead to a questioning of the validity of Keynesian principles. It meant simply a recognition of some of the difficulties in implementing them properly.

Yet another relevant feature of a state's structure was the power of the central bank over economic policy-making. The more powerful was the central bank, Hall argues, the less likely was it that Keynesian policies would be pursued. This, he says, was because central bankers tend to view deficit spending negatively. Their concern is that it leads to an increase in public debt, for which they have to provide the funds, and that it might threaten the value of the currency.

In the 1930s, as I have said, Australia lacked a truly central bank. None the less, the Commonwealth Bank emerged as a dominant force in the determination of economic policy. It acted as a powerful bulwark in the way of those pushing for an expansionary public works policy. It was the great champion of financial orthodoxy. In 1931 it responded to requests from the Scullin Labor Government for additional funds by simply stating that it would be impossible for it to provide further assistance. Theodore, the Labor Treasurer, complained bitterly that this represented 'an attempt on the part of the bank to arrogate to itself a supremacy over the Government in the determination of the financial policy of the Commonwealth'.[25]

The Commonwealth Bank's attitude was in many ways entirely typical of Australian trading banks in general. What stands out, again, is the absence of cooperation among the leading economic institutions and the persistence of hostility and conflict instead. Schedvin says that in their various encounters in the 1930s, the trading banks were informed by well-entrenched principle:

The word 'principles' is probably a misnomer, as they were more accurately a mixture of prejudice, instinct, self-interest and common-sense; but they were applied by the banks as inflexibly as principles. Undoubtedly the most pervasive of these was an abhorrence of all forms of government regulation, particularly in relation to banking. This was more than narrow self-interest, for the bankers genuinely believed that any government interference with banking in general, and the note issue in particular, would inevitably violate the dictates of sound finance, and in the more extreme cases lead to run-away inflation ... Even during the depression when prices were falling bankers were haunted by a fear of inflation ... In their view, a policy of credit expansion could not possibly remedy depression, and would cause the complete collapse of the economic system if allowed to take control.[26]

For the ALP one of the lessons of the 1930s experience was that there was a need to provide the Commonwealth Bank with comprehensive powers with which to exercise control over the activities of the trading banks. The vital corollary was that the bank had to be subservient to the wishes of the government. An attempt was made to give legislative force to these desires with the passing of the Commonwealth Bank Act of 1945. This legislation spelt out the bank's specific duty to exercise its powers in a manner that would simultaneously meet three aims, the traditional one of ensuring the stability of the Australian currency and two novel ones: 'the maintenance of full employment in Australia' and 'the economic prosperity and welfare of the people of Australia'. Even without the onus of meeting these requirements, the fact is that the Australian central bank's role in economic policy advice remained clearly subservient to the Treasury's right throughout the Keynesian era. In any case, those in charge of the bank did not fit into the usual central banker mould. H. C. Coombs was appointed its governor in 1949 and retained this position until 1968. Coombs, as noted, was one of the earliest and keenest supporters of Keynesianism in Australia and remained a devotee of Keynesian principles throughout his governorship.

The notion of administrative viability needs to be set in the context of the structure of state–society relations. Of particular importance in understanding the acceptance of Keynesianism, Halls says,

> was the institutional relationship developed between each state and the capital markets for the purpose of providing public finance. That turned on the kind of financial instruments that each state developed to fund its debt, the regulatory regime it imposed on the banking sector, and the general character of the capital markets at its disposal ... this relationship was crucial to the capacity of a state to sustain high budgetary deficits and one of the principal reasons that Keynesian experiments were not undertaken more quickly or more widely in the 1930s.[27]

Australia was typical of a great many countries in the 1930s in that it had not yet perfected the institutions now in place to facilitate deficit financing. It relied instead on quite rudimentary mechanisms for the provision of public finance. Economic policy in the early 1930s, as mentioned earlier, was severely constrained by a massive build up of public debt during the 1920s, approximately half of which was owed overseas. The need to service this debt was a major governmental preoccupation in the early years of the depression. All of this was compounded by the unfortunate relationship that had developed between governments and banks. Schedvin summarises the situation nicely:

> At the end of 1929 the banks were faced with an acute liquidity crisis which occurred so rapidly that the traditional methods of control were completely ineffective ... Throughout the 1930s the banks struggled to regain liquidity. Increased lending was out of the question, particularly for financing government deficits. The very gravity of the situation later forced them to assist governments, but they did so reluctantly. In the banks' view governments alone were responsible for the disarray of public finance which was a legacy of over-borrowing and lax financial methods, and it was not a banking duty to rescue them. Their responsibilities were towards the stability of their own institutions, and this was not compatible with assisting financially reckless governments.[28]

Schedvin goes on to complain about 'the parsimonious attitude towards works expenditure' in Australia in the 1930s. He criticises 'the modicum of unemployment relief expenditure' sanctioned during the depression, which, he says, was 'totally inadequate'.[29] But as he himself points out in the passage above, funding of additional works expenditure, if that had been the preferred strategy, would have been extremely difficult to achieve with the banks in such a hostile mood. Schedvin also admits that there were additional limitations, primarily to do with what we have referred to above as problems of administrative viability:

> *It cannot of course be denied that an expansionary programme might have been frustrated (at least in part) by exhaustion of international reserves. In view of the persistent low level of export prices and of London funds through the 1930s, it would have required exceptional skill in economic management to guide the economy towards full employment without precipitating a major payments crisis. Even assuming that an expansionary programme had been politically acceptable and there existed scope for additional import replacement, there is no reason to believe that the monetary and fiscal authorities possessed sufficient skill to handle such a delicate operation.*[30]

In short, then, it is by no means clear whether in the early 1930s it would have been possible to pursue a sustained reflationary policy even if governments had been determined to do so. With both governments and domestic banks so acutely sensitive to the burden of servicing overseas debts and, quite apart from this, with such restricted access to funds from overseas and with the domestic capital market so weak, it is difficult to see how Keynesianism could have been made to work in Australia in the 1930s.

Another consideration, relevant to the earlier discussion on the degree to which power over macroeconomic management was concentrated, is that in the 1930s the Federal Government's budget was relatively so small that its impact on the level of economic activity was at best marginal. Even if the Federal Government had embraced Keynesian principles, and leaving aside the question of adequate finance, the size of the federal budget was such that one wonders whether the validity of Keynes' principles could have been properly tested. It was not until World War II, as we have seen, that such a test was possible.

Political viability

In referring to political viability, the third criterion, Hall is making the obvious point that economic theories will need to have some broader political appeal if they are to become policy. In one sense, as Hall points out, politically Keynesianism was polarising in that it was appealing to a great many trade unionists who sought the restoration and maintenance of full employment, and the income security that this brought, but was anathema to many of those in the worlds of public and private finance who interpreted Keynes' message as a form of heresy. It came to be realised, however, that the *General Theory* offered not just a solution to unemployment but one that was in the interests of both capital and labour, and thus it appealed to conservative and labour parties alike in Australia. As Coombs puts it,

> *it was one of the most attractive features of the Keynesian analysis that it seemed to by-pass the most divisive issues within our society. It seemed in everybody's interest that expenditure should be pitched at levels adequate to sustain business activity close to capacity and so to maintain high levels of employment.*[31]

Another attraction was that Keynes' macroeconomic management promised to maintain high employment levels without direct regulation of microeconomic matters; that is, without directly interfering with the exercise of individual choice and initiative. It also promised — a message that Australian economists seized on — to restore vitality to the private sector. They, like Keynes, saw governmental initiative as an essential precondition for the restoration of confidence within the private sector and for the rehabilitation of entrepreneurial dynamism — an attitude influenced perhaps by a long tradition of public enterprise in Australia. This in turn raises questions about the nature of political discourse in Australia.

Hall argues that too often contemporary political analysis is marred by a failure to consider 'a crucial component of the environment in which policy is made':

> *Policy making takes place within an institutional framework, whose configuration varies from nation to nation, but it also occurs within the context of a prevailing set of political ideas. These include shared conceptions about the nature of society and the economy, various ideas about the appropriate role of government, a number of common political ideals, and collective memories of past policy experiences. Together, such ideas constitute the political discourse of a nation. They provide a language in which policy can be described within the political arena and the terms in which policies are judged there.*[32]

Furthermore,

> *The nature of prevailing political discourse can work to the advantage or disadvantage of new policy proposals. In terms of prevailing discourse, some new proposals will be immediately plausible, and others will be barely comprehensible. Therefore ... the nature of national political discourse can have a major impact on the likelihood that a new set of policy ideas will be accepted.*[33]

In Australia, to simplify greatly, political discourse grew out of a tradition of government interventionism. Many years ago the economic historian Noel Butlin popularised the term *colonial socialism* to describe the pervasive nature of state activity in late nineteenth-century Australia. Butlin argued in a later work that for the first forty years of the twentieth century the nature of state activity changed from what he called 'direct market participation' to 'more indirect modes of intervention', especially of a regulatory and allocative nature. Despite this change, there was a noteworthy continuity, namely 'a strongly supportive relationship, almost a partnership, of government towards major business interests and a private acceptance (and use of) this supportive relationship'.[34] Keynesianism was portrayed, and during World War II was accepted, as being consistent with this longstanding relationship between the public and private sectors. To a country long used to government intervention, and ruled at the federal level by a Labor Party enamoured of the virtues of nationalisation and direct wage, price and rental controls as vital tools in managing the economy, Keynesianism seemed a relatively non-interventionist doctrine to those who debated it during the war and in the early post-war years. If one accepts Butlin's views on what happened subsequently the irony is that in practice Keynesianism changed the nature of public–private sector relations in that it led to 'the emergence of public constraint on and even some antagonism towards private business arising out of the requirements of macro-economic management'.[35]

The notion of political viability raises questions about the significance of the orientation of the governing party. This, Hall observes, 'appears to have been the single most important factor affecting the likelihood that a nation would pursue Keynesian policies'. Such policies, he says, 'were much more commonly initiated by parties with particularly strong ties to the working class than by their conservative or bourgeois rivals'.[36] Hall rightly adds that one needs 'to distinguish between the initial introduction of Keynesian policies and their continuation. Social democratic parties have been most responsible for the initiation of Keynesian policies. Once tried, those policies were often maintained by more conservative successors'.[37]

The Australian experience confirms Hall's arguments. Indeed it has sometimes been suggested that the acceptance of Keynesianism in Australia was linked fundamentally with the electoral victory in 1941 of a Federal Labor Government. Emphasis has been placed in particular on the fact that J. B. Chifley, the Labor Treasurer and, from 1945, Prime Minister, was sympathetic to Keynesian ideas. In his biography of Chifley, L. F. Crisp points out that the royal commission on money and banking (1936–37), in which Chifley was a commissioner, happened to begin sitting in the same month that Keynes' *General Theory* was published. Crisp argues that from July 1936 some of the economists giving evidence to the commission began to refer to the book. Under the guidance of a fellow commissioner, Professor R. C. Mills of the

University of Sydney, Chifley 'was perfectly placed to gain an early appreciation of the Keynesian "revolution" ... Chifley in a broad sense became a "Keynesian-of-the-first-hour"'.[38]

Crisp also suggests that 'experience and instinctive inclination had predisposed Labour men to Keynes' approach and general theses'. Although this is asserted rather than argued, it is true that the Labor Party had long been inclined towards interventionism. More especially, the labour movement was obsessed with the so-called 'money power'.[39] Public works expenditure was deemed a useful palliative for dealing with rising unemployment, and it accorded with the underconsumptionist ideas popular among ALP members, but the common conviction in the labour movement was that politically the fight should be about ensuring the nationalisation of the banks.

It has to be remembered also that a predisposition towards interventionism does not necessarily signify a predisposition towards Keynesianism. The point remains nevertheless that the Labor Party was particularly vocal during the war and especially from 1942 onwards in declaring that unemployment could be eradicated and that it was the responsibility of Federal and State Governments to do so (although, again, such arguments do not by themselves indicate an acceptance of Keynesianism). Delegates of the Labor Government preached this message to overseas audiences and attempted valiantly to gain international acceptance of the need to ensure full employment.

The conservative United Australia Party (UAP) Government, by contrast, had been notably reluctant to commit itself publicly to a full employment policy. Nevertheless, an examination of the activities of a host of international committees, various specialist committees and study groups formed in 1941 by the UAP Government reveals quite clearly that a change in attitude towards employment and the notion of economic management predated Labor's electoral victory. As Butlin and Schedvin point out,

> the central concern of both re-establishment and economic committees was post-war employment prospects. With hundreds of thousands of men mobilised and unemployment not entirely eliminated, the vision of a return to mass unemployment after demobilisation was vivid; it was assumed that no government whatever its political complexion could avoid giving employment policy the highest priority.[40]

It would seem, then, that where the ALP differed from the preceding UAP Government was not in accepting the need for and ability of governments to eradicate unemployment but in its willingness to make this commitment explicit. By 1942, however, even Robert Menzies (who had been prime minister at the outbreak of the war and who was to lead the Liberal Party when it was created in 1944) was openly supporting the notion of economic management and control. And, as mentioned earlier, it was a Liberal–Country Party coalition government, under Menzies' prime ministership, that was the first to use budgetary policy based explicitly on Keynesian principles.

Conclusion

The guiding assumption in this chapter, one shared with Hall, is that the role of ideas in political life needs to be taken seriously. Hall concludes by observing that:

> *Over the ages, politics has traditionally been seen as a struggle for power, a contest for control over scarce resources that pits one social group against another in recurring confict for domination. Without denying the truth of this, however, we can see that politics is more than that. In democratic societies especially, it is also a process whereby the basic ideals and identity of a nation are defined, as attempts are made to master the collective problems facing society. Hence, ideas are central to politics in two ways. From the competing moral visions put forward by contenders for political power, a sense of collective purpose is forged; and out of the policy proposals generated by intellectuals and officials alike, solutions to common problems are devised.*[41]

The curious thing is that there has not been much systematic analysis of how economic ideas influence policy. Nor has there been much comparative work. Hall and his contributors have taken a vital first step in filling both these gaps. The strength of Hall's framework is his recognition of the need for economic ideas to satisfy not one but three distinct criteria if they are to have a chance of becoming the basis of policy. These criteria help us to understand why certain ideas become accepted and why others are rejected. They also help us to understand why a particular set of ideas might be warmly embraced in one country but receive a lukewarm reception in another.

Hall's framework is valuable, too, in that it is a counsel against simplification. To suggest, for example, that the adoption of Keynesianism in Australia can be largely attributed to the influence of the economists making up the wartime F & E committee would be to ignore a range of important administrative and political factors. One would also want to know why the economists accepted Keynesianism and why the F & E committee was able to exercise such influence.

The other great benefit of Hall's analysis is that, in talking of economist, state and coalition-centred approaches, Hall provides a useful classificatory schema, one which points to competing interpretations of the nature of the policy-making process and the principal actors involved.

Notes

1. Certain sections here draw on the author's earlier work, G. Whitwell (1986), *The Treasury Line*, Allen & Unwin, Sydney, esp. ch. 3.
2. 'Memorandum on Treasury organisation', Dedman Papers, National Library.
3. G. Whitlam (1985), *The Whitlam Government 1972–1975*, Viking, Ringwood, p. 184.
4. P. A. Hall (ed.) (1989), *The Political Power of Economic Ideas: Keynesianism across Nations*, Princeton University Press, Princeton, pp. 8–10.
5. P. A. Hall (1989), pp. 9–10.
6. P. A. Hall (1989), pp. 10–11.
7. P. A. Hall (1989), p. 11.
8. P. A. Hall (1989), pp. 11–12.
9. P. A. Hall (1989), p. 12.
10. P. A. Hall (1989), p. 13.
11. P. A. Hall (1989), p. 371.
12. *Commonwealth Parliamentary Debates*, 182, 30 May 1945, pp. 2238–9.
13. R. Skidelsky (1975), 'The reception of the Keynesian revolution', in Milo Keynes (ed.), *Essays on John Maynard Keynes*, Cambridge University Press, Cambridge, p. 104.
14. R. Wilson (1940), *Economic Co-ordination*, the Joseph Fisher Lecture in Commerce 1940, University of Adelaide at the Hassell Press, Adelaide, p. 25.
15. P. A. Hall (1989), p. 372.
16. H. C. Coombs (1981), *Trial Balance*, Macmillan, Melbourne, p. 3.
17. C. Clark and J. G. Crawford (1938), *The National Income of Australia*, Angus & Robertson, Sydney.
18. D. B. Copland (1951), 'Development of economic thought in Australia, 1924–50', in D. B. Copland, *Inflation and Expansion*, Cheshire, Melbourne, pp. 16–17.
19. D. B. Copland (1951), p. 18.
20. P. A. Hall (1989), p. 373.
21. P. A. Hall (1989), p. 374.
22. C. B. Schedvin (1970), *Australia and the Great Depression*, Sydney University Press, Sydney, pp. 375–7.
23. P. A. Hall (1989), p. 379.
24. P. A. Hall (1989), p. 378.
25. Letter from E. G. Theodore to Sir Robert Gibson, 15 April 1931, reproduced in E. O. G. Shann and D. B. Copland (eds) (1931), *The Battle of the Plans*, Angus & Robertson, Sydney, p. 48.
26. E. O. G. Shann and D. B. Copland (1931), pp. 79, 80.
27. P. A. Hall (1989), p. 380.
28. C. B. Schedvin (1970), p. 81.
29. C. B. Schedvin (1970), p. 373.
30. C. B. Schedvin (1970), p. 373.
31. H. C. Coombs (1981), p. 146.
32. P. A. Hall (1989), p. 383.
33. P. A. Hall (1989), p. 383.
34. N. G. Butlin, A. Barnard and J. J. Pincus (1982), *Government and Capitalism: Public and Private Choice in Twentieth-Century Australia*, Allen & Unwin, Sydney, p. 10.

35 N. G. Butlin, A. Barnard and J. J. Pincus (1982), p. 10.
36 P. A. Hall (1989), p. 376.
37 P. A. Hall (1989), p. 377.
38 L. F. Crisp, *Ben Chifley* (1961), Longman, Melbourne, p. 169.
39 See P. Love, *Labour and the Money Power* (1984), Melbourne University Press, Melbourne.
40 S. J. Butlin and C. B. Schedvin (1977), *War Economy 1942–45*, Australian War Memorial, Canberra, pp. 626–7.
41 P. A. Hall (1989), p. 389.

6

The arbitration system since 1967

Braham Dabscheck

Throughout the twentieth century industrial tribunals in Australia have played a prominent, if not pre-eminent, role in regulating relationships between workers, unions and employers. Industrial tribunals were created during the period 1890 to 1910 in response to the crisis engendered by the depression and strikes of the 1890s. Their creation resulted from the work of middle-class intellectuals, of lawyers and politicians, who believed that the state had a duty and responsibility to create machinery to regulate relationships between workers and employers.[1] In the words of Henry Bournes Higgins, the second president of the Commonwealth Court of Conciliation and Arbitration (1907–21), industrial tribunals would usher in

> a new province for law and order ... the process of conciliation, with arbitration in the background, is substituted for the rude and barbarous processes of strike and lockout. Reason is to displace force; the might of the State is to enforce peace between industrial combatants as well as between other combatants; and all in the interests of the public.[2]

We can identify two different approaches that industrial tribunals may pursue in seeking to resolve disputes between employers and employees and their representative organisations. The tribunal could tailor its decisions to factors relevant to each case per se. This approach reflects the view that each dispute requires its own solution and that the decision reached should be based on factors peculiar to the dispute in question. However, a decision handed down in a particular dispute has potential effects on other groups of parties which fall under the tribunal's jurisdiction. Such parties may seek a similar decision from the tribunal, even though the factors relevant in the first dispute do not pertain to them. It is conceivable that a decision handed down by a tribunal in one case could be followed by disputes among other groups of parties over which it has jurisdiction. In attempting to overcome this externality problem the tribunal will downgrade the relevance of unique or peculiar factors in making a decision in any particular case and will seek to introduce consistent or general principles or adjudication. This uniform approach emphasises the needs of the system/jurisdiction as a whole, rather than the needs of the particular and different groups of parties that constitute a part of that system.

Higgins enunciated the need for consistent principles in resolving industrial disputes in the following terms:

> *Awards have to be framed on some definite system, otherwise in getting rid of one trouble you create many others ... the Court ... has to deal, not with single isolated disputes, but with a series of disputes. The awards must be consistent one with the other, or else comparisons breed unnecessary restlessness, discontent, industrial trouble. The advantages of system and consistency in the awards are increasingly apparent.*[3]

In developing principles tribunals seek to influence, cajole, push or bully the parties[4] to accept their interpretation of how to approach problems of industrial relations regulation. Tribunals engage in a continual struggle with the parties in trying to win their endorsement, if not acceptance, of their principles.[5] If a tribunal is successful in this quest, where its principles—and their application—are not inconsistent with the expectations and desires of the parties, the relationship between the tribunal and parties will be one of harmony. On the other hand, if the tribunal's principles are unacceptable to the parties, its relationship with them will be one of conflict and discord.

This chapter is concerned with providing an account of arbitration in the period 1967 to early 1993. In doing so the chapter will focus on the activities of the federal tribunal[6] (the commission) and its trials and tribulations in attempting to develop a consistent and coordinated approach to wage determination and industrial relations regulation. The chapter will be organised into five sections. The first section will examine the institutional setting that governs the operation of industrial tribunals and Australia's three-tiered system of wage determination. The second section will examine the era of the total wage between 1967 and 1974. The third section will analyse the period 1975–82, which started with wage indexation and concluded with a wages freeze. The various Accords and the move to enterprise bargaining between 1983 and 1993 will be the focus of the fourth section. The major themes of the chapter will be drawn together in the summary and conclusion.

Institutional setting: Australia's three-tiered system of wage determination

In February 1983 the federal Australian Labor Party, under the leadership of Bob Hawke, and the Australian Council of Trade Unions negotiated an Accord that, among other things, championed a wages and incomes policy as the best means to resolve economic problems experienced in the early 1980s. As will become clear shortly, the ALP, which won the subsequent March 1983 federal election, did not have the power to legislate for the wages side of the Accord. Only the commission had the constitutional power to implement the wages policy enshrined in the Accord.

Most discussions of the Accord have been concerned with whether it represents an Australian version of (neo-)corporatism.[7] Little, if any, attention has been directed to the question of the commission endorsing the wages side of the Accord (which it subsequently did in the September 1983 National Wage Case). Implicit in most writings on the Accord is the view that the commission should simply act as a cipher, rubber-stamping agreements negotiated between the ALP and ACTU.

The Australian Constitution severely limits the ability of the Commonwealth Government to become directly involved in industrial relations. Section 51, paragraph xxxv of the Constitution only empowers the Commonwealth to make laws with respect to 'Conciliation and arbitration for the prevention and settlement of industrial disputes extending beyond the limits of any one state'.

This section of the Constitution provides the Commonwealth Government with an indirect power. It is undoubtedly the only national government in the world that does not enjoy a direct industrial relations power with respect to the private sector. The Constitution forces the Commonwealth Government to delegate powers of conciliation and arbitration to industrial tribunals charged with the responsibility of settling and preventing industrial disputes. If the Commonwealth wants to achieve certain industrial relations outcomes, it is forced, like other parties, to argue its case before industrial tribunals. For example, the Commonwealth lacks power to introduce a wages policy by legislation. It can only make submissions before the commission, which will make a decision based on the merits of the various submissions argued before it.[8] Alternatively, the commission can operate a wages policy notwithstanding the opposition of the government of the day—as occurred with wage indexation between 1975 and 1981 under the Fraser Coalition Government (see below).

State Governments are not precluded from becoming directly involved in industrial relations. On a number of occasions important developments with respect to conditions have been established at the state level by legislation. Despite their direct industrial relations powers, State Governments have legislated for industrial tribunals or brought them into being. At the risk of making a rash historical generalisation, state tribunals have tended to follow the lead of the commission with respect to matters of major importance. State Governments have also enacted legislation requiring their respective tribunals to follow the major decisions of the commission. In addition, legislation and the tribunals themselves have, in the 1970s and 1980s, sought to achieve greater cooperation and coordination between (state and Commonwealth) tribunals.[9]

The commission has consistently maintained and guarded its independence from the government of the day. Members of the commission maintain that they base their decisions on the quality of submissions presented before them and their judgement concerning the best or most appropriate course of action that should be adopted at a particular time. One of the members of the commission perceived its independence so strongly that he referred to himself and his colleagues as the 'economic dictators of Australia'.[10]

Australia has developed what is known as a three-tiered (or level) system of wage determination. The three tiers are national wage cases, industry cases and over-award or direct negotiations between the parties. In national wage cases a full bench of the commission determines or adjusts wages, and/or the rules or principles that govern wage determination, for all workers covered by federal awards. National wage cases (and other important cases heard by a full bench) constitute the major mechanism through which the commission has sought to develop a consistent and coordinated approach to wage determination and industrial relations regulation. In national wage cases the commission determines minimum increases in wages that are believed to be consistent with Australia's industrial relations and economic needs. Major factors considered in national wage cases have been the state of the economy and the equitable distribution of the benefits of economic growth, given levels of inflation, employment, investment, productivity and the balance of payments.

The commission has believed that the fruits of economic growth and productivity should be distributed to all Australian employees (or, to be more correct, those covered by federal awards) via national wage cases. It has eschewed claims for pursuing a more decentralised approach because of its belief in the need, or wisdom, of pursuing a consistent and coordinated approach to industrial relations regulation. In the 1966 *General Motors Holden* and 1970 *Oil Industry* cases the commission rejected union applications that wages should be linked to company or industry profitability respectively.[12] In the *Oil Industry* case the commission stated 'that increased prosperity should be shared amongst employees generally and not be confined to employers in the more prosperous industries'.[13]

In both cases the commission expressed concern about practical problems associated with measuring productivity and profitability and how such increases should be translated into wages. If high profits and productivity meant high wages, then falls in either or both would imply wage reductions, which would bode ill for those on low incomes. Moreover, the commission was worried that if it granted such claims the principle of comparative wage justice—which it later described as 'that universal test which means all things to all men'[14]—would result in similar increases being paid to other workers whose firms or industries had not experienced similar increases in profits or productivity.

Industry cases involve the commission or the relevant tribunal in dealing with wages and working conditions of workers in a particular sector or industry. Such cases are usually heard by individual tribunal members who, in theory at least, are able to fashion decisions to take into account unique circumstances relevant to the industry/sector and workers concerned. They have been referred to as secondary, margins or work value cases. Increases so gained are added to those determined in national wage cases. National wage cases, in both procedural and substantive (money) terms, have the potential to restrict and restrain the decision-making ability of individual tribunal members in industry cases.[15] These problems can be further exacerbated when the parties seek endorsement by an individual tribunal member of an agreement that is inconsistent with principles developed by a full bench in national wage cases. Sir John Moore, commission president between 1973 and 1985, indicated a need to move individual commission members from one industry to another, because 'after looking after particular industries for some years [they] have become proprietorial of those industries and ... ceased to have a proper approach to problems'.[16] Presumably such problems have been resolved, in theory, by the High Court's decision in the 1982 *Phonogram Officers* case, which requires individual commission members to adhere to principles developed by a full bench.[17]

With over-award bargaining wages are determined by direct negotiations between employers and workers/unions. Such bargaining takes account of local and unique factors at a particular workplace and reflects the variance in bargaining power that exists between different groups of workers/unions and their employers. Over-award pay has the potential to reduce the scope of industry and national wage cases and to undermine the commission's quest to operate and maintain a co-ordinated and consistent approach to wage determination and industrial relations regulation.

1967–74: The total wage

The introduction of the total wage by the commission in 1967 heralded a new approach to wage determination. The total wage replaced the basic wage and margins formula established by Higgins in 1907.[18] The basic wage enshrined the principle of the minimum wage that should be paid to adults performing unskilled labour.[19] The commission's criteria in such cases were similar to those used in national wage cases. The margin, or secondary wage, was an additional amount paid for extra skill, responsibility, arduousness and so on.

The determination of margins had become complicated because the fitter in the metal trades was used as a yardstick for the fixation of other margins. Increases awarded by the commission to the fitter seemed to flow on via the principle of comparative wage justice to workers in other awards. Because of these flow-on effects metal trades margins cases had become dominated by national rather than industry considerations—the same criteria considered in basic wage cases. During the 1960s the private employers argued that, because basic wage and metal trades cases were both based on national criteria, they should be combined in a total—or national—wage case. In the 1965 and 1966 basic wage inquiries the commission simultaneously heard metal trades margins cases.[20] In 1967 the commission acceded to the private emplyers' request.[21] The decision foreshadowed that the commission's approach to work value cases, under a total wage regime, would be announced in a forthcoming *Metal Trades* case.

In the 1974 *National Wage* case the commission looked back on its experiment with the total wage with feelings of disquiet. It said:

> *Ever since 1967 it has been the hope of the Commission that the bulk of wage increases would come from national wage cases in which general increases on economic grounds would normally be awarded ever year ... The Commission's hope has not been fulfilled. In 1970, 1972 and again last year the Commission expressed its concern at the development of what has become known as the three-tiered wage system, with increases occurring as a result of national wage cases, industry awards and agreements, and overaward gains of varying amounts obtained from employers.*[22]

The failure of the commission in this regard is amply demonstrated by table 6.1, which shows the percentage contribution of national wage cases to increases in male wages between 1967–68 and 1974–75. The

Table 6.1 National wage case increases as a percentage of changes in male average minimum wages, 1967–68 to 1974–75

Year	Percentage
1967–68	*39.5*
1968–69	*41.4*
1969–70	*52.6*
1970–71	*50.9*
1971–72	*28.2*
1972–73	*37.7*
1973–74	*19.1*
1974–75	*21.1*

Source: W. A. Howard (1977), 'Australian trade unions in the context of union theory', *Journal of Industrial Relations* 19:3, 255–73.

percentage has varied from a high of 52.6 per cent in 1969–70 to a low of 19.1 per cent in 1973–74.

Why was the commission so unsuccessful in its attempt to ensure that the bulk of wage rises flowed from national wage cases? The answer is linked to the condition or health of the Australian economy. During these years the economy enjoyed an annual average growth rate of almost 5 per cent and full employment–unemployment levels ranged from 1.4 to 2.5 per cent (see appendix 6.1). Australia exhibited the symptoms of a classic textbook demand pull inflation. This buoyant economic environment enabled workers and unions to obtain higher wages and/or enabled employers to pay them. At the risk of oversimplifying a complex process, the economic environment in this period was such that the parties were not prepared to wait for the commission to dole out wage increases in an annual national wage case.

On several occasions during the 1960s the commission expressed concern about the phenomenon of over-award payments because of the threat that they posed to its determinations in basic wage and margins cases.[26] While the 1967 *Metal Trades* case was ostensibly concerned with work value considerations, it turned out to be an exercise in which the commission sought to assert control over over-award pay. In awarding a variety of margins for more than three hundred classifications the commission sought to absorb over-award payments into the metal trades award.[24]

Unions objected and initiated a series of stoppages to force employers to pay up the money amounts included in the decision. As a result a new full bench was convened to reconsider the decision. In deferring 30 per cent of the increase to a later period the full bench overturned the earlier decision concerning absorption.[25] In his 1968 annual report Sir Richard Kirby observed that 'absorption in times of full employment is generally not practicable and that in present conditions therefore wage prescriptions should be divorced from assumptions that absorption should take place'.[26]

Following the debacle of the 1967 *Metal Trades* case, private employers asked the commission to determine procedures for the conduct of future work value cases in the 1968 *National Wage* case. The commission deferred such deliberations to the 1969 case because other parties had not had a chance to make submissions concerning the principles of work value determinations.[27] Its decision concerning work value principles is somewhat vague; at best it admonished individual members of the commission to be cautious in their determinations. They should keep an eye on 'other areas of federal wage fixation', and they could no longer expect that over-award pay would be absorbed. The commission also quoted from the 1963 *Metal Trades Margins* case in which it had rejected the development of a detailed code for fixing margins:

> *However convenient it may seem to attempt to lay down for all time precise rules or formulae for the fixation of margins, the assessment of particular margins at particular times must be an act of judgement by the person or persons making the assessment in the light of current knowledge and practice both of which are themselves susceptible of change.*[28]

The commission realised that full employment propelled the movement of wages in over-award and industry determinations but was in a quandary concerning how to proceed in national wage cases. In the 1970 case it decided to be 'generous' in attempting to stem the flow of rises from the other two tiers. The commission stated:

> *If we are not realistic in our attitude to wage fixation, then those who look to the Commission as their main source of wage increases, and there are many who do, will be treated inequitably while more and more of those who are strong enough to do so will seek increases in the field. If in the present state of the economy and in the atmosphere of general affluence which exists in the community we failed to give a reasonable increase we would be failing in our duty. However, we wish to emphasise that the material before us ... disclosed a state of affairs which if continued may inhibit the commission in future national wage cases ... If this large award increase is not followed by restraint in claims in the field, the commission may be frustrated in its desire to ensure that the results of economic progress are distributed as equitably as possible to all.*[29]

The decision, however, did not arrest 'claims in the field' (see table 6.1 above). In subsequent cases the commission adopted a more conservative attitude to the money amounts it awarded, discounting national wage cases, as it were, for movements that occurred in the other two tiers.[30]

The 1974 *National Wage* case is of interest because of a joint claim by the Whitlam Labor Government and the ACTU to reintroduce automatic quarterly cost of living adjustments, or what became known as wage indexation. Such a scheme had operated with respect to the basic wage from 1922 to 1953.[31] The commission was not prepared to accede to this request, mainly because of a lack of consensus on how wage indexation should operate. Nevertheless it was prepared to acknowledge that wage indexation 'could have positively beneficial economic, social and industrial implications'.[32]

1975–82: From wage indexation to a wages freeze

The commission regarded the experiment with the total wage from 1967 to 1974 as a failure. These years were seen as being chaotic and disorderly; a veritable wages wilderness in which it lost control over Australia's three-tiered system of wage determination. The early 1970s witnessed unprecedented increases in wages and prices. To make matters worse, in the latter part of 1974 unemployment increased alarmingly, to levels that had not been experienced since World War II (see appendix 6.1). The major attraction of wage indexation for the commission was that it held out the prospect of overcoming the industrial relations and economic problems experienced between 1967 and 1974. As the commission explained in April 1981:

> *In the ten years or so before 1975, sectional increases flowing from individual awards, without centrally determined constraints, were generally as important as national wage cases.[33] It was principally to avoid the damaging economic and industrial effects of these sectional wage increases which led the Commission to embark on the more centralized system of the indexation principles.[34]*

In its original indexation decision of April 1975 the commission said it would be prepared to link wage rises to movements in prices, each quarter, in national wage cases (after September 1978 adjustments were six-monthly) if wage rises from other sources were kept to a minimum. It warned that 'violation even by a small section of industry whether in the award or non-award area would put at risk the future of indexation for all'.[35]

Table 6.2 indicates that the commission was generally successful in ensuring that national wage cases were the major source of wage movements between 1975 and 1981.[36] In the early years of indexation more than 90 per cent of wage movements, for both males and females, resulted from the national wage case decisions of the commission. In the

Table 6.2 Wage indexation increases as a percentage of change in total wage, 1975–81

Year ended	Male (percentage)	Female (percentage)
August 1976	92	94
August 1977	94	96
June 1978	98	99
December 1978	89	97
June 1979	86	95
January 1980	86	96
June 1980	81	86
January 1981	83	70
May 1981	91	79

Source: Australian Bureau of Statistics (various dates), *Wage Rate Indexes (Preliminary)*, Catalogue No. 6311.0.

second half of the period there is a slight decline for both sexes. This mainly reflected the flow of an $8 per week work value round, consistent with the indexation principles, which began in mid 1978. By April 1981, 80 per cent of the workforce had obtained such increases.[37]

Throughout the six-year life of wage indexation the commission was involved in a continuing struggle with unions, employers and governments to obtain a consensus to ensure its survival. While the ACTU assured the commission that it supported wage indexation, several affiliates sought to obtain wage rises and other concessions over and above those implied by the commission's principles. Both the Fraser Coalition Government and private employers consistently urged the commission not to grant any wage rises at all because of the parlous state of the economy.[38] At one stage the commission ruefully observed that 'one side wants indexation without restraints while the other wants restraints without indexation'.[39]

In its various decisions the commission steadfastly sought to convince the parties of the need to maintain wage indexation, often harking back to the problems which had beset the economy before its introduction. The commission rejected arguments that its indexation decisions had harmful effects on the economy. In December 1977 it said:

> *we do not consider that wage rates can be looked at solely with regard to the economy. Industrial relations aspects must also be considered. In fact the two go hand in hand. To refuse any wage increase might have the effect of increasing demands in the field, supported by strikes, bans and the like. If this happened there would be a further fall in production, employees would have even less money to spend, the economy would further deteriorate and the ranks of the unemployed would swell even more.*[40]

The commission also pointed out, on a number of occasions, that it was not an arm of government policy.[41] Moreover, it warned that its activities 'can ... be prejudiced by government decisions in other areas of government policy'.[42] It was particularly critical of government budgetary decisions that increased prices.[43]

On three occasions—December 1978, June 1979 and January 1981—the commission indicated that it was on the verge of abandoning indexation because of the lack of consensus and support from the parties.[44] Reference has already been made to the work value round, which began in mid 1978. In 1980 unions in the metal trades initiated a campaign to reduce the length of the working week to thirty-five hours. In July 1980 and again in January 1981 the commission contemplated reducing wages for the complying majority because of the actions of the non-complying minority.[45] And in April 1981 it indicated that it would give serious consideration to withholding national wage increases to those unions and workers who had used industrial action to obtain benefits. The commission claimed that:

> *this is not a punitive act. The Principles must apply uniformly and consistently to all our awards. Those who refuse to comply with the rules should not expect to receive the benefits which flow from the rules.*[46]

Australia experienced a short-lived mining and resources boom in the early 1980s. Increasing numbers of employers in growth areas of the economy were prepared to increase wages by amounts higher than those allowed under the commission's indexation principles. In May, June and July 1981 a number of unions and employers, in both the private and public sectors, negotiated wage rises in the vicinity of $20 per week. Given its previous warnings the commission duly brought wage indexation to an end on 31 July 1981. In doing so it announced that it would not countenance hearing another national wage case before February 1982.[47]

As in the period 1967–74, the more buoyant economic times associated with the mining and resources boom of the early 1980s saw the parties eschew the commission's preference for a consistent and coordinated approach to industrial relations regulation as embodied in wage indexation. After July 1981 Australia moved to a decentralised, uncoordinated system of industrial relations regulation. Would the commission's fears concerning the harmful industrial relations and economic effects of such a system be confirmed?

There are indications that the commission might have had second thoughts about its decision to abandon indexation. In a September 1981 decision involving transport workers it indicated that it was prepared to convene a national wage case before its February 1982 deadline. The commission appears to have been worried about wage rises based on work value grounds, which were beginning to flow through awards, precluding its ability to use future national wage cases to increase wages for movements in national productivity.[48] None of the parties, however, took up the commission's offer to convene an early national wage case.

Undoubtedly, the most significant case that occurred during this decentralised period was the agreement negotiated in the metal trades, which was ratified by the commission in December 1981. The agreement granted substantial wage increases, including a mid-term adjustment beginning in June 1982, and introduced a thirty-eight-hour week and a no extra claims during the life of the agreement clause.[49]

Early in 1982 the ACTU initiated a national wage case in which it sought to have the commission award wage rises to those workers who had missed out on the 'community standard' established since the end of wage indexation. The ACTU also sought the reintroduction of automatic quarterly cost of living adjustments, beginning with the December 1981 quarter. The commission refused both parts of the ACTU's claim. It was not prepared to acknowledge that a community standard had been established. Its decision also seems to have been based on an expectation that it would only be a matter of time before wage increases would flow to those workers who had not obtained post-indexation increases. With respect to the latter claim, the commission wanted the decentralised increases that had been negotiated to run their course before returning to a centralised wage-indexation-based system. Furthermore, the commission doubted whether the parties had the appropriate degree of 'collective responsibility' for wage indexation to work. It also wanted the parties to have more time to think about the wage system that should be employed in the future. The decision includes the following statement:

> *The commission has from time to time during the period of indexation emphasised the benefits, both industrial and economic, to be gained from a centralised and orderly system of wage fixation which gave high priority to the maintenance of real wages of all wage and salary earners, the weak and the strong. But it also emphasized repeatedly that such a system imposed obligations on all participants—unions, employers and governments—and called for their commitment to the system and its principles. It ultimately abandoned the system because the necessary degree of commitment for the system's survival was no longer forthcoming.*[50]

In the second half of 1982 drought and a world recession combined to strain the Australian economy severely. Both the level of inflation and unemployment hovered around 10 per cent (see appendix 6.1). Following a by-election held in the seat of Flinders, which had been fought (and won) over a wages freeze, and a subsequent Premiers Conference, the commission agreed in December 1982 to the introduction of a six-month wages pause (it subsequently lasted for nine months). In reaching its decision the commission quoted from a submission by the Victorian Government 'that the pause is the beginnings of a process of re-establishing a centralised wage fixing system'.[51]

1983–93: The Accord(s) to enterprise bargaining

Between 1975 and 1981 the commission had implemented a consistent and coordinated system of wage determination, in the form of wage indexation, in which it sought to ensure that national wage cases were the major source of wage movements in the Australian economy. In its various decisions between 1975 and 1981, and again in May 1982, the commission made it clear that it believed indexation provided the best means for Australia to overcome its associated economic and industrial relations problems. The events of the second half of 1981 and 1982—decentralised wage determination followed by a deteriorating economy, with both inflation and unemployment hovering around 10 per cent—would have served to convince the commission, if only regretfully, of the wisdom of its stance between 1975 and 1981. The commission had forestalled a return to wage indexation in May 1982 because it doubted whether the parties possessed the 'collective responsibility' to make such a system work.

It is in this context that the February 1983 Accord negotiated between the ALP and ACTU needs to be analysed. The Accord provided an electoral platform that would be pursued by the ALP if elected at the forthcoming March 1983 federal election. It advocated a wages and incomes policy as the best means to solve Australia's economic problems. The Accord said that 'the maintenance of real wages is agreed to be a key objective ... over time'.[52] That is, it advocated a return to wage indexation. During the election campaign Hawke pledged that, if elected, he would hold a national economic summit conference of governments, employers, unions and various interest groups that, via consensus and cooperation, would devise a program to bring about economic recovery.

Hawke duly won the election and held his foreshadowed summit in April 1983. The essential function of the summit was to obtain business or broader community endorsement for the broad contours of the Accord.[53] A fifty-six-point communiqué was endorsed by all participants at the summit, except for Queensland Premier Sir Joh Bjelke-Petersen. The summit supported a return to a centralised system of industrial relations regulation based on wage indexation. Clause 21 of the communiqué stated that: 'This Summit ... proposes that the parties should as a matter of priority develop the option of a return to a centralised system under the auspices of the ... Commission'.[54]

In September 1983 the commission duly reintroduced a centralised system based on six-monthly wage indexation, quoting extensively from both the Accord and the summit. In doing so it said that it expected wage indexation 'would lead to a more stable industrial environment and ... provide the basis for a more rapid recovery than would occur in any alternative system'. National wage cases would once again be the major source of wage movements in the economy. And, as it had in April 1975, the commission warned:

> *Increases outside national wage [cases]—whether in the form of wages, allowances or conditions, whether they occur in the public or private sector, whether they be award or overaward—must constitute a very small addition to overall labour costs.*[55]

The issue that will be explored here is the relationship between the Accord and the commission. The above analysis has maintained that the commission desired to re-establish a centralised system based on wage indexation. In 1982 it had decided not to because of the parties' lack of 'collective responsibility'. Given the constitutional protection afforded to the commission, the wage assumptions in the Accord would never have been realised if the commission had been opposed to the reintroduction of indexation. If the commission had decided to adopt a different wages norm, or develop a different system of industrial relations regulation, the Accord would have quickly disintegrated—as is evidenced by the experience of the Accord Mark VI (see below). It will be argued that both the Hawke-led ALP and the ACTU, with their not inconsiderable knowledge of industrial relations, and an ability to gauge the desires of the commission from its previous decisions, assumed that the commission wanted to reintroduce indexation. If this analysis is correct, the major skill of the Accord was the ability of the ALP and ACTU to gain political kudos from appearing to be responsible for a policy that the commission itself wanted to put in place.[56]

The importance of the Accord and the summit for the commission was that they demonstrated that governments and the parties now possessed the 'collective responsibility' to sustain the operation of a wage indexation system. The experience of the early 1980s had taught them the folly of abandoning the commission's coordinated and consistent approach to wage determination.

The commission was successful in ensuring that national wage cases were the major source of wage movements during the early years of the Accord. In June 1986 the commission reported that, between September 1983 and December 1985, 96 per cent of all award wage increases resulted from its decisions in national wage cases, and that it was unable to identify any sizeable movements in over-award pay in this period.[57] The economy also experienced growth and recovery, with reductions in the level of inflation and unemployment, as well as a diminution in levels of industrial disputation (see appendices 6.1 and 6.2).

Notwithstanding the economic growth that seemed to flow from the Accord, the Australian economy was still confronted by major problems. In the mid 1980s Australia was beset by balance of payments, terms of trade, depreciating currency and international debt problems. Given these problems it was believed that Australia could no longer afford wage indexation. The ALP and ACTU negotiated a second Accord that involved a superannuation−wages tax trade-off in September 1985. The Accord Mark II involved the ACTU agreeing to a reduction in wages, which they presumably were entitled to expect given the existence of indexation, in exchange for tax cuts to arrest Australia's international economic problems.[58]

The commission endorsed the wages component of the Accord Mark II in its decisions of November 1985 and June 1986.[59] In doing so it rejected submissions by the Business Council of Australia and others who advocated a move towards an enterprise-based, or award by award, approach to wage determination. It said:

> *The perceived advantage of a decentralised system so eloquently argued by its proponents on the basis of selected countries, is illusory and at best transient in the context of the Australian labour market. This is so clearly exposed in the experiences of the late 1960s and early 1970s and more recently 1981−82, that it is surprising that the proponents of decentralisation should continue to ignore the lessons of history and their underlying institutional basis.*[60]

At the next national wage case all of the major parties agreed that, given current and anticipated economic problems, wage indexation was no longer sustainable. The commission duly brought wage indexation to an end in December 1986.[61] Whereas in 1975 and 1983 indexation was seen as providing a solution to economic problems, in 1986 it was now viewed as contributing to such problems.

Following the abandonment of indexation, Australia's system of industrial relations regulation has been dominated by three interrelated factors. They are a series of wage−tax deals between the ALP and ACTU, the emergence of the structural efficiency principle and a move to enterprise bargaining.

The wage−tax trade-offs negotiated between the ALP and ACTU have served to determine or limit the wage claims of the ACTU before the commission.[62] The structural efficiency principle seeks to bring about a fundamental restructuring of awards to enhance the productivity and performance of Australian firms and industry. The principle is designed to remove provis. in awards that have hitherto placed restrictions or limitations on employers at the workplace. As the commission said in its August 1989 decision, it wants to encourage changes to 'work methods and the application of new technology and ... award provisions which restrict the right of employers to manage their own business unless they are seeking from the employees something which is unjust or unreasonable'.[63] In March 1987 the commission said, 'In our view, it is primarily at the enterprise level that the objectives of this principle will be achieved'.[64] And in May 1989 it stated: 'the main thrust of the principle is aimed at changing those award structures which inhibit measures to improve efficiency in individual establishments'.[65]

The structural efficiency principle, with its emphasis on a decentralised, firm-based system, might create the impression in some minds that the commission has retreated from operating a consistent and coordinated approach to industrial relations regulation. This would constitute a misreading of events. The commission, until the latter part of 1991 at least (see below), in developing the structural efficiency principle has sought to manage the movement to a decentralised system by developing a set of coherent, consistent and coordinated principles. In its structural efficiency principle the commission has not only determined rules and procedures but also set limits on the quantum of increases that might flow from successful applications of the principle. Under the structural efficiency principle national wage cases have been transformed into a vehicle for determining the principles that should apply to second-tier cases.

Before the March 1990 federal election the ALP and ACTU negotiated the Accord Mark IV concerning wages, taxes and other matters. The Accord Mark VI sought to continue the process of award restructuring occurring under the structural efficiency principle, and saw the enterprise as being the appropriate location for the implementation of future wage rises and employment conditions. It also wanted the commission to consider the 'principles upon which enterprise agreements would be determined'.[66] The major features of the Accord Mark VI were tax cuts, an increase in wages equal to the movement of prices in the September 1990 quarter, a $12 per week increase six months later and a 3 per cent increase in superannuation by 1 May 1993. At the time of the negotiation of the Accord Mark VI it was anticipated that the rise in prices in the September 1990 quarter would be in the vicinity of 2 per cent. The actual figure was 0.7 per cent. Following this lower than expected figure the Accord partners decided not to proceed with a national wage case, in exchange for topping-up previously agreed tax cuts. This subsequent agreement has been referred to as the Accord Mark VIa.

The national wage case concerning other aspects of the Accord Mark VI occurred during the end of 1990 and early 1991. Except for the Metal Trades Industry Association, all of the parties supported a move to enterprise bargaining. The Metal Trades Industry Association feared that a system of enterprise bargaining would result in Australia encountering the same problems that had occurred during decentralised periods in the late 1960s/early 1970s and 1981–82.[67]

The case occurred in the context of a worsening economy. Economic growth stagnated and unemployment steadily increased. The only good news was a fall in the level of inflation (see appendix 6.1). In its decision in April 1991 the commission rejected the Accord Mark VI holus-bolus. If nothing else the decision has served to remind us of the commission's independence. The commission refused to grant a $12 across-the-board increase because of the adverse condition of the economy. It was prepared to grant increases 'to a maximum of 2.5 per cent' where the parties could demonstrate that awards had been revised in accordance with the structural efficiency principle. The commission did not act on superannuation because of differences between the parties and difficulties associated with its application. It called on the Commonwealth Government to convene a conference to discuss such issues.

The most interesting parts of the decision involve the commission's findings concerning the structural efficiency principle and enterprise bargaining. The commission found that inadequate progress had been made concerning the structural efficiency principle. It said:

> *It is clear from the material before us that the results of restructuring to date have been uneven. In some areas substantial progress has been made, at least in terms of the framework at award level. In these areas, the stage is set for implementation of award changes at enterprise level. At the other end of the scale, there are areas where little progress has been made either in providing an appropriate framework at award level or in otherwise implementing the structural efficiency principle. In the case of the former, the efficacy of award variations have, generally, still to be tested properly at workplace level. In the case of the latter, more substantial change seems necessary at the award level before a concentrated effort can be made at the workplace level ... even where parties have made substantial changes to their awards, there seems to have been little real impact at the enterprise level.*[68]

Given this, the commission felt disinclined at that stage to endorse the adoption of enterprise bargaining. It said that 'The parties to industrial relations still have to develop the maturity necessary[69] for the further shift of emphasis now proposed'. In addition, the commission noted that the parties possessed different definitions of enterprise bargaining,[70] the existence of problems with its application, the calculation and distribution of benefits, whether there would be a limit on the quantum of benefits and the commission's role in the process. Furthermore, it feared that enterprise bargaining would lead to a wages breakout, with unions in strategic positions winning large increases with spill-over effects in other sectors.

Despite these problems the commission's April 1991 decision did not constitute a rejection of enterprise bargaining—it deferred the adoption of such arrangements to enable the parties to respond to the issues that it had raised. The commission was also concerned that not enough attention had been given 'to the criteria for future wage increases other than those [that] arise from enterprise bargaining'. The commission called on the parties 'to clarify their ideas and objectives' for a further review to be finalised before 1 November 1991.[71]

Both the Hawke Labor Government and the ACTU strongly criticised the April 1991 decision. It was seen as an attack on the Accord and on the needs of low-income earners and as retarding progress towards enterprise bargaining. ACTU Secretary Bill Kelty was particularly vehement, alternatively referring to the decision as 'a rotten egg' or 'vomit'. Tension between the commission and Accord partners was further exacerbated over issues associated with the appropriate level of salaries for commission members.[72]

A subsequent national wage case was held to reconsider the issue of enterprise bargaining. In October 1991 the commission gave its imprimatur to such deals. It would aid the parties in reaching agreements by conciliation (note, not arbitration) that were consistent with the structural efficiency principle. No limitations were placed on the quantum of agreements. The decision said:

> *The submissions again revealed a diversity of opinions and a failure to confront practical problems. Despite this, the parties and interveners once more press us to move towards a more devolved system. Collectively, they have left to us the task of translating a general concept into workable arrangements. There is little prospect, it would seem, that further postponement will lead to more fully developed proposals or to the resolution of points of disagreement. Although the concerns expressed in our April decision have not been allayed, we are satisfied that a further and concerted effort should be made to improve the efficiency of enterprises.*[73]

Following his elevation to prime minister, in February 1992 Paul Keating issued *One Nation*, a charter designed to help achieve economic growth and recovery. For our purposes *One Nation* contains four key factors. First, it supports the continual shift to workplace, or enterprise, bargaining to link wage increases more directly to productivity at the workplace. Second, the Keating Government foreshadowed changes to the *Industrial Relations Act 1988* to enhance the movement to workplace bargaining. Third, there would be a national wage case to commence in the second half of 1992. Fourth, a superannuation guarantee levy would be legislated to increase the level of occupational superannuation from the current figure of 3 per cent to 5 per cent in mid 1992, increasing to 9 per cent by 2000.[74]

Concerns over the state of the economy in mid 1992, with low or negative levels of growth and rapid increases in unemployment (see appendix 6.1), delayed the timing of the increase in the superannuation guarantee levy by six months (i.e. it was increased to 4 per cent in mid 1992 and to 5 per cent in January 1993), with the 9 per cent figure pushed out to 2002 rather than 2000.

Legislation was introduced to give effect to the government's promise to speed up the move to enterprise bargaining. The most significant aspect of this legislation is that, subject to the agreement not disadvantaging existing terms and conditions of employees covered by the agreement, there is no scope for the commission to subject such deals to a 'public interest' test. As long as the parties have reached an agreement consistent with the legislation the commission is required to register it as a certified agreement.[75] This situation can be contrasted with the decision of the commission in the October 1991 national wage case. While that decision recognised or accepted the principle of enterprise bargaining, it required the parties to jump through the hoops of the structural efficiency principle. The 1992 legislation removes this requirement. In his annual report to parliament, Mr Justice Maddern, the commission's president, observed:

> *the [1992] legislation in conjunction with the Commission's October 1991 enterprise bargaining principle does mean that two sets of rules apply to consent agreements. This is contrary to the views expressed by the October [1991] National Wage Case Full Bench and will, at least, create confusion.*[76]

Before Easter 1993 the commission convened a full bench to examine issues, or the 'confusion', associated with competing paths for moving towards enterprise bargaining.

Notwithstanding Paul Keating's statement in *One Nation*, the Accord partners did not initiate a national wage case in 1992. Such a decision appears to have been motivated by concern that an across-the-board wage increase would place undue pressure on a fragile economy, an implicit undertaking by the Accord partners to pursue superannuation improvements over national wage increases and a desire to 'force' or encourage the parties to embrace enterprise bargaining.

During the 1993 election campaign the ALP and ACTU negotiated the Accord Mark VII. The Accord Mark VII needs to be interpreted as a response to the more deregulatory policies pursued by the coalition before and during the election campaign.[77] The key features of the Accord Mark VII are commitments to employment growth and enterprise or workplace bargaining in which wage rises and other concessions are linked to productivity. For those workers on low pay or in weak bargaining positions unable to obtain wage increases via enterprise bargaining, the Accord Mark VII holds out the prospect of safety net increases to be arbitrated by the commission. The Accord Mark VII states than an $8 per week adjustment would be made available after 1 July 1993, and two further readjustments of between $5 and $10 available from 1 July 1994 and 1 July 1995 respectively.[78]

Following the ALP's electoral victory in March 1993 the ACTU announced that it would not initiate a national wage case to trigger the safety net increases foreshadowed in the Accord Mark VII until the latter part of 1993. The rationale for this was to encourage affiliates to make use of enterprise bargaining to obtain improvements in wages and working conditions. Moreover, the decision not to mount a national wage case has the effect of marginalising the commission. In saying this, however, it should be noted that the commission has convened a full bench to examine issues associated with the 'confusion' that exists between its approach to enterprise bargaining via the October 1991 national wage case and that enshrined in the 1992 legislation enacted by the ALP Government.

Summary and conclusion: Can lightning strike in the same place thrice?

Kitay conducted a study of the commission between 1967 and 1981 and maintained that its actions were 'characterised by inconsistent, opportunistic, highly political action'.[79] The material contained in this chapter fundamentally challenges such a view. The commission is not an inconsistent, opportunistic body acting as a cipher in responding to the ever-changing whims of the parties to industrial agreements. Rather, the commission has been involved in a continual struggle with the parties in which it has sought to convince them of the wisdom of adhering to systems of wage determination and industrial relations regulation based on consistent and coordinated principles. The commission's insistence on constructing and maintaining a principled approach to industrial relations regulation has involved it in becoming involved in several clashes with the parties.

The wage indexation experiments of 1975–81 and 1983–86, and the development of the structural efficiency principle between March 1987 and April 1991, were periods in which the commission was able to operate what it would regard as a consistent and coordinated approach to industrial relations regulation. Between 1967 and 1974, and again in the early 1980s, the commission was unable to operate such systems. Both these periods were associated with what the commission regards as harmful industrial relations and economic consequences. The commission fears that if enterprise bargaining is not developed in a way that mitigates or overcomes the traditional coordination problems of Australia's system of industrial relations, it will simply recycle the problems experienced during the years of the total wage and the early 1980s.

Appendix 6.1 Australian economic indicators, 1967–68 to 1991–92

Year	Change in prices %	Change in wages %	Real wage growth %	Real GDP growth %	Employment growth %	Unemployment rate %	Change in real unit labour costs %
1967–68	3.3	5.8	2.5	4.6	2.3	1.7	−1.7
1968–69	2.6	7.3	4.7	7.9	2.5	1.6	−0.9
1969–70	3.2	8.4	5.2	6.4	2.5	1.5	−0.3
1970–71	4.8	11.1	6.3	5.0	4.1	1.4	2.4
1971–72	6.8	10.4	3.6	4.0	2.2	1.7	0.8
1972–73	6.0	9.6	3.6	4.5	1.7	2.5	−0.6
1973–74	12.9	18.1	5.2	4.6	3.1	1.8	3.0
1974–75	16.7	28.3	11.6	1.3	1.2	2.4	4.0
1975–76	13.0	15.2	2.2	2.4	−0.2	4.6	0.0
1976–77	13.8	12.9	−0.9	2.9	1.0	4.7	−0.6
1977–78	9.4	9.9	0.5	0.9	0.6	6.5	0.9
1978–79	8.2	7.7	−0.5	5.0	0.8	6.1	−3.2
1979–80	10.1	9.9	−0.2	1.7	2.3	6.2	−0.8
1980–81	9.4	13.5	4.1	2.9	2.7	5.9	0.4
1981–82	10.4	13.7	3.3	2.1	1.2	6.1	1.9
1982–83	11.5	11.2	−0.3	−1.0	−1.7	8.9	−0.1
1983–84	7.9	8.5	0.6	5.1	0.9	9.5	−5.0
1984–85	5.8	6.9	1.1	5.2	3.0	8.5	−2.1
1985–86	8.4	5.9	−2.5	3.9	4.3	7.9	−0.9
1986–87	9.3	6.2	−3.1	2.5	2.7	8.3	−0.4
1987–88	7.3	6.0	−1.3	4.8	3.0	7.8	−3.1
1988–89	7.3	6.8	−0.5	4.1	4.1	6.6	−3.1
1989–90	8.0	6.6	−1.4	3.4	3.8	6.2	2.0
1990–91	5.3	5.8	0.5	−0.9	−0.4	8.4	2.0
1991–92	1.9	2.9	1.0	0.3	−1.6	10.4	0.6

Source: R. A. Foster and S. E. Stewart (1991), *Australian Economic Statistics 1949–50 to 1989–90*, Reserve Bank of Australia, Occasional Paper No. 8, February; B. Chapman and F. Gruen (1990), 'An analysis of the Australian consensual incomes policy: The Prices and Incomes Accord', Centre for Economy Policy Research, Discussion Paper No. 221, Australian National University, January; and Department of the Treasury, *Economic Round-up* (various issues).

Appendix 6.2 Industrial disputes in Australia, 1967–91

Year	Number of disputes	Workers involved directly and indirectly ('000)	Working days lost ('000)	Working days lost per employee
1967	1340	482.3	705.3	0.176
1968	1713	720.3	1079.5	0.261
1969	2014	1285.2	1958.0	0.458
1970	2738	1367.4	2393.7	0.555
1971	2404	1326.5	3068.6	0.693
1972	2298	1113.8	2010.3	0.449
1973	2538	803.0	2634.7	0.570
1974	2809	2004.8	6292.5	1.320
1975	2432	1398.0	3509.9	0.742
1976	2055	2189.9	3799.2	0.803
1977	2090	596.2	1654.8	0.350
1978	2277	1075.6	2130.8	0.432
1979	2042	1862.9	3964.4	0.785
1980	2429	1172.6	3319.7	0.649
1981	2915	1247.2	4189.3	0.797
1982	2060	706.1	1980.4	0.358
1983	1787	470.2	1641.4	0.249
1984	1965	560.3	1370.4	0.248
1985	1895	570.5	1256.2	0.228
1986	1754	691.7	1390.7	0.242
1987	1517	608.8	1311.9	0.223
1988	1508	894.4	1641.4	0.269
1989	1402	709.8	1202.4	0.190
1990	1177	726.2	1366.9	0.216
1991	1036	1181.6	1610.6	0.265

Source: Australian Bureau of Statistics, *Labour Reports* and *Industrial Disputes Australia* (annual) Cat. No. 6322.0 and (monthly) Cat. No. 6321.0.

Notes

1 For an account of this period see S. Macintyre and R. Mitchell (eds) (1989), *Foundations of Arbitration: The Origins and Effects of State Compulsory Arbitration 1890–1914*, Oxford University Press, Melbourne.
2 H. B. Higgins (1915), 'A new province for law and order—I', *Harvard Law Review*, 29:1, 13–14.
3 H. B. Higgins (1919), 'A new province for law and order—II', *Harvard Law Review*, 32:1, 190–91.
4 The term *parties* as used here is not confined to unions and employers. It also includes governments and other interested groups that become involved in cases before tribunals.

5 This has been referred to as activist arbitration. For further elaboration see B. Dabscheck (1983), *Arbitrator at Work: Sir William Raymond Kelly and the Regulation of Australian Industrial Relations*, Allen & Unwin, Sydney. For a survey of theoretical writings on industrial tribunals see B. Dabscheck (1992), '"A new province for law and order": The Australian experiment with industrial tribunals', paper delivered at Ninth World Congress, International Industrial Relations Association, Sydney, Australia, 31 August–4 September.

6 Over the years there have been four changes in the name of the major federal industrial relations tribunal. From 1904 to 1956 it was called the Commonwealth Court of Conciliation and Arbitration; 1956–73 the Commonwealth Conciliation and Arbitration Commission; 1973–89 the Australian Conciliation and Arbitration Commission; and since 1989 the Australian Industrial Relations Commission.

7 See for example P. Loveday (1984), 'Corporatist trends in Australia', *Politics*, 19:1, 46–51; K. Schott (1985), 'The consensus economy: An international overview', *Economic Papers*, 4:2, 1–22; R. G. Stewart (1985), 'The politics of the Accord: Does corporatism explain it?', *Politics*, 20:1, 26–35; R. Gerritsen (1986), 'The necessity of "corporatism": The case of the Hawke Labor Government', *Politics*, 21:1, 45–54; D. McEachern (1986), 'Corporatism and business responses to the Hawke Government', *Politics*, 21:1, 19–27; J. Pemberton and G. Davis (1986), 'The rhetoric of consensus', *Politics*, 21:1, 55–62; F. Stilwell (1986), *The Accord and Beyond: The Political Economy of the Labour Government*, Pluto Press, Sydney; and G. Singleton (1990), *The Accord and the Australian Labour Movement*, Melbourne University Press, Carlton.

8 See R. C. McCallum, M. J. Pittard and G. F. Smith (1990), *Australian Labour Law: Cases and Materials*, Butterworths, Sydney, for further discussion concerning the role of the Constitution in governing Australian industrial relations and its interpretation by the High Court.

9 For a more detailed examination of these developments see *Australian Journal of Labour Law* (1990), 3:1, which is devoted to 'Joint state/federal arrangements in the settlement of industrial disputes'.

10 Quoted in M. Perlman (1954), *Judges in Industry: A Study of Labour Arbitration in Australia*, Melbourne University Press, Carlton, p. 32.

11 Generally speaking, as already mentioned, other industrial tribunals replicate the national wage case decisions of the commission and increases flow on to workers in their respective jurisdictions.

12 115 *Commonwealth Arbitration Reports* (hereafter CAR) 931 and 134 CAR 195.

13 134 CAR 159, at p. 164.

14 *National Wage* case, 18 September 1975. For a discussion of various meanings attached to 'comparative wage justice' see J. E. Isaac (1986), 'The meaning and significance of comparative wage justice', in J. Niland (ed.), *Wage Fixation in Australia*, Allen & Unwin, Sydney; C. Provis (1986), 'Comparative wage justice', *Journal of Industrial Relations*, 28:1, 24–39; B. Dabscheck (1986), 'Tribunals and wage determination: The problem of coordination' in J. Niland (ed.), op. cit.; and B. Dabscheck (1989), *Australian Industrial Relations in the 1980s*, Oxford University Press, Melbourne, pp. 58–64.

15 Over the years there have been some celebrated clashes among members of the

commission. The most recent example has involved Mr Justice Staples. For details see J. Kitay and P. McCarthy (1989), 'Justice Staples and the politics of Australian industrial arbitration', *Journal of Industrial Relations*, 31:3, 310-33 and M. Kirby (1989), 'The removal of Justice Staples and the silent forces of industrial relations', *Journal of Industrial Relations*, 31:3, 334-71.

16 J. Moore (1983), Submission to Committee of Review into Australian Industrial Relations Law and Systems, December, pp. 12-13 (mimeo).
17 56 ALJR 224.
18 2 CAR 1.
19 The commission had distinguished between the basic wages of men and women; the former being based on a family and the latter an individual. In 1969 and 1972 the commission handed down decisions that incorporated the principle of equal pay for work of equal value. For further details see E. Ryan and A. Conlon (1974), *Gentle Invaders: Australian Women at Work 1788-1974*, Nelson, West Melbourne.
20 See 110 CAR 178 and 115 CAR 93. See B. Dabscheck and J. Niland (1981), *Industrial Relations in Australia*, Allen & Unwin, Sydney, chapter 12 for a history of the commission's approach to wage determination.
21 118 CAR 655.
22 157 CAR 293, at p. 301.
23 For example see comments by Sir Richard Kirby, the commission's president from 1956 to 1973, in the Eighth, Ninth and Tenth *Annual Reports, President of the Commonwealth Conciliation and Arbitration Commission*. Also see Kirby's comments in the 1965 Basic Wages Case, 100 CAR 178, at p. 288.
24 121 CAR 587.
25 122 CAR 169. For accounts of this dispute see J. Hutson (1971), *Six Wage Concepts*, Amalgamated Engineering Union, Sydney, pp. 165-211; and N. F. Dufty (1972), *Industrial Relations in the Australian Metal Industries*, West Publishing Corporation, Sydney, pp. 129-38.
26 *Twelfth Annual Report, President of the Commonwealth Conciliation and Arbitration Commission, Year ended 13 August 1968*, p. 15. For further details concerning his approach to industrial relations regulation see R. Kirby (1965), 'Some comparisons between compulsory arbitration and collective bargaining', *Journal of Industrial Relations*, 7:1, 1-17; R. Kirby (1970), 'Conciliation and arbitration in Australia: Where the emphasis?', *Federal Law Review*, 14: September, 1-29; and R. Kirby (1982), 'Conciliation and arbitration: Can government control it?' in K. Cole (ed.), *Power, Conflict and Control in Australian Trade Unions*, Pelican, Ringwood. Also see B. d'Alpuget (1977), *Mediator: A Biography of Sir Richard Kirby*, Melbourne University Press, Carlton.
27 See 124 CAR 462, at p. 467.
28 102 CAR 138, at p. 140, quoted in 129 CAR 617, at pp. 629-30. Kirby also had a view that individual members of the commission should be free to make their own decisions. He was opposed to the use of conferences, or providing advice to others, concerning their decisions in a particular case. See Kirby (1982), pp. 166 and 171.
29 135 CAR 244, at pp. 247-8.
30 See 143 CAR 290, 149 CAR 75 and 157 CAR 293.

31 For an examination of events and the case (77 CAR 477) that lead to its abolition see B. Dabscheck (1983), pp 135–47.
32 157 CAR 293, at p. 306.
33 Table 6.1 suggests that they were more important!
34 *National Wage* case, 7 April 1981, p. 4.
35 *National Wage* case, 30 April 1975, p. 37.
36 The commission awarded full indexation in seven of its nineteen decisions during this period. In September 1978 it estimated that its partial decisions were equal to approximately 75 per cent of full indexation. *National Wage* case, 14 September 1978, p. 30.
37 *National Wage* case, 7 April 1981, p. 32.
38 For details of their submissions see B. Dabscheck (1989), p. 32.
39 *National Wage* case, 27 June 1979, p. 9.
40 *National Wage* case, 12 December 1977, p. 12. For further discussion of these issues by one member of the commission see J. E. Isaac (1982), 'Economists and industrial relations', *Journal of Industrial Relations*, 24:4, 495–516.
41 For example, see *National Wage* case, 30 April 1975, p. 5.
42 *National Wage* case, 31 March 1977, p. 7.
43 See for example *National Wage* case, 31 March 1977, p. 6; *National Wage* case, 27 June 1979, p. 6; and *National Wage* case, 14 July 1980, p. 14.
44 *National Wage* case, December 1978, p. 6; *National Wage* case, 27 June 1979, pp. 2–9; and *National Wage* case, 9 January 1981, pp. 2–14.
45 *National Wage* case, 14 July 1980, p. 21 and *National Wage* case, 9 January 1981, p. 26.
46 *National Wage* case, 7 April 1981, p. 58.
47 *National Wage* case, 31 July 1981.
48 *Transport Workers Award 1972*, 1 September 1981, especially p. 17.
49 *Metal Industry Award 1971*, 18 December 1981.
50 *National Wage* case, 14 May 1982, pp. 47–8.
51 *National Wage* case, 23 December 1982, p. 10.
52 Statement of Accord by the Australian Labor Party and the Australian Council of Trade Unions Regarding Economic Policy, 1983 (mimeo), p. 5. A copy is reproduced as an appendix in F. Stilwell (1986).
53 For analyses of the summit see D. A. Kemp (1983), 'The national economic summit: Authority, persuasion and exchange', *Economic Record*, 59:166, 209–19; D. McEachern (1985), 'National economic summit: Business and the Hawke Government', *Journal of Australian Political Economy*, No. 19, 5–13; and B. Dabscheck (1989), pp. 51–6.
54 *National Economic Summit Conference Documents and Proceedings*, Vol. 2, *Record of Proceedings*, AGPS, Canberra, 11–14 April 1983, p. 147.
55 *National Wage* case, 23 October 1983, pp. 7–11, 16 and 57.
56 The basic thrust of the ideas contained in this paragraph was confirmed in a conversation with Sir John Moore on 5 November 1987 at the University of New South Wales.
57 *National Wage* case, 26 June 1986, p. 8.
58 Agreement Between the Government and the ACTU for the Discounting of Wages Indexation and Ongoing Wage Restraint, 4 September 1985 (mimeo). A copy is reproduced in an appendix in Stilwell (1986).
59 *National Wage* case, 4 November 1985 and *National Wage* case, 26 June 1986.

The commission's decision concerning superannuation was somewhat confused and contradictory. For a discussion of the decision see Dabscheck (1989), pp. 101–6.
60 *National Wage* case, 26 June 1986, p. 4. The mid 1980s saw the rise of the New Right, who advocated a stance of aggressive anti-unionism and labour market deregulation. See for example J. Hyde and J. Nurick (eds) (1985), *Wages Wasteland: The Australian Wage Fixing System*, Hale & Iremonger and Australian Institute for Public Policy, Sydney; P. P. McGuinness (1985), *The Case Against the Arbitration Commission*, Centre for Independent Studies, Sydney, and H. R. Nicholls Society (1986), *Arbitration in Contempt*, Melbourne. For a critique of their views see Dabscheck (1989), pp. 113–41 and K. Coghill (ed.) (1987), *The New Right's Australian Fantasy*, McPhee Gribble, Fitzroy.
61 *National Wage* case, 23 December 1986.
62 They have also been regarded as variations to the Accord. The two-tiered system introduced by the commission in the 10 March 1987 *National Wage* case has been called the Accord Mark III. For details of the Accord Mark IV and Mark V see P. J. Keating (1988), *Economic Statement May 1988*, AGPS, Canberra, 25 May, and P. J. Keating (1989), *Economic Statement April 1989*, AGPS, Canberra, 12 April. The Accord Mark VI is entitled 'Agreement Between the Federal Government and the ACTU', 21 February 1990 (mimeo). A copy is reproduced in Department of Industrial Relations (1991), *National Wage Case, December 1990–February 1991*, Vol. 2, *Exhibits presented by the Commonwealth Government*, AGPS, Canberra, pp. 27–32.
63 *National Wage* case, 7 August 1989, p. 10.
64 *National Wage* case, 10 March 1987, p. 13.
65 *National Wage* case, 2 May 1989, p. 4.
66 'Agreement Between the Federal Government and the ACTU', 21 February 1990 (mimeo), p. 2.
67 See affidavit by A. C. Evans, Chief Executive, Metal Trades Industry Association, 17 December 1990 (mimeo).
68 *National Wage* case, 16 April 1991, p. 22.
69 Evidence provided by R. Callus, A. Morehead, M. Cully and J. Buchanan (1991), *Industrial Relations at Work: The Australian Workplace Industrial Relations Survey*, Commonwealth Department of Industrial Relations, AGPS, Canberra, pp. 87–9 and 107–9, indicates that there are high degrees of inexperience among union delegates and specialist industrial relations managers at the workplace level.
70 For a discussion of different meanings attached to enterprise bargaining see B. Dabscheck (1990), 'Enterprise bargaining: A new province for law and order', *Australian Quarterly*, 62:3, 240–55.
71 *National Wage* case, 16 April 1991, pp. 38–40 and 63.
72 For reactions see the daily newspapers immediately after the decision; Report of the Committee (1991), *Australian Industrial Relations Commission Review* (Gleeson Report), AGPS, Canberra, March; and *Third Annual Report of the President of the Australian Industrial Relations Commission*, AGPS, Canberra, 1 July 1990 to 30 June 1991.
73 *National Wage* case, 30 October 1991, p. 3.
74 P. J. Keating (1992), *One Nation*, AGPS, Canberra, 26 February, pp. 44–54.

168 *State, Economy and Public Policy in Australia*

75 *Industrial Relations Legislation Amendment Act 1992*, No. 109 of 1992.
76 *Fourth Annual Report of the President of the Australian Industrial Relations Commission*, AGPS, Canberra, 1 July 1991 to 30 June 1992, p. 4.
77 See *Fightback! The Liberal National Parties' Plan to Rebuild and Reward Australia* (3 volumes), 21 November 1991; *Jobsback! The Federal Coalition's Industrial Relations Policy*, October 1992; and *Fightback! Fairness and Jobs*, December 1992. For a critique of the coalition's industrial relations policies see B. Dabscheck (1993), 'The coalition's plans to regulate industrial relations', *Economic and Labour Relations Review* 4:1, 1−26.
78 Accord Agreement, *Putting Jobs First* (mimeo), February 1993.
79 G. B. Kitay (1984), 'Federal conciliation and arbitration in Australia 1967−81', PhD thesis, Australian National University, p. 452. Also see J. Kitay and P. McCarthy (1989).

7

The political economy of federalism since 1970

Peter Groenewegen

As the former communist federations of the Soviet Union, Yugoslavia and Czechoslovakia are falling more or less violently apart in the strain of adjustment to political and economic freedom, Australian federalism is preparing for its hundredth birthday on 1 January 2001. The bicentenary celebrations in 1988 were surrounded by soul-searching as well as ecstasy, and there are already signs that the same will apply to the centenary of federation. Perhaps in imitation of the very gradual federalist movement of the 1890s,[1] major premiers conferences in 1991 were to celebrate the start made in 1891 by the first federal convention. Neither Hawke as Prime Minister nor his premier colleagues, however, could have foretold in October 1990 the temporary setback to federal rejuvenation that occurred in November 1991 when the centrepiece of the new spirit of cooperative federalism—the Premiers Conference designed to tackle fiscal federalism issues—was abruptly cancelled in response to a leaked federal Cabinet decision on the government's stance on tax sharing. In perhaps too close an imitation of the 1890s the premiers instead decided to go it alone without the noxious influence of Canberra centralism as revealed once again through its firm non-sharing decision on income tax.[2] Whether this temporary failure in 1991 will result, as in the previous century, in an ultimate Premiers' Conference that heralds a new federal era for the twenty-first century, time alone will tell. What is certain, however, is that the federal problems to be solved in the 1990s are as complex as those that bedevilled the founding fathers of the Constitution in the 1890s, although in many respects the problems are quite different. At the same time, on some issues, such as free trade and improving interstate mobility and cooperation, the problems are still very much the same.

Explanations of these problems facing the reconstructors of Australian federalism in the 1990s, and suggestions for some potential solutions, form the subject matter of this chapter. Its discussion concentrates on the political economy of federalism because the economic aspects of these problems invariably involved political responses and decisions.

The order of the argument is as follows. After a statistical overview of Australian fiscal federalism, the successive 'new federalism' schemes, which have inspired Prime Ministers Whitlam (1972–75), Fraser (1975–83) and Hawke (1983–91), and evidently also Keating (1991–), will be summarised and appraised. The chapter then briefly canvasses the major Australian fiscal federalism issues. In order of appearance, they can be described as the problems of vertical fiscal imbalance; choosing alternatives for revenue sharing between Commonwealth, states and local government; conditional grants for specific purposes and their potential waste in duplication of services; fiscal equalisation and the relative merits of the Grants Commission's role therein; the role of the Loan Council as a national public investment planning agency; policy coordination for national microeconomic reforms, especially with respect to public enterprises in transport and energy supply but also embracing environmental and other aspects of resource development policy. In conclusion some desirable outcomes for the 1990s are briefly sketched.

A statistical overview of Australian fiscal federalism 1972–93

Tables 7.1 and 7.2 present a statistical overview of the fiscal transfers from the Commonwealth to the states and local government (including borrowing under the Loan Council) for selected years in the two decades from 1971–72. The first year represents the last fiscal year of the pre-Whitlam period, the second (1975–76) the last fiscal year influenced by Whitlam Government policies, the third year (1979–80) one from the period of the Fraser Government in the heyday of its new federalism. The years from 1983–84 reflect the fiscal federalism experience of the Hawke and Keating Governments. The totals in nominal prices need to be interpreted in the light of the vastly different inflation experiences of these decades (see chapter 8); commencing as they do with the low inflation decade ending in 1971–72, followed by the galloping inflation of the Whitlam period, the slower but still substantial inflation from the

Table 7.1 Funds available to state and local government sectors from Commonwealth payments to and borrowings by states and territories, selected years[1] 1971–72 to 1992–93

	1971–72 $m	1975–76 $m	1979–80 $m	1983–84 $m	1987–88 $m	1988–89 $m	1989–90 $m	1990–91 $m	1991–92 $m	1992–93 $m (est.)
Commonwealth payments										
Recurrent purposes										
General revenue funds	1537	3112	5657	10362	14248	12973	13278	13601	13704	14189
Specific-purpose payments	249	2316[2]	3435	4634	6397	8660	9547	10948	12042	12776
Total for recurrent purposes	1786	5428	9092	14996	20646	21633	22825	24550	25746	26965
Capital purposes										
General-purpose capital funds	892	1291	1352	1598	621	704	372	330	372	513
Specific-purpose payments	459	1836	1392	2577	2829	2750	3150	3571	3658	4399
Total (net) capital payments	678	2929	2466	3795	3081	3123	3117	2133	900	2146
Total (net) Commonwealth payments	2464	8463[3]	11558	18791	23727	24756	25942	26683	26824	29541
Borrowing[4]	673	810	2195	6617	5522	4700	3893	4146	6388	4692
Specific-purpose payments as a % of total net Commonwealth payments	28.7	49.1	41.8	39.7	38.9	46.1	48.9	54.4	57.2	58.1
Total Commonwealth payments and borrowing by states and territories	3137	9273	13754	25408	29249	29456	29835	30829	31521	36129

[1] Includes Northern Territory from 1977–78 and ACT from 1989–90.
[2] Includes Medibank prepayment of $215.6 m.
[3] Total includes direct payment to local government.
[4] From 1982–83 includes all state and territory borrowing.

Source: Payments to or for the States and Local Government Authorities 1974–75, 1975–76, Budget Paper No. 7, Canberra, 1975, 1976; Payments to or for the States, the Northern Territory and Local Government Authorities (various issues from 1978–79); Commonwealth Financial Relations with other levels of government, Budget Paper No. 4 (various issues from 1987–88).

Table 7.2 Commonwealth payments to state and local government sectors by function (net basis), selected years 1971–72 to 1992–93

	1971–72 $m	1975–76 $m	1979–80 $m	1983–84 $m	1987–88 $m	1988–89 $m	1989–90 $m	1990–91 $m	1991–92 $m	1992–93 $m (est.)
Defence	7	34	2	6	4	1	2	2	2	−1
Education	205	1406	2100	3366	4436	4530	4867	5388	5868	6452
Health[1]	18	1083	1241	435	1295	3317	3671	3973	4249	4493
Social security and welfare	43	238[2]	71	116	355	389	470	468	521	727
Housing	9	363	258	689	1066	984	927	788	934	1193
Urban and regional development (n.e.i.) and environment[3]	—	263	43	63	—	—	—	—	—	—
Culture and recreation	—	12	6	16	39	13	9	17	25	45
Economic services										
Transport and communication	263	495	616	1241	1282	1300	1377	1628	1297	1888
Water supply and electricity[4]	3	46	29	77	—	—	—	—	—	—
Industry assistance and development	83	110	72	84	190	195	158	156	301	185
Labour and employment	2	6	9	408	154	38	36	25	33	95
Total economic services	350	657	725	1811	1626	1534	1571	1810	1631	2168
General public services	4	8	13	35	82	97	170	257	336	394
Total allocated to function	637	4064	4459	6537	8897	10864	11684	12700	13613	15470
Outlays not allocated to function										
General-revenue funds	1537	3112	5426	9890	14248	12973	13278	13601	13800	14189
State Government Loan Council Program	892	1139	1050	1009	−130	76	58	1246	2142	2050
Assistance related to state debts	65	47	53	61	52	51	50	54	258	161

Table 7.2 continued

	1971–72 $m	1975–76 $m	1979–80 $m	1983–84 $m	1987–88 $m	1988–89 $m	1989–90 $m	1990–91 $m	1991–92 $m	1992–93 $m (est.)
Payments to Northern Territory[5]	—	—	339	648	—	—	—	—	—	—
Payments to local government[6]	—	80	222	459	642	664	689	711	1046	1079
Natural disaster relief	7	25	10	122	−15	30	—	139	65	44
Total not allocated to function[7]	2501	4403	7100	12253	14830	13984	14258	13983	13352	14071
Grand total (net basis)	3137	8467	11558	18791	23727	24848	25942	26683	26965	29541

Source: Payments to or for the States and Local Government Authorities 1975–76, 1977–78; Payments to or for the States, the Northern Territory and Local Government Authorities (various issues from 1978–79); Commonwealth Financial Relations with other levels of government (various issues from 1987–88).

Notes: Totals might not add due to omission of certain items.

[1] Excludes identified health grant from 1982–83.
[2] Comparison affected by inclusion of unemployment relief grant in 1975–76.
[3] Absorbed into other categories from 1987–88.
[4] Estimated from 1987–88 and absorbed in other economic services (not shown in this table).
[5] Absorbed in totals from 1987–88.
[6] From 1987–88 includes 'Other', not allocated to function.
[7] Grants Commission Grant for 1975–76, income tax share until 1986–87, then general purpose assistance.

mid 1970s to the end of the 1980s and the once again quite low inflation of the early 1990s.

The first thing to notice in table 7.1 is the slow relative growth in general revenue funds from the mid 1980s, occasionally even marking negative growth as the Federal Government enforced fiscal restraint on the states by cutting its revenue assistance. Slow growth in general revenue funds for the states while maintaining their funds for specific purposes explains much of the rapid relative rise in the latter from 1988–89. However, the sharp relative rise of such grants in 1975–76 and their subsequent vicissitudes can only be explained by explicit policy choices by Federal Governments. The sharp decline in capital funding for nearly the whole of this period can also be noted. It partly reflects significant changes in the operation of the Loan Council mentioned later in this chapter, but the underlying explanatory factor is the fiscal restraint Treasury had diagnosed as the appropriate response to the current economic situation. Not surprisingly given these trends, growth in total funding to the states and territories slowed down sharply in the five fiscal years until 1991–92 when the trend was reversed to boost public spending during the recession (table 7.1). Stabilisation policy objectives, together with an ideological obsession with reducing the already small Australian public sector, provide the major reasons for the tightening of federal financial assistance in these years.

Table 7.2 reflects the varying priorities in specific-purpose payments since the early 1970s. Overall growth under Whitlam, and subsequent decline under Fraser, reflect the stance of their respective new federalism policies (see next section). The relative shifts under Hawke owe more to the greater flexibility in cutting general revenue assistance for fiscal policy reasons than to a firm ideological, centralist commitment to uniformity in service delivery. Variations in individual functions could reflect drastic policy changes or the necessity of maintaining real service levels in times of fluctuating inflation rates. Education spending by the Federal Government, for example, shows the funding requirements of the Whitlam takeover of tertiary education responsibilities in 1974 as well as the costs of growth in tertiary education places initiated by Dawkins from 1988. Fluctuations in spending on the health function shows the rise and fall of Whitlam's Medibank, the transfer of much specific health payment to an identified health block grant under Fraser and the steady growth in cost of the Medicare scheme from 1984. The fate of urban and regional development as a specific payments category illustrates the enthusiasm with which the Whitlam Government introduced such funding and the indifference, if not hostility, of subsequent governments to this objective. Elimination of water and electricity supply as an identifiable function within the economic services category reflects a similar story. On the other hand, federal funding of social security and welfare, transport (especially roads) and communications reflects steady real growth for what are considered essential functions. The relative merits of specific purpose payments, and of the alternative policy approaches to them which have been adopted, are discussed later in this chapter.

Both tables show the high degree of flexibility in Australia's fiscal federalism arrangements over this relatively short period. Relative shares of conditional grants for specific purposes can alter fairly rapidly as can the functions to which such funds are allocated. Overall financial assistance from the Commonwealth to the states and territories can be changed just as quicky from the considerable largesse of the Whitlam and Fraser years to tight-fistedness and restraint under Hawke and Keating. And even tight-fistedness can be reversed for stabilisation purposes, as shown in the 1992–93 estimates. Irrespective of its various shortcomings, flexibility is a desirable characteristic of the system. From the perspective of recipient governments its drawback is the considerable uncertainty it creates in their forward financial planning.

Three new federalism policies: Whitlam, Fraser and Hawke

The three Australian prime ministers who held office from 1972 to 1991 attempted to stamp their own policy views on Australian federalism arrangements. None of these attempts can be said to have been successful or enduring, although all contain elements which sooner or later might revitalise segments of Australia's federal structure.[3] Given the difficulties of changing Australia's Constituion, most of these new federalism policies have attempted to work within that Constitution, either through cooperative endeavours with the states or through taking advantage of generous interpretations of the federal powers by the High Court. What are the essentials of these efforts at change?

Whitlam saw his new federalism as an exercise in coordination from the centre by independent commissions rather than centralism per se. His commissions for education and health, urban renewal and transport, social security and the arts would establish objective spending priorities to be funded by the Commonwealth for the benefit of the 'men and women of Australia', such funding to be administered by the states, often through newly created regions and local authorities. The 'existing States with their irrelevant State boundaries and malapportioned electoral boundaries' had therefore only a limited role to play in this grand vision.

> *A meaningful decentralisation of power will be effected in this country only when we provide* local *authorities with the means and incentives to associate freely on the basis of shared urban and*

> regional interests. *The new federalism will rest on a national framework for the establishment of investment priorities and a regional framework for a participation in all those decisions which most directly determine the quality of our lives.*[4]

The few parts of this program that were implemented, largely through the rapid increase in specific purpose grants already noted, were almost as quickly dismantled by Whitlam's successors in government, whose vision of federalism was often little more than a direct states' rights reaction to this centralist vision of effective decentralisation.[5] Interestingly, the vision lives on in the hearts and minds of contemporary politicians who see real change in federalism associated with a decline in the power of the states and the construction of a genuine regionalism as a vehicle for effective decentralisation.[6]

Fraser's new federalism was designed to restore to the states the independence they had lost through Labor's centralism. As a starting point, it sought to increase state revenue independence (by lowering their reliance on grants and the vertical fiscal imbalance discussed in the next section) in two stages. The first of these was to introduce a system of designated revenue-sharing by assigning a specified proportion of federal revenue collections to the states. Initially confined to personal income tax, later generalised to include all tax revenues, these revenue-sharing arrangements also promised consultation with the states on federal policy that affected state tax entitlements, a promise rarely implemented. Aggregate state share in tax revenue was distributed to individual states on traditional Commonwealth Grants Commission principles of fiscal capacity equalisation (discussed subsequently) applied to *all* states. The second stage of revenue-raising independence for the states involved enabling legislation for the states to raise surcharges from, or grant rebates to, personal income tax liabilities of their residents. No state took advantage of this revenue-raising opportunity during the dozen years of its existence.[7] Fraser's new federalism also promised curtailment of federal use of specific purpose payments (table 7.1 shows its limited success in this regard), thereby increasing state freedom in expenditure decision-making from transferred revenue. In addition, it set up an Advisory Council for Intergovernmental Relations in Hobart as a government-financed think tank on federalism issues, to be initiated by its governing body, comprising federal, state and local government politicians. Although the Fraser Government explicitly abandoned specific attempts to raise the constitutional stature of regional and local government (in fact it purposefully eliminated all of Whitlam's regional initiatives), it nevertheless institutionalised the federal funding for local government begun under Whitlam. It did so, however, on the basis of different principles, more sensitive to state feelings on this contentious subject.[8] During the second half of Fraser's period in office, the need for fiscal restraint, together with increasingly frequent conflicts between the national and state interests on environmental and other issues, wrecked the conservative attempt at new federalism as well.[9]

The Hawke Government had been in office for seven years before revealing its new federalism dreams in a speech delivered by the Prime Minister at the National Press Club on 19 July 1990. The speech promised to open Australia's federalism arrangements to scrutiny, evaluation and reform within the existing constitutional framework. Such a cooperative review (designed to involve state premiers and representatives from local government from the start) was intended 'to improve our national efficiency and international competitiveness, and to improve the delivery and quality of services governments provide'. This process of change was to be achieved through a series of premiers' conferences in 1991 after an initial conference in October 1990 to set the agenda. However, to start the reform ball rolling the Prime Minister identified the following items as essential components of the review agenda:

- *microeconomic reform (i.e. deregulation and structural change) in the management and pricing policies of essential public sector business enterprises, and greater consistency or uniformity in state regulations which impact on interstate and international trade in goods and services;*
- *reductions in the duplication of effort in, and a rationalisation of, the provision of services—particularly in health and welfare initially, but ultimately in all services—and avoidance of the emergence of overlap and duplication of responsibilities as new challanges emerge;*
- *greater cooperation and coordination between governments in the pursuit of the Commonwealth's national social justice strategy; increased cooperation and coordination in industrial relations systems, with the possibility of transferring ultimate responsibility to the Commonwealth;*
- *the replacement of controversy and conflict with common ground and common purpose (and, where possible, agreed processes and guidelines) in relation to environmental issues; and*
- *a review of at least some aspects of Commonwealth–State financial arrangements (especially the role of tied grants) and of arrangements for the annual Premiers' Conferences at which financial issues, among other things, are regularly discussed and determined.*[10]

The October 1990 Premiers' Conference largely endorsed this prime ministerial agenda for federal reform. Initial premiers' conferences, assisted by ministerial and departmental officers' working parties, reported good progress during much of 1991, especially in the area of microeconomic reform in the regulatory, transport and energy resource areas (discussed subsequently). However, the review of financial arrangements scheduled for November 1991, especially that concerned with the potential for reducing state revenue dependence on the Commonwealth (the degree of vertical fiscal imbalance), was abandoned in acrimonious disagreement over the compatibility of reduced central tax powers with the effective exercise of national economic policy. This obstacle to cooperative federalism was made all the more difficult by the public involvement on the anti-state side of the debate of the former Treasurer, Paul Keating, then backbench contender for the ALP's federal parliamentary leadership. Labor opposition to a potentially reduced role for tied grants was also growing. Fears were expressed by the Caucus about the fate of Aboriginal and welfare programs in such an eventuality, while federal Education Minister Dawkins clouded the horizon precisely at this delicate state of the negotiations by proposing a federal takeover of TAFE.[11] Before examining such current federalism events in more detail, essential aspects of the background to these events can now be systematically investigated starting with the vexed and controversial concept of vertical fiscal imbalance.

Vertical fiscal imbalance

Vertical fiscal imbalance can be simply defined as an imbalance between revenue-raising powers and expenditure responsibilities for various levels of government. In the Australian federation, vertical fiscal imbalance arises because the Federal Government has revenue resources in excess of its expenditure requirements, while at the state and local government levels independent revenue sources fall short of those required to finance expenditure commitments. The premiers defined the situation statistically by noting that:

> *Currently the Commonwealth collects about 80 per cent of all taxation revenue but requires only 50 per cent to fund its own current outlays ... The States, on the other hand, collect around 20 per cent of all taxation revenue but account for more than 40 per cent of public sector own purpose outlays.*[12]

Table 7.3 looks at vertical fiscal imbalance in terms of the sufficiency of own revenue by level government for 1989–90 and the grants imbalance necessary to ensure that all levels of government can meet their expenditure responsibilities.

Vertical fiscal imbalance is deemed to have a number of unfavourable outcomes, which the premiers summarised as follows in November 1991 in their plea for more favourable tax treatment from the Commonwealth:

(a) Promotes duplication and overlap of expenditure responsibilities between Commonwealth and State governments.
(b) Reduces the accountability of both Commonwealth and State governments to the electorate by breaking the nexus between expenditure and revenue raising.
(c) Encourages the growth of inefficient and distorting State taxes.[13]

Theoretically, these detrimental efficiency consequences can be ascribed to the conflict between such revenue disparities and the conventional economics approach to efficient public sector resource allocation. This suggests that benefits from public service delivery should be equalised with the costs of necessary taxation at the margin. A revenue gap of the size disclosed by Australian federalism sits uneasily with such an efficiency perspective, even though the experts[14] fully admit that there is no convincing empirical evidence of detrimental efficiency consequences. In fact, a number of European federations live with such imbalances without demonstrable inefficiencies in their public sectors.

Vertical fiscal imbalance has a number of obvious solutions. One is to transfer expenditure powers from the levels of government with revenue deficiencies; the other is to transfer tax powers from the government level with excess tax power. More subtly, revenue transfers, including the possibility of institutionalised revenue-sharing (discussed in the next section), can be used to eliminate this imbalance. The last is the more realistic possibility, since there are substantial objections to the

Table 7.3 Sources of revenue for each level of goverment, 1989−90 (%)

	Commonwealth	State	Local
Own-source revenue			
Taxes, fees and fines	91	33	53
Net operating surplus[1]	3	9	8
Other	7	16	18
Total own-source revenue	100	58	78
Payments from higher levels of government			
• from Commonwealth[2]	na	42	15
• from state	na	na	7
Total revenue	100	100	100

[1] Net operating surplus (NOS) is included as revenue in the ABS Government Financial Estimates. NOS is calculated as operating revenue (including subsidies received from the general government sector) less operating expenditure.
[2] In 1989−90 Commonwealth payments to local government comprised general revenue assistance (8.9% of local government revenue), direct payments to local government (1.4% of local government revenue) and specific purpose payments to the states that were passed on to local government (4.6% of local government revenue).
Source: Commonwealth of Australia (1991), *Commonwealth Relations with other Levels of Government 1991−92*, Budget Paper No. 4, Canberra, AGPS, p. 15.

first two solutions arising from the theory of efficient function (including tax power) assignment in a federal system. Conventional fiscal federalism theory as developed by Musgrave[15] assigns distributional and stabilisation policy functions to the national government, while the allocative function of public goods provision is assigned to the appropriate level of government according to scale factors, organisational and administrative cost factors, local (including national) preferences and, perhaps most importantly, the geographical diffusion of benefits. Apart from services like defence, trade and international relations where benefits are unequivocally national, this theory supports substantial decentralisation of services on efficiency grounds. In fact, it suggests wider variety in government units than that provided for by states and the typical local government unit in the Australian federation.[16] With taxation, however, assignment rules are skewed in favour of the Federal Government. Progressive personal income tax for distributional reasons, corporate income tax and broad-based consumption taxes tend to be assigned to central government; there is less agreement on proper assignment of resource-based taxes, while the immobile tax base of local government rates and land tax make such taxes ideally decentralised.[17] Thus it could be argued that the high degree of centralisation in the Australian tax structure is defensible on normal rules of tax assignment, while the greater decentralisation in service delivery can be said to approximate expenditure assignment rules. So vertical fiscal imbalance Australian-style can be defended on normative fiscal federalism theory principles.[18]

In addition, the Australian Constitution imposes formidable constraints on solving vertical fiscal imbalance on the tax side. The exclusive excise power it gives to the Commonwealth, combined with its wide interpretation by the High Court, makes a viable solution on the consumption tax side virtually impossible. Only repeal of the exclusive excise power opens such opportunities. Corporate taxation, for a wide variety of practical reasons, needs to stay with the central government. On stabilisation and distributional grounds (both national functions on conventional assignment rules) progressive comprehensive income and general (wealth) taxes need to be federally assigned. In practice this leaves little scope for new state or local taxes.

Alternative revenue-sharing possibilities

There are various ways of conducting revenue-sharing between levels of government. For most of the life of the Australian federation, when revenue-sharing proved necessary, it has been done by providing general revenue assistance to the states, negotiated with the Commonwealth on the basis of various principles. Starting points for such assistance in 1942 were determined by past tax collections of the states; in 1959 and 1985 the base Financial Assistance Grant was determined for individual states by the previous year's grant. Provision for nominal growth in such grants has varied from a minimal assurance of its real value maintenance (adjusted by some agreed inflation factor) or by more elaborate formulae based on population growth, wage growth and sometimes even by including a 'betterment factor' to enable improved quality of service delivery. These two alternatives formed the bases for determining the current financial assistance grants and the earlier system of administering such grants in force from 1959 to 1976.[19]

At other times, Australia has relied on institutionalised revenue-sharing by assigning a specified proportion of the revenue from a particular tax or group of taxes to other levels of government. During Australia's federal history several types of such revenue-sharing have been used. For the first ten years of federation, the Braddon clause (section 87) of the Constitution guaranteed the states at least three-quarters of the customs and excise revenue they had exclusively assigned to the Commonwealth on federation. Revenue was to be distributed according to source and, for its duration, this revenue sharing was constitutionally guaranteed. Although to assist road finance, excise revenue was shared with the states between 1930–31 and 1958–59, the next major initiative in tax revenue-sharing had to await the introduction of Fraser's new federalism in 1976. In its first two years, this assigned 33.6 per cent of current personal income tax collections to the states; from 1978–79 to 1980–81 it assigned 39.87 per cent of previous year collections to the states; and from 1982–83 until its abolition by the Hawke Government in 1985–86 it assigned 20.72 per cent of total tax revenue to the states. However, these shares were never constitutionally guaranteed, unlike the temporary revenue-sharing of the Braddon clause, and the points of understanding negotiated when the new system was introduced were never fully adhered to by the Federal Government. When the system was abandoned in May 1985, therefore, it was with the full consent of the states. A similar system of personal income tax sharing with local government was likewise abandoned in 1985.[20]

To generate genuine revenue independence for State Governments, tax shares from revenue-sharing need to be constitutionally guaranteed while institutional arrangements need to be developed by which states can contribute to framing underlying tax policy. Within a quite different institutional framework, this is the fiscal federalism system in the Federal Republic of Germany. Shares of its major revenue-raisers, income tax and value-added tax, are assigned to levels of government in fixed proportion by its constitution. The German upper house (Bundesrat), genuinely composed of state representatives, can decide on all legislative matters (including fiscal items) that affect state interests.[21] Although Australia cannot simply imitate such institutional arrangements, their impact can be approximated by introducing appropriate institutional changes *within* Australia's existing constitutional and political framework. For example, constitutionally guaranteed proportions in which the major taxes currently levied by the Commonwealth would be shared could be introduced by simple amendment of the concurrent tax power (section 51 (ii) of the Constitution). Such an amendment is likely to prove acceptable to the Australian electorate. German state powers reflected in the Bundesrat can in principle be approximated by alterations to the current premiers' conference arrangements, as appears to be the fundation for current thinking by the premiers on their Council of the Australian Federation proposal.[22]

A revamped system of revenue-sharing in this way would eliminate the real problems associated with the present vertical fiscal imbalance while maintaining the benefits of a centralised, uniform tax system. It also has potential, depending on the degree of local and/or regional involvement in the Council of the Federation, for improved decentralised service delivery. In this way, some of the more innovative features of Whitlam's and Fraser's new federalism could merge to build a better federal system for the twenty-first century.

One further revenue-sharing possibility needs to be mentioned in the context of Australian federalism reform. This is the opportunity to give states access to personal income tax revenue by enabling them to impose a proportional surcharge at the margin. These piggy-back arrangements, envisaged in stage 2 of Fraser's new federalism, have surfaced and resurfaced at frequent intervals in the federalism policy debate. A modified version of this proposal was implied in the premiers' document of November 1991 with its hints at potential freedom for the states to vary their initial '6 per cent' fixed proportion of income tax (in fact more like 20 per cent of collections on 1991–92 estimates).[23] A similar proposal was floated by the Leader of the Opposition in February 1991 and the *Fightback* document the Opposition prepared before the March 1993 federal election. *Fightback* proposed a curtailment of specific purpose payments, a reduction in federal financial assistance to the states for general revenue purposes and a re-examination of the fiscal equalisation procedures on which the federation had been operating for such a long part of its history. Most interesting of its proposals was the abolition of payroll tax (a state tax) to be replaced by a fixed share in the revenue from the goods and services tax the opposition was also advocating.[24]

Tied grants for specific purposes

Specific purpose payments have been a feature of the Australian federation since the 1920s when they were first used to assist state road construction. During the 1950s their importance increased with Federal Government funding initiatives for tertiary and then secondary education. The extensive range of functions they have covered from the

1970s are disclosed in outline in table 7.2. Although specific purpose payments have never been very popular with the states, and reducing their relative importance has been among the terms of reference in discussions of fiscal federalism reform, especially since the 1980s, such grants have an important role in a federal system as a means of removing problems that would otherwise arise. In short, there is a strong theoretical case for including such grants in a federal system for three reasons.

The first reason is that where benefits from a good generally supplied at the subnational level cannot be fully localised, cost-sharing arrangements through specific purpose grants are appropriate to eliminate the temptation for the original provider to undersupply the good in question. By internalising such externalities through cost-sharing, the provision of specific purpose grants secures a more efficient public goods supply for the nation as a whole. Public health and tertiary education are examples to which this type of argument applies. Second, new initiatives in public goods provision can be centrally fostered by specific purpose grants, particularly in cases of publicly provided merit wants the value of which is underappreciated for social or cultural reasons in some, or all, subnational jurisdictions. A substantial number of current specific purpose payments in the Aboriginal, welfare and special education areas fall within this category. Third, the grantor government might attempt to influence the spending patterns of other jurisdictions because constitutional or other rigidities make it impossible for it to do so in other ways. The urban and regional programs of the Whitlam Government, some cultural and recreational programs or, for that matter, the Hawke Government's 1991 Better Cities program, fall into this category. Section 96 of the Constitution gives the Commonwealth Government an unlimited power to make conditional grants to the states and other levels of government.[25]

The unpopularity of such grants with the states and territories rests on the following factors. Through specific purpose payments they fear that the Commonwealth is increasingly involving itself in functions constitutionally assigned to the states. Health and education, which together accounted for almost two-thirds of specific purpose grants in 1990–91, are prime examples. Some conditions, especially that of a matching requirement where the recipient has to fund the specific purpose in question in a specified proportion, might reduce freedom of state and territory decision-making over expenditure from own revenue. Where such matching grants are important, state and territory priorities in public spending are said to be seriously distorted in the process. Finally, it is argued that the system is wasteful because it causes overlap and duplication in administering the programs for which costs are shared. Considerations of this nature have led to frequent state demands for the abolition of specific purpose payments, preferably by absorbing them into funds for general revenue assistance. This, as shown previously, was a substantial aim of Fraser's new federalism.

A number of observations can be made on these complaints. In contrast to United States practice, matching conditions are less frequently used in Australian specific purpose payments. A survey conducted by the Auditor-General's Office found that of forty-five specific purpose payments, only nineteen required contributions by the state or territory government concerned, but in the absence of size this relatively high percentage frequency of matching conditions (42.2 per cent) is rather meaningless.[26] Furthermore, most specific purpose payments in practice have such easy conditions that their overall effect is to free state revenue for other purposes thereby enhancing freedom in expenditure decision-making at the state level. This was often found to be the case in Jay's examination of such grants in the 1970s; his result seems not to be contradicted by the Auditor-General's 1990 survey already mentioned.[27] The cost savings of administrative duplication are often emphasised when eliminating specific purpose payments is contemplated, but in practice such savings tend to be insignificant. The Finance Department estimated total Commonwealth administrative costs of specific purpose payments at $30 million, with only a fraction of this sum potentially saved if the requisite Commonwealth functions were completely transferred to the states.[28] The cry of eliminating waste from duplication of services is part of federalism reform rhetoric from the right in Australian politics and rarely, if ever, based on hard empirical evidence.

Specific purpose payments have a well-recognised role in making essential fiscal adjustments in a federal system. What evidence there is suggests that they have not induced expensive duplication and waste in their administration and only infrequently do they result in distorting state priorities in spending. What is essential for the purpose of securing continuing accountability and responsible decision-making is that their effectiveness is continuously monitored by the relevant government auditing agencies.

Fiscal equalisation: What role for the Grants Commission?

From its establishment in 1933 the Commonwealth Grants Commission has attempted to remove fiscal disabilities from partners in Australia's federation to secure them a 'fair go'[29] through fiscal capacity equalisation. Some see the suitable methodology for fiscal equalisation developed by the Grants Commission over the years as one of the major Australian contributions to applied economics during this century; others describe it as an unwarranted cause of further distortions in the economy and one further example of government-induced resource allocation inefficiency. Nevertheless, fiscal equalisation is a principle of Australian fiscal federalism akin to that of motherhood and, given the extensive power of the smaller states to prevent constitutional or other change to Australia's federalism arrangements, it is a principle not likely to disappear in a hurry.

The general formulation of the principle of fiscal equalisation can be quoted from one of the commission's more recent reports:

> ... *each State is entitled to receive a level of general revenue funding from the Commonwealth which would enable it to provide, without having to impose taxes and charges at levels appreciably higher than the levels imposed by the other States, government services at standards that are not appreciably different from the standards provided by the other States.*[30]

This principle enables the commission to recommend a distribution of federal funding to equalise the fiscal capacity of the states in terms of an Australia-wide standard, based on the averaging of actual state budgetary policies in such a way that each state is free to determine its own policy.

For much of the first half century of its existence, the commission did this by recommending special grants to assist fiscally disadvantaged states: Tasmania, Western Australia, South Australia and, briefly during the 1970s, Queensland. From 1981 onwards it has recommended the per capita relativities appropriate for determining the distribution to individual states of general revenue assistance provided by the Commonwealth. Initially such recommendations were based on three-yearly reviews of state finances by the commission; from 1988 they were replaced by five-yearly reviews combined with annual updates in the light of changing circumstances. Reviews have recently been the commission's major task, although it has also been occasionally involved in assessing funding requirements for the territories, for local government and for Australian dependencies such as the Cocos (Keeling) Islands. The remainder of this section ignores these more minor aspects of the commission's work and is confined to explaining the essentials and drawbacks perceived in the way the commission estimates per capita relativities as the basis for distributing general revenue assistance to individual states.

These relativities are estimated on the basis of commission calculations of the revenue-raising and cost disabilities experienced by particular states relative to the national standard and adjusting the aggregate disability for the degree of equalisation implied in the per capita differentials with which grants for specific purposes are paid to the states. Revenue-raising disabilities are calculated for all taxes levied by states, arising from differentials in tax bases such as land values, motor vehicles in use, gambling turnover and so on, as well as those from other revenue resources like operating surpluses or losses from public business enterprises. Cost disparities are estimated in terms of scale, dispersion, isolation, urbanisation and units of use. Aggregate disabilities, adjusted for the specific purpose payment equalisation component, are then used as weights to alter the outcome for individual states from that achieved by an unadjusted per capita division of general revenue assistance. The relativities determine the distribution of the overall financial assistance grants pool, taking into account population estimates, the aggregate Commonwealth revenue assistance and a number of other factors adjusting entitlements agreed to over the years.

Using Victoria, the state with least aggregate fiscal disability, as the base of 1.000, the weights applied to the other five states and the Northern Territory in distributing general revenue assistance in 1991–92 were as follows: New South Wales, 1.015; Queensland 1.335; Western Australia, 1.408; South Australia, 1.526; Tasmania, 1.731 and the Northern Territory, 5.673. However, the commission's five-year review of relativities, released in April 1993 as a basis for adjustments to Commonwealth grants in 1993–94, involved some redistribution towards New South Wales (and to a lesser extent Victoria) and away from the smaller-population states.[31] The actual relativities to be implemented will be subject, as usual, to intergovernmental bargaining at the financial Premiers' Conference.

The commission's attempts to equalise fiscal capacity, often described as the most comprehensive and explicit in the world, have increasingly been criticised, particularly on efficiency grounds. Federal Treasury, for example, has queried the concern with equity in current Grants Commission procedures, preferring an equal, rather than weighted, per capita distribution of federal general revenue assistance to the states. This suggested change is partly based on simplicity (elimination of the Grants Commission would save its administrative costs)[32] and on efficiency grounds. Cost equalisation in particular distorts government expenditure decisions both within and between states, while it can also be said to distort private locational choices. The net welfare loss of such distortions has been alternatively estimated at around twenty per cent of the aggregate cost equalisation transfers or at $600 million in present value terms.[33] Not surprisingly, the Grants Commission has defended its procedures. Its emphasis on equity is justified in terms of governments' continuing high priority to social justice and equity in spite of growing awareness of efficiency issues; given the high dislocation costs to states like Tasmania, Western Australia and South Australia if the present system was abandoned, the estimated welfare losses from its distortions are small. It seems unlikely in any case that fiscal equalisation principles of Australian federalism will be abandoned altogether, although their continuing modification and refinement seems certain.[34]

The Loan Council and public investment

Another unique feature of Australian federalism is the Australian Loan Council, which was designed as a means for coordinating public investment and borrowing. It was formed voluntarily by the states and the Federal Government in the early 1920s, and initial success ensured that it was given constitutional recognition by an amendment passed in 1927. The state premiers, the prime minister and federal treasurer remain the members of the council to this day; attempts at gaining local government representation have failed. The operation of the Loan Council has seen many modifications since its foundation, particularly in the wake of deregulation of the financial system from the late 1970s. Its former controls over interest rates on public loans, for example, are gone. Separate controls over overseas borrowing and aggregate domestic loan-raising by semi-government and local authorities have been merged into a global approach to regulating aggregate public authority borrowing from 1984. Setting the global limit to public authority borrowing is now the Loan Council's major function. These results are shown in table 7.1.[35]

To use this valuable institution better it has been suggested that the Loan Council should examine infrastructure investment proposals on a national basis, thereby coordinating the setting of priorities in this crucial area for effective restructuring of the Australian economy. Given the concerns expressed about potential shortfalls in essential parts of Australia's infrastructure stock, including replacement of some of its parts inherited from the previous century, and providing complementary public works to the private sector, the assignment of a national investment planning role to the Loan Council could considerably enhance the efficiency by which Australia's scarce capital resources are allocated. At the same time, it would combine oversight of the uses of sources of finance for public works with control over them, thereby at last making effective one of the original aims of the organisation which, for one reason or another, was never actually implemented.[36]

Policy coordination for national microeconomic reform[37]

Much of Hawke's new federalism proposal stemmed from a desire by federal bureaucrats to harness state officials to the task of much-needed microeconomic reform. State cooperation is essential to any major reform of the road freight industry on lines advocated by the Industry Commission, to national rationalisation of rail freight operations and rail passenger traffic outside urban centres, and to the coordination of electricity generating and distribution on the eastern seaboard to prevent a repetition of the massive excess generating capacity constructed in the early 1980s. In addition, this process would clear the way for streamlining regulations in consumer protection covering food, other manufactured goods and credit; removing remaining vestiges of interstate trade barriers; and setting national standards for environmental protection, the recognition of trade and professional qualifications and performance criteria for state business enterprises. Harmonisation can likewise be usefully extended to the criminal code, defamation law and gun controls, similar to attempts in previous decades at greater uniformity in corporate control. Much useful work had been done in previous decades on such projects by dedicated working parties of ministers and officials. They removed many of the more ludicrous aspects of state sovereignty through harmonising legal provisions and regulations. Hawke's initiative in July 1990 was designed to accelerate this process and to steer it in the direction of the market-orientated microeconomic reform measures which his government, and like-minded governments in states such as New South Wales, were already pursuing.

The July 1991 Premiers' Conference subsequent to the Hawke new federalism proposals moved purposefully on several of these issues. It agreed to establish a National Rail Corporation designed as a single company responsible for interstate rail freight. Its initial 'shareholders', the Commonwealth, New South Wales, Victoria and Western Australia, will contribute the starting equity of $400 million, with South Australia willing to participate and Queensland supportive with a small contribution to equity. The corporate nature of the new federal authority is in line with the corporatisation principles by which the Federal Government and the states are organising their own business enterprises. This includes a commitment to full cost recovery from users, designed to eliminate the current rail freight deficits aggregating $375 million a year. This experiment with a supranational form of corporation is an interesting one, since there are few precedents. Meetings of the Council of Australian Governments and the Transport Ministerial Council in 1992 facilitated the provision of considerable Commonwealth funding to enable the National Rail Corporation to upgrade its infrastructure.

Full cost recovery is also a major factor in the agreement of a national pricing policy to force owners of trucks to pay for the damage trucks cause to roads. Control will be exercised by a new National Road Transport Commission. It will move towards full road cost recovery charges through tax on diesel fuel and registration fees based on weight of the vehicle and distance travelled. In order to reduce the burden on remote areas, more reliant on trucking services and hence more affected by a rise in road freight costs, Australia has been divided into two registration zones, with lower trucking charges applying to the lower-cost zone of Western Australia, South Australia and Queensland. In addition, the new commission will eliminate state differences in regulations affecting the road haulage industry. Full agreement between all the parties was not achieved on this issue at the July 1991 Premiers'

Conference (the Chief Minister of the Northern Territory, the government area most dependent on road transport, was a lone dissenter to these reforms). During 1992 further progress was made but full cost recovery was not recommended, a strong indication of the strength of the trucking industry and its importance to the economies of states with less populated remote areas.

The third major microeconomic reform agreed to at the July 1991 conference established a National Grid Management Council, to advise on coordinating generating capacity and eventually to link all the eastern states including Tasmania. This will save costs by reducing the need to install additional capacity by pooling generating resources.

These examples of microeconomic reform illustrate the value of cooperative federalism and show that much can be achieved without resorting to the often frustratingly difficult device of constitutional change. Such managerial achievements, of which there are many examples, together with initiatives like the Council of the Australian Federation (proposed by the premiers in November 1991 and agreed by Prime Minister Keating in May 1992 under the title Council of Australian Governments) can play a constructive role in streamlining the arrangements of federalism in future.

Is there a federalism agenda for the 1990s?

The previous sections of this chapter have highlighted both the stability and the change in Australian federalism since the 1970s. The chapter has also illustrated the lack of success in designing new federalism schemes on a unilateral basis, particularly if they are to be imposed from the top of the federal pyramid in Canberra. In fact, the thrust of the chapter provides support for the evolutionary hypothesis that true institutionalist students of federalism prefer: federal arrangements develop and grow, inspired by ideas from the bottom and the top, from politicians, officials and the public at large, and by responding in the best possible way to external circumstances as they arise within the constraints of a difficult-to-change Constitution and not always rational High Court. It is difficult, therefore, to predict a future course for Australian federalism, even during the 1990s, with any degree of certainty. This uncertainty is heightened by Keating's replacement of Hawke in December 1991 and subsequent re-election in March 1993. How far his federalism reforms will continue those of Hawke is difficult to say.

However, the outcomes of the December 1992 Council of Australian Governments meeting suggests that intergovernmental consultations on topics of national interest will continue to increase as an ongoing sign of healthy cooperative federalism. Such consultation will be particularly useful for settling politically sensitive issues associated with the environment (forests and greenhouse emissions), Aboriginal affairs, water resources, transport and energy policy and, with an eye to the centenary of federation in 2001, transforming Australia's monarchical form of government into a republic. The December 1992 meeting also showed, as was to be expected from his record as Treasurer, that Keating would strongly support Hawke's push to secure faster microeconomic reforms in transport and energy policy through intergovernmental cooperation. Drastic alterations in fiscal federalism, through new forms of revenue-sharing, are less likely under Keating as Prime Minister, particularly now that his replacement by a Liberal or Coalition prime minister has been postponed to 1996 at the earliest. For reasons explained in this chapter, such proposals are likely to continue to surface from within the bureaucracy, especially the Treasury and Finance Department.

The last remark indicates that there are still quite a few desirable aims to be pursued to improve existing arrangements. Federalism research now increasingly accepts that federations can benefit from a highly centralised tax system combined with decentralised service delivery, provided that adequate steps have been taken to ensure revenue independence for other levels of government. Constitutionally guaranteed revenue-sharing of major taxes, combined with initiatives like the Council of Australian Governments, are capable of achieving this objective. Together with more effective decentralisation possibilities through innovative arrangements involving local and regional government reforms, this creates real potential for lasting improvements in Australian federalism. A by-product of this manner of solving revenue imbalance is the ability to confine specific purpose payments to their proper role of securing essential fiscal adjustments in a federal system.

The probability that new federal institutions such as the Council of Australian Governments will work is strong. This prediction finds support in other elements stressed in the chapter. The Grants Commission, the Loan Council and the Premiers' Conference itself are all institutions of Australian federalism that have stood the test of time, adapting to changing circumstances and weathering the occasional storms which have sought to destory them. In addition, given the strength of Australian federalism in its flexibility, and the steady growth and development of intergovernmental cooperation, a new federal institution might well succeed in ending regular financial wrangling without undesirable tax transfers. However, as experience from the federal movement of the 1890s suggests, it might take many years of patient, and occasionally turbulent, negotiations, with setbacks and recoveries, before such a goal is reached.

Notes

1 For a useful discussion of the 1890s background to federation see R. L. Mathews and W. R. C. Jay (1972), *Federal Finance*, Nelson, Melbourne,

chapter 2, and for a detailed bibliographical outline see L. F. Crisp (1979), *The Later Australian Federation Movement 1883–1901*, Sopal Printery, Canberra.
2 For a long-term statistical overview of Australian federalism see P. Groenewegen (1983), 'The political economy of federalism 1901–81', in B. Head (ed.), *State and Economy in Australia*, Oxford University Press, Melbourne, pp. 169–75, and Mathews and Jay (1972).
3 For useful surveys of the new federalisms of Fraser and Whitlam, see P. Groenewegen (1979), 'Federalism' in *From Whitlam to Fraser*, A. Patience and B. Head (eds), Oxford University Press, Melbourne, esp. pp. 55–67; P. Groenewegen (1989), 'Federalism', in B. Head and A. Patience (eds), *From Fraser to Hawke*, Longman Cheshire, Melbourne, esp. pp. 257–69.
4 E. G. Whitlam (1977), 'The future of Australian Federalism' in *On Australia's Constitution*, Widescope, Melbourne, pp. 147–61; the quotations come from p. 161.
5 For a survey of Whitlam's regional initiatives failures see P. Groenewegen (1990), *Public Finance in Australia, Theory and Practice*, 3rd ed., Prentice Hall, Sydney, pp. 274–6 and references.
6 Examples are the former Premier of New South Wales, Neville Wran (reported, *Sydney Morning Herald*, 11 October 1991), John Howard (reported, *Sydney Morning Herald*, 4 November 1991) and earlier, before he entered federal parliament, Bob Hawke (1979), *The Resolution of Conflict, 1979 Boyer Lectures*, ABC, Sydney, especially lectures 1 and 2.
7 The policy would therefore maintain commitment to the uniform income taxation Australia had enjoyed since 1942. It also provided for equalisation procedures to compensate below-average-income states for the lower yield of a percentage income tax change relative to high-income states.
8 These local government finance arrangements are discussed in detail in National Inquiry into Local Government Finance (1985), *Report*, AGPS, Canberra, esp. chapters 3–5.
9 For a discussion see P. Groenewegen (1983), 'The fiscal crisis of Australian federalism' in A. Patience and J. Scott (eds), *Australian Federalism: Future Tense*, Oxford University Press, Melbourne, ch. 9 and Groenewegen (1989).
10 R. J. Hawke, 'Towards a closer partnership', speech at the National Press Club, Canberra, 19 July 1990. The speech marked Hawke's abandonment of his earlier Whitlamesque vision of federalism expressed in the 1979 Boyer Lectures.
11 Keating's condemnation of proposals for increasing state tax powers was widely reported on 23 October 1991; by the middle of November the premiers had abandoned the November Premiers' Conference (substituting a meeting without the Commonwealth) in response to federal Cabinet rejection of tax-sharing on Monday, 5 November. The takeover of TAFE was proposed on 15 October, while fears about services for Aborigines, the elderly, the disabled and the homeless were reported on 11 and 18 November 1991.
12 Proposals for the Special Premiers' Conference in Perth (mimeograph), November 1991, clause 20.
13 Ibid., clause 21. This position is part of a populist federalism ideology, uncritically accepted by business and the media. See, for example, BCA (1991), 'Paying for the new federalism', in *Business Council Bulletin*, 81,

pp. 7–8, and M. Steketee (1991), 'Keating wrecks chances of a saner federalism', *Sydney Morning Herald*, 16 November.
14 See W. Oates (1991), 'A survey of recent theoretical and empirical research', paper for OECD seminar, Fiscal Federalism in Economies in Transition, Paris, 2–3 April. Professor Oates in discussion confirmed that there was no convincing empirical evidence for the detrimental efficiency consequences of vertical fiscal imbalance. An Australian test case would best use historical comparative analysis of the 1920s and 1930s with the 1960s and 1970s to show unequivocally the high allocative efficiency of public expenditure decisions in the first as compared with the second period, but no one as yet has taken up this challenge.
15 See R. A. and P. B. Musgrave (1989), *Public Finance in Theory and Practice*, 5th edition, McGraw Hill, New York, chapter 27.
16 See P. Groenewegen (1990), pp. 236–9.
17 See C. E. McLure (ed.) (1983), *Tax Assignment in Federal Countries*, Canberra, Centre for Research on Federal Financial Relations and International Seminar in Public Economics, especially introduction, pp. xiii–xv; for a detailed evaluation of the costs and benefits of tax decentralisation, see P. Groenewegen (1990), 'Taxation and decentralisation' in R. J. Bennet (ed.), *Decentralisation, Local Government and Markets*, Clarendon Press, Oxford, ch. 6.
18 See P. Groenewegen (1991), 'Decentralising tax revenues: Recent initiatives in Australian federalism', University of Sydney, Department of Economics Working Papers, No. 159, April, esp. pp. 6–9.
19 For a more detailed overview see P. Groenewegen (1983), 'Tax assignment and revenue sharing in Australia' in C. E. McLure (ed.), p. 304. The whole of this article is a useful supplement to much of this section.
20 See P. Groenewegen (1983), pp. 304–6, P. Groenewegen (1979) and P. Groenewegen (1989).
21 See P. B. Spahn (1991), 'Financing federal and state governments: The experience of Germany', OECD seminar, *Fiscal Federalism in Economies in Transition*, Paris, OECD, 2–3 April; and J. Fiedler (1991), 'The experience of Germany', ibid.
22 See 'Proposal for the special Premiers' Conference in Perth' (mimeograph), November 1991, paragraphs 15–19; this resembles an earlier proposal by the author for a national tax council. See P. Groenewegen (1977), 'A proposal for an Australian tax council', in R. L. Mathews (ed.), *State and Local Taxes*, Centre for Research on Federal Financial Relations, Canberra, esp. pp. 370–80, and P. Groenewegen (1981), 'Apportioning tax powers in a federation', in R. L. Mathews (ed.), *State Taxation in Theory and Practice*, Centre for Research on Federal Financial Relations, Canberra, esp. pp. 19–24.
23 'Proposals for a special Premiers' Conference in Perth' (mimeograph), November 1991, paragraphs 24–8.
24 J. R. Hewson (1991), 'Commonwealth–state relations', 6th Norman Cowper Oration, Sydney, 15 February, reprinted in *Australian Quarterly*, 63:1, 4–14; *Fightback*, 21 November 1991; and for an evaluation of the federalism proposals it contained, R. Albon and J. Petchy (1983), 'Federal aspects of Fightback' in J. Head (ed.), *Fightback: An Economic Assessment*, Australian

Tax Research Foundation, Sydney, Conference Series No. 12, pp. 551–65.
25 See P. Groenewegen (1990), pp. 243, 260–63.
26 Commonwealth Auditor-General, Audit Report No. 18, 1990–91, *Specific Purpose Payments to and through the States and Northern Territory*, AGPS, Canberra, p. 58, question 2.12.
27 See W. R. C. Jay (1975), 'The shift to specific purpose grants', in R. L. Mathews (ed.), *Responsibility Sharing in a Federal System*, Centre for Research on Federal Financial Relations, Canberra, Research Monograph No. 8, pp. 42–9.
28 See the Auditor-General, Audit Report No. 18, pp. 31–2; EPAC Discussion Paper (1990), *Towards a More Cooperative Federalism*, EPAC, Canberra; and see also Commonwealth Grants Commission (1990), *Report on Issues in Fiscal Equalisation*, Vol. 1, *Main Report*, AGPS, Canberra, chapter 9, esp. pp. 92–5.
29 See E. Gramlich (1984), 'A fair go: Fiscal federalism arrangements', in R. E. Caves and L. B. Krause (eds), *The Australian Economy: A View from the North*, Allen & Unwin, Sydney, chapter 6; Commonwealth Grants Commission (1983), *Equality and Diversity: Fifty Years of the Commonwealth Grants Commission*, AGPS, Canberra; and R. L. Mathews (1986), 'Fiscal federalism in Australia: Past and future tense', Centre for Research on Federal Financial Relations, Canberra, Reprint Series No. 74.
30 Commonwealth Grants Commission (1990), *Report on Issues in Fiscal Equalisation*, Vol. 1, p. 3.
31 Ibid., chapter 3; Commonwealth Grants Commission (1993), *Report on General Revenue Grant Relativities 1993*, AGPS, Canberra; *Commonwealth Financial Relations with Other Levels of Government 1991–92*, Budget Paper No. 4, AGPS, Canberra, pp. 54–60 and esp. table 17. A simplified discussion of the principles is in P. Groenewegen (1990), pp. 253–60.
32 Treasury submissions as cited in Commonwealth Grants Commission (1990), *Report on Issues in Fiscal Equalisation*, Vol. 1, p. 11, Vol. 2, p. 217.
33 R. Williams (1990), 'Quantifying the effects of cost equalisation in a federal system', University of Melbourne, Department of Economics, Research Paper 255, esp. pp. 12–13; Commonwealth Grants Commission (1990), *Report on Issues in Fiscal Equalisation*, Vol. 2, pp. 284–5.
34 Commonwealth Grants Commission (1990), *Report on Issues in Fiscal Equalisation*, Vol. 1, pp. 26–7, 46–51; Commonwealth Grants Commission (1993).
35 For a brief account see P. Groenewegen (1990), pp. 292–3, as well as P. Groenewegen (1979) and (1989) for more detail.
36 See House of Representatives Standing Committee on Transport, Communications and Infrastructure (1987), *Constructing and Reconstructing Australia's Public Infrastructure*, AGPS, Canberra; EPAC (1988), *Economic Infrastructure in Australia*, EPAC Council Paper No. 33, Canberra.
37 This section relies heavily on press reports of the Premiers' Conference as well as official communiqués from the conferences in 1990, 1991 and 1992.

8

Employers' associations, corporatism and the Accord: The politics of industrial relations

Trevor Matthews[1]

Two momentous changes occurred in Australia's system of industrial relations under the Hawke and Keating Labor Governments. First, a historic 1983 agreement between the Australian Council of Trade Unions and the Australian Labor Party enabled the newly elected Labor Government to introduce a corporatist-style incomes policy. Guaranteeing trade union wage restraint, this agreement (commonly known as 'the Accord') became the centrepiece of the Labor Government's economic strategy. Second, Australia moved decisively away from a centralised wages system grounded in compulsory arbitration towards a more decentralised one centred on the needs of the enterprise. The Accord process facilitated that shift in the focus of industrial relations from the industry or occupational level to the enterprise or workplace level.

When viewed from an international perspective, however, these momentous changes in Australian industrial relations are unusual, indeed paradoxical. For one thing, Australia embraced its form of corporatist policy-making at the very time that the European countries with corporatist policy-making systems—notably Sweden, Austria and the Netherlands—were retreating from corporatism.[2] For another, the Accord was a distinctive form of corporatism in that it did not 'incorporate' business. For yet another, the Accord gave the Australian trade union movement unprecedented political influence at the very time that the initiative in industrial relations in other countries was shifting to the employers.[3]

In exploring these puzzles, this chapter gives particular attention to the way organisational and party political factors shaped these industrial relations changes.[4] It concedes that the changes were a response to severe economic problems—stagflation in the case of the 1983 Accord and falling international competitiveness in the case of enterprise bargaining—but argues that the form of the changes and their pace were shaped less by economics than by politics. The chapter gives special emphasis to one explanation that has been advanced to account for Australia's corporatist experiment: that it was the result of Australia's peak economic interest groups becoming 'encompassing organisatons' and so acquiring the organisational capacity that enabled them to pursue collective gain strategies. The chapter argues that while that explanation is plausible, it (1) fails to account for or notice the organisational asymmetry of organised labour and organised business in Australia, and (2) fails to account for two striking features of the Accord: its partisan character and the fact that, as a corporatist arrangement, the Accord did not 'incorporate' business.

The chapter is divided into four sections. The first section examines the 'encompassing organisaton thesis' and addresses the question of why business and employer representation is so fragmented in comparison with the organisation of the trade union movement. The second describes the present structures of employer representation. The third considers the Accord as corporatism without business. The fourth section argues that the shift towards enterprise bargaining exemplifies a resurgence of employer initiative in Australian industrial relations. The conclusion argues the importance of party government in shaping the form, if not the direction, of industrial relations change in Australia.

Australian employers and the problem of collective action

In an effort to explain the marked variation in economic performance among industrialised market economies since the end of the 'long boom', many analysts have argued that interest groups hold the key. Two contrasting viewpoints can be distinguished. The first explains poor economic performance and 'ungovernability' by laying the blame at the door of sectional interest groups. According to this argument, the attempt by sectional groups to secure policies that will protect and benefit their members has led to 'government overload' and 'pluralistic stagnation'. The second, in contrast, argues that the concerted participation of organised labour and business in corporatist (or more accurately neo-corporatist)[5] policy-making arrangements has contributed to the better economic performances of countries with such arrangements.

Political scientist Samuel Beer and economist Mancur Olson typify the first viewpoint. According to Beer, Britain in the 1970s suffered from 'pluralistic stagnation' because its interest groups were too aggressive, too self-serving and too numerous.[6] With governments offering 'subsidies for all' in an effort to win the cooperation of economic interest groups, and with the political parties competitively bidding for votes by offering welfare benefits to a widening circle of groups, the logic of British politics allowed pluralistic process to triumph over public purpose. Olson has similarly ascribed the economic ills of countries such as Britain, the United States and Australia to the self-defeating pursuit of distributional gains by narrowly based special-interest groups.[7] So long as groups are small in relation to society as a whole, Olson argues, it will be economically rational for them to lobby for policies that will ensure that their own group gets a bigger slice of society's pie and not for policies that will increase the size of that 'pie'. Labelling these groups 'distributional coalitions', Olson posits that the smaller and more numerous interest groups are, the more negative their effect on economic growth and the efficient allocation of resources will be.[8] Australia's historical pattern of group–government dynamics, he claims, fits his theory 'like a glove'.[9] Australia's unimpressive economic growth and its failure in the 1960s and 1970s to export more than a small fraction of its manufactures stemmed, he asserts, directly from the high levels of tariff protection that manufacturers and their workers enjoyed in the decades since Federation.[10]

Other analysts, in contrast, have argued that it is the very existence of centralised, comprehensive and hierarchically organised economic interest groups, together with their participation in policy-making, that explains why a number of the smaller corporatist states in Western Europe have been able to return better economic performances than a number of more 'liberal' market economies.[11] Some also argue that cooperation between organised labour, organised business and the state has enabled these states to avoid destructive distributional conflict and to pursue effective and consensual economic restructuring.[12] They also argue that these countries have been less prone to ungovernability and to an overload of group demands than countries that lack corporatist forms of 'interest intermediation'.[13]

Olson's notion of 'encompassing organisations' resolves the apparent contradiction between these two judgements about the impact of interest groups on a country's economic and political performance. *Encompassing organisations* are interest groups whose size and comprehensive coverage make it economically rational for them to consider the effect their demands have on society as a whole. They possess the outlook and authority to engage in collaborative positive-sum bargaining with the state and with other similarly centralised and broadly based peak interest groups. Olson notes a high degree of overlap between the corporatist countries of Western Europe—such as Austria, Sweden and Norway—and countries with encompassing interest organisations.[14] He also notes 'that none of the English-speaking countries has anything approximating neo-corporatist arrangements and none of them has any encompassing interest groups either'.[15] And, he adds, none of them have performed well economically.

Australia in the 1980s would appear to disprove Olson's sweeping generalisation that the English-speaking market economies lack encompassing organisations and neo-corporatist policy-making arrangements. That decade saw a transformation in the organisation and objectives of Australia's economic interest groups. The Australian Council of Trade Unions and the National Farmers' Federation gained an organisational monopoly in their sectors. Both acted as encompassing organisations by espousing collective-gain solutions to Australia's economic problems. So too did the newly formed Business Council of Australia, which consisted of the chief executive officers of the largest corporations operating in Australia.

The decade also saw the emergence of a corporatist-style of policy-making under the Hawke Government. To many observers, the Hawke Labor Government's pursuit of 'consensus politics', its early enthusiasm for summoning labour, business and governmental leaders to national summit conferences, its decision to create a number of tripartite consultative and planning bodies and, above all, its 1983 prices and incomes Accord with the ACTU were all evidence of a historic shift towards corporatist policy-making.[16]

Some analysts have drawn on Olson's concept of encompassing organisations to explain the radical reorientation of economic policy that took place during the years of the Hawke Government. Prominent in that policy reorientation were the decisions to deregulate the financial market, to float the Australian dollar, to dismantle Australia's historically high tariff barriers, to implement an incomes policy based on the government's Accord with the ACTU and to endorse a shift to enterprise or workplace-centred industrial relations. These analysts argue that the newfound organisational capacity of peak interest groups to pursue a collective gain strategy, to engage in policy trade-offs and to sell the outcomes to their members made possible the 'bargained consensus' on which the new policies were based.[17]

While plausible, the application of the 'encompassing organisation thesis' to explain the reorientation of economic policy under the Hawke Government overlooks the distinctive organisational asymmetry of Australia's economic interest groups.[18] Australian business was far less organisationally integrated than was the trade union movement and the farm sector, each of which had been able to weld together a single encompassing organisation to advance and protect its sector's interests. No single association enjoyed a dominant and unchallenged position as the voice of business or as the voice of employers. No clearly established division of labour pertained between the various national business groups. Nor does any arrangement ensure that the scores of regional industry and employers' groups are integrated vertically and horizontally into a cohesive national system. Why does Australian business lack a single association able to speak on its behalf?

Fragmentation and the lack of organisational unity have always been the hallmarks of business and employer representation in Australia.[19] Until the late 1970s three federally structured national associations spoke for business: they were the Australian Council of Employers' Federations, the Associated Chambers of Manufactures of Australia and the Associated Chambers of Commerce of Australia. In addition, and often competing with them, were a variety of sectoral associations, such as the Metal Trades Industry Association, the Australian Mining Industry Council and the Australian Bankers' Association. The rivalry between many of these national associations is seen most clearly in the field of industrial relations, where all attempts to create a single confederation of Australian employers to serve as a counterbalance to the ACTU have foundered.

That Australian business lacks a single encompassing organisation coherently integrating the plethora of sectoral and regional business associations is not unusual. After all, organisational overlap and rivalry, together with weak vertical integration among groups, are characteristic features of business representation in all the industrialised English-speaking democracies — the United States, Canada, New Zealand and, to a lesser degree, the United Kingdom.

Some writers have advanced a number of theoretical reasons why business can be expected to have a lesser need for organised collective action than labour. First, as two Marxist scholars, Offe and Wiesenthal, claim, there is an inherent class asymmetry in the organising capacities of business and labour.[20] Because business, as firms and corporations, is already organised at the economic level, it has a lesser need than labour or farmers for organised collective action. Rather than relying on business associations, individual firms can choose to use their own market power and their existing organisational resources when dealing with their workers, trade unions or the government. In addition, Offe and Wiesenthal suggest, business can act collectively in a non-associational manner by coordinating its stand on policy issues through informal contacts. This idea has been developed by sociologist Michael Useem who argues that the collective interests of business are effectively articulated and coordinated by the 'inner circle' of the capitalist class — the interlocking directors of the country's largest companies.[21] Supplementing these arguments about a class bias in producer group representation is the view that business does not need to rely on national general-purpose associations for its interests to be attended to by the state. The very importance of business profitability in a capitalist economy means that its interests are privileged: governments, whether radical or conservative, must necessarily attend to the long-term needs of business.[22]

A quite different set of arguments to account for the fragmentation of business representation are advanced by writers who adhere to 'pressure group pluralism' in political science, to theories of the product cycle and to Marxist ideas of 'class fractions'. According to these writers, conflicts of interest within business, not least market competition between firms, are formidable obstacles to business unity. Among these conflicts are those based on size (small firms being pitted against large corporations), on nationality of company ownership (domestic versus transnational corporations), on industrial sector (especially finance versus manufacturing), on market orientation (whether production is mainly for domestic or export markets) and on stages in the product cycle (whether an industry faces declining or expanding markets). The 'diverse and competitive' character of Australia's business sector is the reason given by a former executive director of the Business Council of Australia why it would be unwise for Australia's major business associations to attempt to 'agglomerate' in order to speak with 'a single common voice'. Such a voice, he suggested, could be better achieved through inter-associational policy coordination.[23]

Despite these various arguments, the fact remains that business in a number of industrialised market economies is comprehensively organised into a cohesive and integrated set of business interest groups.[24] Arguments based on the class logic of collective action or the necessarily centrifugal effects of business competitiveness are in themselves unable to explain national variations in effective business mobilisation. Other factors need to be brought into the analysis, in particular the institutional and historical context in which business operates. Given that business associations are intermediaries between firms on the one hand and the state and the trade union movement on the other,[25] collective action by business must be seen as a response to two separate but interrelated imperatives: the need not only to attract and retain the support of members but also to respond to and to exercise adequate influence over governments and trade unions. Particularly significant in shaping Australia's fragmented structure of nation-wide business organisation have been the federal system of government, the distinctive policy instruments for determining wages and allocating tariffs, and the character of the labour movement.

Federal system of government

The division of economic powers between the Commonwealth Government and the states has resulted in a system of business interest groups shaped by federalism. The vast majority of business groups in Australia are state-based; and most nationally organised groups possess a federal (or more accurately a confederal) structure. Federalism has promoted a proliferation of state-based business groups; it has also created problems of cohesion and integration for federally structured national groups.

The unity of these groups has on occasion been seriously fractured because of two types of internal conflict. The first is conflict over the distribution of powers between the national organisation and the branches. The larger and wealthier branches were often reluctant to cede any of their powers and prerogatives to the national level. The second is conflict between the branches over whether the national organisation should support proposals to increase the Commonwealth Government's industrial relations powers. Branches took different stands on that issue depending on whether their members benefited from or suffered under the industrial relations policies of the State Governments.[26]

Policy instruments

Australia's distinctive policy instruments for determining wages and allocating tariff protection have also helped to fragment organised business. In the case of industrial arbitration, the legalism of the system and the complexity of its industrial awards offered competing umbrella groups in the states the opportunity to use selective incentives in their struggle for organisational survival and growth. Employers' federations and chambers of manufactures sought to tap this market in the years 1910–20 by appointing industrial officers to provide members with information about industrial awards and to represent them before the tribunals. Thus was entrenched a rivalry between these two associations that has continued to this day.

The creation of the Tariff Board in 1921 similarly prompted the chambers of manufactures in Victoria and New South Wales to appoint staff to advise member firms on the intricacies of the tariff and to help them present submissions to the board. Tariff services were an important impetus in the organisational growth of these two chambers, and for that reason they were never willing to surrender that function to their national organisation, the Associated Chambers of Manufactures.

The arbitration and tariff systems underpinned the organisational competition between the employers' federations and the chambers of manufactures in yet another way. As a means of augmenting their membership, they vied with each other to enrol the plethora of small and poorly funded employers' and industry associations that were spawned by the occupation- and craft-based system of industrial awards and the 'made to measure' system of tariff protection. In return for the affiliation of an employers' group or a trade association, the peak groups offered to undertake their secretarial work. This competition between the employers' federations and the chambers of manufactures resulted in complex networks of affiliations among business groups that vary markedly from one state to another. It is largely responsible for the lack today of any clear and consistent pattern of vertical and horizontal integration among the labyrinthine confusion of Australia's state-based employers' and industry associations.

Labour movement

In accounting for the absence of encompassing business associations in Canada and the United States, observers have stressed the weakness of organised labour.[27] How relevant is trade union organisation in explaining the fragmentation and competition among peak business groups in Australia? Plowman rejects the applicability of the 'countervailing power thesis' as an explanation for employer organisation in Australia.[28] He argues that employers in Australia have never mobilised to check and balance the industrial powers of trade unions. The reason, he suggests, lies in the Australian system of industrial relations. Compulsory arbitration has lessened the significance of sheer union muscle in industrial relations: it has enabled a weak union to bring employers before the tribunal through the simple expedient of serving a log of claims on employers. Consequently, it has been far more important for employers' organisations to be effective in advocacy before the tribunal than to be able to take on the unions in direct industrial confrontation.

This is true. But to argue that countervailing power and organisational parallelism have not been major forces in the development of Australian business representation is to take too narrow a view of the question. By only considering the employers' response to the *industrial* power of trade unions, Plowman disregards the employers' response to the *political* power and influence of the labour movement.

In a number of countries, business has mobilised in reaction to what it sees as a direct threat to its hegemony by social democratic and labour parties. In other countries (again Canada and the United States are the prominent examples) the absence of social democracy has removed the incentive for business to create 'strong' peak associations. In Australia, reaction to the Labor Party has prompted business mobilisation on four distinct occasions when Labor governments (or Labor Party influence) was seen as particularly threatening to business interests. The first occurred during the first decade of Federation when the presence in the national parliament of three parties enabled Labor to trade its parliamentary support for legislative concessions. It was to counter this early and unexpected legislative influence of the Labor Party—not simply to 'counter the activities of the state'[29]—that led employers both to organise and to campaign prominently in electoral politics under the 'antisocialist' banner. The second took place when Labor first held office in its own right (1910–13). The third occurred in reaction to the centralist policies of the Curtin and Chifley Governments (1942–49), particularly the Chifley Government's attempt to nationalise the banks. The Whitlam Government's three years in office (1972-75) witnessed the fourth period of business mobilisation. The inability of business to influence the Whitlam Government or to match the effectiveness of the ACTU was a major spur to the merger negotiations that eventuated in the formation in 1977 of the Confederation of Australian Industry.

Why, though, has the Labor challenge never been sufficient to induce business to create an effective encompassing organisation? One reason is that Labor governments in Australia have been relatively infrequent. Periods of heightened concern have been followed by lengthy periods of non-Labor rule. Following the Chifley Government's defeat in 1949, the two decades of conservative Liberal–Country Party government removed the need for business to be strongly and cohesively organised. A second reason is that not all Labor governments have challenged business. The big business orientation of the Hawke Labor Government meant that in the 1980s organisational unity appeared to lose its urgency. A third reason is the absence of a corporatist tradition in Australian politics. Unlike social democratic governments in Scandinavia, Austria and West Germany, Australian Labor governments have historically not relied on tripartite corporatist arrangements for making and implementing economic policy. As a consequence, Australian business has not been faced with the imperative, as has business in those Western European countries, to organise cohesively and comprehensively in order to bargain effectively with its corporatist 'partners'—the state and organised labour.

Nevertheless, given the Hawke Government's allegedly corporatist style of decision-making, why was business not 'incorporated' into the Accord process? As one might infer from Hawke's criticism of employers for having failed to 'match the trade union movement in reorganising themselves into a more effective force for change',[30] was it because business was simply too fragmented to engage in corporatist bargaining with the ACTU and the government? Before those questions can be answered, it is necessary to describe the structures of business representation during the Hawke and Keating Governments.

The structures of business representation

When the Hawke Government came to office in 1983, three peak national groups spoke on behalf of Australian business. They were the Confederation of Australian Industry, the Australian Chamber of Commerce and the National Farmers' Federation. A decade later, the field is occupied by seven more or less national business groups. The 'big seven' include the Australian Chamber of Commerce and Industry, the Business Council of Australia, the Australian Chamber of Manufactures, the Metal Trades Industry Association, the Australian Mining Industry Council and the National Farmers' Federation. No single association enjoys a dominant and unchallenged position as the voice of business. No clearly established division of labour pertains between the national business groups. Nor does any arrangement ensure that the scores of national, regional and industry groups are integrated horizontally and vertically into a cohesive national system. Indeed the overwhelming majority of Australia's seven hundred or so national trade and industry associations are not affiliated with any of the 'big seven'.

The Confederation of Australian Industry, formed in 1977 with the merger of the Australian Council of Employers' Federations and the Associated Chambers of Manufactures of Australia, was intended to be an encompassing organisation along the lines of the Confederation of British Industry. By 1979 the CAI had enrolled more than forty national employers' and industry associations representing a wide cross-section of the economy. Alongside its 'founding members'—the employers' federations and chambers of manufactures—were affiliated groups as diverse as the Australian Bankers' Association, the Metal Trades Industry Association, the Australian Woolgrowers and Graziers' Council and the Australian Council of Local Government Associations.

The CAI encountered organisational problems from the very start. First, it was never fully representative. Absent from its membership were not only most of the country's large public sector employers but also a number of important industry groups such as the Australian Mining Industry Council, the Australian Finance Council, the Federal Chamber of Automotive Industries and the Australian Chamber of Commerce.

Second, unlike the Confederation of British Industry, it did not allow large corporations to be members in their own right. With this rule, it shut the door on the active involvement in its affairs by the chief executives of many of the country's major corporations. (Some large monopolistic companies, however, got around the bar on individual company membership by establishing industry associations in which they were the dominant members: CSR sponsored the Australian Sugar Refiners' Industry Association; BHP, the Iron and Steel Industry Association.) In general, however, large corporations soon came to see the CAI as oriented too much to the interests of small business.

Third, its division into two secretariats—one in Melbourne handling industrial relations and one in Canberra handling trade, tariff and industry matters—created tensions. Some rural sector affiliates (such as the National Farmers' Federation) resented having to pay for the upkeep of the Canberra secretariat, which they saw as a manufacturers' lobby; they also objected to the CAI's lingering commitment to protectionism. Other affiliates that competed with the CAI in representing the interests of manufacturing industry (such as the Metal Trades Industry Association) wanted the CAI to confine itself to industrial relations. Others again (such as the National Farmers' Federation) criticised the CAI for supporting the centralised wages system.

Fourth, the CAI ran into financial difficulties. Dissatisfaction with the confederation's policy and with hefty hikes in affiliation fees led to many resignations. Among the powerful associations that chose to walk out were the National Farmers' Federation, the Australian Retailers' Association, the Metal Trades Industry Association and the Insurance Council of Australia. It suffered a particularly severe blow in 1989 with the resignation of the Australian Chamber of Manufactures—formerly the Victorian and New South Wales Chambers of Manufactures. That departure deprived the CAI of a quarter of its income.[31]

During the 1980s the CAI's authority as the voice of employers was challenged by its failure to be fully representative; by the spate of resignations; by a number of 'New Right' groups claiming to speak for small employers; by independent appearances at national wage cases by, among others, the National Farmers' Federation, the Australian Chamber of Commerce and the Metal Trades Industry Association; and, most importantly, by the growing stature and influence of the Business Council of Australia (BCA). To meet these threats to its standing, the CAI rationalised its operations in 1989 when it decided to devote itself to its industrial relations role and to move its secretariat from Canberra to Melbourne.

In an effort to shore up its financial base and strengthen its ties with small business, the CAI joined forces in 1992 with the Australian Chamber of Commerce to form the Australian Chamber of Commerce and Industry (ACCI). The merger was facilitated by amalgamations in the states between employers' federations and chambers of commerce and by the CAI's shift in policy from being a supporter of the centralised wage system to being an advocate of decentralised enterprise bargaining. At its launch the ACCI claimed to be 'Australia's peak council of employers', consisting of forty affiliated associations representing more than 300 000 firms.[32] In an attempt to attract manufacturers' associations back into the fold, the ACCI announced its intention to establish a new manufacturing division. Three important groups, however, still stood apart from the ACCI. They were the Australian Chamber of Manufactures, the Metal Trades Industry Association, the National Farmers' Federation and the Business Council of Australia.

Under the Hawke and Keating Governments, the Business Council of Australia (BCA) eclipsed the CAI as the generator of broad business strategy on public policy questions. The catalyst for the formation of the Business Council in September 1983 was the damaging lack of cohesion among business representatives at the National Economic Summit Conference convened by Prime Minister Hawke earlier that year. The business contingent at the conference consisted of five representatives from the CAI; a group representing fourteen assorted business groups; and eighteen 'independents', all of whom were the chief executives or chairmen of some of the country's largest corporations. The contingent lacked leadership and a consistent position on the central issues on the conference agenda: the *Financial Review* described it as a rabble. This experience convinced big business of the need for a forum, backed by a sophisticated research capacity, through which the largest companies could articulate a 'first best' position on issues concerning the future direction of the Australian economy.[33]

Modelled on the Business Roundtable in the United States, the BCA (like its Canadian and New Zealand counterparts) consists of an invited group of chief executive officers from the largest corporations in the country, public as well as private. Membership numbers around eighty. These corporations (in 1989) earned more than $216 billion in sales revenue, gave work to more than a million employees and possessed assets in excess of $500 billion. If we rank corporate enterprises, governmental as well as private, in terms of their 1989 sales revenue, twenty-three of the top thirty were members of the BCA. The BCA's members also included twenty-three out of the thirty biggest corporate employers and seventeen out of the thirty corporations with the largest asset holdings. Along with such corporate giants as BHP, Elders IXL, Coles Myer, BTR Nylex and Pacific Dunlop, the BCA's membership list includes the CEOs of four banks (ANZ, Commonwealth, NAB and Westpac), three life insurance companies (AMP, Colonial Mutual and National Mutual), five oil companies (BP, Caltex, Esso, Mobil and Shell), five automobile manufacturers (Ford, GMH, Mitsubishi, Nissan and Toyota), three government trading enterprises (OTC, Telecom and Qantas) and seven mining companies (Alcoa, CRA, MIM, North Broken Hill Peko, Renison Goldfields, Santos and Woodside Petroleum).[34] If productive capacity can be taken as an index of whether an organisaton is 'encompassing', there is little doubt in the case of the BCA: the collective gross revenue of its eighty members amounts to more than 60 per cent of Australia's GDP.

Partly because of their dependence on tariff protection, Australian manufacturers have always been represented by strong associations. Two important groups stand aloof from the ACCI. The first is the Metal Trades Industry Association, the major employers' group in the metal and engineering industry. It covers almost seven thousand companies. The second is the Australian Chamber of Manufactures. This is essentially the former Victorian Chamber of Manufactures, which adopted the national name in 1985. For a period the Australian Chamber included the New South Wales Chamber of Manufactures. In 1992, however, the two parted ways, the result of personality clashes, state rivalries and disagreements over how the assets of the two organisations should be controlled.[35] The New South Wales Chamber has since reaffiliated with the ACCI.

Although based on autonomous commodity groups, the National Farmers' Federation has created a remarkably centralised, hierarchical and integrated system of representation for Australia's farmers. Formed in 1979, the NFF brought together twelve federally organised national commodity councils and ten general-purpose state-based organisations. Its coverage was broad—no major commodity group was outside its fold—and its membership density is high. Representing more than 80 per cent of Australia's 170 000 farms, the NFF can rightfully claim an organisational monopoly in representing Australian farmers.

Despite its organisational achievements, the NFF faces an uncertain future. Since the 1950s the importance of agriculture to the economy has been declining. Its contribution to gross domestic product has fallen from around 24 per cent (in 1949–50) to 5 per cent today; and its contribution to export earnings has fallen from 80 per cent to less than 40 per cent over the same period. Its pool of eligible members is also diminishing: since the mid 1960s, farmers have been leaving the land at the rate of 2 per cent a year, a rate that agricultural economists predict will continue as farmers face an increasingly severe cost–price squeeze. The NFF will also have to manage the conflicting interests of two sets of members: traditional farmers operating small family farms and the new 'agribusinesses' on which farmers are increasingly dependent for inputs (machinery, seeds, fertiliser) and for the processing and distribution of their output. The organisation will also have to handle internal policy differences between its affiliates. It encountered such differences in the early 1990s over tariffs. Tobacco growers, cane growers, dried fruits producers and dairy farmers criticised the federation's policy that all protection be phased out by 1995. The Tobacco Growers' Council actually quit the federation on this issue.

Since the strikes of the 1890s Australian employers have experimented with various mechanisms of national coordination through which they could present a united front to the union movement and to governments.[36] A century later they were still seeking the appropriate model.

During the years of the Hawke and Keating Governments, employers' associations pursued two approaches. As its name suggests, the Confederation of Australian Industry (and its successor, the Australian Chamber of Commerce and Industry) has espoused the confederation model, striving to become the pre-eminent encompassing peak association of Australian employers. This goal has proved elusive, with important industry associations, such as the Metal Trades Industry Association and the Australian Chamber of Manufactures, unwilling to come under its umbrella.

The second approach, favoured by the Business Council, has involved informal coordination and ad hoc coalitions among the major employer and business associations on issues of general concern to business. The 1990 national debt summit, organised by the BCA and attended by three hundred business leaders, is an example. So too is the informal consultation among the so-called national employer group before national wage cases. That group is made up of the ACCI, the Business Council, the MTIA, the Australian Chamber of Manufactures and the National Farmers' Federation.

The differing stands taken by employers' groups at those wage cases suggests that coordination is easier said than done. More importantly, it suggests that the organisational diversity and fragmentation among Australian employers is a major impediment to their participation in corporatist-style bargaining. Does that explain why business was never a party to the Accord?

The Accord: Corporatism without business

To explain interest group strategy solely in terms of organisational factors is to overlook the political conditions that permit an organisation to adopt an encompassing strategy. A strong and comprehensive trade union confederation is unlikely to pursue a collective-gain strategy unless it has some guarantee that workers will benefit from their industrial restraint. One form this assurance may take is a commitment by government to use welfare and taxation policy to compensate workers for their wage restraint. Because such assurances are far more likely when a social democratic or labour party government is in office, some analysts now argue that corporatism is contingent on the coexistence of a social democratic government with a strong centralised trade union confederation.[37] It is this commitment by social democratic (and labour) parties to full employment, to the welfare state and to trade union participation in policy formation that allows trade union leaders (and members) to turn their long-standing attachment to such parties 'into the offer and practice of wage restraint for social democratic governments facing economic or electoral difficulties'.[38]

This approach is central to an understanding of the 1983 Accord between the Australian Labor Party and the ACTU on economic policy.[39] In its origins, purpose and implementation, the Accord was embedded in the politics of the labour movement. It was, as Gwynneth Singleton argues, 'a strategy for advancing the objectives of the political and industrial wings of the labour movement through the political process'.[40] For the ALP, the Accord was part of its strategy of wresting office from the Coalition parties at the 1983 elections. Electorally the ALP needed a credible commitment from the trade unions that they would act 'responsibly' under a Labor Government. It was crucial that the party be able to demonstrate to voters that a new Labor Government would not be blighted in its attack on stagflation by a wages scramble as had occurred in the mid 1970s when Labor last held office. For their part, the unions, chafing under the Fraser Government's wage freeze and anxious about rising unemployment, were determined to see the Labor Party elected to office. To enable a Labor Government to address the twin problems of unemployment and inflation effectively, the ACTU was willing to offer wage restraint to the Labor Government in return for a reciprocal commitment to full wage indexation, employment creation and welfare policies to benefit low wage-earners. In its subsequent formulations under the Hawke and Keating Governments, the Accord has remained 'a partnership in government' between the union movement and the Labor Party 'that serves their discrete but interrelated ... economic, electoral and social objectives'.[41]

Over the next ten years the Accord was renegotiated six times to reflect changing economic and political circumstances. Continued deterioration in Australia's foreign trade performance severely tested its durability. Accord Mark II in 1985 moved away from full wage indexation. It embodied a 2 per cent real wage cut to protect the competitive benefits of the 1985 devaluation of the Australian dollar. Faced with a fall in the terms of trade, a continued depreciation of the Australian dollar, a rapid growth in foreign debt and a balance of payments deficit, the Accord partners acknowledged the need for enterprise bargaining and award restructuring as essential elements in achieving improved productivity, workplace flexibility and rapid structural change. For that reason, Accord Mark III in 1987 introduced the idea of a two-tier wage structure, giving a flat increase to all workers but tying additional (second-tier) increases to improved efficiency at the workplace. These second-tier wage increases were to be negotiated between unions and individual employers and ratified by the Industrial Relations Commission. This approach, with its emphasis on workplace reform, was maintained in the following two versions, Mark IV in 1988 and Mark V in 1989. In return for productivity-based wage restraint, the government committed itself to substantial cuts in personal income tax and increases in family allowances. Enterprise bargaining became an increasingly central feature of Accord Mark VI (1990) and Mark VII (1991). The importance of political considerations is seen in the timing of the last two versions of the Accords. Each was deliberately negotiated so that it could be announced on the eve of a federal election.

The bilateral character of the Accord distinguishes it from the tripartite forms of corporatist policy-making found in Western Europe.[42] At no time did the ACTU or the Labor Government ever invite organised business to join them as an Accord partner or to participate in renegotiating the terms of the Accord.[43] At best business associations, such as the BCA, the ACCI and the MTIA, have occasionally been consulted during the Accord negotiations. More typically they are simply informed of the outcomes. As Bob White, chief executive officer of Westpac and president of the Business Council, commented in 1985: 'When business is consulted we usually find that the die is pretty much cast.'[44]

Business was made fully aware of its peripheral role in the Accord process at the 1983 National Economic Summit Conference, convened by Prime Minister Hawke one month after the Labor Government's election to office. Business realised, to quote Sir Peter Abeles, managing director of TNT, that it had been invited 'to play singles tennis against a championship doubles combination'.[45] The summit was adroitly used by the government to orchestrate corporate endorsement of a return to centralised wage fixing, as set out in the Accord, and to gain corporate support for the government's strategy of fighting inflation and unemployment simultaneously. The communiqué embodied that endorsement. That, however, was the last time business was a player, albeit a subsidiary and reluctant one, in the Accord process. Thereafter it was a spectator on the sidelines.

This is not to say that business has been economically disadvantaged by its formal exclusion from the Accord process. Although the Accord did not 'incorporate' business, the Accord was not hostile to business. There is no doubt that business benefited economically from the unions' strategy of wage restraint. During the period of the Accord, strike activity declined markedly, real wages fell and the profit share increased. While economists debate the degree to which these outcomes can be attributed to the Accord itself rather than to other factors (such as the high level of unemployment), there is little doubt that the Accord prevented a wage explosion at the end of the 1980s when demand increased significantly.[46] To the extent that corporatism is, as David Cameron argues, essentially 'a system of institutionalised wage restraint in which labour, acting "responsibly", voluntarily participates in and legitimises the transfer of income from labour to capital',[47] the Accord can be said to have operated as a form of corporatism. But it has been 'corporatism without business'.

Even though business has been a beneficiary of the Accord process, and even though the business representatives at the economic summit endorsed the Accord, it is misleading to argue that business in effect became an Accord partner.[48] Simply put, the partisan nature of the Accord has precluded business from being a full Accord partner. In any case, to many small employers the Accord was anathema: it simply symbolised union power. In addition, the larger employer groups knew that, even if they were to negotiate a wages deal with the ACTU, there was no guarantee that other business groups, especially the numerous 'New Right' groups speaking for small employers, would accept the deals. In that sense the organisational weakness of business, as Streeck has argued elsewhere,[49] can act as a source of political strength. Because of its organisational weakness, business was able to avoid having to make bargained concessions on such matters as investment, executives' salary levels and managerial prerogatives at the workplace. It is true that Sir Peter Abeles challenged the government at the economic summit to incorporate business as a third, and equal, partner in the Accord. But his was a lone voice among business representatives at that time and in the decade since. Despite the economic benefits the Accord has conferred on business, the business world has remained politically suspicious of and, in some quarters, actively hostile to the Accord.

Business misgivings have rested on political, economic and policy grounds. Politically, the economic summit taught business to be wary about being 'roped in' by the two Accord partners to legitimise arrangements intended to benefit the Labor Party electorally. Business was also disturbed by the political power and insider status that the Accord process conferred on the ACTU. This was most manifest in the vigorous opposition by business to the ACTU's claim in the 1986 national wage case for a nationwide superannuation scheme based on union-based funds. Business groups saw the scheme as a device to strengthen the power of trade unions greatly by giving them the capacity to make decisions about the levels and patterns of investment.[50] A number of the policy concessions offered by the government to the ACTU in return for wage restraint also disturbed business. Among the concessions were the superannuation scheme and a 3 per cent training guarantee levy.

Even the economic benefits flowing from the Accord soon lost their gloss. By the late 1980s business wanted more from the Accord than wage restraint and industrial peace. After all, the recession and high unemployment were delivering those benefits. Faced with declining international competitiveness, business became increasingly critical of the centralised system of wage fixing and the Accord's commitment to it. Business leaders blamed the Accord for failing to deliver improved productivity and for impeding labour market reform. They also called for rapid microeconomic reform and labour market deregulation. The catchcry was flexibility, particularly at the enterprise level. The next section examines the role played by business and employers' associations in putting enterprise bargaining on the industrial relations agenda in the late 1980s.

Employers take the initiative: Enterprise bargaining

Since the early years of the century the institutional basis of Australia's centralised wages system has been a network of conciliation and arbitration tribunals established under federal and state laws to deal with industrial disputes. By the late 1950s the federal tribunal (then known as the Commonwealth Conciliation and Arbitration Commission) had assumed primary responsibility for determining a national wages policy. The state tribunals generally followed its lead. By developing a set of wage-fixing principles—'needs', 'industry capacity to pay' and 'comparative wage justice'—which it applied in different disputes as well as in national test cases, the federal tribunal saw its role change from ad hoc dispute resolution to national wage prescription.[51]

The commission's major vehicle for determining wages policy was its decisions in periodic national wage cases. These decisions (and the enunciated principles on which they are based) were applied in a multiplicity of individual craft, industry and enterprise 'awards'. In the 1980s around 80 per cent of workers were covered by minimum wage awards set either by the commission or by the state tribunals.

Under the Hawke and Keating Governments, Australia has experienced a critical shift from the centralised wages system to one focused on workplace bargaining. That shift has been reflected in the evolution of the Accord. A fundamental and unquestioned tenet of the 1983 Accord was the centralised wages system. The Accord partners took it for granted that the federal tribunal (now known as the Australian Industrial Relations Commission) would have the role of implementing the wages implications of the Accord. By Accord Mark VII, however, the emphasis had moved to productivity-based workplace bargaining, with the Industrial Relations Commission being relegated to the role of providing a safety net for employees unable to negotiate enterprise agreements.

This shift in focus in Australian industrial relations was the product of a number of intertwined influences: the contempt that the New Right had for the arbitration system and for groups—employers as well as unions—that willingly worked within the system;[52] the spreading acceptance of the economic rationalist case for the deregulation of Australia's product and labour markets; the public awareness in the mid 1980s of Australia's declining international competitiveness and the poor export performance of its manufacturing sector; and, last but not least, the success of the Business Council in presenting an intellectually respectable, detailed and empirically researched rationale for enterprise bargaining.[53]

The centralised system of compulsory arbitration came under concerted attack in the mid 1980s from the New Right, in particular from the H. R. Nicholls Society.[54] Consisting of industrial lawyers, conservative politicians, employers, farm and small business leaders, polemicists and academics, this society represented a reaction against the Hawke Government's corporatist style of consensus politics. Its targets were union power and the arbitration system. In speeches and publications, members of the H. R. Nicholls Society aggressively argued for labour market deregulation as the solution to Australia's economic ills. They also advocated confrontational tactics, particularly the use of the common law to claim strike damages from unions. By suing unions at common law and by resorting to the secondary boycott provisions of the Trade Practices Act,[55] the New Right won a number of spectacular industrial victories in the mid 1980s against militant unions. These victories demonstrated that direct legal action could be used to remove inefficient (and in some cases corrupt) practices in the workplace.

Among employers' groups, the National Farmers' Federation was most closely aligned with the New Right's hard-line stance against union power. Its massive fighting fund financed a number of the legal cases. The New Right's arguments were also taken up by economic rationalists in the Liberal Party who, after a bitter battle with supporters of the centralised system, managed in 1986 to rewrite the party's industrial relations policy. The new policy sought to reform the centralised system by encouraging the emergence of an alternative system based on voluntary workplace contracts.

Despite these free-market arguments, it was the rapid deterioration in Australia's international competitiveness in the mid 1980s that persuaded the government, the ACTU and the mainstream employers' groups of the urgency of labour market reform if Australian enterprises were to succeed in global markets. The structural and competitive weaknesses of the Australian economy were made increasingly apparent in 1986 with the release of each new set of economic indicators showing the collapse in Australia's terms of trade, the rise in net foreign debt, the rapid depreciation of the Australian dollar and the growing balance of payments deficit. Treasurer Paul Keating starkly highlighted the country's economic predicament when he warned in May of that year that Australia risked becoming a 'banana republic'. From 1986 the government and the ACTU conceded that enterprise bargaining was the route to improved productivity.

The BCA's contribution has been to help shift the terms of the debate from whether there should be change to the precise institutional form that the change should take. Early in its life the BCA adopted a strategic approach to public policy advocacy. It committed itself to becoming involved in issue politics but not party politics; to avoid ad hoc responses to passing issues; to concentrate on winning fundamental long-term change; and to pursue long-term change on the basis of objective, research-based advocacy.[56] Its stand on industrial relations reform conformed to that strategy.

After an internal BCA survey revealed that Australia's centralised and adversarial industrial relations system was one of two public policy issues of greatest concern to its members,[57] the BCA decided to fund (at a reported cost of $2 million) an Employee Relations Study Commission. The study commission had the task of advising the BCA on the precise institutional and legal changes that were needed to improve employee relations, and hence productivity and competitiveness, in Australia's business enterprises. The four-member commission, chaired by Frederick G. Hilmer, Dean of the Australian Graduate School of Management and former senior partner of McKinsey & Co.,[58] commissioned survey and case-study research into the workplace, consulted with management and industrial relations experts in companies, universities and government, and prudently briefed senior politicians, public servants, union leaders and members of the federal industrial tribunal on its work. The commission presented three reports to the Business Council, which the Business Council published. The first two (1989, 1991) argued that the occupational and craft basis of most unions—and the fact that most enterprises were host to several competing unions and to several industrial awards—had an adverse effect on enterprise productivity, on skill development, and on the capacity of enterprises to adapt to change.[59] These reports recommended the establishment of enterprise-based bargaining units. Senior management was also urged to pay greater attention to improving employee relations at the workplace. The third report (1993) proposed a radically new legislative framework to speed up the shift to a fully fledged system of enterprise-based bargaining.[60]

The study commission's proposals, adopted by the BCA, are predicated on a number of interconnected propositions:

- that enterprises, not nations or industries, will become the critical economic units of the future;
- that Australia must nurture a greater number of globally competitive industries if it is to remain a 'first-division' country;
- that leading-edge enterprises trying to compete in the global marketplace must have more flexibility than is available under the multi-employer award system;
- that a major overhaul of bargaining structures, both union and employer, are essential to true labour market reform;
- that the issue is not centralisation versus wage chaos, but one of successfully managing greater diversity in the industrial relations system; and
- that to achieve flexibility and diversity at the enterprise level, legislative changes to the formal institutions of the industrial relations system are in themselves insufficient. Flexibility and diversity also require:
  — a fundamental reform of management practices, including the refocusing of managerial attention on maximising productivity rather than minimising labour costs; and
  — the continued opening of the economy to international competition.

In terms of its specific reform proposals, the BCA study commission advocated:

- reducing the number of bargaining units in the workplace, with the objective of having no more than one union per workplace;
- permitting the registration of enterprise unions;
- providing for an alternative stream of enterprise-based agreements to exist alongside traditional multi-employer awards;
- rewriting the legislative framework. The new framework would (1) allow enterprises and their employees to leave the award system if they wanted to determine the terms of their employment relation by

agreement; (2) permit employees to determine who should represent them in their dealings with their employees; (3) permit employees and their employers to decide how their agreements would be adjusted and enforced; and (4) provide for the establishment of statutory minimum conditions of employment to protect individual employees;
- developing among employers, employees and unions an acceptance (1) that awards and agreements should have a specified duration; (2) that they should be largely unalterable for that specified period; and (3) that industrial action over the content of awards and agreements should be prohibited during that period.

In demanding a flexible and decentralised system of industrial relations, Australia's corporate leaders were responding to the uncertainties and challenges posed by rapid structural change, change brought about by new production technologies, deregulated financial markets, the dismantling of industry protection, shortening product cycles, the shift of competitive strength from price to product quality, volatile exchange rates and increased international competition, particularly from the newly industrialising countries in North-east and South-east Asia. However, by stressing productivity enhancement rather than price minimisation, the BCA's recipe for industrial revitalisation was quite distinct from that advanced by many in the small business sector. For example, by accepting a role for unions, the BCA divorced the big business case for enterprise bargaining from the union-crushing zealotry of the New Right. And by advocating a two-stream evolution of the industrial relations system, the BCA made it clear that the big business case for enterprise bargaining did not entail the acceptance of a completely unregulated system of wage-cutting. Considering the traditionally reactive stance of employers' groups in Australia both to the arbitration system itself and to unions' wage demands—as David Plowman[61] argues, the employers' traditional strategy was basically one of 'holding the line' against union demands—the BCA's decidedly proactive role was a major new development in employer politics.

The decision of the BCA to advocate fundamental reform in Australian industrial relations was, however, not just a response to structural change in the international economy. It was also an attempt to wrest the initiative in the debate abut structural adjustment policy and industrial relations policy from the ACTU. Since 1983 the ACTU had played a dominant role in determining the direction of these policies through the Accord process and through its blueprint for corporatist industry policy set out in the document *Australia Reconstructed*.[62] Just as that activist role embodied the ACTU's notion of 'strategic unionism', so the BCA's involvement in the issue of industrial relations reform can be seen as embodying 'strategic managerialism'—an attempt by Australia's corporate leaders to exercise critical choice in order to reshape the power relations between business and labour in the industrial relations system.[63]

The strategy was to do so by redefining the very bargaining structures of the industrial relations system.

In that sense, the BCA's advocacy of enterprise bargaining and its goal of having 'no more than one union per workplace' have problematic implications for the union movement. Despite the BCA's disclaimer that 'Whether that one union [be] an enterprise union or a reasonably autonomous branch of a larger, probably industry, union is not something that is sensible or necessary to prescribe in advance',[64] the BCA's goal raises doubts about the immediate and the longer-term role unions should play in industrial relations. What relationship will autonomous enterprise unions have with industry unions? How much autonomy should enterprise branches of unions have to bargain at that level? What should be the legal status of agreements made in non-union workplaces, given that only 30 per cent of the private workforce is unionised? Should unions continue to have guaranteed rights to represent specified groups of employees, regardless of the service they offer members and potential members in a particular enterprise? Should enterprise agreements continue to need the approval of a union for them to have legal status?

By the same token, enterprise bargaining also represents a difficult challenge to many employers' associations. As single-enterprise agreements supplant multi-employer awards, will employers' associations be able to retain their members? Will large corporations, which presently play a prominent part in the affairs of employers' associations, decide to go it alone? After all, they can rely on their own staff specialists in negotiating an enterprise agreement. Will large firms, which often find it necessary to belong to more than one employers' association—either because their activities embrace more than one industry or because their employees are covered by more than one industry award—shed most or even all of those memberships under enterprise-based bargaining? Will smaller firms also depart, especially if the associations find it necessary to offer specialist industrial relations assistance on a fee-for-service basis rather than as an entitlement of membership? Will the associations be able to compete effectively with industrial relations consultants, legal firms and accountants in offering fee-for-service consultancy?

Or, on the other hand, will many associations experience 'something of a membership and organisational boom' in the wake of enterprise bargaining as they did when the Industrial Relations Commission introduced the structural efficiency principle and the industry training levy?[65] Might not smaller firms, for whom price advantage is a prime consideration, wish to rely on employers' associations to set the parameters in which enterprise negotiations can take place? When unions are strong, small employers might well want the security of a multi-employer formula (such as the MTIA's blueprint for enterprise bargains in the metal industry) to guard against the flow-on potential of enterprise bargaining. And when union bargaining power is weak, they might prefer multi-employer bargaining to prevent their rivals undercutting them on labour costs. They might even choose, as has happened occasionally in New Zealand under the Employment Contracts Act, to have their association act as the bargaining agent. The main effect of the New Zealand Act, however, has been to reduce the role of employers' associations in industrial relations. A survey among employers shows that while 45 per cent used the services of an employers' association in their contract negotiations, another 21 per cent used outside sources of assistance. Of those who sought assistance from an association, only a fifth used an association advocate for negotiations.[66] In response, New Zealand employers' associations are finding it necessary to shift from a representative to a consultancy role. Australian employers' groups will likewise be forced to reassess and redefine their role.

Conclusion

The Accord process—the various understandings between the ACTU and the Labor Government in the 1980s and early 1990s on the broad parameters of incomes policy—was Australia's version of corporatism. The Labor Government's unprecedented and unexpected re-election in 1993 for a fifth term showed the Accord to be a durable and distinctive feature of Labor's decade in office.

This chapter takes issue with observers who explain the origins and longevity of the Accord in terms of the ACTU's centralised and encompassing character. To focus only on interest group structure is to neglect the political conditions that prompt and permit an interest group to pursue a positive-sum strategy. More specifically, it is to neglect the links between party politics and a trade union confederation's willingness to commit its members to a policy of wage restraint. The Accord has to be seen as embedded in Labor politics.

The origins of the Accord are rooted in the industrial and political objectives of the Australian labour movement. Because of the organic links between the industrial and political wings of that movement, the ACTU was prepared to commit its member unions to wage restraint. It was willing to do so because such a commitment would be electorally and politically advantageous to a *Labor Party* government. Equally important, the ACTU was prepared to endorse wage restraint because it knew it could rely on a *Labor* government to provide increases in the social wage to compensate workers for their wage restraint. The stability and persistence of the Accord arrangement has depended not only on Labor's remaining in office but also on the two Accord partners judging that the trade-offs embodied in the Accord are still in their interests. That judgement is largely informed by a partisan calculus. For the ACTU the costs of continued wage restraint and a weakening of the centralised award system of wage-fixing have to be balanced against the benefits of being able, under a Labor government and through the Accord process, to control the pace and institutional form of labour market deregulation. Following the rise of the New Right, and the Coalition's adoption of an industrial relations policy designed to erode the unions' power base, the ACTU has had even more incentive to see a Labor government remain in office.

Despite the Accord's 'labourist' origins, some analysts argue that in terms of actual economic outcomes the Accord demonstrates the structural power of business.[67] They argue that business power is seen in the way that the ACTU and the Labor Government were constrained to accommodate and facilitate the conditions necessary for business to flourish. Because it was predicated on the need to stimulate private business investment in order to promote the creation of jobs, the Accord was highly beneficial to business. Under the Accord, business enjoyed a substantial redistribution of national income from wages to profits and an unprecedented period of industrial peace. Similarly, reflecting the degree to which the Accord partners attended to the needs of business was their willingness to embrace (in Accord Mark III and its successors) a greater focus on enterprise-based wage-fixing. These 'capitalist imperatives', we are told, 'form the terrain on which the politics of the Accord have been played out'. They have enabled business, as the passive beneficiaries of the Accord process, 'to stand aloof from the exhausting politics of the Accord and yet still gain substantial benefits'.[68] Business, in short, was not an Accord partner because it had no economic need to be.

Such an approach to business power is valuable in emphasising how in periods of economic crisis governments are obliged to accommodate the needs of business, notably by giving a freer reign to market forces. It is in that sense, as Streeck shrewdly observes, that 'economic weakness constitutes a source of political strength for capital in its power game with labour'.[69] Nevertheless, to say that it is the structural power of business that permitted business to 'stand aloof' from the Accord process is misleading on two counts.

First, because it suggests that business could have been involved in the Accord bargains had it chosen to be. This overlooks the way that the Accord's partisan character largely precluded business ever becoming a 'party' to the Accord. As a 'partnership in government' between the ACTU and the Australian Labor Party, there was very little political space in the Accord arrangement to include business. Even in the unlikely event that business had been invited to become a formal Accord partner, business was simply not prepared to bargain with the ACTU and the Labor Government when the point of the bargaining was to boost the Labor Party's electoral stocks. This bears out Lehmbruch's observation that tripartite consensus building on economic and social policy is incompatible with party conflict over those issues.[70] Indeed, with industrial relations having become a prominent partisan issue at the 1990 and 1993 elections, business had no incentive whatsoever to underwrite the Accord. In fact, by the time of the 1993 election, the policy of the larger employers' groups in favour of replacing the centralised wage-fixing system with a system based on enterprise bargaining was very close to the Coalition's 'Jobsback' industrial relations policy. Convinced that the ACTU would veto any attempt by the government to jettison the centralised award system—the system on which much of the union movement's power rested—organised business pinned its hopes on (and, in the case of the ACCI and the Housing Industry Association, publicly campaigned for) a Coalition victory. It was Australia's adversarial and divisive style of party politics, and not just the imperatives of capitalism, then, that formed the terrain on which the politics of the Accord were fought out.

Second, because it gives little weight to the political mechanisms whereby business's structural power is transformed into outcomes beneficial to business. To talk of business 'standing aloof' from the Accord is to give the impression that business was a passive and satisfied bystander. That impression conceals the degree to which business deliberately went on the offensive to reshape the structures of industrial relations bargaining and to redefine the terms of the industrial relations debate. That the Accord has been transformed because unions 'now accept fundamental business precepts regarding the primacy of profits, labour market flexibility, union discipline and the need to focus on productivity issues'[71] is true. But by the late 1980s that transformation was as much the result of overt political action by business as it was of the structural power of business. The BCA's active advocacy of enterprise-based bargaining is hardly consistent with 'standing aloof' from the Accord. Its involvement in that issue, moreover, indicates that by the late 1980s business wanted more from the Accord than wage restraint and industrial quiescence. It wanted higher labour productivity and greater labour market flexibility. In terms of those yardsticks it found the Accord wanting, just as it found the slow pace of labour market reform under the Accord too costly. Dissatisfaction with the Accord and its outcomes explains why employers did not simply stand aloof from the politics of the Accord but actively sought to transform the very basis of wage-fixing in Australia. The degree to which business is successful in securing such a transformation—particularly under a Labor Government—will be the real test of its political power.

Notes

1 I wish to thank Michael Angwin, Mark Bray, Ron Callus, Merilyn Bryce and Barry Watchorn for help with aspects of this paper.

2 P. Gerlich (1992), 'A farewell to corporatism', *West European Politics*, 15, 132–46; S. Lash (1985), 'The end of neo-corporatism: The breakdown of centralized bargaining in Sweden', *British Journal of Industrial Relations*, 23, 215–39; M. Micheletti (1991), 'Swedish corporatism at a crossroads: The impact of new politics and new social movements', *West European Politics*, 14:3, 144–65; J. Visser (1992), 'The coming divergence in Dutch industrial relations', in A. Gladstone et al. (eds), *Labour Relations in a Changing Environment*, Walter de Gruyter, Berlin and New York, pp. 251–64.

3 G. Strauss (1984), 'Industrial relations: Times of change', *Industrial Relations*, 23:1, 1–15; T. A. Kochan, R. B. McKersie and P. Cappelli (1984), 'Strategic choice and industrial relations theory', *Industrial Relations*, 23:1, 16–39; W. Streeck (1987), 'The uncertainties of management in the management of uncertainty: Employers, labour relations and industrial adjustment in the 1980s', *Work, Employment and Society*, 1:3, 281–308.

4 For an extended argument interpreting economic policy in terms of a country's distinctive socioeconomic and political institutional structures, see P. A. Hall (1986), *Governing the Economy: The Politics of State Intervention in Britain and France*, Polity Press, Cambridge.

5 The term *neo-corporatism* is used by some writers to distinguish contemporary forms of corporatism in liberal democracies from the authoritarian forms of corporatism found in Fascist Italy and Salazar's Portugal. For a comprehensive discussion of corporatism, see P. J. Williamson (1989), *Corporatism in Perspective: An Introductory Guide to Corporatist Theory*, Sage Publications, London.

6 S. H. Beer (1982), *Britain Against Itself: The Political Contradictions of Collectivism*, Faber & Faber, London.

7 M. Olson (1982), *The Rise and Decline of Nations: Economic Growth, Stagflation and Social Rigidities*, Yale University Press, New Haven and London; M. Olson (1984), *Australia in the Perspective of the Rise and Decline of Nations*, Centre for Economic Policy Research, Discussion Papers No. 109, Australian National University, Canberra.

8 Some commentators have interpreted the term *distributional coalition* to mean a collaborative coalition between sectional interest groups (e.g. a coalition between manufacturers and trade unions in favour of tariff protection). In Olson's usage, however, the term simply refers to any narrow special-interest group.

9 M. Olson (1984), p. 135.

10 J. J. Pincus (1987), 'Government', in R. Maddock and I. W. McLean (eds), *The Australian Economy in the Long Run*, Cambridge University Press, Cambridge, pp. 291–318.

11 R. M. Alverez, G. Garrett and P. Lange (1991), 'Government partisanship, labor organization and macroeconomic performance, 1967–1984', *American Political Science Review*, 85, 539–56; A. Martin (1986), 'The politics of employment and welfare: National policies and international interdependence', in K. Banting (ed.), *The State and Economic Interests*, Toronto University Press, Toronto, pp. 157–241; H. Paloheimo (1984), 'Distributive struggle and economic development in the 1970s in developed capitalist countries', *European Journal of Political Research*, 12:2, 171–90; H. Paloheimo (1990), 'Between liberalism and corporatism: The effect of trade

unions and governments on economic performance in eighteen OECD countries', in R. Brunetta and C. Dell'Aringa (eds), *Labour Relations and mic Performance*, Macmillan in association with the International Economic Association, London, pp. 114–36; K. Schott (1984), *Policy, Power and Order: The Persistence of Economic Problems in Capitalist States*, Yale University Press, New Haven. For a collection of studies examining the relationship between corporatism and economic performance see J. Pekkarinen, M. Pohjola and B. Rowthorn (eds) (1992), *Social Corporatism: A Superior Economic System?* Clarendon Press, Oxford.

12 P. J. Katzenstein (1984), *Corporatism and Change: Austria, Switzerland and the Politics of Industry*, Cornell University Press, Ithaca; P. J. Katzenstein (1985), *Small States in World Markets: Industrial Policy in Europe*, Cornell University Press, Ithaca.

13 P. C. Schmitter (1981), 'Interest intermediation and regime governability in contemporary Western Europe and North America', in S. Berger (ed.), *Organising Interests in Western Europe*, Cambridge University Press, Cambridge.

14 M. Olson (1986), 'A theory of incentives facing political organisations: Neo-corporatism and the hegemonic state', *International Political Science Journal*, 7, 165–89.

15 M. Olson (1986), p. 179.

16 R. Gerritsen (1986), 'The necessity of "corporatism": The case of the Hawke Labor Government', *Politics*, 21:1, 45–54; R. G. Stewart (1985), 'The politics of the Accord: Does corporatism explain it?', *Politics*, 20, 26–35; F. Stilwell (1986), *The Accord and Beyond: The Political Economy of the Labor Government*, Pluto Press, Sydney; K. West (1984), *The Revolution in Australian Politics*, Penguin Books, Ringwood.

17 See M. Keating and G. Dixon (1989), *Making Economic Policy in Australia 1983–1988*, Longman Cheshire, Melbourne.

18 For a more detailed examination of that asymmetry see T. Matthews (1991), 'Interest group politics: Corporatism without business?', in F. G. Castles (ed.), *Australia Compared: People, Policies and Politics*, Allen & Unwin, Sydney, pp. 191–218.

19 T. Matthews (1983), 'Business associations and the state, 1850–1979', in B. W. Head (ed.), *State and Economy in Australia*, Oxford University Press, Melbourne, pp. 115–49.

20 C. Offe and H. Wiesenthal (1980), 'The two logics of collective action: Theoretical notes on social class and the political form of interest organisation', in M. Zeitlin (ed.), *Political Power and Social Theory Vol. 1*, JAI Press, Greenwood, Conn., pp. 67–115.

21 M. Useem (1984), *The Inner Circle: Large Corporations and the Rise of Business Political Activity in the US and the UK*, Oxford University Press, New York.

22 C. E. Lindblom (1977), *Politics and Markets*, Basic Books, New York.

23 P. A. McLaughlin (1991), 'How business relates to the Hawke Government: The captains of industry', in B. Galligan and G. Singleton (eds), *Business and Government Under Labor*, Longman Cheshire, Melbourne, pp. 147–67.

24 W. D. Coleman and W. Grant (1988), 'The organisational cohesion and political access of business: A study of comprehensive associations', *European Journal of Political Research*, 16, 467–87.

25 P. C. Schmitter and W. Streeck (1981), *The Organisation of Business Interests: A Research Design to Study the Associative Action of Business in the Advanced Industrial Societies of Western Europe, Discussion Paper IIM/LMP 81-13*, Wissenschaftszentrum, Berlin.
26 T. Matthews (1990), 'Federalism and interest group cohesion: The case of Australian business groups', *Publius: The Journal of Federalism*, 2:4, 105-28.
27 W. D. Coleman and W. Grant (1988), 'The organisational cohesion and political access of business: A study of comprehensive associations', *European Journal of Political Research*, 16, 467-87; W. D. Coleman and W. Grant (1988); G. K. Wilson (1981), *Interest Groups in the United States*, Clarendon Press, Oxford.
28 D. H. Plowman (1989), 'Countervailing power, organisational parallelism and Australian employer associations', *Australian Journal of Management*, 14:1, 97-113.
29 D. H. Plowman (1989), p. 109.
30 *Australian Financial Review*, 11 October 1989, p. 3.
31 In 1992 the New South Wales Chamber of Manufactures withdrew from the ACM.
32 *CAI Industrial Review*, No. 91, September 1992.
33 The BCA in effect was a merger of two groups that had been attempting to perform this role: the Australian Industries Development Association and the Business Roundtable.
34 Missing from its membership are the three media giants (News Corporation, Consolidated Press and Fairfax); the large New Zealand-based paper and packaging company, Fletcher Challenge; the two Japanese trading companies with extensive Australian operations (Mitsui and C. Itoh); all the state banks and state superannuation funds; and most government-operated utilities, even though they are among Australia's largest employers (e.g., Australia Post, the Victorian SEC and Queensland Rail).
35 N. Way (1992), 'Employers leave ACM in the cold', *Bulletin*, 28 February, pp. 30-31.
36 D. H. Plowman (1987), 'Models of national employer coordination, 1890-1980', *Journal of Industrial Relations*, 29:4, pp. 493-518.
37 D. R. Cameron (1984), 'Social democracy, corporatism, labour quiescence and the representation of economic interest in advanced capitalist society', in J. H. Goldthorpe (ed.), *Order and Conflict in Contemporary Capitalism*, Clarendon Press, Oxford, pp. 143-78; P. Lange and G. Garrett (1985), 'The politics of growth: Strategic interaction and economic performance in advanced industrial democracies', *Journal of Politics*, 47:3, 792-827; C. S. Maier (1984), 'Preconditions for corporatism', in J. H. Goldthorpe (ed.), *Order and Conflict in Contemporary Capitalism*, Clarendon Press, Oxford, pp. 39-59; L. Panitch (1986), 'The tripartite experience', in K. Banting (ed.), *The State and Economic Interests*, Toronto University Press, Toronto, pp. 35-119.
38 L. Panitch (1986), p. 45.
39 The full text of the Statement of Accord is reproduced in F. Stilwell (1986), *The Accord and Beyond: The Political Economy of the Labor Government*, Pluto, Sydney, Appendix A.
40 G. Singleton (1990), *The Accord and the Australian Labour Movement*, Melbourne University Press, Carlton, p. 200.

41 G. Singleton (1990), 'Corporatism or labourism? The Australian labour movement in accord', *Journal of Commonwealth and Comparative Politics*, 28:2, 180.
42 P. J. Katzenstein (1984); P. J. Katzenstein (1985); G. Lehmbruch (1984), 'Concentration and the structure of corporatist networks', in J. H. Goldthorpe (ed.), *Order and Conflict in Contemporary Capitalism*, Clarendon Press, Oxford, pp. 60–80; L. Panitch (1986).
43 Rumours circulated in 1992 that the MTIA would be a party to Accord Mark VII. Had the MTIA actually become an Accord partner, the move would not have signified that the Accord had become a genuine tripartite arrangement; rather, it would have indicated a tactical move by the government and the ACTU in the run-up to the federal election to show that at least one major employers' group was not fully committed to the Coalition parties' 'Fightback' industrial relations policy.
44 *Financial Review*, 30 December 1985, p. 2.
45 NESC (1983), *National Economic Summit: Documents and Proceedings*, vol. 2, Australian Government Publishing Service, Canberra.
46 For assessments of the Accord see R. Archer (1992), 'The unexpected emergence of Australian corporatism', in J. Pekkarinen, M. Pohjila and B. Rowthorn (eds) (1992), *Social Corporatism: A Superior Economic System?* Clarendon Press, Oxford, pp. 377–477; B. Chapman and F. Gruen (1990), *An Analysis of the Australian Consensual Incomes Policy: The Prices and Incomes Accord*, Discussion Paper No. 221, Centre for Economic Policy Research, Australian National University, Canberra; B. J. Chapman (1988), 'Some observations on wage setting practices in the Australian labour market system', *Australian Journal of Management*, 13:2, 161–76; F. Gruen and M. Grattan (1992), *Managing Government: Labor's Achievements and Failures*, Allen & Unwin, Sydney.
47 D. R. Cameron (1984) and R. Kuhn (1991), 'The Accord and business: The distinctiveness of the Hawke Government's approach to capital accumulation' in B. Galligan and G. Singleton (eds), *Business and Government under Labor*, Longman Cheshire, Melbourne, pp. 47–74.
48 For the argument that business in effect became an Accord partner, see R. G. Stewart (1985) and F. Stilwell (1986).
49 W. Streeck (1991), 'Interest heterogeneity and organising capacity: Two logics of collective action?', in R. M. Czada and A. Windhoff-Héretier (eds), *Political Choice: Institutions, Rules and the Limits of Rationality*, Westview Press, Boulder, pp. 161–98.
50 D. McEachern (1986), 'Business and the trade union superannuation campaign', paper presented to the 1986 Conference of the Australasian Political Studies Association.
51 See chapter 6 of this book.
52 H. R. Nicholls Society (1986), *Arbitration in Contempt*, H. R. Nicholls Society, Melbourne.
53 F. G. Hilmer et al. (1989), *Enterprise-based Bargaining Units: A Better Way of Working*, Report to the Business Council of Australia by the Industrial Relations Study Commission, Business Council of Australia, Melbourne; F. G. Hilmer et al. (1991), *Avoiding Industrial Action: A Better Way of Working*, Allen & Unwin in association with the Business Council of

Australia, North Sydney; and F. G. Hilmer et al. (1993), *Working Relations: A Fresh Start for Australian Enterprises*, Information Australia in association with the Business Council of Australia, Melbourne. The objectivity and methodology of the research undertaken for the BCA has been questioned. See the critiques by S. Frenkel and D. Peetz (1990), 'Enterprise bargaining: The BCA's report on industrial relations reform', *Journal of Industrial Relations*, 32:1, 69–99 and by B. Dabscheck (1990), 'Industrial relations and the irresistible magic wand: The BCA's plan to Americanise Australian industrial relations', in M. Easson and J. Shaw (eds), *Transforming Industrial Relations*, 117–30, Pluto Press in association with Lloyd Ross Forum, Sydney. For the ensuing debate, consult F. G. Hilmer and P. McLaughlin (1990), 'The BCA report: A response to Frenkel and Peetz (1)', *Journal of Industrial Relations*, 32:3, 403–12; R. Drago and M. Wooden (1990), 'The BCA report: A response to Frenkel and Peetz (2)', *Journal of Industrial Relations*, 32:3, 413–18; and S. Frenkel and D. Peetz (1990), 'The BCA report: A rejoinder', *Journal of Industrial Relations*, 32:3, 419–30.
54 For accounts of the H. R. Nicholls Society, see B. Dabscheck (1989), *Australian Industrial Relations in the 1980s*, Oxford University Press, Melbourne, pp. 116–24; P. Kelly (1992), *The End of Certainty: The Story of the 1980s*, Allen & Unwin, Sydney, chs 6 and 13; D. H. Plowman (1987), 'Economic forces and the New Right: Employer matters in 1986', *Journal of Industrial Relations*, 29:1, 84–91.
55 The New Right's victories were in disputes with unions at the Mudginberri abattoirs in the Northern Territory, at the South-East Queensland Electricity Board, at the Dollar Sweets company in Melbourne and at Peko-Wallsend's iron ore operation at Robe River.
56 P. A. McLaughlin (1991). See also Sir Roderick Carnegie (1988), 'Issue politics: No longer a spectator sport for CEOs', *Business Council Bulletin*, 44, 23–5.
57 P. A. McLaughlin (1991). The other issue of concern was Australia's rising national debt and its falling international competitiveness.
58 The other members were John Rose, director of the Graduate School of Management at the University of Melbourne, David K. Macfarlane, a former managing director of James Hardie Industries, and Peter McLaughlin, the executive director of the BCA, who was seconded to work full-time with the commission and to head its secretariat.
59 F. G. Hilmer et al. (1989) and (1991).
60 F. G. Hilmer et al. (1993).
61 D. H. Plowman (1988), 'Employer associations and industrial reactivity', *Labour and Industry*, 1:2, 287–305; D. H. Plowman (1989), *Holding the Line: Compulsory Arbitration and National Employer Coordination in Australia*, Cambridge University Press, Melbourne.
62 ACTU and Trade Development Council (1987), *Australia Reconstructed: ACTU/TDC Mission to Western Europe*, Australian Government Publishing Service, Canberra.
63 The idea of strategic choice is discussed by T. A. Kochan, R. B. McKersie and P. Cappelli (1984).
64 P. A. McLaughlin (1991), p. 58.
65 D. Plowman and M. Rimmer (n.d.), 'Bargaining structure, award respondency

and employer associations: A report to the Business Council of Australia', University of NSW Studies in Australian Industrial Relations, No. 33.
66 BCA (1993), 'New Zealand workplace reform: Lessons for Australia', *Business Council Bulletin*, Supplement to No. 94, 9.
67 D. McEachern (1991), ch. 7; F. Stilwell (1986); S. Bell (1992), 'Structural power in the manufacturing sector: The political economy of competitiveness and investment' in S. Bell and J. Wanna (eds), *Business–Government Relations in Australia*, Harcourt Brace Jovanovich, Sydney, pp. 194–7.
68 S. Bell (1992), p. 195.
69 W. Streeck (1984), 'Neo-corporatist industrial relations and the economic crisis in West Germany', in J. Goldthorpe (ed.) (1984), *Order and Conflict in Contemporary Capitalism*, Oxford University Press, Oxford, p. 296.
70 G. Lehmbruch (1984), 'Concertation and the structure of corporatist networks', in J. H. Goldthorpe (ed.), *Order and Conflict in Contemporary Capitalism*, Clarendon Press, Oxford, p. 77.
71 S. Bell (1992), p. 196.

9

Can the state 'manage' the macroeconomy?

John Wanna

Can the Australian state effectively and successfully manage the macroeconomy? Does the state have the capacity to manage the once highly protected domestic economy now increasingly buffeted by global economic forces? Is 'the economy' something manageable in aggregate or is it increasingly disaggregated, compartmentalised and responsive to many influences, including a disparate range of state policies? These are fundamental questions that cannot be answered by looking solely at immediate policy approaches or measuring the success of policies according to isolated economic indicators. Rather, such questions call for a general appreciation of the changing dynamics of state–economy relations. This suggests that any assessment of the state's capacity to manage the macroeconomy is premised on a range of evaluations including: the general impact of the state on economic life, an appreciation of those aspects of economic life beyond the reach of the state, the historical dimensions of state activity, the changing nature of the economy, prevailing orientations to economic policy-making and the specific policy responses to economic problems. These themes provide a context in which to analyse the state's performance in managing economic activity.

This chapter is not an exhaustive coverage of the policy twists and turns over the past decade; detailed accounts charting this history already exist.[1] Instead, this chapter argues that the state's aspirations over macroeconomic management tended to outweigh the state's capacity to achieve intended outcomes. Evidence for this assertion is drawn largely from federal policy responses to the fluctuating economic conditions of the 1980s and early 1990s. Economic policy was often driven by a belief that change was essential and the hope that improvement would result. A floating dollar and manipulated interest rates became the major elements of macroeconomic policy, but these 'levers' operated in the context of fiscal policy (public sector spending, taxing and borrowing) and a centralised wage-fixing system. The drift into 'economic rationalism', while appealing to many policy-makers, did not rectify Australia's poor economic performance. Moreover, an indifferent economic response to policy settings, and the problems of restructuring across many industry sectors, tended to cause frequent policy readjustments even within a broad policy orientation towards less protectionism and microeconomic reform. Changing economic circumstances and changing forms of state provision also had an impact on investment patterns and employment levels across various industries with considerable socioeconomic implications.

Frustration and uncertainty appeared to be the norm. As something of a coping strategy, policy-makers reacted to Australia's poor economic performance by switching emphasis from one target economic indicator to another (from job creation to debt levels, to deficits or balance of payments). Federal governments were anxious to demonstrate to business and the electorate that they were in control. Political rhetoric became preoccupied with the economy and with communicating the implications of economic trends in simple terms to a more literate electorate. Finally, the chapter points to the reassertion of political imperatives in guiding economic policy considerations as 'economic rationalist' solutions became discredited and especially as levels of unemployment continued to rise in the deep recession of the early 1990s.

State–economy relations

General arguments about the 'state's capacity' to manage the economy tend to focus on the possibilities and limits of state power relative to the constellation of power relations in the wider economy. The strength and cohesion of interest groups over particular issues or periods can invite or constrain state solutions to problems. Thus, the concept of 'state capacity' attempts to gauge the state's degree of autonomy over other powerful interests in society, and this has allowed analysts to identify 'strong' or 'weak' state capacities over time. The analysis of state capacity also attempts to gauge state administrative resources that can be used to exert influence in ways that correspond with state interests. State capacity is often predicated on institutional cohesion, state centralisation, decisional experience, surviving patterns of policy-making or policy 'legacies' and inherited bureaucratic resources. Some writers see the state exercising long-term 'deliberative capacities', charting directions of socioeconomic development based on perceived obligations or responsibilities. Others have tended to see 'state capacity' as a dimension of political contingency where the scope for state activism changes according to the latitude of 'give' in state–economy relations.[2]

State capacity arguments also presuppose some appreciation of the specific nature of state–economy relations. In particular the state's general influence on the economy can be assessed in a number of different ways. First, the state's quantitative economic impact can be gauged by considering its size, the amount and directions of expenditure allocations, the forms of resource raising, interest on public debt and the size of public sector borrowing.[3] Thus, irrespective of the state's performance in managing economic activity, the state continually exerts significant influence over the economy and patterns of economic activity. The state is by far the largest economic agent within the nation, responsible for taxing, spending and employment. The state serves as a provider of economic and social services and consumes or transfers resources equal to (in Australia) around 40 per cent of gross domestic product.

Second, the internal structure of the state is significant to economic development and the nature of state–economy relations.[4] The federal/ state/local structure of the Australian state produces a diverse mix of institutions, with different roles and value systems and problems of coordination. Key federal agencies, such as Treasury and Finance, set the general parameters within which more specialised agencies conduct policy-making, but there is scope for different approaches and alternative priorities.

Third, patterns of regulatory intervention and customary bureaucratic practices shape industry, sectoral and firm decisions, as do the day-to-day relations between public officials and private sector economic decision-makers. Regulatory reform through bodies such as regulatory review units, together with cultural adjustments within departments, have occurred at federal and state levels.[5]

Fourth, general state policies (including those with less immediate economic orientation such as education, health services, law and order, and safety net policies for social welfare) also have an impact on the economy, imposing longer-term constraints on the economy or influencing levels of economic growth.[6] They also serve to supplement economic services, provide for selected workforce needs, enhance consumption and, to a lesser extent, redistribute income.

Fifth, specific economic policies or interventions (from annual budgets and economic statements to specific industry proposals) intended to guide the economy can be examined and evaluated against performance criteria or their degree of success or failure. Over time this allows us both to explore the changing historical contours of policy settings and to focus on the main turning points of policy.[7]

Sixth, in times of crisis, war or major dislocation the state often extends its previous operational activities, exploiting the greater authority ceded to the state in such times. Statist responses to military or socioeconomic problems generally change the basis on which previous economic relations were premised.[8]

The state exercises various influences over the economy through each of these dimensions irrespective of whether particular economic policy settings are judged to be effective. Hence, the policy responses of particular governments should not be considered in isolation when attempting to assess the state's capacity for economic management.

Economic management before 1983

The role of the Australian state in managing the macroeconomy has changed substantially since the early 1960s. The post-war experience of economic management was a combination of expansionary economics, demand management and regulatory protection. Indeed, in many ways the Australian state built its own form of 'bastard Keynesianism' based on undirected state intervention.[9] Post-war aspirations towards macroeconomic management were derived from the depression-born paradigm of Keynesian economics in which national government action was advocated as a means of 'correcting' levels of economic activity, particularly demand in the private sector.[10] Keynesian theory ascribed national managerial responsibilities to the state, but in practice this often implied a degree of control over the private sector economy not possessed by elected governments or state agencies.[11] Nevertheless, the Australian state continued to aspire to manage the economy even where its policy levers were deficient or where it exercised insufficient power to achieve its intentions. As late as 1982, after years of anti-Keynesian monetarist rhetoric, the Fraser Government still resorted to Keynesian economics in an attempt to break a particularly deep recession. The post-war 'managerial' legacy was therefore difficult to dispel, partly because many sectors within the economy had grown to expect state intervention, and partly because senior managers in state agencies became accustomed to working within the paradigm of national state economic management.[12]

In the Menzies era of the 1950s to the mid 1960s, when economic growth rates were high and markets were available, the 'protective state' assisted key industries through high levels of protection (tariffs, regulation and marketing authorities).[13] Thus, manufacturing protection was intended to secure industries, provide jobs, encourage migration and reduce the need for imports. Such protection became known as McEwenism after John McEwen, the deputy prime minister and trade minister, who was responsible for tariffs and import licences. However, in retrospect these decades have also been regarded as a period of lost opportunities, the so-called 'forgotten years'. While actively protecting industry on the one hand, the state also tended to neglect sustainable economic development and the competitiveness of Australian industry. Economic efficiency or the viability of protected industries was not typically a concern of state policy.[14]

By the 1970s economic problems became more pressing as rising inflation and unemployment (stagflation) both coincided. The state responded with various configurations of crisis management, including abrupt policy changes, selective cuts in public expenditure, attempts to hold or reduce wages and anti-union attacks.[15] Across-the-board tariff cuts of 25 per cent were made in July 1973 by the reformist Labor Government under Whitlam. The Labor Government also attempted to introduce, by referendum, a prices and incomes policy in 1973, but was defeated by a constellation of opponents including the ACTU, the Liberal Party and business associations. After 1975 the Coalition Fraser Government sought to restrain wages (via centralised partial indexation introduced in mid 1975) in the hope of curtailing inflation and creating jobs. Rhetorical commitments to cut aggregate spending were largely unheeded as outlays continued to grow, unemployment numbers rose and tax receipts crept upwards.[16] The Fraser Government's confrontationist approach to industrial relations, together with its contradictory policies leading to the 1982–83 recession, made its economic medicine electorally unpopular. Elected governments were susceptible to economic downturns and the 'certainties' of post-war Keynesian economic management seemed to have evaporated.

By the early 1980s, then, the remains of a 'protectionist consensus' had broken down with the end of the post-war boom and the onset of stagflation. An intense distributional conflict emerged between various sectors of the economy as firms and industries were confronted with profit crises or problematic markets.

Macroeconomic problems and policy responses of the 1980s and early 1990s

Throughout the late 1980s and early 1990s governments have wrestled with the notion that the macroeconomy can be managed. Economic policies increasingly became reactive to economic trends and market indicators that in many areas appeared to be beyond effective state control. Governments, meanwhile, conditioned the electorate (and key markets) to accept bad economic news as inevitable. Crisis management meant manipulating economic messages to prepare different publics to modify their expectations.[17] The state gradually attached considerable significance to 'normalising' adverse economic trends (e.g., persistently high unemployment), so that by the 1990s the state often performed a messenger role rather than that of a decisive manager. This represented a significant historical shift in state–economy relations.

Today the pressures on the economy have changed significantly since the 1960s, and the contours of international trade and economic globalisation have eroded the viability of many sectors of industry. Thus, on top of problems of macroeconomic management have been added problems of structural economic adjustment. The legacy of the forms of protectionism used in Australia all contributed to weakening the economy in the international context and to constraining the private sector's ability to adjust to changing economic conditions. Previous economic structures, rather than consolidating or providing springboards for new economic growth, proved to be major impediments to restructuring. Australia's specialisation in primary production for export, the limited processing of primary products, together with import substitution policies for domestic manufacturing, and a dependent or complacent service sector, tended to limit growth opportunities and produce structural unemployment. Moreover, the insular character of Australian industry did not encourage strategic management and the paucity of managerial talent in both the private and public sectors contributed to the problems of structural adjustment.[18] State policies had to address the problem of how to restructure an economy that was ill-prepared for economic change, especially where sectors were most reliant on direct forms of state intervention. Given the magnitude of adjustment needed, there were no simple or ready solutions to Australia's economic problems.

Economic data indicate the relatively poor performance of the Australian economy during the 1980s and early 1990s. Compared to other OECD nations, Australia's gross domestic product (GDP) per head has fallen substantially since 1970 and is now well below the OECD average.[19] GDP has remained relatively stable, increasing generally by between 2 and 4.5 per cent per annum throughout the 1980s and early 1990s (in constant 1984–85 prices). Only twice did economic growth exceed this range (the post-recession 'catch-up' of 1983–84 with 5 per cent and 1984–85 with 5.1 per cent), while over another two years Australia recorded negative growth (in 1982–83 recording −1.6 % and again in 1990–91 with a decline of −1.1%).[20] Since 1983–84 profitability has remained relatively buoyant (at around 15–16 per cent gross operating surplus) but high corporate debt and high interest rates tended to erode profit rates, limiting new investment or business expansion.[21] The rate of business investment, which had risen throughout the mid 1980s, began to dive after mid 1989 as business firms attempted to reduce debt levels, wind back credit and run down assets and stock. Lower investment in turn resulted in lower demand for domestic goods (especially consumer durables and vehicles). Moreover, if a major aim of structural adjustment policies has been to boost exports, particularly manufactured exports, the results here have also been mixed. Australia's share of manufactured imports into rapidly growing Asian markets has actually fallen since the early 1980s, and the level of manufactured exports as a percentage of all merchandise exports, after collapsing in the mid 1980s, has only recently climbed back to the mediocre levels of the early 1970s.[22]

With the economy making an unsteady recovery after the 1982–83 recession, the Hawke Government generally followed a mild expansionary policy throughout the mid 1980s, based on moderate inflation, employment growth, public sector spending and wage restraints.[23] But the Federal Government increasingly became concerned about the growth of outlays and successively reduced the budget deficit until two years of budget surpluses were recorded at the federal level. In part this disciplined fiscal approach was sustained by increasing tax returns, spending cutbacks, reduced grants to the states and restrictions on public sector borrowings. Moderate economic growth during the mid 1980s led to rising imports, which Treasury economists regarded as evidence of excessive demand. By the late 1980s the economy was overheated. It was generally slow to respond after the stock market crash of October 1987, and some entrepreneurs increasingly searched for speculative gains. The government turned to monetary policy (using rising interest rates and lowering the value of the dollar) to dampen demand. Given the (electorally) limited scope for constraining fiscal policy further by the late 1980s, there was little left in the government's policy tool kit other than relying on a tight monetary policy. In the event, the government imposed a severe monetary policy, which saw interest rates soar to 17–18 per cent in the late 1980s before dropping more than 10 percentage points by January 1992.[24] Government policies during the 1980s were, therefore, a confusing mixture of messages and signals, indicating a concern to stimulate the economy, encourage industry restructuring, hold down inflation, raise growth and dampen demand.

Yet the policy levers used in the 1980s tended to be relatively indirect modifiers of economic activity. For instance, monetary policy is necessarily an indirect and blunt instrument that often does not achieve the desired results. Because monetary policy is indiscriminate in its effects, it has an impact both on those sectors of the economy that governments wish to encourage and those activities to be discouraged; successful firms went under along with the less competitive. Higher interest rates were usually advocated by financiers, economists and bureaucrats who either stood to gain or would not personally suffer from the consequences of the policy.

A further indirect policy tool of the Hawke–Keating Governments known as the Accord was a series of 'voluntary' incomes policies intended to contain labour costs in order to encourage business to invest. In securing industrial peace along with substantial reductions in real wages from the unions, the government hoped for new investment, progress towards economic restructuring and improved business confidence. From the outset of its first term Labor was committed to a centralised wage-fixing system relying on 'bargained consensus' between the government and ACTU leaders as a way of incrementally adjusting wages policy and other industrial relations matters. Initially the government presented 'consensus' (or more accurately consultation) as a political alternative to the divisiveness of the Fraser years.[25] However, despite claims that the voluntary incomes policy would collapse, the Accord became the enduring centrepiece of Labor's economic policies.[26]

Initially there is evidence that some increases in investment occurred, especially as real wages fell in the mid 1980s.[27] But investment levels were fickle and initially in many sectors barely reached the levels of the late 1970s. It soon became apparent that wage levels and industrial relations were not the only factors impeding growth and investment; managerial limitations, lack of vision, a failure to explore new markets and short-term horizons also curtailed investment rates. Hence, while the Accord under various phases (Marks I to VI with VII negotiated just before the 1993 election) was effective in reducing industrial disputes and restraining real wages, it was less effective in enhancing growth, providing full-time employment or redressing structural and generational unemployment (i.e., unemployment affecting one generation after another). In fact while the labour force grew from 6 284 000 in 1980 to 7 727 000 in 1989, much of the job growth occurred in part-time employment (rising from one in seven jobs to one in five by the end of the period).[28] Moreover, increased profits taken in the mid 1980s were often drawn into speculative investments and property markets rather than into long-term productive ventures.

Other regulatory-inspired interventions similar to the Accord were adopted, particularly in the initial years of Labor rule, in relation to specific industry sectors in the form of collaborative 'industry plans'. These 'plans' usually required commitments from industry (firms and unions) in conjunction with a supportive policy framework from government (including some subsidies). During the 1980s the Labor Government extended or negotiated a range of plans with manufacturing sectors including motor vehicles, steel, clothing and textiles, and heavy engineering. Based on planning and consultation, such regulatory policies provided a marked contrast to the general direction of macroeconomic policies affecting other industries. In these other areas, the government adopted a selective deregulation approach where consultation was absent or perfunctory and market-based or 'guided' market policies were pursued. Policy decisions were imposed without 'consensus', often against Labor Party official policy. For instance, a series of decisions to deregulate various industry sectors (such as financial markets, the media, aviation and selected agricultural products) were taken without much consultation with relevant interests or the ACTU.[30] Such policy was 'top-down', emanating from Treasury (often on specialist advice through government reports) and other bodies such as the Industry Commission. Inconsistencies between Accord-style intervention and guided market approaches did not overly worry the government, although the opposition parties and media commentators were occasionally critical, especially from the perception that greater progress could be made in labour market deregulation.[31]

Labor's overall economic strategy during the mid 1980s was to hope for a quick economic upturn while medium-term policies began to have effect and the economy increasingly adjusted to become more internationally competitive. The onset of a second and deeper recession, from about 1989–90 and worsening in the early 1990s, caught the government on the horns of a dilemma: should they simply try to cope with the recession or renew their determination to restructure the economy? Existing economic policies were either not working as expected or were too slow in working. Monetary policy had hurt business and other borrowers without producing the intended results. But the government chose to persevere, maintaining monetary policy for a time while increasingly directing its attention to restructuring the internal cost structures of various industries through microeconomic reform. Since around 1987 Labor's microeconomic agenda has involved targeting for policy attention sectors of the economy (such as transfer or distribution industries) that were fundamental to extending market opportunities and improving the competitiveness of other commodity-based industries. Transport, roads, rail, shipping and aviation were identified as key industries requiring reform, as were the communication areas, including telecommunications, satellite operations and postal services. Other aspects of this agenda consisted of attempts to introduce greater consistency within the federal system between different jurisdictions. A series of premiers' conferences were held during 1990–92 at which directions of microeconomic reform were agreed in principle.[32]

Moreover, in the late 1980s and early 1990s the trade problem and the current account imbalance became increasingly of concern. Because of its commitment to market liberalisation, the government had greatest difficulty with finding room to manoeuvre over trade policy. Domestic policies aimed at reducing barrier protection and creating a so-called 'level playing field' exposed the Australian economy to foreign competition. While export volumes tended to rise, prices generally fell, whereas rises in import volumes were accompanied by rising prices.[33] To counter this, some export incentives were introduced or extended while the Federal Government attempted to gain access to other markets through pressure exerted at international forums, particularly the General Agreement on Tariffs and Trade (GATT). But a growing current account deficit appeared to be the price of policy consistency, and the market-inspired central agencies such as Treasury became the main opponents of a return to import restrictions.

Nevertheless, the depth of the recession of the early 1990s surprised policy-makers. Unemployment continued to increase, peaking at around 12 per cent (or more than a million unemployed in early 1993), industrial production was stagnant, export volumes increased while prices declined, imports were more erratic but were generally considered too high, the current account was permanently in deficit, foreign debt was increasing by around $1.5 billion per month and topped $168 billion by early 1993 (of which around $123 billion or 70 per cent was private sector debt) and investment fell after 1989. Policies intended to restructure the economy were problematic because of the state's relatively weak influence over the direction of investment and became more so perhaps as a result of the withdrawal of selected interventionist strategies. Only the steady decreases in inflation could be perceived as a success, even though the lower levels of inflation were due more to the severe recession and the impact of high interest rates than a direct outcome of deliberate policy initiatives. In short, the Australian economy was reluctant to respond to the policy levers, or policy levers were too indirect to encourage sustained economic commitment.

Limits of policy: Having impact but not necessarily managing

Australia's recent record in macroeconomic management is consequently not impressive. Policies introduced since 1974 have generally been reactive, partial, stop-go and, at times, somewhat arbitrary. Indeed, the increasing focus on microeconomic reforms was in itself an admission that macroeconomic policy had lost considerable effectiveness.[34] Many of the macroeconomic policies have not worked or produced lasting results, and some were tried as a last resort with little knowlege of the likely consequences (e.g., high interest rates in the late 1980s or financial deregulation during the mid 1980s). Fiscal and monetary policy orientations were often counteracted by short-term considerations or by simultaneous contraction and expansionary adjustment. General directions in policy were also contradicted by expedient relaxations (e.g., the Kodak subsidy in 1990 and the 1993 sugar tariff moratorium). Economic policy, in fact, appeared to be a succession of frustrations rather than a means of control.

Underlying broad aggregate indicators, three cases illustrate more precisely the limitations of policy: financial deregulation, tariff reduction and the sudden panic when unemployment levels rose during the recession of the early 1990s.

Financial deregulation

The decisions to float the dollar in 1983 and introduce financial deregulation from 1985 were taken on optimistic economic advice from Treasury (based in part on the reports of two major government inquiries under Campbell and Martin) without sufficiently heeding realistic assessments of the likely outcomes.[35]

The government's policy of deregulation was premised on the assumption that foreign banks would immediately wish to locate in Australia, thereby expanding the amount of capital available for business investment. In addition, other domestic financial institutions (such as building societies) were encouraged to expand their activities and provide capital for commerical purposes. The Commonwealth Treasury assumed that increased competition or at least contestability would trim the profit margins levied by banks and thus reduce the costs of borrowing capital for businesses. However, contrary to Treasury's expectations, foreign banks were not very interested in trading in Australia, and in the domestic financial scramble that occurred after deregulation many institutions lent recklessly to risky commercial ventures or for dubious property speculation.

All of these consequences were predictable and were raised by critics of deregulation from the outset.[36] But such considerations were not adequately addressed or seen as significant in the process of policy formation. Here was a case of state policy-makers not wishing to see, preferring instead to extrapolate outcomes from sterile economic models.

Tariff reduction

In the second case, tariff reductions were progressively announced to give industry a longer-term planning framework.[37] Manufacturing, which had traditionally relied on the 'protective state' to provide barrier protection to limit imports, was given a schedule of reductions over the late 1980s and 1990s.[38] Influential government reports supported this course of action with perhaps the most significant regularly emanating from the Industry Commission along with other specialist investigations such as the Garnaut Report of 1989.[39] The main tenor of this advice was that tariff reduction was a quick way of shaking out the non-performers and inducing a more competitive and export-oriented industrial sector.

However, these projections were based on a fairly positive but naive view of trade and the way international trade markets worked. The policy therefore represented a unilateral commitment to liberalise inward trade without securing similar agreements or access for Australian products from our major trading partners. As imports rose and exports were slow to expand, the 'excessive demand' experienced by the

Australian economy was a logical consequence of reducing tariff barriers. State policy to make manufacturing more competitive allowed cheaper imports into Australian markets, thereby worsening the balance of payments problem, increasing foreign debt and ultimately creating a drastic deflation due to tight monetary policy.

Recession, unemployment and panic

No matter how rhetorically committed to 'economic rationalism' governments have sounded, they have still shown a propensity to hit the panic button when confronted with harsh economic data or if required to salvage political credibility. Thus, when elections fall due governments resort to conventional forms of political expediency offering immediate policy concessions. These electoral cycle adjustment (which seem inconsistent with preceding rationalist orientations) provide not just a short-term 'fix' to the economy but are also intended to restore electoral confidence in the government. More importantly, however, irrespective of election timing, the state has been forced to reassert political interventionism over 'rationalist' economic policy during periods of severe recession. Hence, while market-inspired policy approaches often prevailed during the years 1983–88, political imperatives after 1990 were of greater import. The main reason for this was the post-1989 recession. In short, the government lost its political nerve.

After a phase of rationalism that produced indifferent results and contributed to a prolonged recession, the government gradually began to advocate a more positive role for the state in stimulating economic development. Rather than simply embracing short-term expediency, official policy reflected a partial rehabilitation of neo-Keynesian initiatives. Government became more prepared to spend, to entertain deficit fiscal policy and to use the state actively especially for long-term infrastructural and employment-generating capital works projects.[40]

Yet the expected political spin-off from 'fast-tracking' these projects did not always materialise as many proved very slow to start despite political encouragement. Infrastructural projects in particular tended to require long lead times, meaning that they could not be turned on instantly to provide jobs. Hence, policies tended to see-saw by reacting to market conditions; in practice they risked being too little too late or, because of the lag effect, risked overheating the economy as business cycle conditions improved.

Winners and losers: Sectoral impacts of economic policy

Policy interventions are never neutral in their effects; they allow new winners and losers to emerge within the economy. Policy shifts, even if relatively ineffective, still have the capacity to affect subsequent economic decisions and distributional politics between industries or economic groups. Thus, the state might not be an effective overall manager of the economy but can still have major sectoral impacts (and influence sectoral patterns of investment) via specific policies. A case in point is the mining sector whose cost structures depend on the prices of imports. When it appeared that the government might respond to pressure from the car industry and halt announced tariff cuts, the mining magnate, Sir Arvi Parbo, strenuously opposed any dilution of tariff cuts undertaken for political purposes:[41]

> *I write to express my growing concern about the way in which the controversy on car-industry tariffs is confusing the issues and distracting attention from questions which should be addressed. There has been a broad consensus within business, the political parties, and the community generally in support of a marked reduction or phasing out of tariffs on imports by the end of this century ... Any watering down or postponement of planned tariff cuts will be seen by investors as a weakening of will and loss of commitment to achieving a world competitive economy ... We must stop playing short-term political games, on car tariffs or anything else, and refocus on what really matters. The alternative is that we will continue going downhill as a country.*

The losers were equally predictable. The management of Ford Australia informed their employees in September 1992 through a company memo[42] displayed on the assembly line noticeboards that:

> *At zero tariffs we believe we'll have zero investment. What would be the effect on our balance of payments if we lost our car industry? If all Australian-made cars were replaced by imports, the adverse effect upon the balance of payments would be $5.5 billion. How many jobs would be lost if we lost our car industry? Probably a total of about 60,000 jobs.*

So there is a perception at least that favourable state policies are required to facilitate continued (or new/expanded) investment in industry sectors. Such statements from industry chiefs are not simply a manifestation of the trench warfare of vested interests in which each side seeks partisan adjustments for their own benefit.[43] They are also an acknowledgement that particular investment patterns often depend on longer-term supportive frameworks of state policy as well as on specific commercial considerations.

Government macroeconomic and microeconomic policy settings since the mid 1970s have contributed to very different patterns of investment *between* industry sectors. Gross fixed capital expenditure tripled in the finance and property sector and the mining sector between 1976–77 and

1990–91 ($2.4 to $7.1 billion and $1.1 to $3.8 billion respectively). In wholesale and retail trade and transport and communications investment virtually doubled over the same period ($2.4 to $4.4 billion and $1.1 to $2.1 billion respectively). However, in manufacturing investment rose by only two-thirds from $3.7 billion to $6.1 billion, while in agriculture, forestry and fishing investment levels dropped from $2.5 billion to $2.1 billion.[44] The cuts in the effective rates of assistance to manufacturing (from above 35 per cent in the late 1960s to less than 15 per cent by the early 1990s) seem to have discouraged high levels of investment relative to other industries such as finance and property and mining.[45]

Can the state manage the 'economy'?

Given that there are problems with the effectiveness of macroeconomic policy we come back to the core questions raised at the outset of this chapter: Is there still a role for state management of the economy? How might we judge whether state capacities can be effective in economic management? Did the state have more capacity to manage the economy in the past and is it losing that capacity today? And how have state policy-makers responded in the face of frustrations over the policy directions?

Posing these questions raises the issue of what we might mean by the term *economy*. Should the economy be seen as a national entity, the domestic economy with account taken of imports and exports; or should it include other international considerations (e.g., credit ratings, dollar values, market access)? Does the economy consist of all market transactions, all organisations and individuals involved in buying or selling, supplying or demanding, or does the economy involve just the key industry sectors taken together? Clearly, how we define the economy (whether in aggregate or in sectoral terms) will greatly affect how we see and judge state capacities to manage it. In conventional terms, macroeconomic management tends to view the economy in aggregate, often apprehended in sets of composite economic data such as the gross domestic product. This might not be an appropriate or very useful way of conceiving of state–economy relations in a contemporary policy sense. For instance, the state is not capable of managing the economy in toto and rarely attempts to do so. The state does not 'manage' gross domestic product, and even slight shifts in policy (e.g., higher interest rates) can markedly affect different sectors but add nothing to GDP. Instead, state policies attempt to manage or influence specific components of economic relations (such as wage-setting or interest rates), over which the state has more or less power and over which its influence will fluctuate over time. These components of the economy often cut across entire industry sectors, with the effect of either improving or worsening conditions of production. Over some components of the economy the state will exercise statutory authority (e.g., specific regulations), over others its size and operations will be a determining factor (e.g., government contracts) and in other areas the state's collective presence or persuasive powers will prove influential (e.g., in setting the exchange rates for the dollar).

One of the main ways in which the state has attempted to cope with the complexity of economic management during the 1970s and 1980s is to focus on specific indicators or targets. This is a less ambitious objective than attempting to manage and restructure the entire economy. Government, state agencies and market spokespeople tend to identify surrogate indicators and preferred trends against which macroeconomic policy can be judged. Attention might focus on government spending, public sector borrowing, foreign debt or the balance of trade, and each indicator assumes a dominant importance until it is met or superseded. Such indicators provide prisms through which governments and policy operators can assess their specific policy adjustments, on occasions even influencing general public sector activities (as with concerns about excessive public sector borrowing). Thus, during the 1970s and 1980s, federal governments addressed a succession of indicators, often for relatively short periods. In the late 1970s 'inflation-first' strategies were in vogue, followed by campaigns to reduce the size of the state.[46] In 1984 Labor identified a 'trilogy' of fiscal commitments (not increasing taxes, expenditure or borrowings as a percentage of GDP), but this approach gave way to an explicit preoccupation with the size of the federal deficit.[47] Once surplus budgets were achieved attention swung to interest rates, escalating foreign debt levels, the declining value of the dollar, then the balance of payments problem and eventually unemployment. Such forms of crisis management required continual policy modification and flexibility, often accompanied by policy somersaults in which short-term considerations prevailed.

In this context, the Commonwealth's annual August budget has become an inadequate means of responding rapidly to changing economic trends. Increasingly, governments have relied on mini budgets and economic statements to announce adjustments to policy. Some of these statements, like the 1987 May economic statement, *Building a Competitive Australia* (1991), *One Nation* (1992) and *One Nation Mark II* (1993), were presented at the time as essential adjustments needed to tackle selected problems and key indicators, even though they were quickly displaced by subsequent statements according to political expediency.[48]

Increasingly, it seems, markets have emerged as a more potent force impeding the state's capacity to manage. With increased global integration, markets have tended to overrule declared policy objectives. Although socially created, markets tends to operate according to their own internal logic and might be responsive or unresponsive to policy changes or operate in predictable or unexpected ways because of prevailing norms. The state can devise seemingly sound policy only to find it undermined by 'imperfect' markets (displaying perhaps any number of distorting characteristics such as oversupply, speculation, vertical integration, price-fixing, power imbalances, insufficient or wrong information, environmental considerations, 'externalities' or decisions taken on corporate whim). Thus, market mechanisms and the economic power of the private sector can severely limit the scope for state policy-making over economic matters, and this factor seems to have become more apparent in recent decades.[49] As a consequence, the state has often found it necessary to manage through second-best policy options. This is not because state managers lack experience or are totally devoid of ideas about appropriate policies (for instance, an investment drive to create employment or increased export growth to redress trade problems). Rather, the state often lacks the power to tackle problems directly. Examples include the above-mentioned ALP–ACTU Accord (which to encourage investment focused on restraining wages) or the reduction in tariffs on manufacturing (which was intended as a means of inducing competitiveness). State economic policies, therefore, tend to be shaped by institutional considerations and opportunities — the possibilities of implementation, policy legacies and administrative resources — not potential effectiveness.

Other limits to the effectiveness of macroeconomic policy derive from the long-standing structural constraints on the state itself.[50] The configuration of state agencies with responsibilities for the economy disaggregate policy approaches and create problems of coordination. But given the uneven track record of central agency policy settings, such disaggregation might not necessarily be a bad thing, allowing different policy frameworks to develop according to the different industry pressures (for instance, the split between the Treasury and the Department of Industry, Trade and Regional Development (DITARD) over industry policy). In a federalist state like Australia, national economic policies also continually face the prospect of being countered by State Government actions. Provincial states often pursue parochial economic concerns, which from a national viewpoint might be both ineffective and inefficient. Such regionally based parochialism contributes to the geographic spread of industries, often involving low economies of scale, insufficient clustering, counterproductive competition for investment or surplus production maintained under state-protected marketing regimes. State Governments often seek to relocate firms within their regions, adding to the problems of national coordination and planning for industries.

Recognising the difficulties of macroeconomic management, some state agencies have adopted seemingly coherent economic ideologies as a means of making policy choices.[51] Such ideological perspectives do not necessarily enhance the state's capacity for economic management but will shape the types of policy advanced by state managers and influence which groups are winners or losers. For example, during the 1980s economic rationalism significantly shaped the policy choices of the Hawke and Keating Governments.[52] The economic rationalism of this period was a market-inspired set of assumptions often reduced to abstract principles, which did not acknowledge the high social costs associated with policy recommendations. Moreover, professional economists tended not to recognise that their models often did not fit the particular institutional arrangements in Australia or that they were dealing with the lives of real people. The resulting microeconomic policies tended to become determined less by sectoral or democratic preferences than by the influence of prevailing economic ideologies.

Some institutions within the state were more susceptible to capture by economic rationalists than others.[53] While some agencies (e.g., in industrial relations or DITARD) maintained relative continuity in policy orientations, 'rationalist' economic ministers rose to the fore (including Keating, Walsh, Willis and at times Dawkins), and a new economically literate Senior Executive Service was formed in the higher echelons of the public sector.[54] Persistent economic problems and the financial constraints on the state encouraged many other state agencies to follow a more economic rationalist line, including the federal Treasury, the Reserve Bank, departments like Transport and Communications, Finance, Employment, Education and Training, Prime Minister and Cabinet, plus other influential agencies such as the Industry Commission and to a lesser extent the Bureau of Industry Economics. The managers of public trading enterprises also tended to embrace economic rationalist and commercial thinking as a means of 'liberating' their agencies from government controls and public service norms.

Furthermore, both major political parties tended to drift towards economic rationalism over the 1980s and early 1990s, generating bipartisan support on major policy issues. In general there was normative agreement over a less interventionist role for the state and over the means of economic restructuring. There were disagreements over some priorities and over the extent or speed of reforms, but generally the policy approach adopted by the Labor Government was broadly in line with that proposed by the conservative opposition. Hence, while both agreed in principle to dismantle protectionism, there were still disagreements over whether tariffs should eventually be abolished altogether, with the Liberals preferring close to zero by the turn of the century while Labor opted for retaining some tariff protection (e.g., 25 per cent for imported clothing and 15 per cent for motor vehicles and a general tariff of 5 per cent).[55] Given broad bipartisan agreement, opposition to the economic rationalist strategy had to emerge from extra-parliamentary sources (excepting the Australian Democrats and the occasional Labor or National Party dissident). These opponents included the ACTU and disillusioned unions, some tripartite industry bodies (such as the Australian Manufacturing Council), environmental bodies, charity and religious leaders and ad hoc pressure groups formed to address economic issues such as excessive interest rates on house mortgages).[56]

The achievements of macroeconomic management were probably easier to sell in the past than in recent years. But the credibility of governments is still forged by how well they appear to be managing the economy. With an increasingly economically educated electorate, political leaders have found it more convenient to condition the audience than try to control the economy. During the 1980s they began in earnest to educate Australians about the economy and the inevitable consequences of economic trends. Governments modified expectations via preparatory warnings (such as that unemployment or interest rates will rise, debt will continue to grow or the balance of payments will worsen); in effect talking authoritatively about trends while not having much success often in influencing them. Governments successfully presented rising levels of unemployment as unfortunate but 'acceptable'; so that, in the early 1970s, 2 per cent unemployment was high, by the mid 1970s 5 per cent was acceptable, while for the late 1980s and 1990s, 10 per cent or above has seemingly become the 'norm'. A contemporary role for the state, therefore, became to communicate unpleasant news sufficiently ahead of time to allow expectations to be adjusted. This strategy was intended to translate the complexities of economic phenomena into language and imagery that ordinary Australians could understand — so that unpleasant economic news was at least greeted with tacit acceptance.[57]

Accordingly, government policy became tinged with economic fatalism; if macroeconomic policy-making was increasingly problematic then it was less politically damaging if people were resigned to their fate. Moreover, given bipartisan agreement over the direction of policy (and a cynical electorate with little confidence in either side), there were attempts, particularly by Labor, to distract attention from the economy as the political battleground for electoral politics. Thus, the Labor Government successfully resorted to royalty, Britain's conduct in World War II, republicanism, the Australian flag and the national anthem to shore up political support and provide alternative copy for a grateful media receptive to stories not about economics.

Conclusions

From the early 1970s the Australian state has struggled to retain its grip on the macroeconomy as a combination of external pressures and internal impediments came together to retard growth rates and our trade position significantly. Yet since that time, after intense policy interest in macroeconomic management, evidence suggests that the state appears no closer to retaining its grip or solving the major structural problems of the economy. In the final decade of the twentieth century, the management of the macroeconomy seems generally beyond state capacities.

Economic policies have rarely met with unambiguous success, and poor results from policy have been legion. In part the state's policy frustrations have been caused by limitations arising from the changing nature of state–economy relations after the post-war 'long boom', global pressures for increased competitiveness, trade 'liberalisation' and different norms of state intervention. The state's capacity to manage selected components of the economy is itself premised on the power relations within the economy operating at international, national and sectoral levels. The nature and extent of private sector power serves as the reciprocal dimension of state capacities. And in peripheral capitalist economies like Australia, the state has historically tended to operate with relatively limited capacities to shape macroeconomic developments.

However, a history of policy frustration does not necessarily entail an absence of state capacity. In the past, state preferences concerning the structure of the economy were significant in shaping at least some industry profiles. Both protectionist politics and Keynesian economics lent credence to the notion that active state interventionism was a necessary and successful means of 'managing' the economy, and some have interpreted this as 'nation-building'.[58] Today the dynamics of state–economy relations are dominated by serial attempts by the state to make and remake economic policies more out of frustration than a clear sense of purpose. State policy has sought to guide markets by establishing less overtly regulatory frameworks within which markets operate. State policy-makers have in many ways dispensed with the notion of a 'national' economy and with the idea that a Keynesian central government could effectively manage nation state economies. Indeed, most state policy-makers now content themselves with addressing the consequences of economic decisions taken outside the state. And state macroeconomic policies have become as much about reconciling expectations as about steering the economy.

Nevertheless, political decision-makers necessarily remain preoccupied with economic problems; the economy cannot be ignored even if the forms of state action and policy approaches have changed. Business cycles and electoral cycles ensure that the economy remains a key political matter. Government performance in economic policy still serves as a major criterion of overall performance evaluation and credibility. Business is ever cognisant of a particular government's ability to work within an accepted set of economic expectations. Thus, the drive for credibility obliges governments to reinvent economic policy continually and adjust policy settings continually, even invest in the pretence of economic management; and all to sustain segmentalised business confidence. The state's management of the economy appears to be a Sisyphean task, endlessly rolling the policy stone but not necessarily achieving sustained progress up the hill.

Notes

1 See M. Stutchbury (1990), 'Macroeconomic policy' in C. Jennett and R. Stewart (eds), *Hawke and Australian Public Policy*, Macmillan, Melbourne; M. Keating and G. Dixon (1989), *Making Economic Policy in Australia*, Longman Cheshire, Melbourne; K. Davis (1989), 'Managing the economy' in B. Head and A. Patience (eds), *From Fraser to Hawke*, Longman Cheshire, Melbourne; Indecs (1990), *State of Play 6*, Allen & Unwin, Sydney; and D. Clarke (various dates), *Student Economic Briefs*, Fairfax, Sydney.

2 For general arguments about state capacities see E. Nordlinger (1981), *On the Autonomy of the Democratic State*, Harvard University Press, Cambridge, Mass.; P. Evans, D. Rueschemeyer and T. Skocpol (eds) (1985), *Bringing the State Back In*, Cambridge University Press, New York (especially chapters 1, 2, 4 and 11); G. Almond, E. Nordlinger, T. Lowi and S. Fabbrini (1988), 'The return to the state (and critiques)', *American Political Science Review*, 82:3, 853–901; S. Krasner (1984), 'Approaches to the state', *Comparative Politics*, 16, 223–46; T. Mitchell (1991), 'The limits of the state: Beyond statist approaches and their critics', *American Political Science Review*, 85:1, 77–98. For Australian studies operating from within a state capacity tradition see M. Pusey (1991), *Economic Rationalism in Canberra*, Cambridge University Press, Melbourne; and A. Capling and B. Galligan (1992), *Beyond the Protective State*, Cambridge, Melbourne. A more contingency-based approach is S. Bell (1993), *Australian Manufacturing and the State: The Politics of Industry Policy in the Post-War Era*, Cambridge, Melbourne.

3 For an accessible account of the issues see G. Dow (1992), 'The economic consequences of economists', *Australian Journal of Political Science*, 27:2, 258–81; H. Emy and O. Hughes (1991), *Australian Politics: Realities in Conflict*, 2nd ed., Macmillan, Melbourne.

4 Representative studies in this area include: B. Head (ed.) (1986), *The Politics of Development in Australia*, Allen & Unwin, Sydney; M. Wood et al. (eds) (1989), *Governing Federations: Constitution, Politics, Resources*, Hale & Iremonger, Sydney; A. Peachment (ed.) (1991), *The Business of Government: Western Australia 1983–1990*, Federation Press, Adelaide; S. Bennett (1992), *Affairs of State: Politics in the Australian States and Territories*, Allen & Unwin, Sydney; P. Drake and J. Nieuwenhuysen (1988), *Economic Growth for Australia: Agenda for Action*, Oxford University Press, Melbourne; J. Warhurst (1982), *Jobs or Dogma?*, University of Queensland Press, St Lucia; G. Whitwell (1986), *The Treasury Line*, Allen & Unwin, Sydney.

5 L. Zines (1990), 'Federal power to regulate economic matters', *Publius*, 20:4. On regulatory reform see C. Coady and C. Sampford (1993), *Business, Ethics and the Law*, Federation Press, Adelaide; B. Head and E. McCoy (eds) (1991), *Deregulation or Better Regulation*, Macmillan, Melbourne (especially chapters 1, 2 and 16).

6 See F. Castles (ed.) (1991), *Australia Compared: People, Policies and Politics*, Allen & Unwin, Sydney; R. Kennedy (ed.) (1989), *Australian Welfare*, Macmillan, Melbourne.
7 See M. Stutchbury (1990); also C. Walsh (1991), 'The national economy and management strategies', in B. Galligan and G. Singleton (eds), *Business and Government Under Labor*, Longman Cheshire, Melbourne; F. Castles (1988), *Australian Public Policy and Economic Vulnerability*, Allen & Unwin, Sydney.
8 See F. Block (1977), 'The ruling class does not rule: Notes on the Marxist theory of the state', *Socialist Revolution*, 7:3, 6–28; a general introduction is P. Dunleavy and B. O'Leary (1987), *Theories of the State*, Macmillan, London; on Australia see R. Catley and B. McFarlane (1983), *Australian Capitalism in Boom and Depression*, Alternative Publishing Cooperative, Chippendale.
9 G. Whitwell (1986); M. Pusey (1991). For a recent selection of views see G. Hooke and R. Reilly (eds) (1991), *Macroeconomic Policy*, Allen & Unwin, Sydney.
10 G. Whitwell (1986) and chapter 4 of this book.
11 P. Hall (1986), *Governing the Economy*, Polity Press, Cambridge; W. Grant and S. Nath (1984), *The Politics of Economic Policymaking*, Basil Blackwell, Oxford.
12 M. Keating and G. Dixon (1989); H. Coombs (1982), 'Economic change and political strategy', *Social Alternatives*, 2:4, 12–18.
13 L. Glezer (1982), *Tariff Politics*, Melbourne University Press, Melbourne; J. Warhurst (1982); A. Capling and B. Galligan (1992); S. Bell (1993).
14 K. Anderson and R. Garnaut (1987), *Australian Protectionism: Extent, Causes and Effects*, Allen & Unwin, Sydney; S. Bell (1993), chapter 2.
15 On the state's general responses to crisis management see C. Offe (1984), *Contradictions of the Welfare State*, Hutchinson, London.
16 On the political economy of Fraserism, see A. Patience and B. Head (eds) (1979), *From Whitlam to Fraser*, Oxford University Press, Melbourne.
17 For details of the 1987 mini budget, see D. Clarke (1987), *Student Economic Briefs 1987/8*, Fairfax, Sydney.
18 On the conservatism and lack of managerial talent in Australia, see Department of Industrial Relations (1991), *Industrial Relations at Work*, AGPS, Canberra.
19 OECD (1992), *Australia: Economic Survey*, Paris, p. 57. In relation to the OECD's index of GDP per head (average=100), Australia dropped from 101 in 1970 to 94 in 1990 (well below average). Japan over the same period increased from 81 to 104, while Germany (remaining steady on 108) and France (rising from 102 to 103) were relatively unchanged but above average. Like Australia, the USA also fell during the period (from 136 to 126) but remained well above average.
20 ABS, *Australian National Accounts*, Catalogue Number 5206.0 (1984–85 prices).
21 OECD (1992), p. 14–15.
22 Australia (1992), *Budget Papers, No 1, 1992–93*, AGPS, Canberra (see also OECD (1992), pp. 13–14). On our export performance, see D. O'Reily (1993), 'The revolution that wasn't', *Australian Business Monthly*, April.
23 OECD (1985), *Australia: Economic Survey 1985*, OECD, Paris.

24 OECD (1992), pp. 30–33.
25 On the contrast between Fraser's economic management and that of the Hawke–Keating Government, see K. Davis (1989), 'Managing the economy' in B. Head and A. Patience (eds), *From Fraser to Hawke*, Longman Cheshire, Melbourne.
26 An early assessment of the Accord is ACTU (1986), *Accord Update '86*, TUTA, Albury Wodonga, 1986. See also D. McEachern (1991), *Business Mates: The Power and Politics of the Hawke Era*, Prentice Hall, Sydney; G. Singleton (1990), *The Accord and the Australian Labour Movement*, MUP, Melbourne; M. Gardner (1990), 'Wage policy', in C. Jennet and R. Stewart (eds).
27 OECD (1992), *Australia: Economic Survey*, OECD, Paris, p. 14.
28 ABS (various dates), *The Labour Force, Australia*, Catalogue No. 6203.0.
29 On industry plans see R. Stewart (1990), 'Industry policy', in C. Jennet and R. Stewart (eds); A. Capling and B. Galligan (1992); and E. Jones (1993), 'The heavy engineering adjustment and development program', *Australian Journal of Public Administration*, 52:1, 40–53.
30 Critical assessments of financial deregulation include M. Suich (1991), 'Bankruptured', *Independent Monthly*, May and K. Davidson (1992), 'The failures of financial deregulation in Australia', in S. Bell and J. Wanna (eds), *Business–Government Relations in Australia*, Harcourt Brace Jovanovich, Marrickville.
31 For example, K. West (1984), *The Revolution in Australian Politics*, Penguin, Ringwood.
32 The waterfront reform was regarded by the government as one of the major achievements of microeconomic reform in this period; see Australia, Report of the House of Representatives Standing Committee on Transport, Communications and Infrastructure (1992), *Efficiency of the Interface Between Seaports and Land Transport: Wharehouse to Wharf*, AGPS, Canberra. For a sanguine view of the special premiers conferences see B. Galligan (1993), 'Which way Australian federalism', paper to the Public Policy Network Conference—Policymaking in Volatile Times, University of Southern Queensland, Toowoomba, January.
33 OECD (1992), p. 25. See generally H. Emy and O. Hughes (1991), *Australian Politics: Realities in Conflict*, 2nd ed., Macmillan, Melbourne, chapter 2.
34 Thus, business was active in reflecting their concerns (see M. Howard (1989), 'A big business "line" on the public sector?', Public Sector Research Centre Discussion Paper No. 2, UNSW, September) while governments paid greater attention to microeconomic management; see G. Banks (1990), 'Economic gains from improved government "management" of the microeconomy', paper to Centre for Australian Public Sector Management Conference, Improving Public Sector Management, Griffith University, July. The Industry Commission has persistently reaffirmed its commitment to further microeconomic reform; see Industry Commission (1992), *Annual Report 1991–92*, AGPS, Canberra.
35 Major governmental reports included the Campbell Report (1981) and the subsequent Martin Report (1984); see Australian Financial System Inquiry (1981), *Final Report*, AGPS, Canberra and Australian Financial System (1984), *Report of the Review Group*, AGPS, Canberra.

36 Warnings of the consequences of financial deregulation included OECD (1985), *Australia: Economic Survey*, OECD, Paris; cf also M. Hall (1987), *Financial Deregulation: A Comparative Study of Australia and the UK*, Macmillan, London. For alternative strategies see ACTU/TDC (1987), *Australian Reconstructed*, ACTU, Melbourne.

37 DITAC (1991), *Annual Report 1990–91: Building a Competitive Australia*, AGPS, Canberra.

38 A revised tariff schedule was announced by Senator J. Button (1991), 'Statement by the Minister for Industry, Technology and Commerce', in R. J. Hawke et al., *Building a Competitive Australia* (Ministerial Statements by the Prime Minister, Treasurer and Industry Minister), AGPS, Canberra.

39 R. Garnaut (1989), *Australia and the Northeast Asian Ascendancy*, AGPS, Canberra; R. Garnaut (1991), 'The end of protection and the beginnings of a modern industrial economy: Australia in the 1990s', *Australian Quarterly*, 63:1, 15–23.

40 Some $2.3 billion was promised under the *One Nation* package and around $800 million on city infrastructure; see P. Keating (1992), *One Nation*, AGPS, Canberra; and B. Howe (1991), *Building Better Cities Program*, AGPS, Canberra.

41 Letter to the editor of the *Australian Financial Review* (1992), 29 September, p. 17.

42 See *Australian* (1992), 19–20 September, p. 1.

43 M. Olson (1982), *The Rise and Decline of Nations*, Yale University Press, New Haven.

44 ABS (1992), *Australian National Accounts: Estimates of Capital Stock*, Cat. No. 5221.0.

45 Pappas, Carter, Evans, Koop/Telesis (1990), *The Global Challenge: Australian Manufacturing in the 1990s*, AMC, Melbourne.

46 A. Patience and B. Head (eds) (1979) and B. Head and A. Patience (eds) (1989), *From Fraser to Hawke*, Longman Cheshire, Melbourne.

47 See M. Stutchbury (1990) in C. Jennett and R. Stewart (eds).

48 D. Clarke (1987), pp. 22–4; R. J. Hawke et al. (1991), *Building a Competitive Australia*; P. Keating (1992), *One Nation*, AGPS, Canberra. Such patterns of political adjustment or indecisiveness could be seen as evidence that state managers seem to be losing control of the economy compared to the 1950s — and, indeed, that the statements increasingly appear reconciled to this fact. However, not all commentators have drawn the same conclusions from this development. For example, M. Pusey (1991) considers that the Australian state has lost control of the economy because the modern state has 'changed its mind' and is now pursuing 'anti-social' economic policies. The post-war reconstruction state guided by Keynesian economists, he argued, maintained a balance between economic policy and social responsibility, and in doing so preserved state integrity. The 'economic rationalist' state, in his view, not only surrendered control of the macroeconomy but also abrogated its social responsibilities allowing distributional issues to be determined by the vagaries of the market. While there has certainly been a change of emphasis in state activity, this view overlooks the mediation of politics on economic policy. Seemingly 'rationalist' state managers may respond periodically to economic exigencies, but political imperatives have been the major driving force

behind the pattern of adjustments in economic policy even during the 1980s.
49 C. Lindblom (1977), *Politics and Markets*, Basic Books, New York; P. Hall (1986), *Governing the Economy*, Polity Press, Cambridge.
50 EPAC (1990), *The Size and Efficiency of the Public Sector*, Council Paper No. 44, EPAC, AGPS, Canberra.
51 L. Whitehead (1990), 'Political explanations of macroeconomic management: A survey', *World Development*, 18:8, 1133–46. States have turned to professional economists for policy advice precisely because they are prepared to quantify trends, make calculated predictions and give governments detailed forecasts. Their credibility rests not so much on successful outcomes/predictions as on the assuredness derived from their models.
52 B. Head (1988), 'The Labor Government and "economic" rationalism', *Australian Quarterly*, 60:4, 466–77; R. Gerritsen and G. Singleton (1991), 'Evaluating the Hawke Government's industry agenda: Democratic economic planning versus economic rationalism?', in B. Galligan and G. Singleton (eds), *Business and Government Under Labor*, Longman Cheshire, Melbourne. For a collection of critiques see J. Carroll and R. Manne (eds) (1992), *Shutdown: The Failure of Economic Rationalism and How to Rescue Australia*, Text Publishing, Melbourne.
53 M. Pusey (1991).
54 Not all these economic rationalist state managers necessarily agreed on politics or policy orientations. On the basis of Pusey's evidence, state managers were far from being in agreement as indicated in their responses to a range of questions about the economy, such as labour market deregulation, the distribution of resources, the power of trade unions or the relationship between capital and labour. Economically literate state managers were not inevitably right-wing, anti-state or anti-social (although some clearly were). They were likely to approach problems from similar economic assumptions, methodological approaches and sets of concerns—but such orientations did not inherently prescribe their ideological stance.
55 ALP (1992), *Poles Apart: Australia's Future—It's Your Choice*, ALP, Barton, ACT.
56 Pappas, Carter, Evans, Koop/Telesis (1990).
57 Perhaps the most proficient communicator of economic jargon into everyday parlance was Paul Keating, federal Treasurer from 1983 to 1991 and Prime Minister after December 1991. Keating's political talent lay in the semiotics of economic policy, encapsulating developments or policy intentions in pithy and memorable phrases (usually repeating them until they stuck in the popular consciousness). Keating continually referred to the economy as the 'main game', principally in order to maintain fiscal constraints and internal discipline in the government and Labor Party. During the 1980s Australians were treated to a litany of economic catch-phrases, many of which resonated with the public. When the government's policies were not working Australia was in danger of becoming a 'banana republic' or going down the 'Argentinian road' (as Peter Walsh, the former Finance Minister, added). The 'world's greatest Treasurer' was concerned to 'bring home the bacon', keep us focused on the 'main game' and, after the speculative booms of the mid 1980s, ensure that the economy came down with a 'soft landing'. As the recession of the early 1990s lengthened, Keating likened Australia's position to 'surfing in

on a weak wave' (not much of a wave and with lots of paddling to do). Not all Keating's populist translations, however, were positively perceived; his most famous remark—that the post-1989 slump was 'the recession we had to have'—stayed around to haunt him and was used by political opponents as an admission of failure. See M. Gordon (1993), *A Question of Leadership*, UQP, St Lucia (especially chapter 5). For an alternative assessment see H. Emy (1990), 'Economic development versus political development: Another view of the "main game" in Australia', in H. Emy and A. Linklater (eds), *New Horizons in Politics*, Allen & Unwin, Sydney.

58 M. Pusey (1991) and A. Capling and B. Galligan (1992).

10

State strength and state weakness: Manufacturing industry and the post-war Australian state

Stephen Bell[1]

In some ways it is a relatively straightforward task to construct a broad historical picture of the evolution of post-war federal manufacturing industry policy. Essentially, there has been a major shift in focus from an insular, inward-looking industry strategy based on a highly protected domestic market to what is now virtually a 'post-protectionist' strategy aimed at exposing local industry to international market pressures. Restructuring and boosting the competitiveness of Australia's cosseted and ramshackle manufacturing sector in the face of mounting trade imbalances has been the aim.

Yet this is but one possible (and purely descriptive) characterisation of the process as a whole; one that focuses only on policy instruments and policy aims. This chapter suggests that such an overt focus on policy does not really go far enough in uncovering more enduring and more critical aspects of the state's role in industry. Indeed, the key dynamics of industry–state relations often do not boil down to *which* particular policies are used but *how* they are used. For example, in the post-war period, protectionist policies were used in both Japan and Australia. But the way they were used was very different. In Japan, protectionism formed part of a coherent industrial strategy aimed at international competitiveness.[2] This did not happen in Australia. Indeed, for much of the post-war era, industry competitiveness was not really an issue in this country. In both countries, then, similar policy instruments were handled in different ways, and certainly in Japan a relatively hands-on, interventionist policy style, involving a substantial emphasis on policy coherence and purposefulness, was apparent.

Thus, beyond the choice of policy instruments, three broad aspects are critical in defining the state's industrial role. The first is the degree of coherence, coordination and purposefulness the state imparts to its policy role. The second is the state's autonomy; that is, its capacity to confront opposition and press ahead with policy initiatives. The third is the state's degree of intrusiveness or its willingness and capacity to play a detailed role in the affairs of industry. These aspects of the state's industrial role — state coherence, state autonomy and state intrusiveness — are used in this chapter to characterise and analyse the Australian state's industrial role.

My purpose, then, is to abstract from the details of policy in order to characterise more broadly Australia's pattern of post-war industry policy and the changing pattern of industry–state relations. This is a useful task for the purposes of comparative analysis. A clearer aggregate-level view of industry policy and of the apparent limits and possibilities of state action in the Australian context is also useful for developing evaluative and prescriptive arguments about what is desirable and politically feasible for Australia's industry policy. The analytical tools to be used here draw on Atkinson and Coleman's distinction between 'reactive' and 'anticipatory' industry policy regimes, on Zysman's so-called state-led, tripartite-negotiated and company-led models of industrial adjustment, and on the comparative literature dealing with state strength and state weakness.[3]

In their own study of Canada (a country featuring a federal parliamentary political structure and a commodities economy similar to Australia), Atkinson and Coleman conclude that 'Canadian industrial policy corresponds almost entirely to the reactive model'.[4] This chapter argues that the same straightforward conclusion cannot be derived for Australia. The content of Australian industry policy has changed significantly over time and, furthermore, even in terms of more fundamental properties of industry policy and state action, there has been a mixing of elements, which has produced variable combinations of reactive and anticipatory industry policy forms, as well as variable combinations of Zysman's three models of industry adjustment, particularly the company-led forms and, in some cases, versions of the state-led form.

Yet beneath the surface ambiguity it is possible to discern some underlying patterns. It will be argued that, overall, Australia has moved during the post-war era from a reactive model to a weak version of the anticipatory model. This reflects underlying dynamics of state action in the Australian context which, throughout, have stressed the autonomy of the firm, producing something like a state-supported model of company-led adjustment. More recently, especially since the early 1980s, the level of state assertiveness has increased to produce something like a state-cajoled model of company-led adjustment. Despite such bouts of state assertiveness, however, it is argued that the Australian state displays more characteristics of so-called state weakness than strength. Indeed, it is suggested that Australia does not have the right kind of state or industrial culture to be able to mount a full-blown anticipatory or state-led industry policy.

Reactive and anticipatory industry policy, weak states and strong states

Comparative research on industry policy shows that all of the advanced industrial economies deploy a wide range of industry policy instruments. On some assessments, even nominally 'non-interventionist' countries such as the United States have active and wide-ranging industry policies.[5] But if all countries engage in industry policy, there is also a wide diversity of policy goals, of policy instruments and of ways of assembling and administering these instruments. There is also wide variation in the relative activism and intrusiveness of the state in the process of industrial change. In the face of such complexity, Atkinson and Coleman's models of reactive and anticipatory industry policy provide a useful way of categorising and analysing national styles of industry policy as idealtypes. The same applies to Zysman's models of industrial adjustment. Such typologies are useful for heuristic purposes. We should not necessarily expect to find pristine examples of such policy typologies in the real world, and often industry policy strategies at times involve some blending or variation of the constituent elements of these typologies.

There are three broad dimensions of industry policy that Atkinson and Coleman use to build their typology: policy objectives, state intrusiveness and policy integration.

Policy objectives
Policies that aim to protect or insulate industry from the need to adjust or attempt to shield industry from competitive pressures are categorised as reactive in nature. On the other hand, policies that aim to promote change in industry and to help adapt industry to emerging competitive pressures are categorised as anticipatory in nature. Atkinson and Coleman argue, however, that in most cases industry policy will involve both elements. Thus, even aggressively anticipatory policy styles can involve reactive elements designed to soften the immediate impact of adjustment pressures. Similarly, a policy stance that emphasises reactive protection can also include elements that aim to help industry to adjust

eventually to new competitive pressures. In both cases, the issue of how to characterise the overall policy stance—in terms of the reactive or anticipatory models—depends on which *overall* policy objective is stressed.

State intrusiveness

The second dimension of Atkinson and Coleman's typology is the degree of *state intrusiveness* in the industry policy process and in the broader pattern of industrial change. Here, the reactive policy style insists on an arms-length relationship with industry and on a narrow rationale for intervention based on strict cases of market failure. Such a mode of intervention respects the autonomy of firms and management prerogatives. In this sense, the reactive model accords with Zysman's model of the 'company-led' process of industrial adjustment.[6] Given the stress on the private, autonomous character of industrial firms, the reactive model eschews the notion of active state selectivity between industry projects and insists instead on the use of broad-based, industry-neutral policies aimed at what Atkinson and Coleman refer to as 'environmental intervention'.

Anticipatory approaches, on the other hand, insist on a more fine-grained and intrusive state role aimed at 'structural intervention'. Here the rationale for intervention is based on a more sceptical assessment of the market's ability to promote national goals. Typically, policy-makers have a clear view of where the economy should be going in structural terms and are prepared to intervene with selective or targeted measures to assist what are considered to be strategically important industries or directions for industrial change. The process of industrial adjustment in this model accords with Zysman's model of 'state-led' adjustment, which explicitly 'politicises and centralises the process of industrial change'. It also broadly accords with Zysman's model of 'tripartite-negotiated' adjustment, which 'involves an explicit and continuing negotiation of the terms of industrial change by the predominant social partners'.[7]

'In either case', Atkinson and Coleman argue, 'structural intervention presumes a considerable degree of technical expertise and a set of political institutions capable of engineering the necessary degree of consensus.'[8]

Policy integration

The third and final dimension of Atkinson and Coleman's typology is the degree of *policy integration*. Reactive industry policy, as the name implies, is typically constructed through a series of ad hoc responses to particular crises or challenges; particularly those that become electorally relevant. This patchwork approach tends to produce a policy pattern with little overall coherence or integration, and often there is little attempt or little in the way of administrative capacity to assess how the various arms of policy fit together.

The anticipatory model, on the other hand, places particular emphasis on the coordination of policy responses according to an overall planned framework for the industry policy process as a whole. Such an approach presumes a well-developed bureaucratic apparatus possessing considerable information resources and technical skills for monitoring industry developments. It presumes a relatively autonomous state not the captive of industry interests. It also presumes the presence of some kind of centre to the political or bureaucratic apparatus which is able to plan authoritatively and coordinate myriad industry interventions according to an overall policy agenda.

Weak and strong states

These industry policy categories resonate with another method of characterising national styles of industry policy and industry–state relationships: namely the distinction made between so-called 'weak' states and 'strong' states. Indeed, for writers such as Krasner, the 'defining feature of a political system is the *power* of the state in relation to its own society'.[9] This kind of 'statist' approach marks a departure from earlier pluralist and Marxist formulations, which tended to see the state largely reflecting societal demands or as wholly constrained by the imperatives of a capitalist economy. For statist writers, the state itself, particularly its variable forms of structure and organisation, become an important focus for analysis in characterising, assessing or explaining state–economy relationships.

According to the weak state/strong state framework, state strength can be measured in terms of the state's power and autonomy in relation to societal actors and its ability to act in a coherent manner. State strength is underpinned by particular state attributes, which include (among others) the state's control over financial resources, the character of the state's bureaucratic élite and the degree of centralisation of the state apparatus. Atkinson and Coleman argue that perhaps one of the most important distinguishing attributes of a strong state is centralisation. 'The emergence of multiple centres of authority', they argue, 'is the quintessence of state weakness.'[10] Dyson continues this line of argument by stressing that so-called 'stateless' societies, or those with weak state traditions and structures, have typically experienced more peaceful and less stringent forms of political development, which has given rise to liberal political traditions emphasising individual rights, not political obligation to the state or a stark sense of national purpose.[11]

In societies such as Britain and the United States (and one might add Australia), Dyson argues that the very concept of the state as some kind of separate, authoritative entity is only very weakly developed. In such systems, state authority is diffuse; state structures are typically fragmented, and politics and administration are seen as separate activities. Moreover, the concept of the 'government', not the state, is predominant in political discourse, with the former typically being seen as something from which resources might be extracted. Weak states, then, have only a very limited capacity to provide strong leadership or direction for the economy or society as a whole.

'State' societies, on the other hand (Dyson refers to France and Germany, but the argument could be extended to countries such as Japan and many of the new industrial Asian economies), are those with a political history marked by conflict and insecurity. Typically, these 'strong' states have experienced authoritarian or absolutist regimes that have stressed national solidarity, the primacy of national interests and national security, as well as nationalist conceptions of economic development. In these states, successive regimes have built powerful and authoritative legal and administrative structures and traditions in which the pre-eminence of public authority and state responsibility in national affairs is central. In such a setting, the state is seen as an abstract embodiment of national purpose with the state apparatus standing above and somewhat aloof from society. The institutional dimensions of such a statist regime typically involve an entrenched bureaucratic culture, élite training of officials, a centralised bureaucratic apparatus, strong distinctions between public and private law and a notion that officials have a degree of autonomy from and rule alongside, but do not directly serve, elected politicians.[12] Given the historically entrenched concerns about national security and national purpose in such regimes, the state is legitimately seen as having an activist, leadership role to play in economic development. Indeed, the state is typically seen as a central and legitimate economic player in the market. In France, for example, when business executives were asked in a 1985 poll 'who should be the decision-makers for very large investments', two-thirds of the respondents chose the state, either alone or in combination with corporate management; only a third chose the market or corporate management alone.[13]

It is useful to note the considerable correspondence between weak states and reactive industry policy on the one hand, and strong states and anticipatory industry policy on the other. As Wilks and Wright argue, within such an analytical framework:

> *Britain and the United States are 'weak' states marked by liberal traditions, a reactive government which intervenes very reluctantly, and national attitudes which strongly reject any need for the state to intervene extensively in the market. France and Japan, by contrast, are 'strong' states with authoritarian traditions, where the market is regarded as suspect, and government intervention is regarded as in the natural order of things.*[14]

It is important to note that various authors have criticised the weak state/strong state formulation as too aggregate. Wilks and Wright, for example, argue that such an approach can be 'positively misleading'.[15] The implication is that such misgivings must also apply to attempts, such as Atkinson and Coleman's above, to characterise national styles of industry policy. The force of the critique developed by Wilks and Wright stems from the fact that any national or aggregate characterisation of the state's role or of modes of industry policy runs the risk of failing to capture cases that run counter to aggregate-level depictions. For example, cases can be cited of agency capture by industry in nominally strong states or of so-called weak states becoming heavily involved in the affairs of sectors of industry.[16] Such a critique is important in alerting us to the need to distinguish between the use of aggregate-level concepts and concepts that are more useful at the micro or sectoral level of analysis. Wilks and Wright, for example, point to the utility of fine-grained analysis of policy networks in different industry sectors.[17] Atkinson and Coleman extend this idea and provide a useful typology of different policy networks, including (among others) pressure pluralism, corporatism and state-led forms.[18] Yet Atkinson and Coleman see the need not to focus only on fine-grained sectoral analysis and stress the importance of macro-level analysis as well. As they argue: 'The idea that several levels of analysis coexist in the conduct of policy is only weakly developed in comparative political economy'.[19]

The problem with the Wilks and Wright critique, then, is that it attacks aggregate-level concepts for failing to explain detailed sectoral or micro-level events comprehensively, which is, arguably, something that the aggregate-level concepts were not designed to do in the first place. In any case, if national-level comparisons are to be made at all, or indeed, if we are to stand back and assess the broad pattern of national approaches to industry policy, we clearly need national-level analytical categories. Yet following Wilks and Wright, the potential descriptive or explanatory limits of such concepts, particularly at the sub-aggregate level, always need to be kept in mind.

Australia's pattern?

The analytical frameworks and issues discussed above point to the importance of the concept of levels of analysis. As just argued, it is often important to distinguish between macro-level developments and sectoral or micro-level developments. Here the focus is on broad macro-level characterisations and developments, yet even within this macro-level framework it is important to distinguish between what might be called 'surface-level' policy developments and more intrinsic underlying patterns. One way of characterising this more fundamental reality, at least at the level of aggregate models of the policy process, is the reactive/anticipatory formulation (which is discussed above). An even more fundamental level of analysis is the intrinsic nature of state action and capacity, as in the weak/strong state categorisation (also discussed above).

In assessing how the Australian pattern fits into all this, it is important, then, to recognise that even quite drastic shifts in policy at the surface level need not necessarily be associated with more fundamental changes in the state's basic role or its basic capacities. In the Australian context, there have certainly been significant changes in the direction of industry policy in the post-war era, but the question remains of whether this implies a more basic shift in the modis operandi of federal industrial policy or, indeed, more basic shifts in the character of the state's industrial role. The issue, then, is one of distinguishing between surface policy changes and more fundamental state characteristics. In the paragraphs that follow it will be argued that the quite drastic changes which have occurred in the type and direction of industry policy in post-war Australia have not been geared directly to corresponding shifts in the more basic modis operandi of industry policy-making nor to fundamental shifts in the industrial role of the state.

It is possible to distinguish four broad phases of industry policy in post-war Australia. The first, in straight policy terms, was the broad span of post-war protectionism. A more fundamental characterisation, in terms of Atkinson and Coleman's industry policy typology, would stress the 'reactive' nature of the post-war protectionist framework. Thus, the goals of the policy were protectionist, and the state was not particularly intrusive in the affairs of industry, relying instead on broad 'environmental' policy settings. Moreover, as far as industry policy was concerned, there was little in the way of central policy coordination, and the whole approach to post-war industrial development — beyond achieving raw growth — lacked focus, direction and detailed oversight.

At an even more fundamental level, does the general correspondence noted above between reactive industry policy and a 'weak' state hold in this case? Here the issue becomes more complex because it is clear that for much of its history Australia has not been a classic laissez-faire state and that the state's role in the economy in formative periods of economic development and under the impact of protectionism had indeed been very significant.[20] Moreover, the twentieth-century pattern in Australia of loosely tying together various broad strands of policy, including protectionism, arbitration, immigration and welfare policies, into a protective 'domestic defence' model was not just a historic class settlement; it also bore the clear imprint of state purpose and initiative.[21] Nowhere was this clearer than in federal Trade Minister McEwen's central brokerage role in the post-war protectionist policy coalition.

Clearly, then, settling key questions about the state's role is not straightforward and, in the post-war era in particular, we have a pattern of strong state activism in terms of overseeing 'domestic defence' and in profoundly reshaping the industrial economy through high protectionism, together with a pattern of state 'weakness' in terms of limited state intrusiveness and the reactive industry policy model.

The second phase of industry policy from the late 1960s until the onset of recession in late 1974 was brief but significant. It was the half decade or so when the Tariff Board (and later the Industries Assistance Commission) asserted a new policy agenda based on a fundamental attack on post-war protectionism.[22] Although not corresponding fully to the defining elements of an anticipatory policy framework, there is enough in the make-up of the policy approach during this period to move the focus of the approach closer to the anticipatory style of policy than to the reactive approach. The anti-protectionist change-oriented policy framework was one aspect, but perhaps as important was the activist and relatively autonomous role of the state (or at least a key state agency) in initiating what was later to become a revolution in industry policy. Does this swing towards an anticipatory policy framework imply state 'strength'? In many ways it does, particularly if we see the state during this period as having a good deal of autonomy from and power over recalcitrant societal interests, particularly manufacturing interests.

But this phase of anticipatory policy and the state strength and autonomy that underpinned it did not last long. Despite some success in reducing protection in the late 1970s, as well as attempts to support this process with new positive forms of industry intervention,[23] the overall model of industry policy from late 1974 until the re-election of Labor in 1983 best fits the reactive model. This is particularly so in terms of the criterion of policy incoherence, in terms of the protectionist decisions in key areas of industry (such as textiles, clothing and footwear (TCF) and motor vehicles), and in terms of the unwillingness by policy-makers to take much in the way of active responsibility for the process of industry restructuring. These outcomes reflect the lack of an authoritative political or bureaucratic centre able to assert a clear policy direction. It also reflects a state that was unable to assert much coherence over the policy process as a whole, in part because it lacked autonomy from powerful cross-cutting economic interests amid bitter tariff politics.

A fourth phase of federal industry policy has occurred under Labor since 1983. There are two possible policy interpretations. One stresses Labor's policy gyration and uncertainty as reflected, for example, in Labor's swing from initial protectionism to free trade later in the decade. The image of the state that underpins this potential interpretation stresses the state's limited autonomy amid the cross-fire of contradictory free trade and protectionist policy pressures. This kind of assessment has been adopted by Atkinson and Coleman. As they see it:

In the United States, Britain, Canada, Australia and New Zealand, the most common arrangement involves a reactive approach to industrial policy and a pressure pluralist network. Even at the sectoral level, where business organisation is often mobilised and state structures more variable, the state is predisposed to leave business alone. Policies are responses to political pressures from business. They tend to be ad hoc, uncoordinated with previous decisions, and oriented almost entirely to the short term.[24]

A second and more generous interpretation of Labor rule since 1983 would see the broad pattern of Labor's industry policy as indicating a capacity for policy governance and a capacity to impose a degree of direction over the policy process as a whole. This is so particularly in terms of what ultimately became a determined push to cut protection and to support this process with a range of positive assistance policies.

Added to this, Labor's special sectoral policies in areas such as steel, TCF and motor vehicles reveals a willingness to intrude in at least some areas of industry. This suggests a pattern of policy underpinned by a degree of state autonomy and by an attempt to impose political direction from the centre of government.[25] Such an assessment, of course, points to an anticipatory industry policy model and a relatively strong state.

Yet, as with the early post-war era discussed above, there are inevitable ambiguities in any characterisation of the Labor era. Most importantly, the degree of state autonomy achieved under Labor was of a relatively modest type. Indeed, the type of state autonomy that has underpinned Labor's trade liberalisation is best seen as an example of Nordlinger's type 3 state autonomy: a relatively weak type of state autonomy and a form in which the state acts on its preferences but in a context where the most powerful preferences in the state and society are generally in accord.[26] To be sure, Labor did need to overcome significant opposition in its push to reduce protection, but its autonomy from recalcitrant groups was buttressed by coalition with other powerful groups and by a general economic and policy context in which continued protectionism was becoming untenable. Such an account of state autonomy considerably softens the image of a starkly autonomous state and instead stresses the idea that the state's autonomy is arranged through active coalition with other powerful groups.[27] Moreover, despite areas of intrusiveness at the sectoral level, there has been an *overall* tendency to adopt where possible an arms-length 'environmental' form of intervention. Labor also experienced major problems in coordinating key arms of policy into a coherent whole, particularly the mismatch between attempts to boost industry investment in a context of high interest rates and/or domestic deflation, together with the determination to push ahead with tariff reductions despite tardy progress with microeconomic reform.[28]

Beyond these particular phases of industry policy, in overall terms, it can be argued that Australia has a relatively weak state in both the key ideological and institutional dimensions discussed above by Dyson. The Australian state system has a deeply ingrained liberal and parliamentary character. Political rule stems more from the institutions of cabinet and party rule than from powerful or autonomous bureaucracies and, in this sense, Australia stops well short of being a 'state' society. On the contrary, little in Australia's political development, save for a statist penal first step, has steered Australia away from the classic liberal notions of government. Parties and cabinet government have ruled Australia and, although key federal bureaucracies such as Treasury, the Tariff Board and later the Industries Assistance Commission have exerted considerable influence in the post-war era, our liberal Westminster traditions, federalism and a fragmented administrative apparatus have limited state authority and centralisation: the hallmarks of state societies. Ideologically, the Australian state lacks a definitive state ethos, and the very idea of state intervention is highly politicised. There has also been a marked proclivity on the part of state and economic élites to stress certain key liberal principles of economic management; particularly in terms of preserving the sanctity of private sector management prerogatives, the concept of the autonomy of firms, as well as a determination not to become too involved in the detailed workings of the economy. In this regard, the overall stress has been on arms-length forms of 'environmental' intervention, not on detailed forms of state activism in which the state becomes an active market player. Atkinson and Coleman reach similar conclusions about the Canadian state:

> *It is the combined institutional legacy of the Westminster model of parliamentary government and federalism that fosters a weak state tradition and discourages anticipatory industry policy ... It is this weak state tradition that has encouraged the broad diffusion of political power and provided only the thinnest of bases on which to erect consensus-building institutions. It has led Canadian politicians and bureaucrats away from projects based on state intervention and towards the liberal, continentalist option in industry policy making. Given that the present pattern of industry policy is rooted in this tradition—that is, in the structures of Canadian government and in the belief systems of bureaucrats—changing the direction and content of policy will be an exceptionally long and difficult chore.*[29]

Yet if Australia does have many of the general hallmarks of a weak state, how can such a model account for cases that clearly reveal instances of state autonomy and leadership? For example, the major and deliberate economic impact of Australian protectionism and, more recently, the apparently successful efforts to dismantle protectionism both reveal a determined and purposeful state. Indeed, there has developed a body of writing that depicts the Australian state as something of a prime mover. This depiction embraces not only protectionism but also notions of 'colonial socialism' in relation to earlier, historically high patterns of public infrastructure investment, as well as Australia's unique package of domestic economic 'defence' arrangements (protection, arbitration, wage-earner welfare and immigration controls), which shielded both capital and labour for much of the twentieth century from market perturbations.[30] Accordingly, Pusey argues that:

> *Australia was 'born modern' ... Through its controls over tariffs and industrial relations, and a direct control over wages and thus over the distribution of national income, the state held and used its power both to resist private capital interests and, within that large measure of 'relative autonomy', to form or at least protect the social structure. Consequently, it was a state that ... looks rather like a very 'strong' state or even a 'dominant' state.*[31]

Pusey's characterisation goes too far. Yet the evidence just cited, with its depiction of an activist state in some arenas and at various levels in the economy, does pose the puzzle of how such a pattern is to be explained within the context of what is, arguably, Australia's weak institutional state system; one, moreover, that has never really challenged the sanctity of the autonomous firm, except in the area of wage determination (which, in part, reflects the historical strength of the trade union movement). How is it, then, that an essentially weak state apparatus has been able to 'act strong' at various points? One part of the answer lies in the nature of the economic exigencies that have confronted the Australian state. Another part of the answer lies in the intermittent bouts of determined party leadership within government, which has at times propelled the state in coalition with external political groupings.

To what extent do economic exigencies shape patterns of state action? Here we come to a second key element in Dyson's concept of state strength and weakness; one that draws on the work of economic historians such as Gerschenkron, who argues that the later a country industrialises the more active and assertive the state's role tends to be.[32] This is but one slice of the more general argument that suggests that the nature of economic conjunctures or key national economic problems is one factor that shapes state–economy relations.

According to Dyson's rendering of Gerschenkron, early industrialisers such as Britain and the United States had relatively open competitive frontiers and were able to rely on a company-led, market-based pattern of industrial development in which the state played only a minimal role. Late industrialisers, by contrast, faced more of an uphill battle with more competition and higher industry start-up costs, and this tended to put pressure on the state to support, underwrite or protect industrial development. Historically, argues Dyson, state societies such as France and Japan were also late industrialisers so there was a double historical impulse to propel state activism.

The contrast here with countries such as Britain and the US could not be more profound in the sense that both Britain and the US both have weak state traditions and structures and both were early industrialisers. In these countries there is entrenched scepticism about the value and the ability of the state to play an active leadership role in the economy and, as Dyson argues, 'neither administrative nor business culture has absorbed the concept of a benevolent "public power"—the state— acting in the name of the common good'.[33] Accordingly, such an industrial culture emphasises private management prerogatives, the autonomy of the firm, an unwillingness to plan economic development explicitly and a company-led process of industrial change.

There is much here that resonates with Australian experience. Without pushing too far the argument that certain forms of economic exigency will cause certain predictable state responses, it is clear that Australia's peculiar economic experiences, at least historically, have at times prompted the state to play a major economic role. Thus, the challenges of pioneer colonial development and, following Dyson and Gerschenkron, of Australia's relatively late industrialisation, have seen the Australian state intervene, often significantly, in the economy. As suggested above, the role of large public infrastructure investments in colonial and pre-war economic development, together with high protectionism and arbitration, were the key ingredients in this regard.[34] Critically, however, such interventions have been mediated through liberal (weak) state institutions and traditions that have generally insisted on maintaining the autonomy of economic actors and an arm's-length relationship between state and economy. As mentioned above, the only case where such principles have been breached is the arena of centralised wage determination, and in recent years this too is beginning to weaken under the impact of decentralising market tendencies.

Overall, then, Australia's pattern has historically involved economically driven impulses towards state intervention, which have been mediated by weak state traditions and structures, which in turn have generally eschewed the notion of detailed, selective or directive intervention and have produced instead a pattern of 'environmental' or framework-setting economic intervention. Australia's historical pattern of state–economy relations is probably best described as one where the state has played a structuring role at the macro level, but with laissez-faire at the micro-level: a kind of statist–laissez-faire amalgam.

The second key element that has occasionally propelled the state to act assertively has been determined party leadership within government. The classic comparative case here might be the Thatcher Government's assertive leadership of what on most dimensions is a relatively weak liberal state. Much the same pattern has emerged, intermittently, in Australia. The Menzies–McEwen and the Hawke–Keating Governments have been prominent in this regard. In both cases, the major push for high protection and, subsequently, for low protection was driven by determined government leaders in coalition with other groups. Indeed, only on one major occasion in the post-war era has the drive and initiative for change come from the bureaucratic apparatus of the state itself; notably the Tariff Board under Rattigan in the late 1960s.[35]

In terms of readjusting Dyson's model, then, Australia has a weak state tradition that at times receives an injection of state activism from determined political leaders and, on occasion, from key bureaucratic élites. Moreover, as argued above, the powerful and autonomous image of such bouts of state assertiveness or activism need to be softened to some extent because, typically, they rely on state leaders forming politically effective coalitions with powerful non-state actors or groups.

The image of a strong state also needs to be softened because the relatively weak structures and fragmented character of the Australian state produces a very uneven pattern of administrative capacity. In areas such as industrial relations or protection policy, the state developed, over time, a tradition of activism and administrative expertise. But in other areas, for example in areas such as positive industry policy, microeconomic or training policy, a tradition of purposeful and co-ordinated state intervention is lacking. This means, then, that bouts of state activism will tend to be built around areas of administrative capacity. Notably, tariffs and other forms of protection policy have been at the centre of bouts of state activism under McEwenism and during the anti-protectionist push by Labor in the late 1980s and early 1990s.

All this suggests that we should stand back for a moment from Dyson's model in order to modify it to better account for the Australian experience. Thus, in terms of the state's economic role, Australia has historically produced simultaneous elements of state strength and weakness in the economy; a pattern marked by what at times has been substantial intervention, but of a kind featuring classic weak state characteristics, particularly the proclivity of state élites not to challenge the autonomy of firms and not to become too involved in the detailed workings of the economy. In this sense, the pattern and ethos of intervention has been decidedly pragmatic. Such a pattern of active though circumscribed state economic intervention can be explained by the historic combination of various pressing economic exigencies with what in fact has been the classic liberal, 'stateless' character of the Australian state in an institutional sense. To borrow from Dunleavy's depiction of the British case, Australia's pattern of economic intervention was never 'grounded' in a supportive strong state tradition.[36] In such a setting, the intervention that did occur (particularly protectionism) was poorly administered for want of effective state institutions capable of coordinating industry policy and for want of a tradition of detailed state oversight of the economy. The economic problems and inefficiencies that flowed from Australia's brand of high protectionism have in more recent times set in train an ideological reaction that has further strengthened the liberal elements of what was already a weak state tradition. In this sense, the recent push to reduce protection, to reassert the autonomy of market players and the apparent retreat of the state from a long-term shaping role in the economy, represents a historic realignment of the state's (now more minimalist) economic role with its inherent weak state ideological and institutional character.

Such developments also point to the need to stress the limits of any explanation that pushes the 'economic exigency shapes state action' argument too far. State responses to the economy are always highly mediated by political and historical factors. If it is true, as Gerschenkron suggests, that late industrialisation is a powerful impulse towards state activism in the economy, it is also true that other forms of economic challenge, in different economic or historical contexts, might well produce quite different responses. For example, early industrial development and subsequent industrial restructuring could be seen as equally challenging economic exigencies, both of which call forth an activist state response. Yet if this is true in general terms in Australia, the earlier shaping role of the state in the economy during initial industrialisation has since been replaced by attempts to reduce the state's shaping role as part of recent efforts to restructure industry. In both cases, the state confronts an economic exigency, in both cases there is a relatively high degree of state assertiveness and activism, yet in both cases quite different responses occur, largely because the political and historical context of state action has changed. Indeed, in the Australian case, the political and ideological legacy flowing from earlier forms of state activism in the economy have produced a powerful aversion to any subsequent attempts to promote the state as an active shaper of the economy and has led instead to a more determined effort to increase the autonomy of market players.

So far, then, we have an aggregate model of state action that stresses the role of state formation, state tradition, economic exigency and the role of ideologies concerning state action, all of which are contained within Dyson's general model of industrial culture and state strength and weakness. It has been argued that Australia has neither a strong state or a weak state in any universalist or unambiguous sense, but that essentially it has a weak state capable of being propelled towards certain forms of state strength from time to time, depending on the economic and historical conjuncture and on the capacities or determination of party leadership in government, together, on some occasions, with key bureaucratic élites. Moreover, as stressed above, Australia's intermittent bouts of state activism have never really been grounded in a supportive state structure capable of sustaining a purposeful or coordinated state role in the economy.

Conclusion

Atkinson and Coleman's characterisation of Australia as having a purely reactive industry policy model is incorrect, then. But it is also true that Australia falls a long way short of the far more capable and 'interventionist' industry policy regimes in countries such as Japan, France and a number of East Asian economies; economies with states displaying purposeful state support for industry and sophisticated policy integration aimed almost singly at industry competitiveness, and which provide far more robust examples of the anticipatory industry policy category. Another key difference is the general unwillingness of Australian policy-makers to adopt a strategic vision for Australian industry.[37] It is clear, then, that Australia does not have a full-blown anticipatory industry policy and, certainly, it does not fit Zysman's model of 'state-led' industry adjustment. Nor, at the aggregate level, does it fit his model of corporatist or 'tripartite-negotiated' adjustment, the type found in many small northern European states.[38] Atkinson and Coleman argue that it is these two models of adjustment that are typically found in anticipatory industry policy regimes. Yet Australia does not fit this pattern.

Instead, the Australian pattern, although very different in policy terms from what it was twenty or thirty years ago, has not, in broad terms, shifted much beyond the preference by policy-makers for an arms-length relationship with industry and a pattern of industry adjustment that emphasises the autonomy of firms and 'company-led' adjustment. In this sense, changes at the level of policy have not been directly geared to what in fact have been more limited changes in the overall modis operandi of industry policy and state action. This suggests that it is probably best to see recent Australian experience as a *weak* version of the anticipatory approach to industry policy. It was suggested above that, in ideal-typical terms, anticipatory industry policy regimes tend to be underpinned by strong states. As we have seen at times in the post-war era, Australia has displayed limited manifestations of something approaching a strong state role in industry. Yet it is important to stress that, from a comparative perspective, such manifestations of state strength have indeed been limited and sporadic, and that bouts of state assertiveness have been counterbalanced by limited intrusiveness and by difficulties in coherently integrating policy initiatives. Given all this, we might tentatively conclude that Australia has something like a strong version of a weak state or, better still perhaps, a weak state that at times can 'act strong'.

In terms of recent experience, Australia's pattern of state activism — particularly the determined push to reduce protection and efforts to support this with state assistance measures — is by no means a pure company-led model: a good deal of state activism has been apparent. Perhaps the best way to interpret the recent Australian situation is to see it as a process of using the state, in a start-up or prodding fashion, to drive what is hoped will ultimately become a company-led adjustment process. Certainly, this pattern accords with the recent rhetoric of industry self-reliance used by government policy-makers. Such a pattern also accords well with Grant's model of 'partisan state-led' adjustment. This is a strategy that reflects the presence of a state with sufficient autonomy to be able to resist objections from protected industries and from trade unions, and one that is determined to push industry into a less protected market environment. As Grant explains:

Unlike company-led adjustment where the task of change is left in the hands of companies operating in an approximation of a market economy, partisan state-led adjustment involves interventions by government in order to create the conditions in which ultimately, such company-led adjustment can occur. State intervention is necessary because companies lack the political will and capacity, and the management determination, to see adjustment through on their own. Conditions must be created in which free enterprise can flourish, but business cannot do this by itself, partly because of what is seen as spinelessness, partly because the obstacles are so great that they can only be tackled through the determined use of state power.[39]

Notes

1. This chapter draws on work contained in chapter 7 of S. Bell (1993), *Australian Manufacturing and the State: The Politics of Industry Policy in the Post-War Era*, Cambridge University Press, Melbourne.
2. See I. Magaziner and T. Hout (1980), *Japanese Industrial Policy*, Policy Studies Institute, London.
3. M. M. Atkinson and W. D. Coleman (1989), *The State, Business and Industrial Change in Canada*, University of Toronto Press, Toronto, pp. 23–7; J. Zysman (1983), *Governments, Markets and Growth: Financial Systems and the Politics of Industrial Change*, Cornell University Press, Ithaca, pp. 91–3.
4. M. M. Atkinson and W. D. Coleman (1989), p. 30.
5. D. Vogel (1987), 'Government–industry relations in the United States: An overview', in S. Wilks and M. Wright (eds), *Comparative Government–Industry Relations*, Clarendon Press, Oxford.
6. J. Zysman (1983), p. 92.

State Strength and State Weakness 267

7 J. Zysman (1983), p. 92.
8 M. M. Atkinson and W. D. Coleman (1989), p. 25.
9 S. Krasner (1978), 'United States commercial and monetary policy', in P. Katzenstein (ed.), *Between Power and Plenty: Foreign Economic Policies of Advanced Industrial States*, Harvard University Press, Cambridge, Mass., p. 57 (my emphasis).
10 M. M. Atkinson and W. D. Coleman (1989), p. 54.
11 K. Dyson (1985), 'The cultural, structural and ideological context', in K. Dyson and S. Wilks (eds), *Industrial Crisis: A Comparative Analysis of the State and Industry*, Basil Blackwell, Oxford.
12 See also J. Zysman (1983), p. 300.
13 P. Hall (1986), *Governing the Economy*, Polity Press, Cambridge, p. 279.
14 S. Wilks and M. Wright (1987), 'Conclusion: Comparing government–industry relations: States, sectors and networks', in S. Wilks and M. Wright (eds), *Comparative Government–Industry Relations*, pp. 281–2.
15 S. Wilks and M. Wright (1987), p. 284. See also Zysman (1983), pp. 295–9.
16 See the case studies in Wilks and Wright (1987).
17 Wilks and Wright (1987), pp. 294–307.
18 M. M. Atkinson and W. D. Coleman (1989), chapter 4.
19 M. M. Atkinson and W. D. Coleman (1989), p. 26.
20 N. G. Butlin, A. Barnard and J. J. Pincus (1982), *Government and Capitalism*, Allen & Unwin, Sydney.
21 F. G. Castles (1989), *Australian Public Policy and Economic Vulnerability*, Allen & Unwin, Sydney.
22 S. Bell (1989), 'State strength and capitalist weakness: Manufacturing capital and the Tariff Board's attack on McEwenism', *Politics*, 24:2, 23–38.
23 S. Bell (1992), 'Policy reponses to manufacturing decline: The limits of state economic intervention, 1974–83', *Australian Journal of Politics and History*, 38:1, 41–61.
24 M. M. Atkinson and W. D. Coleman (1989a), 'Strong states and weak states: Sectoral policy networks in advanced capitalist economies', *British Journal of Political Science*, 19:1, 60.
25 M. A. Capling and B. Galligan (1992), *Beyond the Protective State: The Political Economy of Australia's Manufacturing Industry Policy*, Cambridge University Press, Melbourne; S. Bell (1993), *Australian Manufacturing and the State: The Politics of Industry Policy in the Post-War Era*, Cambridge University Press, Melbourne.
26 E. Nordlinger (1981), *On the Autonomy of the Democratic State*, Harvard University Press, Cambridge, Mass.
27 For a 'coalition' account of state autonomy see C. J. Martin (1989), 'Business influence and state power: The case of the US corporate tax policy', *Politics and Society*, 17:2, 189–223.
28 S. Bell (1993), chapter 6; see also J. Power (1990), 'Mandarin hits out at govt's industry policy', *Australian Financial Review*, 2 July; and L. Tingle (1990), 'Employers demand action on reforms', *Australian*, 11 April.
29 M. M. Atkinson and W. D. Coleman (1989), p. 76.
30 N. G. Butlin, A. Barnard and J. J. Pincus (1982).
31 M. Pusey (1991), *Economic Rationalism in Canberra: A Nation Building State Changes its Mind*, Cambridge University Press, Melbourne, p. 213.

32 A. Gerschenkron (1962), *Economic Backwardness in Historical Perspective*, Harvard University Press, Cambridge, Mass.
33 K. Dyson (1985), p. 31.
34 N. G. Butlin, A. Barnard and J. J. Pincus (1982); Castles (1988).
35 S. Bell (1993), chapter 3.
36 P. Dunleavy (1989), 'The United Kingdom: Paradoxes of an ungrounded statism', in F. G. Castles (ed.), *The Comparative History of Public Policy*, Polity Press, Cambridge.
37 C. Carter (1992), 'A vision targetted on Asia', *Australian*, 13–14 June.
38 P. Katzenstein (1985), *Small States in World Markets*, Cornell University Press, Ithaca; F. G. Castles (1989).
39 W. Grant (with J. Sargent) (1987), *Business and Politics in Britain*, Macmillan, London, p. 246.

11

Microeconomic reform

Rolf Gerritsen

During the twentieth century the nineteenth century's institutional and economic bases of Australia's political economy and prosperity were gradually eroded. Because of the comprehensive victory of the Deakinite Liberal–Labor 'Australian settlement' in the early 1900s (involving elements such as arbitration and protectionism), it was not generally realised throughout the policy community that this was happening until the close of the 1970s. In reaction, during the latter half of the 1980s, microeconomic reform became a central icon of Australian public policy. Like most icons, it has been inconsistently applied and has become a legitimating device for a variety of (usually partisanly defined) prescriptions for action. Nevertheless, marking this seminal political agenda shift, microeconomic reform will continue to be a central issue during the 1990s as various prescriptions to shape public policy outcomes are advanced under its banner.

This chapter examines the subsequent and continuing endeavours to render the Australian economy more economically efficient, as currently measured by indices of international competitiveness. It seeks to explain why microeconomic reform was the chosen response to Australia's incipient (though relative) economic decline and why this reforming process was so selective of its targets and ambitions. The chapter develops the parameters of a simple general explanation of both why microeconomic reform proposals became dominant on the Australian policy agenda and what determines their individual success or failure (though it is less strictly applicable for the latter exercise). Ultimately the politics of microeconomic reform depends on the complex, three-way interaction between definitions of the public interest, the politics of partisan coalitions and the political party contest for control of the political agenda. These three elements have to come together for so-called 'microeconomic reform' to ensue.

The Australian political economy and microeconomic reform

During the nineteenth century, the Australian state was a profitable entrepreneurial enterprise. The sale of land—following the initial non-recognition and then destruction of Aboriginal society, cheaply assumed by the Crown—provided ready revenues to pay for such governmental services as existed. In addition, the Australian colonies undertook large-scale direct investment in infrastructure provision in order to facilitate the expansion of the frontier and produce an expanding primary commodity exports base. Positive terms of trade for the rural commodities sold to the imperial metropole enabled the user charges on this public investment not only to repay the London bond holders who supplied the capital but also to provide a general subsidy to the consolidated revenue of the colonies. Excise and customs duties further strengthened the fiscal position of Australian governments. The level of income and other taxes were consequently low, despite this period of relatively big government being traditionally characterised as 'colonial socialism'.[1]

During the twentieth century this fiscal legacy was gradually eroded, coincidentally at the same time as the terms of trade for agriculture—and primary commodities generally—gradually declined. The alarms of two world wars and the Great Depression obscured this structural deterioration. By the late 1970s—notwithstanding production increases and the diversification of mineral exports with the addition to gold of iron ore, bauxite and coal—the Australian political economy was facing fundamental challenges as prosperity threatened to decline relatively together with the terms of trade for primary commodities. After 1980, when European Community-subsidised agricultural surpluses spilled on to world markets, this relative decline accelerated.

However, this structural economic decline was obscured until relatively recently. Because of Australian governments' disinclination to raise substantial taxes, plus the decline in the fiscal efficiency of public enterprises, the twentieth century saw a shift from direct public sector provision to regulatory imposts on the economy aiming at a variety of social and economic objectives. These fed on the economic rents created by nineteenth-century prosperity. Policies such as White Australia protected labour from international competition, while tariffs compensated employers for the relatively high wage costs contingent on labour shortages, the introduction of the arbitration system and centralised wage-fixing, and the use of wage-fixing to achieve social welfare objectives. By the end of the 1970s Australia consequently had an inefficient and declining manufacturing sector. The disinclination of governments to raise taxation to fund social welfare measures was not generally seen as a problem because the wage-fixing regulatory system was used to achieve social welfare, in effect creating a wage earners' welfare state that mostly ignored those not actually or potentially in the workforce. Also, government business enterprises, through the extensive imposition of electorally inspired Community Service Obligations, gradually became inefficient and overstaffed, relying on hidden and often inequitable cross-subsidies to retain profitability.[2] The economy and government of Australia had become riddled with endemic microeconomic inefficiencies. So long as protection-all-round existed and economic growth continued, these inhibitions on economic efficiency were accepted.

In the post-1945 period the worldwide boom of the capitalist economies created sufficiently strong growth in the Australian economy to continue the illusion that it was systematically sound. Immigration was accommodated by the further expansion of regulatory restrictions on foreign competition through ever-higher manufacturing tariffs and quotas. Fortuitous new markets, mostly in Asia, both for traditional agricultural exports and for a burgeoning minerals exports sector, defused the external account challenge posed by Britain's entry into the European Community.

Economic growth—albeit at a relatively low real level in comparison with most Western economies—created, through inflation, the fiscal drag that allowed a relatively modest expansion of the Australian Government in education, health, housing and welfare expenditures. Regulatory intervention in markets continued apace, the efficiency costs of this activity obscured by general economic growth. The economy became progressively both less efficient and (less obviously) not as effective in sustaining internally generated economic growth.[3]

In the 1970s—for a combination of reasons, some domestic although most were international—this politico-economic system came under severe pressure, although it took a decade until the mid 1980s for Australian policy-makers to understand the urgency of restructuring the economy. The politics of microeconomic reform become fundamentally about achieving this objective. Microeconomic reform in neo-classical economics is the application of market disciplines to the provision of products and services to improve the volume of outputs obtainable from inputs available.[4] But the policy agenda of microeconomic reform in Australia has gone beyond simple economic reforms. As discussed below, its agenda shifts incorporate multifaceted institutional and policy reforms as well as—during the Hawke–Keating Labor Governments—paradoxically subsuming what in a previous era was called manufacturing industry policy. The breadth of the definition of microeconomic reform in Australia owes much to its being subsumed within the political agenda management of contestation between private, partisan interests. This renders the politics of achieving microeconomic reform amorphous and analysis tentative and imprecise.

Microeconomic reform now seeks to return the economy to internationally comparative efficiency, as much for the future of the Australian state as for the intrinsic merits of the superior allocative and productive economic efficiencies of such reform. Microeconomic reform is a process the definition of which is contested; it has winners and losers, and they are differently configured depending on which political party carries out such reforms. Consequently, microeconomic reform has been subsumed into the normal political agenda contests of party politics. The pressures of such politics inclines Australian reform practices towards incrementalism and bounded, partisanly defined interventions, rather than the Simon-style rationalism implicit from its theoretical base in neo-classical microeconomics.

In retrospect it appears simple to explain the current political agenda favouring microeconomic reform. Following the current account difficulties of the mid 1980s the Australian economy was seen as being at a watershed. There was a popular acceptance that something needed to be done. The then Treasurer, Keating, following his 1986 'banana republic' comment, initiated the new policy agenda after the 1987 election. The institutional signal of the new agenda was the transfer of authority over the Industry Commission from the Minister for Industry (then Senator Button) to the Treasurer. The new agenda signalled the arriving policy dominance of economists in the institutional advisory structures of Australian government. The first comprehensive policy expression of the new agenda was in the 1988 Industry Statement, which began the process of lowering manufacturing tariffs. Then microeconomic reform was, erroneously,[5] assumed to be required to tackle the current account problem. That policy context has since shifted; currently the microeconomic reform agenda is still about economic efficiency but also includes a complementary 'laborist' social equity element.

This focus on microeconomic reform reflects, in part, a historic paradigm change in Australia's economic policy community. Orthodoxy among economists—and, following them, the general community—has shifted towards a greater insistence on market solutions since Australia's last comparable economic policy watershed in the mid to late 1940s. Then quotas and the policy package of 'domestic defence'[6] found widespread support in the economic policy community. During the 1980s that same community mostly accepted market-based microeconomics as orthodoxy, with the consequent change in the proposed solutions to Australia's current crisis.[7] Cutting tax rates and abolishing concessional tax regimes to remove distortions of investment incentives was an important aspect of the new policy agenda. Within the public sector this was expressed in the managerialist notion of achieving more with fewer inputs.

Modelling microeconomic reform

Explaining microeconomic reform has hitherto relied on a simple model: the pre-existence of political agendas that overthrow previous orthodoxy and achieve policy dominance under the impetus of an exogenous shock. This model has little explanatory power. It offers post hoc explanation but has little predictive value. At most it could lead to a hypothesis that a future exogenous shock such as the formation of protectionist world trade blocs would probably revive either Australian protectionism—presently politically represented under the rubric of 'strategic trade' theory—or else a further expansion of Labor's interventionist, European-style managed industry policy and trade regimes.[8] Although the latter is possible, a better model is required. This analytical model should be able to explain past instances of microeconomic reform as well as having some predictive value for the future of such reform in general.

The contemporary Australian microeconomic reform agenda seems relatively specific: it is primarily about economic policy, specifically industrial, transport and communications infrastructure and labour market policies. However, the instruments of reform are less certain. While deregulation was an important aspect of this agenda under Labor, governmental regulatory activity simultaneously expanded, especially in the areas of labour market training (the compulsory training levy) and education and environmental policy. Notwithstanding the dominance of the rhetoric of economic rationalism, selected cases of industry planning also (paradoxically?) became enmeshed in Labor's reform policy agenda.

In addition, whole areas of public policy—principally under the jurisdiction of State Governments—seem relatively immune from the strictures of microeconomic efficiency. Specialist surgeons continue profitably to control the high distorted markets for their services. In most states lawyers, likewise, have so far successfully campaigned against no-fault accident compensation, deregulated conveyancing and liberalising access to the Bar. The microeconomic reform debate concentrates more on centralised wage-fixing's inefficiencies than on deficiencies in capital markets (exposed by the behaviour during the

1980s of the directors of Bell, Quintex, Adsteam etcetera) with equally serious macroeconomic consequences, in this case for the costs of investment capital. Conversely, in much of its social policy Australia has traditionally had microeconomic efficiency, via the medium of our highly selective, targeted welfare system. In that they are targeted and means-tested, the welfare benefits of Australia's poor have always been the bipartisan object of productive fiscal efficiency.

So the demand for microeconomic reform is neither universal, uniform nor socially neutral. It has significant relationships with power and the political opportunities created by shifting public agendas. In the language of public policy, microeconomic reform operates within a bounded rationality, and that is mostly determined by interaction between the partisan preferences and linkages of the governing party and its political agenda control.

A more systematic attempt to deduce the parameters of an explanatory model for the contemporary microeconomic reform agenda would need to focus on two questions: (1) why do particular proposals for microeconomic reform arise at particular times? and (2) what conditions can lead to success or failure for such proposed microeconomic reforms? Below it is proposed to examine these questions in a preparatory fashion before briefly investigating three types of microeconomic reforms. In the conclusion some further hypotheses will be advanced in answer to the second question. To do this we need to start with a preliminary general outline of microeconomic reform. This model has three elements: a public interest variable, a private interest variable and an element of agenda politics. The interaction between these variables provides the basis of the microeconomic reform agenda.

The public interest variable

In the policy field of microeconomic reform, as for any other policy domain, there is a policy 'community'. The microeconomic reform policy community aggregates several industry and sectoral policy networks.[9] These groupings of 'involved publics' are defined by relation to their interest in this specific area of policy rather than in the polity as a whole. The networks of the microeconomic reform policy community fluctuate by issue but include politicians, bureaucrats (particularly the so-called 'econocrats'), representatives of powerful economic interest groups such as the Business Council of Australia and the Australian Chamber of Commerce and Industry, a number of journalists, trade union officials, some academics and sundry others.

Despite varying perspectives resulting from different institutional loci and interests, since the mid 1980s there have usually been broad areas of agreement within that policy community. Often these overrode partisan political differences. The policy community, in a semi-public fashion, provides an arena in which the (alleged) public interest in any policy field is defined and articulated. The policy community—focused on the politicians and the bureaucracy as its institutionally defined implementation agents—is an elitist, non-Westminster, profane reality of Australian politics.

The private interest variable
The politics of private interests has been documented in an extensive literature on how the concentrated benefits from governmental action encourages groups (often successfully) to advance their private interests against more diffuse general interests, such as consumers, patients, voters, etc. An example is the success during the 1950s to the 1970s of manufacturing industry groups in securing tariffs from governments' regulatory powers, these tariffs being electorally invisible because they were paid for by Australians as consumers rather than as taxpayers. So pressure groups are inevitably important in any policy field because the incentives for political intervention are supposedly structured in their favour.[10]

In explaining the political shape of microeconomic reform the most important private interests are the governing party's allies, its 'partisan coalition'. This coalition comprises both formal and informal interests. For example, under Labor the institutionally affiliated trade unions represented by the ACTU were in the former category. As with the operation of the Prices and Incomes Accord, they usually had to be incorporated into the microeconomic policy-making process. The 1993 federal election revealed that the business associations—in particular the Housing Industry Association and the Australian Chamber of Commerce and Industry—together with the AMA comprise part of the Liberal Party's partisan coalition.

But a governing party's traditional voting support is an equally important, albeit informal, interest. During the late 1980s, while the Labor Government was engaged in microeconomic efficiency redirections from its historically more usual statist interventionism, reassuring its core constituency voters was as important as securing the allegiance of swinging voters. Labor's choice of instruments of microeconomic reform impaired the universal applicability of Downsian median voter models (i.e. that policy choices are determined by the preferences of the so-called swinging—or median—voters). So, broadly based partisan coalitions shape the implementation of the microeconomic reform process, in particular the pace of reform in certain areas. Thus, under Labor, labour market reforms—such as enterprise-based bargaining—and manufacturing industry programs (like the exports offsets policies in the automotive manufacturing industry) were instituted cautiously and consensually with the ACTU.

For Labor this partisan element inevitably also involved questions of social justice. The logic of the operation of the Hawke–Keating Labor

Government's Accord arrangements was that its supporters accepted declining real wages to achieve the restoration of the historic profit share of GDP, but only if this was linked to social policies aimed at reducing unemployment and maintaining the levels of real social welfare benefits. Thus, for Labor voters, equitable policies were inseparable from microeconomic efficiency reforms. In this context initiatives such as the Higher Education Contribution Scheme were indistinguishably part of the total process of microeconomic reform, even if not specifically labelled as such (nor entirely accepted by Labor voters).

Conversely, in policy areas where the principal private interests and voter constituencies did not belong to Labor's partisan coalition—all other things being equal—sweeping reforms were more easily implemented. The agricultural and financial sectors' deregulation (discussed below) are examples.

The agenda-setting variable

Agenda-setting is a concept developed by political scientists to explain why issues arise at particular times and why they might then cyclically appear and disappear from political saliency: the issue 'attention cycle' phenomenon. It is also used to illuminate the politics of issue management by governments.[11]

In the agenda-setting of microeconomic reform, most agenda items occur in what the literature characterises as the 'inside-initiative' manner. 'Inside' in this case refers to inside government, although the policy community would be involved in shaping options. Thus, in the mid 1980s, the Labor Government's senior economic ministers largely created the microeconomic policy agenda in response to the public agenda of Australian economic crisis. Similarly, as the 1993 federal election campaign revealed, the Liberal Party attempted to create a public agenda of the necessity for a planned assault on Australia's economic problems in order to implement an 'inside' policy agenda—the GST and sweeping public sector cutbacks—that actually had very limited popular support. As will be seen below, this inside-initiative factor profoundly affects the agenda-management and policy implementation of microeconomic reforms.

During the 1980s the public agenda-setting for microeconomic reform was supposedly achieved by extensive reliance on public inquiries such as the Campbell Committee on the financial sector, the McColl Royal Commission on grain handling and the Interstate Commission report on the waterfront. However, in reality these were exercises in educating the policy community. On the whole, the general citizenry remained unaware of the import of their recommendations, indicating the elitist nature of policy targeting and selection, which is intrinsic to microeconomic reform.

Although agenda management is the stuff of successful politics, controlling the agenda is difficult and perpetually contested.

First, for reasons of electoral advantage an opportunistic Opposition might seek to redirect the agenda. Thus in 1988 the Liberals shifted the timed local telephone calls issue on to a public agenda of disadvantage to the elderly (even though this contradicted the facts). In the excitement of the Adelaide by-election campaign, broad policy agenda agreement among the élite policy community proved irrelevant. Timed local calls were jettisoned. This political complication of an opportunistic Opposition made the agenda management of the totality of the process difficult for the Labor Government because of the consequent suspicion of microeconomic reform within Labor's partisan coalition. In reaction to the Adelaide by-election, and with some success, Labor reshaped the public agenda of microeconomic reform to subsume government regulatory interventions to make Australian industry more internationally competitive. This—paradoxically, given that neo-classical microeconomic theory eschews such interventionism—allowed the incorporation of planned industry restructuring under the rubric of microeconomic reform. The Liberal Party, predictably, rejected such interventionism, also in the name of microeconomic reform. From late 1991 it proposed instead the abolition of a range of taxes on business (such as payroll tax) as part of its GST package.

Secondly, the state of the governing party's electoral support, in the context of particular situational exigencies, encourages caution and incrementalism over time. After 1983, as Labor's popular support eroded, it was more frequently forced to act within parameters created by the Liberal Opposition's public agenda. This was first exhibited by the 'trilogy' commitment during the 1984 election campaign. Again, it occurred in 1986, when the Robe River dispute forced Labor to address the work practices issue by allowing productivity increases to force their way into wage-fixing estimation. In 1991 the Industrial Relations Commission's refusal to endorse the Accord Mark VI in the national wage case led to an attempted wholesale decentralisation of wage-fixing. In effect to pre-empt the Liberal Opposition's labour market policy agenda, the Labor Government endorsed the ACTU decision to negotiate the Accord Mark VI at the individual enterprise level.

This three-part model can now be used to examine the two questions raised above.

Why did microeconomic reform issues arise in the 1980s?

It can be argued that particular cases of microeconomic reform arose in the 1980s because, as the model hypothesised here proposes: (1) the policy community was convinced that change was necessary and inevitable; (2) the point had been reached where the costs of market distortions outweighed or threatened the maintenance of the benefits accumulated over decades by private interests; and (3) agenda-setting effects interacting with exogenous pressures—the threat of perpetual balance of payments crisis.

Necessity for change

The leadership élites of both the Opposition and government's partisan coalitions had absorbed the policy community's values—namely, that microeconomic reform was required to regenerate the competitiveness of the economy and the necessary efficiency of its public sector. So reform developed the imprimatur of the public interest. Contrary views could then be represented as those of private, vested, interests and so delegitimised.

Status quo threatened

The private interests likely to be disadvantaged by any changes abandoned hope that the preservation of the status quo would protect their interests. For example, from the late 1970s, it was obvious that tariffs were preserving neither manufacturing enterprises nor jobs as this sector went into what appeared to be terminal decline. Also the regime of farm supports created in the fifty years after World War I obviously were inappropriate (as was accepted by the National Farmers Federation) in maintaining export market share in a situation where international agricultural produce markets were increasingly corrupted by trade restrictions and dumped subsidised surpluses.

Labor's partisan coalition reluctantly accepted the policy agenda initiated by the policy-makers and advanced by the policy community because there was no convincing alternative; the status quo was obviously failing. This opinion shift was made easier because of the successful incorporation of planned and phased industry restructuring—which pre-dated the microeconomic reform agenda—into this new policy agenda. During this period the Liberals were even more wholehearted about the microeconomic reform agenda because their partisan coalition was less likely to be adversely affected.

Political agenda-setting

In this context Treasurer Keating's 'banana republic' comment in 1986 dramatised the new public agenda of economic urgency. Such microeconomic reforms as then occurred were the policy agenda-management expression of that broadly accepted public agenda. Agenda politics are about perceptions of reality, not necessarily about reality itself. Microeconomic reform became enmeshed with the issue package of Australia's current account difficulties. For this agenda it matters not that microeconomic reform will not affect Australia's current account position; it makes importing more efficient at the same rate as it improves export efficiency.[12]

The case of tariff policy will briefly illustrate the process of the above model in action. Because of such efforts as those of the Liberal backbencher, Bert Kelly, various academics and the Industries Assistance Commission, the deleterious effects of Australia's tariff regime had been accepted for thirty years. Despite this widespread agreement in the policy community, tariffs still increased.

This can be explained by seeing industry policy as controlled by powerful pressure groups successfully passing costs on to politically amorphous consumers. These pressure groups formed a policy alliance between manufacturing capital, the Victorian Liberal Party and (covertly) the unions, with the Department of Manufacturing Industry usually acting as the bureaucratic midwife of this distributional coalition. The public accepted the costs to them as consumers because they were convinced that tariffs created jobs (as they did in the 1950s). So the policy community was marginalised by politically powerful private interests that controlled the policy agenda. The Fraser Government's maintenance, on average, of real tariff levels during the late 1970s supports this interpretation.

Following the collapse of manufacturing from the mid 1970s it became obvious that tariffs were neither preserving firms and jobs nor any longer slowing the decline of secondary industry. Thus the principal private interests—manufacturing capital and trade unions—became susceptible to the new policy agendas of microeconomic efficiency via 'industry restructuring'.

The conditions for success or failure?

From the above, we assume that the policy agenda of microeconomic reform (however defined) was set during the 1980s and the policy community almost unanimously convinced of its merits; that Australia's macroeconomic situation provided the externally derived impetus; and that the vested private interests were in discredited retreat or, however reluctantly, accepted the new directions. In other words, the policy agenda (and, generally, the public agenda) was unambiguously in favour of microeconomic reform.

What about the pace of microeconomic reform? Many have judged it to be proceeding too slowly, but this assertion only raises questions about the factors that determine the rate of such a reform process. It is proposed here that this factor will be governed by three elements: the partisan coalition element, the institutional impediments to authority in the Australian polity and the (partly consequent) policy-making system.

The partisan coalition element
Where partisan coalitions exist they shape the implementation of microeconomic adjustment. Because these linkages proliferate for any government, reform requires inevitably protracted cajoling of individual groups into cooperation. The vehicle for reform of the waterfront, for example — the Waterfront Industry Reform Authority — incorporated the principle private interests, the Waterside Workers' Federation (WWF) and the stevedoring firms, into its negotiated, compensatory policy process. The private firms were included because Labor required a consensual, negotiated process of reform with the WWF. Consequently, the conflict between employers and employees spilled over into the institutional mechanisms of reform of the industry at large, resulting in a protracted, incremental reform process.

The reform of the waterfront and coastal shipping was also prolonged under Labor because of the influence within the labour movement of the Waterside Workers Federation and the Seamen's Union respectively. Similarly the New South Wales Liberal Government has declared an intention to reform the New South Wales Bar Association's monopoly over the provision of legal services in that state. This process will prove similarly protracted because of the influence of lawyers within the Liberal Party's partisan coalition.

The institutional impediments of the Australian polity
Australia's institutional framework often allows private interests to delay, defer or even defeat the public interest (however defined).

The Commonwealth Government does not have overwhelming direct power but shares constitutional sovereignty with the states, whose formal jurisdiction — particularly over economic infrastructure, such as public water and electricity utilities, railways and ports — covers many of the areas requiring microeconomic reform. In addition, a uniquely Australian plethora of statutory agencies and judicial (and quasi-judicial) bodies circumscribe or replace the authority of the central state. Usually Commonwealth Governments do not even control the federal parliament because of a voting system that virtually guarantees that the government will constitute a minority in the Senate.

The political system makes comprehensive, rapid reform difficult. Australia's federal structure enhances this phenomenon by providing competitive political arenas between which pressure groups can 'jurisdiction shop' to their own particular advantage.[13] Alternatively, it allows groups under attack to retreat to bastions under another level of jurisdiction. This tactic was touted by the trade union movement following the Victorian Kennett and Tasmanian Groom Liberal Governments' labour law reforms. Its possibility led to those State Governments eventually resiling from some of their more radical prescriptions.

During the 1980s the relatively more sweeping — compared with

Australia—deregulatory initiatives in New Zealand were because of such institutional factors. The New Zealand Government's unicameral institutional framework allowed the unilateral top-down imposition of national government policy decisions.

The structure of the microeconomic reform process: 'Rationalism' versus 'incrementalism'

Once the public agenda is accepted, the question of implementing a policy agenda arises. Simonian rationalist models of policy-making postulate that decision-makers assemble the available data, evaluate all the options and then select the best course of action. Alternatively, risk-averse policy-makers instead tinker with the existing format of policy, only incrementally changing the status quo as opportunities arise. This latter course reduces the consequences of failure (and, conversely, the likelihood of success). The distinctiveness of these two models has been overstated, but they do illuminate the political possibilities for microeconomic reform policy-makers. The rationalist model assumes global optimisation, with consequent problems in obtaining all the requisite information and anticipating the reactions of all affected interests. Incrementalism—optimising locally by implementing policy in stages—is generally more attractive in Australia, where governments have to deflect an opportunist opposition carefully and manage both their recalcitrant partisan coalition and an institutional environment that inhibits the swift exercise of unbounded authority.

In addition, the incremental nature of governmental policy also arises ineluctably from special relationship with supportive group interests (like the doctors or lawyers for the Liberals or the trade unions for Labor). But the informal relationship between a government and its partisan voters—who require constant reassurance that microeconomic reform is not threatening their immediate interests—is equally important. Both these influences, formal and informal, incline policy-making in this area towards cautious incrementalism. This tendency might grow over time as the government's position in the opinion polls deteriorates. So microeconomic reform might initially be slow, or it might become increasingly difficult, because of the policy system by which it is implemented. This was the case for Labor in the period 1989-93. It remains to be seen whether Labor's surprise electoral triumph in 1993 changes that, although I doubt the policy pattern will alter much.

Significant political will is required to make progress, however incremental. Alternatively, ministers seeking to control the political agenda might attempt to control the definition of the task, setting compromise targets in order to be able to announce that 'reform' has been achieved. In April 1990 the Labor Cabinet announced that microeconomic reform compromised tariff reform, waterfront reform, increasing competition in the telecommunications industry, deregulating air transport and reviewing the role of the Broadcasting Tribunal. These policy items were by then mostly already designed and partisan support organised. The problem—as the Greiner Government discovered in the 1991 New South Wales state election—is that microeconomic reform does not provide the quick and obvious pay-offs that gain popular support.

Three sets of microeconomic reform case studies

Let us now exaimine three of the areas of recent microeconomic reforms to see whether the paradigm advanced above applies. These areas are probably indicative although not entirely representative of the totality of policy concerns labelled as microeconomic reform. They certainly represent the breadth of the activities that have come under that rubric. Their only common thread is that they sought to improve the input–output ratio in particular sectors of the political economy.

Public sector microeconomic reform

Microeconomic reform was initially only a subsidiary policy agenda in the public sector changes of the 1980s. In part public sector reform was initially a Labor policy community response to the perceived failures of public administration under the Whitlam Labor Government. The reforms of the Australian public service in 1983 and the Budget in 1984 were part of the whole process, although they were not then labelled as microeconomic reform because that public agenda had not yet been created. Then the dominant economic agenda was neo-Keynesian macroeconomics. In 1986–87 followed reforms of government business enterprises, which saw the allowance of increased competition, the introduction of rate-of-return targets, reduced investment and personnel controls, and financial restructuring. Not all of these changes unambiguously enhanced microeconomic efficiency, although they generally attempted to make the public sector more productive to overcome the long-term erosion of its fiscal base. These changes principally reflected a conviction within the policy community that such reforms were required and a corresponding inertia on the part of the public sector's 'private' interests, the trade unions, which acquiesced through lack of an appealing alternative approach. Labor's partisan coalition was inert, partly because the government was still popular, seemingly successful and in control of the political agenda.

Equally, the policy community-driven asset sales—privatisation of public enterprises—was an area both of mixed success and mixed motives. Labor's privatisation of the Commonwealth Bank was impelled by fiscal imperatives. By then the microeconomic reform agenda was established and provided a convenient label to legitimate Labor's budgetary deficit-reducing motive. Paradoxically, the price Labor set for its sale of the public airlines indicated that the purchaser would have to be proofed against wholesale air route deregulation (real microeconomic reform?). Conversely, the price the Liberals set for the privatisation of AOTC (which was required for their broad policy strategy) indicated that the purchasers—unlike those who would have bought the airlines under Labor, and contrary to Liberal assurances during the 1993 elections—would be allowed to 'rationalise' their operations (i.e. through removing cross-subsidising consumer service obligations and labour shedding) to achieve maximum profitability. Privatisation, while presented under the rubric of microeconomic reform, has in reality usually been a budgetary strategy. In this case the policy community's convictions, abetted by a surprising diffidence from the private interests, succeeded in controlling the public agenda defining the public interest.

By 1993 Labor (both its policy community and the unions) had become less enthusiastic about privatisation. It was convinced that the AOTC should not be privatised, for broader industry policy reasons; telecommunications being seen as technologically a sunrise industry and so a valuable component of a future manufacturing base. Microeconomic efficiency was to be achieved by introducing a competitor, Optus, the very industry structure that had previously been rejected for the airlines industry! By the 1990s the simple neo-classical microeconomic nostrums of the 1980s were subject to increasing contestation, as the combination of growing policy community divisions over policy (encouraged by the Liberals' continuing purist stance) and increasing resistance from Labor's partisan coalition—in particular the ACTU—began to bite in policy-making forums.

Other failures to privatise reflected purely institutional difficulties. State Governments' reluctance to privatise their more profitable enterprises could be explained in terms of fiscal disadvantage under present federalist arrangements: these enterprises provide State Governments with substantial revenues. New South Wales was paid $121 million by the State Bank and the GIO in 1987–88. In Victoria successive State Governments have used the Gas and Fuel Corporation as a contributor to consolidated revenue (about $290 million in 1988–89). If privatised, these enterprises would provide a one-off capital sum to the state, but the Commonwealth would be the net long-term beneficiary through its monopoly of company tax receipts from the newly privatised enterprises. The vertical fiscal imbalance created by the Australian federation's fiscal division of powers provides a powerful disincentive to privatisation. State-based policy communities thus have been reluctant to advance this microeconomic reform policy. Instead they have focused on the vertical fiscal imbalance in the Australian federation, further revealing that 'microeconomic reform' has become a legitimating device in the contest for the political agenda.

Industry reorganisation

A decade ago most observers were pessimistic about the prospects for substantial reform of Australia's manufacturing industry structure. This pessimism existed despite the dramatic troubles of these industries indicating that decisive action was required. Yet much has been achieved in the heavy engineering, steel and automotive industries. This is mainly because of two factors in our model: the influence of exogenous variables in creating a public agenda favouring new policy directions—with which Labor's partisan coalition was sympathetic—together with the ability of the ministers of the Hawke Government, principally Button, to persuade the private interests to accommodate steady, incremental and negotiated change.

This industry policy of 'microeconomic incrementalism', as epitomised by the 1986–89 Heavy Engineering Plan, produced varied results from the standpoint of improved microeconomic efficiency. The Steel Plan was probably partly responsible—together with the improvement in the world steel market and the post-1986 depreciation of the dollar—for the renewed international competitiveness of BHP's steel division. Progress under the Car Plan was slower, although there were results in improved productivity and exports under Button's offsets arrangements. The Liberals' determination to reduce automotive tariffs to zero, while the superior option in microeconomic theory, merely served to encourage otherwise unwilling private interests in their acceptance of gradual but continuous change. Labor's car plan, while inferior in microeconomic theory, produced results superior to those likely under the Liberal purists because it accommodated the private interests in negotiated predictable reform. Consequently Labor was able to retain the legitimacy of the public interest in its policy agenda management.

Industry deregulation

Financial sector deregulation is the best documented of the Labor Government's deregulatory endeavours.[14] Academic explanations for this phenomenon focus on three, interrelated factors: first, that government was no longer advantaged by the regulatory system. The original prudential, monetary and redistributive goals of regulation were no longer being served. Second, the banks' costs were raised by regulation, while it no longer prevented some of the rent so created in the industry from being captured by the non-bank financial institutions. Finally, the previously advantaged consumers of the regulatory system—farmers, bank employees and home buyers—saw its benefits dwindling and so were prepared to countenance change.

In this schema, for exogenous reasons, the major private interests were no longer advantaged by regulation and consequently pursuit of a public interest policy agenda advantageous to the government became possible. The absence of any element of a partisan coalition between

Labor and the finance industry made the imposition of a dispassionate public interest policy agenda both easier and more attractive.

Other deregulatory successes confounded recognised experts. In the early 1980s commentators on agricultural policy were pessimistic about agricultural deregulation. Since then considerable deregulation of agricultural subsidies and institutional arrangements has been achieved. Two private interest variables explain this success. The first is the lack of partisan linkages between the ALP and farmers. Thus Labor was able to implement the public interest without needing to mollify any supporters. Equally importantly, the representatives of the major private interest, the National Farmers' Federation, proved cooperative. This was a surprise and is best explained by a combination of two factors: that the NFF's leaders had been recruited to economic rationalism, and as an NFF response to the exogenous trade crisis, in particular the need to combat global agricultural protectionism from a standpoint of relative virtue.

None the less in the 1990s the deregulation of agriculture—as seen in the issue of sugar tariffs—attracted more opposition, indicating that reform processes are not irreversible. Another pointer to the future of agricultural deregulation can be seen in the recent behaviour of the 'self-regulating' wool industry. After 1987 the Wool Council's floor pricing strategy disastrously 'chased the market' rather than stabilising prices. The conflicting sectional interests of the wool industry—a powerful producer-controlled authority (aided by the brokers) versus relatively powerless private markets—are permanent. Kerin's reforms of Australia's commodity marketing authorities, designed to make them more efficient by self-regulating their industries' management, were impaired by the wool marketing fiasco and the persistence of producer interests—particularly among wool, dairy and sugar farmers—hostile to agricultural deregulation.[15] The recently renewed partisan connections between farmers and the Coalition parties indicates that future microeconomic deregulation of agriculture will be contested.

The future 'politics' of microeconomic reform?

Improving domestic economic efficiency is essential to achieve the post-1980s redirection of Australia's political economy towards international competitiveness (and through economic growth securing the fiscal base of the state). But focusing on microeconomic reform obscures the fundamental difficulty of Australia's political economy: economic vulnerability because of our narrow export base. Only recently have elements of the policy community realised that microeconomic reform, although necessary, is not sufficient for that fundamental task. As the above example of the AOTC indicates, more multiplex calculations now figure in policy-making; microeconomic reform is no longer an end in itself.

There are also numerous aspects of microeconomic reform that make its achievement difficult and contrary to usual Australian political practice. It is arguably contrary to what Castles identifies (see note 6) as Australia's historical tradition of domestic defence against our economic vulnerability. So economic efficiency has no guaranteed priority in future policy agendas; new private interest distributional coalitions might emerge to vitiate the microeconomic efficiency of the gains of recent reforms. The policy agenda is now increasingly divided on partisan lines, so the definition of the public interest is increasingly contested within the policy community.

Also exogenous environments are not uniform in their effects. For the car industry, exogenous variables, such as the depreciation of the Australian dollar, have not always produced the 'correct' microeconomic response. During the late 1980s, instead of Australian-built cars increasing market share over imports, the local manufacturers maintained cash flows by either chasing import prices or else (e.g. in the case of Toyota) manipulating the offsets policy to maximise import profitability. The car industry case indicates that perverse responses (from the national 'public' if not the individual firm's 'private' perspective) are just as likely as efficient responses to environmental changes.

Microeconomic reform, as a principle, enjoys a wider degree of popular acceptance than do the particular instruments for its realisation. For example, perhaps reflecting the rise of unemployment, tariff cuts do not now enjoy popular support. This makes Labor's management of its partisan coalition doubly difficult in comparison with the bipartisan 1980s. Political conflict over instruments has confused and inhibited the reform process. A recent illustration of this phenomenon is in the volte face performed by the Labor Government and the ACTU after the Industrial Relations Commission failed to endorse the Accord Mark VI agreement in the 1991 national wage case. The unions, with Labor Government support, reacted by superficially adopting the Liberals' stated strategy for labour market reform and engaged in decentralised wage-bargaining at the enterprise level to attempt to achieve the implementation of the elements of Accord Mark VI. The day-to-day realities of political advantage and demand satisficing allows (if not encourages) such policy reversals. Governments faced with declining electoral support are powerfully encouraged in such opportunism. That both parties backed off their sugar tariff policies in the 1993 federal election is indicative of this 'political' factor.

Another problem is that the costs of microeconomic reform are often focused, while the benefits are more diffuse. Also the reforms themselves might create new sets of interests that seek to redress disadvantage. The re-emergence of farmer protectionism is a predictable consequence of Australia's exasperation with the slow pace of international agricultural trade reform. Here there is also a problem of definition: costs and benefits to whom? The success of Button's Car Plan has been undoubtedly corrupted by the structure of ownership in the car industry. Australia's branch office manufacturers pursue strategies that are internationally rational for themselves while being allocatively irrational for Australia.

The progress and targets of microeconomic reform will continue to be shaped by the major parties' partisan coalitions. Again, this is the politics of diffuse benefits and concentrated costs: the problem of extensity versus intensity. Labor in the decade 1983–93 required that its partisan coalition pay most of the price for both macroeconomic policy and microeconomic reform. With the post-1990 recession, this almost proved electorally fatal; Labor was only saved by an electoral perception that the Coalition would be even more hard-line. Maintaining a winning electoral coalition and implementing policy through a political system seemingly designed to prevent decisive government requires political skills, will and luck of a high order. In reaction to its 1993 loss, the Opposition can be expected to offer siren calls to weaken the resolve of governments to implement 'rational' policy about which the electorate might be unenthusiastic and ill-informed. The 1991 New South Wales election, with the reversals suffered by the economically rationalist Greiner Government in face of an opportunist Labor campaign, indicates that—like the 1993 sugar tariffs imbroglio—the 1988 timed local phone calls episode was not a unique incident.

The very elitism of the policy-community-driven microeconomic reform policy process threatens continually to derail individual reforms. There is no inevitable transfer ('mobilisation' in the political science vocabulary) from specific policy agendas on to broader public agendas. Private interests continually seek to reshape the policy agenda to their advantage. For instance, the Business Council of Australia seeks tariff reductions but resists pro-competitive and anti-monopoly regulation, arguing that Australian firms need economies of scale to be internationally competitive. The former policy is microeconomically rational; the latter is not. Like the sugar and dairy farmers, other private interest groups also selectively nominate microeconomic reforms that suit their private interests while ignoring those that have short-term deleterious effects on those interests. Since the recession of the 1990s began, microeconomic reform has degenerated into the self-interested contestation normal to Australian politics.

Conclusion

It is proposed that the politics of microeconomic reform can be roughly structured using three independent variables endogenous to the policy process: the public interest/policy community nexus; the private interest through partisan coalitions and pressure groups; and the agenda-setting variables. These have interacted with the exogenous environment, producing the policy results discussed above. Applying this model has become less simple since the early 1990s recession eroded the policy community's previously bipartisan cohesion. In addition, because the exogenous variable is subject to such a large range of influences, predictive generalisations about the future possibilities of microeconomic reform have to be confined either to single sectors or else to be of such a low order as to be virtually useless. Unfortunately improvement on that dismal methodological conclusion appears elusive.

For a variety of 'political' reasons—the presence of two adversarial (and opportunist?) sets of partisan coalitions, the institutional features of the Australian polity, the persistence of private interests and popular credulity—microeconomic reform will continue to be contested and mostly incrementally implemented. The Simon-style rationalism required for such reform—the financial and agricultural sector deregulations aside—is not a usual feature of Australian political practice. Changes in the 'dependent' variable of my microeconomic reform politics model—the exogenous imperatives—could easily halt the process, a result increasingly likely as the 1990s progress.

It will become ever more obvious that Australia's economic problems cannot be resolved by selective and partisanly defined application of a nostrum that avoids calculation of its distributional outcomes and cannot solve the fundamental economic question facing Australia: our vulnerability to external forces.

Notes

1 For the period up to the 1980s this account depends on the seminal contributions of Noel Butlin and his colleagues. See, for example, N. G. Butlin, A. Barnard and J. J. Pincus (1982), *Government and Capitalism: Public and Private Choice in Twentieth-Century Australia*, Allen & Unwin, Sydney. The commentary in this chapter also relies heavily on various contributions to R. Maddock and I. W. McLean (eds) (1987), *The Australian Economy in the Long Run*, Cambridge University Press, Melbourne.
2 For an exposition of the politics of the 'workers' welfare state' see F. G. Castles (1985), *The Working Class and Welfare*, Allen & Unwin, Sydney. For a description of the evolution of public sector enterprises see part 4: 'Public enterprise', in Butlin, Barnard and Pincus (1982).
3 For a concise analysis of this period see F. H. Gruen (1986), 'How bad is Australia's economic performance and why?', *Economic Record*, 62:177, 180−93. See also chapter 5, 'All the restrictive practices known to man 1945 to 1975', in Butlin, Barnard and Pincus (1982).
4 For a discussion of the definition of microeconomic reform see P. Forsyth (1992), 'A perspective on microeconomic reform', in P. Forsyth (ed.), *Microeconomic Reform in Australia*, Allen & Unwin, Sydney.

5 P. Forsyth (1990), 'Competitiveness, microeconomic reform and the current account deficit', *Discussion Paper No. 228*, Centre for Economic Policy Research, ANU, Canberra.
6 Francis Castles (1988), *Australian Public Policy and Economic Vulnerability*, Allen & Unwin, Sydney.
7 For influential summary accounts see Industries Assistance Commission (1987–88), *Annual Report*, AGPS, Canberra and Economic Planning Advisory Council (1988), *An Overview of Microeconomic Constraints on Economic Growth. Paper No. 32*, AGPS, Canberra.
8 For expositions of this interventionist tendency see C. Hamilton (1989), 'Does free trade produce the goods?', *Economic Papers* 8:2, 23–36 and R. Gerritsen and G. Singleton (1991), 'Evaluating the Hawke Government's industry agenda: Democratic economic planning versus economic rationalism?' in B. Galligan and G. Singleton (eds), *How Labor Governs: The Hawke Government and Business*, Longman Cheshire, Melbourne, or A. Capling and B. Galligan (1992), *Beyond the Protective State: The Political Economy of Australia's Manufacturing Industry Policy*, Cambridge University Press, Sydney.
9 For illustrations of the concept of policy communities see M. Atkinson and W. Coleman (1990), 'Strong states and weak states: Sectoral policy networks in advanced capitalist economies', *British Journal of Political Science* 19:1, 47–67, and M. Wright (1988), 'Policy community, policy network and comparative industrial policies', *Political Studies* 36:4, 593–612.
10 The literature in this area owes much to Olson. See M. Olson (1965), *The Logic of Collective Action*, Harvard University Press, Cambridge, Mass., and his (1984) 'Australia in the perspective of the rise and decline of nations', *Discussion Paper No. 109*, Centre for Economic Policy Research, ANU, Canberra. For an analysis pertaining to the recent period of Labor government see T. Mathews (1991), 'Interest group politics: Corporatism without business?', in F. G. Castles (ed.), *Australia Compared: People, Policies and Politics*, Allen & Unwin, Sydney.
11 For an introduction to the model of political agendas see R. Cobb, J. Keith Ross and M. Ross (1976), 'Agenda building as a comparative political process', *American Political Science Review* 70:1, 126–38. For an application of the concepts see R. Flickinger (1983), 'The comparative politics of agenda setting: The emergence of consumer protection policy as a public policy issue in Britain and the United States', *Policy Studies Review* 2:3, 429–44. For an illustration of issue attention cycles see A. Downs (1972), 'Up and down with ecology—the issue attention cycle', *Public Interest* 7:1, 38–50. For a description of agenda management: A. Harding (1985), 'Unemployment policy: A case study in agenda management', *Australian Journal of Public Administration* 44:3, 224–46. And for a description of the allied process of 'issue packaging', see M. Hogan (1986), 'Issue packaging: A link between pressure groups and political parties', *Politics* 21:1, 94–103.
12 For a conventional account of this linkage see Economic Planning Advisory Council (1988), *An Overview of Microeconomic Constraints on Economic Growth. Paper No. 32*, AGPS, Canberra. For a rebuttal of this argument see P. Forsyth (1990), 'Competitiveness, microeconomic reform and the current account deficit', *Discussion Paper No. 228*, Centre for Economic Policy Research, ANU, Canberra.

13 R. Gerritsen (1990), 'A continuing confusion: A comment on the appropriate dispersal of powers in the Australian federation', *Australian Journal of Political Science* 25:2, 228–40.
14 For accounts see: I. Harper (1986), 'Why financial deregulation?', *Australian Economic Review* 1st Quarter, 37–49; S. Leung (1989), 'Financial liberalisation in Australia and New Zealand', *Discussion Paper No. 208*, Centre for Economic Policy Research, ANU, Canberra, and J. O. N. Perkins (1989), *The Deregulation of the Australian Financial System: The Experience of the 1980s*, Melbourne University Press, Melbourne; K. Davidson (1992), 'The failure of the financial deregulation in Australia', in S. Bell and J. Wanna (eds), *Business–Government Relations in Australia*, Harcourt Brace Jovanovich, Sydney.
15 See L. McQuire (1992), 'Interest networks or sub-sectoral corporatism in wool marketing authorities?' in S. Bell and J. Wanna (eds), *Business–Government Relations in Australia*, Harcourt Brace Jovanovich, Sydney.

12

The welfare state and economic adjustment

Lois Bryson

Processes of economic adjustment during recent decades have had a profound effect on the Australian welfare state. The changes, which will continue through the 1990s, amount to nothing less than a fundamental restructuring of the very form of the welfare state, the foundations of which were laid in the first decade of the twentieth century. This state structure, as Castles has pointed out, relied on a highly centralised system of employment regulation that delivered a degree of economic security and equality, although initially it applied to white males only. The national economy was sheltered from competition, and employment was protected by restricted immigration. Because of this reliance on the employment system, rather than the social wage, to deliver economic security and equality, Castles suggests that Australia would have been appropriately termed a 'wage earners' welfare state'.[1] Income security measures, as they evolved in the 1940s, were rights-based, although selective and means-tested. Few obligations attached to their receipt once eligibility was established, although there was, and remains, an ever-present concern to ensure that de facto relationships were declared.

Economic adjustment, described in detail elsewhere in this volume, has brought with it a number of key effects. First, and fundamentally important, has been a weakening of the centralised regulation of wages and employment conditions, particularly through the introduction of enterprise bargaining.

Second, alterations to tariff protection and changes in immigration policy have linked the Australian economy more closely to the international economy.

Third, the income security system, the traditional safety net of those outside the employment system, has been transformed. The result is a more comprehensive set of entitlements, which now includes additional groups such as the working poor and carers as well as the more established categories of welfare recipients. However, some groups are now without support, for example some young unemployed and those who leave employment voluntarily. Also the sole 'universal' provision, the family allowance, has been means-tested since 1987, and there is generally more stringent targeting of benefits. The financial level of many entitlements has, none the less, improved. In the early 1990s pension rates reached the Labor Government's target of 25 per cent of average weekly earnings for the first time, and they are indexed to the Consumer Price Index.[2]

Fourth, there has been a more detailed development of the coverage of entitlements, surveillance has been intensified and eligibility increasingly linked to explicit demonstrations of commitment to labour force participation, through the government's 'active labour market' strategy.[3] Weatherley describes this change in policy as a move from 'entitlement to contract'.[4] This if effect amounts to a revival of the historic obsession of distinguishing between the deserving and the undeserving poor, a distinction largely made on the grounds of perceived preparedness to work. Similar revivals can be found in the pages of history at similar times, when fiscal demands on public support become heavy.[5] Dean has recently traced the construction of the poor in social policy throughout the last five hundred years of British history. He points to the persistent constitution of the poor according to 'first, those that cannot work; second, those that will work; and third, those that will not work'.[6] Social policy has been keen to rid the public purse of responsibility for this latter group.

A casualty of economic adjustment has also been the implicit assumption of the post-World War II economic growth period that there would be a gradually expanding welfare state with increasing social rights and the progressive extension of state-provided services. The reversal of this assumption has been evident since the late 1970s in a fixation on reduction of government expenditure, rationing of benefits and services, greater reliance on user-pays principles and privatisation. Not coincidentally, these patterns are very much of a piece with changes in other advanced capitalist societies.

As Castles' analysis of the links between employment regulation and welfare demonstrates, the concept of 'welfare state', in its broadest form, is not confined simply to those elements traditionally denoted by the term *welfare*, that is, pensions and benefits and services to the poor. In its broadest sense a welfare state should be concerned with the well-being of all citizens and the degree of equality, or redistribution, that is achieved through all of the state's actions or lack of actions. At its broadest, then, the concept should be just as concerned with the effects on the well-being of citizens of, for example, monetary and tariff policies, support for the arts and sciences and the framework and enforcement of criminal and civil law as with the effects of unemployment benefits and public housing. Such an ideal approach is even broader than the much-quoted tripartite approach proposed by the eminent British social policy analyst, Richard Titmuss, during the 1950s. Titmuss proposed three elements of concern: social welfare (that is, welfare provisions in the narrow traditional sense), occupational welfare (which involves benefits related to occupational status over and above wages) and fiscal welfare (which covers benefits that accrue through the taxation system).[7]

A comprehensive coverage of all areas of redistribution affected by state action is beyond the scope of this chapter and, therefore, the major focus will be on traditional social welfare. After a brief consideration of the broad context of the recent changes, this chapter will essentially focus on three areas: changes to income security entitlements, some key changes in the provision of services themselves and finally the implication for the Australian welfare state of these changes in conjunction with the changes to the system of employment regulation. In relation to service provision, the focus will be mainly on services for the aged and people with disabilities and the provision of child care.

Increasing demands on the welfare state

In most advanced capitalist societies in the late 1970s and early 1980s, the rising cost of welfare state provisions together with a downturn in the economy led commentators, particularly conservative commentators, to suggest that the welfare state was in crisis and question whether it remained an affordable goal.[8]

Pressures on welfare states have come from demographic, social and economic sources. At the demographic level, an almost universal trend in the advanced capitalist societies has been an ageing population and an increase in the numbers with disabilities, which result in an increase in the numbers eligible for income support and more demand for services. Less pressure to remain in unsatisfactory marriages, or to marry at all, in many countries has led to a significant increase in the numbers of single parents in the population, particularly female single parents, another group eligible for support from the state. Moreover, economic recession in many advanced industrial societies produced fluctuating, but relentlessly increasing, numbers of unemployed.

Significant pressure on welfare states, from the 1970s onwards, also came from steadily increasing citizen demands for an expanded view of the nature of social rights. Internationally, although to differing degrees in different countries, there has been a gradual recognition of the legitimacy of the rights of a diverse range of groups including women, indigenous peoples, ethnic minorities, people with disabilities and homosexuals. The expansion of such demands is hypothetically limitless, and this has placed strains on welfare states and their claims to legitimacy as they juggle competing demands.[9] Certainly these newer demands have the potential to alter patterns of distribution of welfare resources and benefits with an associated likelihood of resistance from those whose advantages or cultural norms are threatened. The development of the so-called 'backlash' against the welfare state by neo-conservatives and market liberals must, therefore, at least partly be recognised as a reaction to the New Left political movements of the 1960s and 1970s. As J. K. Galbraith put it, this is a 'revolt of the rich', whose traditional inequitable share of resources is potentially threatened by the claims of the New Left and a range of social movements.[10]

Australia shows clear signs of all these pressures, and demands from conservatives to reduce public expenditure take on a singular significance given the historical context. This is so because, despite frequently expressed conceptions to the contrary, public expenditure in Australia has been quite low when measured against that of comparable affluent societies. On a range of measures Austraila is very rarely above the OECD average and often among the tail-enders. This can be explained partly because the wage-earners' welfare state delivered considerable benefits that in other countries were delivered through the public or social wage. However, this wage-earners' welfare system has been deteriorating since the signing of the Accord in 1983. Except for high-status workers, wage levels deteriorated from that point and other employment benefits diminished.

When we consider the relative size of the public sector, using government outlays as a percentage of GDP as a measure, we find that for Australia government outlays reached a high point of about 39 per cent of GDP in 1985. By 1989 they had fallen to 34.3 per cent. Such a reducing pattern is typical of OECD countries, but not typical is Australia's level of expenditure, which remains well below the average. The 1989 Australian figure was 10 percentage points below the OECD average. Of twenty-one countries, only Japan, Switzerland and Turkey had lower outlays, while the outlays of the top-ranking country, Sweden, was at 60 per cent. Canada, a country with which Australia is often compared, expended 44.2 per cent of its GDP on government outlays.[11]

If we turn to public sector employment, a favourite whipping boy of market liberals, we find that in 1989 in Australia general government employment was 15.7 per cent of total employment. This figure is down from a high of more than 17 per cent in 1985. Again, this is well below the OECD average, which for 1989 was 18.2 per cent, with Australia ranking twelfth among the twenty-one countries. Sweden is also the top-ranking nation here at 31.5 per cent, double the Australian figure.[12]

Despite the historical relative underdevelopment of the Australian welfare state and an increasing demand for services, since the mid 1980s there has been a concerted and, as the preceding figures suggest, partly successful attempt to reduce expenditure. Governments at both federal and state levels have introduced changes that have affected virtually all strands of the welfare state. Interpretations of the effects of the changes vary considerably, although some have increased the financial well-being of certain groups, allowing the then Minister for Social Security, Brian Howe, to claim in 1989, 'We have rebuilt the safety net'.[13]

Demands on the Australian social security system

Outlays on income maintenance as a proportion of GDP almost doubled between 1970 and 1987, rising from 3.8 per cent to 7.3 per cent.[14] Demographic trends graphically illustrate the nature of the pressures on the social security system that largely account for the increase. For example, the number of age pensioners rose from 840 207 in 1972 to 1 407 005 in 1991, an increase of roughly 67 per cent. During the same period the total population expanded by only about 20 per cent. Over that period the number of people receiving income security in respect of disabilities increased also—by more than 170 per cent.[15]

For unemployment and sickness benefits, the rises have been staggeringly large. The annual average number of beneficiaries in 1972 was just under 30 000. By 1991 a large increase in the numbers of unemployed was compounded by an extension of the time spent receiving benefit. The 1991 annual average number of beneficiaries had grown to considerably more than half a million, or seventeen times the figure for 1972.[16]

Demographic and policy changes reduced the extent of claims in relation to one major provision, the family allowance. In 1976 the allowance was instituted through combining tax concessions in respect of children and child endowment (a change that incidentally resulted in a saving for the government). Family allowance was a universal payment and the only one in the Australian income security system. Payments at the time were made to a little more than two million families. This figure remained relatively stable, rising by only about 100 000 to 1987 when means testing by income was introduced. The number of families receiving the allowance then declined by a little less than 100 000 and stayed, with only minor fluctuations, at just under the two million mark. Because of a drop in the birth rate, the number of children in respect of whom family allowance is paid dropped even more significantly. At its highest point in 1978, the figure reached 4.3 million; by 1991 it was down to 3.7 million.[17]

Responses to increasing demands in a time of economic adjustment

This increased demand for income support coincided with the rise of the market liberal conviction that the economic adjustment process must involve cuts to government spending. These competing directions led to the adoption of myriad 'welfare efficiency' strategies. Drawing on the careful analysis undertaken by the Social Security Review (1986–89) and other reports commissioned by the Labor Government in the latter half of the 1980s,[18] these strategies did produce increased income for certain target groups, thus promoting social justice at the same time as they attempted to contain a potential blow-out of public funds. For example, one new measure, the Child Support Scheme, aimed to sheet home some financial responsibility for offspring to non-custodial parents. This provision offers both financial support to custodial parents (a demonstrably poor group) and economies to the state.

A second innovation was the development of provisions to assist sole female parents into the labour force. Before leading the Social Security Review Bettina Cass had demonstrated that full-year, full-time work was the best long-term way of avoiding poverty.[19] Thus, the JET (Jobs, Education and Training) labour market program introduced for sole parents in 1988 could be demonstrated to be in women's best interests. However, very conveniently, it simultaneously reduced claims on the state and reinforced the commitment of the population to paid employment.

Some moves to achieve greater social justice notwithstanding, what can be detected in many recent changes to the social security system is a revival of that well-documented obsession with ensuring that the availability of welfare benefits does not compete with the imperative to undertake paid employment. This obsession in turn leads to a determined separation of the deserving poor from the undeserving, that is, those whose commitment to paid work is in doubt. Some elements of what is happening in Australia today, particularly in relation to the detection of fraud and the straight requirements of those claiming unemployment benefit, resonate with the efforts of the Poor Law reformers in Britain in 1834. The Poor Law Report of 1834 noted that the intention of the reforms was to ensure that any benefits provided by the state would be less attractive than 'the situation of the independent labourer of the lowest class'.[20] George's comment that this fear of undermining people's preparedness to labour has become a 'ghost haunting many a well-intentioned piece of social reform'[21] certainly applies to the Australian reforms of the late 1980s and early 1990s.

This revival of the classic obsession with a work orientation is an international phenomenon. It has been observed that the economic adjustment occurring in most OECD countries involved a concerted effort in the late 1980s and early 1990s 'to ensure that social security systems do not unduly weaken the incentives to work, to save and to change jobs'.[22] In Australia the pursuit of this goal can be seen in respect of many provisions, particularly unemployment benefits, sole parent pensions, disability allowances and the provision of the Family Allowance Supplement to the working poor.

In Australia today the separation of deserving from undeserving social security recipients involves a three-pronged transformation of provisions, which is discussed below. The first separates the undeserving through strict scrutiny of eligibility for benefits via checks for fraud. The second involves the insertion of a range of both voluntary and compulsory programs that aim to assist entry into the labour market. The third element of the approach develops better benefits for those who, for 'acceptable' reasons, are not in the labour force. In this case, deservingness is largely associated with caring for children and old age. An emotive rendering of children as 'deserving' was injected into the debate about social security provisions in the flamboyant and much publicised commitment of Prime Minister Hawke in 1987, that 'by 1990 no child will be living in poverty'.

Fraud control

The most straightforward way to ensure that recipients are 'deserving', and to cut costs and prevent benefits from interfering with commitment to the labour market, is by meticulously ensuring that only directly targeted groups receive benefits. Since the mid 1980s the Department of Social Security has increasingly applied creative fraud control measures. As the department's 1990–91 annual report puts it with rather fudging logic, 'a perception by the community that it is difficult to abuse the income security system and that abuse is likely to result in penalties if detected helps to improve the level of "voluntary compliance"'.[23]

Fraud and administrative reviews take various forms, including office reviews of files, mail reviews, reconciling records with files of the Australian Taxation Office, interviews at regional offices or jointly with the Commonwealth Employment Service and interviews in the recipient's home. In 1986 mobile review teams were introduced 'to verify efforts of unemployment beneficiaries to find work'. This surveillance was extended in 1987 to sole parents and intensified to provide the facility to check information volunteered by the general public. By 1990 sickness beneficiaries had become subject to the net with long-term beneficiaries the focus of specific attention. All told, reviews of more than two million cases were conducted during the 1990–91 period, about a quarter of which were field reviews involving interviews. Around 10 per cent of the reviews of unemployment beneficiaries and sole parents, the two major target groups, led to cancellation.[24]

By 1991 a total of sixty mobile review teams were in operation around the continent. The teams dealt with just on 130 000 reviews in 1991, leading to cancellation of 11.6 per cent of the cases reviewed (unemployment, sickness and sole parent). The rate of cancellation was lowest, at 7.3 per cent, for the long-term unemployed and highest, at 19.5 per cent, where the public had passed on information.[25]

Reorganisation of benefits to enhance labour market participation

Family Allowance Supplement

Throughout the 1980s almost all social security provisions were revamped with a view to enhancing their capacity to encourage recipients to join the labour market. Perhaps the most significant change was the introduction of the Family Allowance Supplement (FAS), which when it was first introduced in 1983 was entitled the Family Income Supplement. It provides additional income, over and above the family allowance, for each child when a family's income is very low ($18 000 per year with one child in 1991), whether derived from the labour market or from social security. The amount per child is higher for older children, and an additional rent allowance is available for those in the private rental market.

FAS is aimed at ensuring that receiving pensions or benefits is not a disincentive to making the transition to paid employment. This aim is also achieved through the establishment of transitional payments, which are attached to certain benefits to ease the cost of returning to employment. FAS is also meant to remove any temptation for people employed on low wages to become social security recipients.

The interface between the Family Allowance Supplement as an income security mechanism and the labour market is its most important and innovative feature. The FAS represents the first time that an Australian provision has explicitly supported the working poor—a highly significant break with the past. The foundations of the Australian welfare state were based on the concept of employers supplying a living wage, with social security only providing a safety net for times when paid employment could not be undertaken.

After an effective publicity campaign in 1987 the number of FAS recipients rose steeply, from about 30 000 families in 1986 to almost 190 000 in 1991.[26] It seemed to be effective in raising low incomes and reducing the disincentive effects of social security. An evaluation of the FAS program undertaken between 1988 and 1990 found that FAS was playing 'a vital role in helping working families make ends meet'. Without FAS, 'one quarter of FAS families would consider stopping work and try to get a pension/benefit'. It was also found that 'the amount of the FAS does not in itself act as a significant workforce disincentive for the second income earner, but rather offers a greater choice about whether to stay at home with children'.[27]

Those receiving social security benefits and those with very low incomes did experience a significant increase in their disposable incomes between 1983 and 1991 (for example, a sole parent with two children renting privately recorded an increase of 24.9%). While most social security recipients' income rose significantly during this period, most income groups outside the social security system and the lowest income quintile actually recorded a drop in income. The top income group, like social security recipients, was an exception in also recording an increase. Thus the only groups recording a real increase were the bottom and the top groups.[28]

Unemployment entitlements

Changes to provisions for the unemployed have also been inspired by a concern to remove any disincentive to seek paid employment. The unemployment benefit has been modified in favour of a more ramified system that spells out a number of categories of unemployed—for example, young, long-term, medium-term—with differing eligibility conditions, particularly for training requirements. This modification challenges the previous unified system with its lack of distinction between claimants and the absence of a time limit on receipt of benefits. These hallmarks of the original provision introduced in the 1940s made the Australian unemployment benefit system less restrictive than those of most other welfare states, which are time-limited and earnings-related and, therefore, dependent on a considerable previous employment record. The Australian benefit has, however, always been modest in its economic value.[29]

Unemployment benefit was abolished, in 1987, for those younger than 18 in favour of a much lower Job Search Allowance (JSA), which is means-tested according to parental income. Even where the person is considered independent, the allowance takes account of parental assets. To cope with a residual group of youth who would have finished up without support, the Youth Homeless Allowance was instituted for young people who are unable to live at home.

Apart from the obvious cost-saving effects of forcing people into employment or transferring primary economic responsibility back to their parents, the reform is partly aimed at removing any disincentive effects that unemployment benefit might have for staying at school or undertaking other forms of training. This strategy formed part of the federal Labor Government's general emphasis on raising the education and skill levels of the labour force, a key element of the current approach to managing adjustment of the Australian economy. As the Department of Social Security expressed it:

> *the central purpose of the JSA is to support (and require) active job search, combined with appropriate training or other job preparation activities where there is a risk of long-term unemployment.*[30]

For those older than 18 who have been unemployed for less than twelve months the unemployment benefit remains, although it is much more stringently administered. There are increasingly regular work tests, requiring periodic job applications, or training which must be documented. A graduated system of non-payment periods has been introduced for 'failing the work/activity test, voluntary job-leaving' or failure 'to attend an interview or respond to correspondence'.[31]

People who have been unemployed for more than twelve months are reassigned to the Newstart Allowance, which was introduced in 1989. This program, together with the earlier JET scheme, marked the beginning of the Federal Government's new labour-market-oriented strategy, something that many other welfare states, particularly the Scandinavian states, have had for many years. In the first year of its operation the proportion of unemployment beneficiaries who were long-term fell from 37 per cent to 26 per cent. This led the government to claim some success for its 'active labour market assistance, including improved access to employment, education and training opportunities'.[32] None the less, it is difficult to disentangle this effect from the effects of the more punitive system of reviews. With the onset of recession, the rate of increase of the long-term unemployed in 1990-91 remained lower than the rates for the shorter term. But this effect is to be expected in the short term, making it difficult to assess the validity of the department's claim to positive results.

Another development that seems to support labour market strategies is the extension of support for students through the AUSTUDY program in 1988. It was made more necessary by the reintroduction of fees for tertiary education. The number of recipients across the educational sectors rose from 200 000 in 1983 to 500 000 in 1991.[33]

Sickness benefits
In relation to sickness and disability, as well as unemployment, the government has wrestled with the fact that the degree of difficulty of returning to work increases with the time a worker has spent out of the labour market. In 1991 the sickness benefit became the sickness allowance and, like the unemployment benefit, became limited to a twelve-month period, except in unusual circumstances. It is linked to labour market programs through rehabilitation and referral schemes. The invalid pension, which became the disability support pension, is now also part of a much more complex package—the disability reform package. It is linked with rehabilitation, active vocational training and labour market programs.[34]

Sole parent benefits
The effects of economic adjustment and the encouragement of labour force participation are nowhere more dramatic than in relation to women. Throughout the 1980s there was a gradual but fundamental

reconstruction of social policy affecting women. The traditional form of gender construction within social policy has been to cast women as legitimate dependants and men as workers.[35] Despite the fact that these patterns have deep historical roots, significant changes have been wrought, with support from many feminists who see them as promoting women's economic independence. While such changes might offer greater gender equality, they are also consonant with ensuring that the social security system does 'not unduly weaken the incentives to work'.[36]

In 1978 the transformation of the supporting mother's benefit into the supporting parent benefit represented a partial reconstruction of the role of fathers in social policy through the recognition of the caring role as well as the breadwinner role. Further developments in these directions occurred during the 1980s with the instatement of the worker role for mothers. There has been a diminution of support available for the wife and mother role and a variety of systematic efforts to direct female social security recipients into the labour force. Until the late 1980s women were eligible for support from the state, as wives, widows or mothers. For women who had been partnered but were no longer in a relationship, the state was prepared to step into the role of economic supporter.

Changes to social security policy aimed at reducing women's dependency involved a number of steps. First the widow's pension was restricted to mothers with dependent children, where formerly widows older than 45 could receive a pension whether or not they had dependants. The latter form of support for older women has been abolished, and older women must now support themselves or qualify for the unemployment benefit. At the same time the age to which offspring in full-time education can be counted as dependent was reduced from 24 to 16 years. The next step, announced in the 1988 federal Budget, was the introduction of the Jobs, Education and Training (JET) scheme. The minister's introduction to the scheme explicitly recognises the drive to reduce women's dependence on the state:

> *JET will offer concerted, practical support and direction to improve sole parents' job skills and help them into the labour market ... JET will build on previous government moves to encourage sole parents out of dependence on the social security system and into economic independence.*[37]

This scheme, however, unlike the Newstart program, remains a voluntary training and income support provision.

Child care services
The provision of child care, and particularly the fee relief offered to low-income parents, represents another strand of policy that encourages women into employment and reduces the workforce disincentives of the

social security system. Yet public provision of child care would appear in the first instance to have negative implications for state budgets. Given the Labor Government's commitment in the mid 1980s to reducing overall expenditure, there was a clear ambivalence about expanding child care services. This attitude changed in 1988 when it was discovered that the government's aims to get women into the workforce and maintain public revenues could be combined. Official commitment to the provision of child care increased with remarkable speed when it was demonstrated that the direct costs to government could be more than compensated and not only from that nebulous factor 'increased productivity'. Revenue, it was shown, would benefit quite directly from increased taxes paid by the women joining the workforce and from direct savings on the dependent spouse rebate and social security outlays.[38]

In 1988 government-funded child care only catered for 9.5 per cent of pre-school children.[39] During the Labor Government's term of office places increased from 70 000 to 250 000 in 1991, or around 180 000 places.[40] The intention was to meet 66 per cent of the demand by 1996, an intention that highlights the government's enthusiasm to encourage women out of the home.[41] Such an increase would put Australia up with the leading Western countries in relation to child care provision.

Child Support Scheme

The Child Support Scheme represents an attempt to cut costs by shifting responsibility for economic support of children and at the same time increasing the income of those in need. It sheets home financial responsibility for support of children of separated parents to the non-custodial parent, a responsibility that was recognised earlier but not enforced. Child maintenance is now collected through employers and distributed through the Australian Taxation Office along with pay-as-you-earn taxation. Before the introduction of this scheme in 1989, individual custodial parents were responsible in the first instance for the collection of maintenance even where it had been ordered by the courts. The officially stated aims for the Child Support Scheme are:

- *that non-custodial parents should share the cost of supporting their children according to their capacity to pay;*
- *that adequate support be available for all children of separated parents;*
- *that the Commonwealth expenditure be limited to what is necessary to ensure that those needs are met;*
- *to ensure that neither parent is discouraged from participating in the workforce; and*
- *that overall arrangements should be simple, flexible, efficient and respect personal privacy.*[42]

The aims of the project clearly reveal three major concerns of the government: to increase the income of the poorest families, to ensure that disincentives to employment are minimised and to reduce public spending. In this case, as in relation to the young unemployed, cost saving is achieved through a re-emphasis on the responsibilities of families, rather than the exercise of collective responsibilities.

The coverage of non-custodial parents by the scheme is still far from complete. Indeed, in 1990 only 35.6 per cent of sole parent pensioners were receiving maintenance, although this was up from 25.6 per cent before the scheme began.[43] While it is too soon to make an overall evaluation of the scheme, and there are clearly still teething problems, it seems likely that the outcomes will at least partially meet all three major objectives.

Entitlements for the aged

The main effect of economic adjustment on income security for the aged has been through the introduction of a national superannuation scheme. The introduction of the Superannuation Guarantee Charge in 1992, with the ultimate aim of providing superannuation for all employees, represents a major departure for a social security system that has, since the first decade of the century, met the cost of age pensions from recurrent revenues.

It must be noted, however, that there has persistently been another source of government support—through tax concessions for payments to superannuation funds—for the retirement incomes of the self-employed and professionals earning higher incomes and of relatively privileged groups of salaried workers. This costly form of public support remains in place.

Award superannuation increased the number of workers covered by some form of superannuation from 40 per cent in 1983 to 72 per cent in 1991. This was further increased to almost complete coverage (although only for those earning more than $450 a month in 1992), from mid 1992 with the institution of the Superannuation Guarantee Charge, a compulsory employer payment.[44]

This Federal Government intervention has helped to extend superannuation to women and low-paid workers, but their coverage on retirement will remain inadequate for the foreseeable future. However, it has not fundamentally changed the unequal distribution of advantages to men and to higher-income earners arising from taxation concessions for personal superannuation contributions and disadvantages caused by women's distinctive employment patterns.[45]

An element of the logic of encouraging private pensions in Australia, as part of the economic adjustment process, was to promote savings and thus encourage investment and reduce inflation. The official position also suggests that private pensions would offer fiscal savings on age pensions, especially as the population ages during the coming decades.

However, this is a contested point. It has been demonstrated that the government will not save money, especially where higher-income earners are concerned, unless it does away with the available tax concessions for private superannuation contributions. The tax subsidy to the private pension contributor in reality is often greater than would be paid out to them through the social security system, partly because the rate of the basic pension remains low, at around 25 per cent of average weekly earnings in 1992. Calculated in relation to the current rates, Toohey has estimated that it would not be until near the end of the twenty-first century that budgetary savings on pensions, through pay-outs from the superannuation system, would outweigh the tax concessions for superannuation.[46]

Carers pensions and the Home and Community Care Program

Another significant change that affects the aged and those with disabilities has been the increasing recognition of the importance of informal caring through the provision of carers pensions.[47] The circumstances under which carers can receive benefits have been broadened, and the take-up rate is increasing. This policy direction can be seen to signal contradictory messages. It represents an appropriate recognition of unpaid caring labour as well as simultaneously flagging a move towards its privatisation, away from collective solutions.

The recognition of informal care, which underpins the carers pension, represents another arena in which the effects of economic adjustment can be observed and where there is considerable international convergence of trends. Internationally we find the promotion of the 'ideals of community support'.[48] As a number of researchers have pointed out, this is an 'area of government policy in which the apparent preferences of the people and the interests of government happily coincide'.[4] People requiring a range of types of support prefer to stay at home rather than live in institutions. Community care is based on the notion that those who are frail or disabled will be assisted to stay in their homes through the provision of some formal services but with, at the same time, a reliance on informal carers who in turn receive formal support. The notion of community care, therefore, involves informal care in combination with professional services rather than care almost exclusively provided by state-run, professionally staffed services, a much more expensive option. This trend is widespread and observable in areas such as children's welfare,[50] adult and juvenile corrections and mental health. But the largest target groups have been the elderly and the disabled. Government policy is heavily influenced by the increasing costs of providing residential professionalised care, particularly given predicted growth in both the aged population and the disabled.

Before the 1980s there was little Commonwealth provision for the support of the aged except for the funding of residential arrangements, mainly in nursing homes. In a move aimed at reducing reliance on residential facilities, the Home and Community Care program (HACC) was initiated in 1985. Its official goal was:

> *To enhance the quality of life of the frail aged and younger people with disabilities and their carers, by providing high-quality and cost-effective care in the community, so that appropriate services are provided according to the assessed need of the individual, and inappropriate admission to residential care avoided.*[51]

The architects of the HACC program (who incidentally were mainly women) did conceive of it as a program responsive to the needs of both clients and their carers (also mostly women) and sensitive to particular interests such as those of Aborigines and people of non-English-speaking backgrounds. However, these aims, as Yeatman points out, have been subverted by economic adjustment agendas 'favouring the privatisation of services where possible and where people cannot afford them, tighter targeting of kinds which subject their users to undemocratic, bureaucratic controls'.[52] An additional issue is the development of non-professional, low-paid and often part-time jobs in the area, which are usually filled by women.[53] Residential and centralised services tended to be developed around the services of better-paid and more powerful professional workers such as nurses, social workers, physiotherapists and doctors.

Although increased funds have been devoted to the HACC program, they are a long way from meeting the demand. The joint funding arrangement between Commonwealth and states, which was intended to be a fifty–fifty sharing, affected by the poor financial circumstances of the states, was closer to sixty–forty in 1990–91.[54] There has been nowhere near enough formal services to meet demand, and the availability of services varies from state to state. Between the financial years of 1985–86 and 1990–91, Commonwealth funding for aged care increased overall, but the rate of increase was very uneven. Funding of residential care, by far the largest item ($1.9 billion) in 1990–91, had increased by 20 per cent over five years while the HACC program received a 95 per cent increase ($278.9 million). Although the geriatric assessment program received the smallest amount of funding ($25 million), it was subject to the largest increase over the period, 346 per cent.[55] Given the shortage of services, geriatric assessment services are effectively becoming 'a means of rationing services, an administrative procedure most concerned with the management of an organisation's limited resources',[56] rather than really being concerned with a comprehensive understanding of the needs of individual clients.

A recent review by the Department of Health, Housing and Community Services has raised the possibility of dealing with the demand through the institution of what amounts to a form of national insurance. This form of funding fits neatly with an economic adjustment agenda and parallels the moves to fund retirement through the national superannuation insurance scheme.[57] It is intriguing that despite a piecemeal drift towards insurance solutions, a national insurance scheme covering all social security and welfare entitlements, as is typical of most European countries, was not seriously debated by the Social Security Review. Clearly such a scheme would require a substantial special fund-raising effort, and times of economic adjustment are times when taxation increases are not politically attractive ideas.

The HACC program illustrates a number of problems inherent in social policy development and service delivery caused by the federal nature of governmental structures in Australia. Since the 1940s the Federal Government has had the majority of fund-raising powers, yet the states have many service-delivery responsibilities. Much state finance has been delivered through tied grants, as with the HACC program, which requires certain performance standards from the states. As has happened with the HACC program, it is not always easy for the Commonwealth Government to enforce these standards, and there is a perpetual tussle between federal and state public services.[58]

The states have perennially argued for greater control of their own finances and, during the early 1990s, the Commonwealth Government offered to meet their demands partly through a program termed the 'New Federalism'. It had the attraction for the Commonwealth of meeting the demands of the states as well as fitting the rhetoric of devolution and would probably have allowed the reduction in government spending that the Federal Government was concerned to achieve. Welfare organisations and service providers were concerned that the 'new federalism' would also have had the disadvantage for citizens that minimum standards for service delivery could not be maintained across Australia. Moreover, history has shown that the Commonwealth is more likely to take a progressive approach to social policy and collective expenditure and to be more attuned to the interests of disadvantaged groups than the states.

The overtaking of the wage-earners' welfare state

The changes to the Australian welfare state wrought during the current period of economic adjustment have involved complex and contradictory elements. The direction of change was set in motion before the commencement of the Hawke Government and is consonant with international trends. The Labor Government, particularly through the portfolios held by Brian Howe,[59] partly followed a traditional Labor path of careful social engineering to improve the lot of the lowest echelons of the working class. The Social Security Review and other projects such as the National Housing Stategy (1990–92) are true to this planned social justice approach. That the resulting changes to social security were in terms of strictly targeted, or selective, assistance also follows a traditional Australian path. Apart from the brief Whitlam period (1972–75), there has been little attempt to take a universal approach to the provision of income security.

The Federal Government's strategies have had some notable success. The basic pension rate reached 25 per cent of average weekly earnings, which is a considerable increase on the 22.7 per cent of 1983.[60] This increase was partly due to a drop in average weekly earnings over the period. However, even allowing for this, there was also a significant rise in the incomes of the poorest due to improved rates of income for those on social security and the provision of assistance to the working poor. Between 1983 and 1991 the rate of real disposable income increased for social security recipients. The rates of increase varied from about 12 per cent for the unemployed on Job Search and Newstart Allowance who were not eligible for rent assistance to around 23 per cent for sole parents and the unemployed who received rent assistance. The income of those earning below-average weekly earnings also rose considerably. For example, for those earning 75 per cent of average weekly earnings in a dual-income family (with income split 70/30 per cent), there was an increase of more than 9 per cent. For dual-income couples earning between 100 and 400 per cent of average weekly earnings, there was, however, a drop in real disposable income.[51] As mentioned earlier, and paradoxically for the pursuit of equality, the incomes of the highest income groups, those earning more than 600 per cent of average weekly earnings, also rose.[62] This notwithstanding, the Labor Government did deliver an improved standard of living to some of the poorer groups, particularly families with dependent children, a group suffering considerable poverty when Labor came to power.

The decade since 1983 has seen a veritable revolution in the social security system, especially at the level of detailed policy. Almost no provision remains unchanged. Some perennial problems have been attacked, such as poverty traps, and the needs of some groups recognised, such as carers and those requiring child care. In the HACC program, the principle of keeping people in their homes was recognised, although insufficient funding has meant that the promise has been far from fulfilled.

In the process of meeting the needs of the poorest, and at the same time keeping costs down, however, the system has become a highly controlling one. There is everywhere evidence of implementing that international goal 'to ensure that social security systems do not unduly weaken the incentive to work, to save and to change jobs'.[63] A great deal of effort has been expended to ensure that no one with a questionable entitlement receives assistance. A sizeable and increasing proportion of all recent annual reports of the Department of Social Security is devoted to a discussion of fraud control measures. A similar pattern can be noted in the annual reports of the Department of Veterans Affairs since 1987, although the degree of concern shown is far less.

The option to quit a job has been curtailed by a consequent denial of the right to unemployment benefit until a certain period has elapsed. All categories of eligibility have been scrutinised for those who might conceivably be channelled into the workforce. Mechanisms for this channelling have been put in place, and entitlements most depend on making every effort to return to paid work. The age pension remains outside this requirement, while for sole parent pensions compliance with employment-seeking behaviour remains optional while there are dependent children under the age of 16.

The social security reforms have not, contrary to former Social Security Minister Brian Howe's pronouncement, 'rebuilt the safety net'. The intention must be seen more accurately as an attempt to turn the social security system into a channel, a conveyor belt, to the employment system. The reality is that the active labour market strategy is not working very well, but the objective is not in doubt. Such an approach has merit because income from employment in the past has been the only safe mechanism for ensuring a reasonable standard of living. However, this focus on employment does mean that collective values have taken a back seat to the imperatives of the economic system. Given the difficulties of returning the long-term unemployed to the labour market, the emphasis on compliance with the active labour market strategy has all the hallmarks of victim blaming.

Attempts to channel people into the employment system come at the very time when the progressive abandonment of central control of wages and conditions promises to reduce the conditions of paid work, at least for those in vulnerable sections of the workforce. In both Australia and other Western societies, the numbers involved in part-time and intermittent work, and work involving poorer working conditions, are gradually increasing.[64] While the Industrial Relations Commission still ensures that basic awards are maintained this trend might develop comparatively slowly. But even if centralised awards remain, with enterprise bargaining the earnings of the weakest workers are likely to hover around the minimum.

Paradoxically the Family Allowance Supplement might encourage this trend because employers might rely on it as a back-up for low wages. Indeed its availability has been explicitly welcomed by some employers. The FAS is effectively a replacement of the family element of the 'family wage', a concept which was abandoned by the Arbitration Commission in 1974. The commission at the time suggested that concern for the needs of families was essentially a function for the welfare system,[65] and the welfare system has taken up the challenge. However, this leaves open the possibility of a new role for the social security system, the subsidisation of low wages, which would clearly be a two-edged sword. In itself such subsidisation is a direct cost to the state, and its very availability might encourage employers to lower wages, leading to a magnification of the number of claimants and the amounts of their claims.

Another element of the same problem is that the Australian welfare state was premised on achieving a measure of equality through the wages system, hence Castles' phrase a 'wage-earners' welfare state'. The arbitration system was premised on employers paying a living wage. At the same time centrally fixed standard awards kept relativities between occupations within a narrow range by international standards. Enterprise bargaining will spread that range. Powerful workers in lucrative industries will be able to command high wages. People in service industries and weakly organised workers will fall behind. Women, particularly those in small organisations and those of non-English-speaking backgrounds, are likely to do badly. The FAS can address problems of survival; it does not, however, address the more general issues of equality.

Furthermore, while there is currently an FAS to fall back on, this might not always be the case. Castles has pointed to the 'reversible' nature of the Australian welfare state.[66] This reversibility is an ever-present possibility because of the oscillation of government between left- and right-leaning political parties in conjunction with the absence of strong middle-class support for most elements of the welfare state. Because the welfare safety-net has provided only meagre (by OECD standards) and means-tested benefits, it has not commanded strong support from the better off whose resources normally preclude their claiming any benefits.

Public support for the social wage seems to oscillate with the state of the economy and, no doubt, in tune with the commentaries which are an ever-present accompaniment. Public opinion polls conducted between 1967 and 1988 show that a clear majority supported increased government spending until the poll of 1979. Since then, and not surprisingly, given the publicity received by the official economic adjustment agenda, support for increased spending has more than halved—from a high of 71 per cent in 1969 to a low of 23 per cent in 1987.[67] Such opinion polls, however, present a simple picture while more detailed research suggests that the situation is both complex and often confused. A recent extensive survey by Elim Papadakis showed that there was considerable support for various provisions and services, both public and private. Only a minority was in favour of an expansion of the private sector at the expense of the public and vice versa. A majority 'appears to want both government and private welfare'.[68] That these relatively positive opinions have not been activated within the political arena does support the assessment that in Australia the welfare state has only weak support from the middle classes.[69]

Thus, while it is clear that some of the recent Labor reforms have delivered benefits to the poor, these are likely, through lack of active defence, to languish with a change of government. What is less likely to languish are the more punitive and privatised elements of a welfare state transformed within an economic adjustment agenda. The new 'contract' elements of the employment and social security systems are likely to prove the most lasting legacies of a reforming Labor Government.

Castles and Mitchell[70] have argued against Esping-Andersen's classification of Australia as a liberal type of welfare state. They suggest that the early achievement of a measure of equality through the employment system set Australia (and New Zealand) apart from the international category of liberal, or residual, welfare states, such as the USA, the United Kingdom and Canada.[71] They propose that Australia historically represents a 'radical' version of the liberal welfare state, which normally assumes responsibility only when the market has failed. However, the changes occurring to the Australian welfare state through economic adjustment are having a deradicalising effect. Esping-Andersen might indeed be proved to be right in the longer term.

The government's program of economic adjustment has accorded priority to fiscal efficiency and harnessed welfare efficiency to this agenda. It has been assumed that fiscal efficiency is to be attained through allowing the market a greater role in the determination of wages and conditions of work and through reducing taxation and cutting back on collective expenditure. Welfare efficiency has been sought by means of an active labour market strategy, careful scrutiny of claims for income support and finer targeting of benefits. For the Labor Government this focus on the efficiency of the welfare system has been tempered by traditional concerns for the poorest, which in itself makes clear the contradiction of deregulating the wages system at the same time as subsidising the working poor.

Reduced taxation levels imply leaving funds with individuals and transferring collective responsibilities to the market, since a smaller government sector can no longer deliver the same range of services. Yet this very contraction, and the apparent savings implied, might prove illusory. In a time of recession, with a great deal of hardship, dealing with the problems engendered by financial stringency might prove more costly than the money saved. Already we have found increased rates of imprisonment and increased expenditure on other forms of enforcement such as social security fraud. Other costs in terms of health, reduced educational achievement, increased homelessness and so on are difficult to quantify but are very real outcomes.[72]

As taxation is reduced and people are left to seek their own services within the marketplace they are likely to find that the market is not oriented to the provision of many formerly available government services. Also the market might not be oriented to produce services in a collective manner, sensitive to the needs of diverse groups. Women's and community health services are two obvious examples of the type of service it is almost impossible to envisage being offered by the market, except to the better off, and there are many others. Hence fiscal calculations of costs of replacement services can never estimate the real social costs.

The 1970s and early 1980s saw a focus by governments on issues of participation, equity and democracy and the inclusion or empowerment of formerly excluded and powerless groups. As attention was transferred to fiscal and welfare efficiency these goals were de-emphasised. A fundamental cost is the pursuit of social justice. Economic adjustment has resulted in a radical restructuring of Australian welfare but this restructuring promises greater inequality in the longer term.

Notes

1 F. Castles (1985), *The Working Class and Welfare: Reflections on the Political Development of the Welfare State in Australia and New Zealand, 1890–1980*, Allen & Unwin, Wellington.
2 Commonwealth of Australia (1992), *Towards a Fairer Australia: Social Justice Strategy 1992–93*, AGPS, Canberra, p. 26.
3 Department of Social Security (DSS) (1991), *Annual Report 1990–91*, Canberra, AGPS, p. 111.
4 R. Weatherley (1992), 'From entitlement to contract: Reshaping the welfare state in Australia', Administration, Compliance and Governability Program, Research School of the Social Sciences, Australian National University, Canberra.
5 M. Dean (1991), *The Constitution of Poverty*, Routledge, London.
6 M. Dean (1991), p. 25.
7 R. Titmuss (1974), 'The social division of welfare: Some reflections on the search for equity', in Titmuss, *Essays on 'The Welfare State'*, Allen & Unwin, London, pp. 34–55.
8 C. Offe (1984), *Contradiction of the Welfare State*, Hutchinson, London; R. Mishra (1984), *The Welfare State in Crisis*, Wheatsheaf, Brighton, UK.
9 See C. Offe (1984); L. Bryson (1992), *Welfare and the State: Who Benefits?* Macmillan, London; and J. Habermas (1975), *Legitimation Crisis*, Beacon Press, Boston.
10 M. Sawer (ed.), *Australia and the New Right*, Allen & Unwin, Sydney, p. viii.
11 P. Saunders (1992), 'Recent trends in the size and growth of government in OECD countries', Social Policy Research Centre Discussion Paper No. 34, University of NSW, September, pp. 6–9.
12 P. Saunders (1992), pp. 6–9.
13 B. Howe (1989), 'The challenge of social policy', in P. Saunders and J. Jamrozik (eds), *Social Policy in Australia: What Future for the Welfare State?*

SWRC Reports and Proceedings No. 79, Social Welfare Research Centre, University of New South Wales, pp. 1-5.
14 P. Saunders (1992), p. 14.
15 DSS (1991), pp. 293 & 296.
16 DSS (1991), p. 303.
17 DSS (1991), p. 309.
18 The report on the Child Support Scheme was particularly important here: Commonwealth of Australia Child Support Evaluation Advisory Group (1990), *The Child Support Scheme: Adequacy of Child Support and Coverage of the Sole Pensioner Population*, AGPS, Canberra. See also publications of the Social Policy Research Centre (formerly the Social Welfare Research Centre) and the Australian Institute of Family Studies.
19 B. Cass (1985), 'The changing face of poverty in Australia', *Australian Feminist Studies*, No. 1, 67-90.
20 E. Evans (ed.) (1978), *Social Policy 1830-1914: Individualism, Collectivism and the Origins of the Welfare State*, Routledge & Kegan Paul, London, p. 62.
21 V. George (1973), *Social Security and Society*, Routledge & Kegan Paul, London, p. 12.
22 D. Henderson (1989), 'Perestroika in the West', in J. Nieuwenhuysen (ed.), *Towards Freer Trade Between Nations*, Oxford University Press, Melbourne, p. 34.
23 DSS (1991), p. 49.
24 DSS (1991), pp. 50-1.
25 DSS (1991), pp. 50-1.
26 DSS (1991), pp. 121 & 272.
27 DSS (1991), pp. 125-6.
28 A. Harding and J. Landt (1992), 'Policy and poverty: Trends in disposable incomes March 1983 to September 1991', *Australian Quarterly* 64:1, 42-3; B. Bradbury and J. Doyle (1992), *Family Incomes and Economic Growth in the 1980s*, SPRC Reports and Proceedings No. 102, Social Policy Research Centre, University of New South Wales, pp. 44-5.
29 F. G. Castles and D. Mitchell (1992), 'Three worlds of welfare capitalism or four?' *Governance* 5:1, 1-26.
30 DSS (1991), p. 106.
31 DSS (1991), p. 106.
32 DSS (1991), p. 111.
33 Department of Employment, Education and Training (DEET) (1991), *Annual Report 1990-91*, AGPS, Canberra, p. 85.
34 DSS (1991), pp. 93-5.
35 L. Bryson (1983), 'Women as welfare recipients: Women, poverty and the state', in C. Baldock and B. Cass (eds), *Women, Social Welfare and the State in Australia*, Allen & Unwin, Sydney, pp. 130-45.
36 D. Henderson (1989), p. 34.
37 Minister for Employment, Education and Training (1988), media release: '"Jet" help for sole parents', Canberra, 23 August.
38 R. Anstie, R. G. Gregory, S. Dowrick and J. J. Pincus (1988), *Government Spending on Work-related Child Care: Some Economic Issues*, Discussion Paper No. 191, Centre for Economic Policy Research, Australian National University, Canberra.

The Welfare State and Economic Adjustment 313

39 C. O'Donnell and P. Hall (1988), *Getting Equal*, Allen & Unwin, Sydney, p. 65.
40 R. Ross (1991), 'Child care for the 1990s', *SPRC Newsletter*, No. 40, p. 2.
41 M. Clyde (1991), 'Social and economic demands—a balancing act?' Paper presented to conference, Ensuring our Futures: The Fabric of Childhood in Australia, Adelaide, 15–17 May.
42 Commonwealth of Australia Child Support Evaluation Advisory Group (1992), *Child Support in Australia: Final Report of the Evaluation of the Child Support Scheme*, Cat. No. 92 14047, AGPS, Canberra, p. 1.
43 Commonwealth of Australia Child Support Evaluation Advisory Group (1990), *The Child Support Scheme*, p. 3.
44 Commonwealth of Australia (1992), *Towards a Fairer Australia*, p. 28.
45 E. Cox and H. Leonard (1992), 'Superfudge or subterfuge?' Women's Economic Think Tank, Camperdown.
46 B. Toohey (1992), 'Super's billion-dollar incentive', *Modern Times*, June, p. 3.
47 DSS (1991), pp. 92–102.
48 M. Fine (1992), *Community Support Services and their Users: The First Eighteen Months*, Social Policy Research Centre, Reports and Proceedings No. 100, University of NSW, p. 1; G. Dalley (1988), *Ideologies of Caring: Rethinking Community and Collectivism*, Macmillan, London; J. Finch and D. Groves (eds) (1983), *A Labour of Love: Women, Work and Caring*, Routledge & Kegan Paul, London; W. Waerness (1984), 'Caring as women's work in the welfare state', in H. Holter (ed.), *Patriarchy in a Welfare Society*, Universitetsforlaget, Oslo, pp. 67–87.
49 S. Graham (1992), 'Community support services', *Newsletter*, Social Policy Research Centre University of NSW, March, p. 4. See also L. Bryson and M. Mowbray (1984), 'Women really care', *Australian Journal of Social Issues* 19:4, 261–73.
50 M. Mowbray (1992), 'Not a care in the world', *Modern Times*, September, p. 3.
51 Department of Health, Housing and Community Services (1991), *Annual Report 1990–91*, AGPS, Canberra, p. 55.
52 A. Yeatman (1993), 'Women and the state' in K. Pritchard Hughes (ed.), *Contemporary Australian Feminism*, Longman Cheshire, Melbourne.
53 M. Steer (1991), 'Policy horizons for Victorians with disabilities: A Delphi study', in P. Saunders and D. Encel (eds), *Social Policy in Australia: Options for the 1990s*, Report and Proceedings No. 98, Social Policy Research Centre, University of NSW, p. 193.
54 M. Fine and S. Graham (1991), 'Home and community care: A new deal for older people?' *Newsletter*, Social Policy Research Centre, University of NSW, December, p. 3.
55 M. Fine and S. Graham (1991), pp. 1–3.
56 M. Fine and S. Graham (1991), p. 3.
57 Department of Health, Housing and Community Services, (1991), *Aged Care Reform, Mid Term Review, 1990–91*, AGPS, Canberra.
58 A. Yeatman (1991), 'The "new federalism", or the selective devolution of the public sector', *Canberra Bulletin of Public Administration*, 67, pp. 56–9.
59 Howe had responsibility for the portfolio of Social Security from 1985 to 1990 and then that of Health, Housing and Community Services. Health was transferred out of Howe's portfolio after the March 1993 federal election.

60 Commonwealth of Australia (1992), p. 26.
61 A. Harding and J. Landt (1992), pp. 42–3.
62 A. Harding and J. Landt (1992); B. Bradbury and J. Doyle (1992), pp. 44–5.
63 D. Henderson (1989), p. 34.
64 G. Esping-Andersen (1990), *The Three Worlds of Welfare Capitalism*, Polity Press, Cambridge.
65 B. Cass (1985), 'Rewards for women's work', in J. Goodnow and C. Pateman (eds), *Women, Social Science and Public Policy*, Allen & Unwin, Sydney, pp. 67–94.
66 F. G. Castles (1989), 'Australia's reversible citizenship', *Australian Society* 8:9, 29–30.
67 F. Gruen (1989), 'Australia's welfare state: Rearguard or avant garde?' in P. Saunders and A. Jamrozik (eds), p. 36.
68 E. Papadakis (1990), *Attitudes to State and Private Welfare: Analysis of Results from a National Survey*, SPRC Reports and Proceedings No. 88, Social Policy Research Centre, University of NSW, December, p. 126.
69 L. Bryson (1992), pp. 94–5.
70 F. G. Castles and D. Mitchell (1992).
71 G. Esping-Andersen (1990).
72 A. Yeatman (1991).

13

The greenhouse effect and the politics of long-term issues

Ian Lowe

Awareness of the climate changes known as the 'greenhouse effect' is now widespread. Although there remain some sceptics, most atmospheric scientists accept the view that human actions are changing various aspects of the Earth's climate.[1] This issue has the twin complexities of being international in scope and long-term in its time dimension. Thus no nation can adequately address the problem by itself; instead, a coordinated global approach is needed. Moreover, the long time horizon needed for policy changes to have any discernible impact does not encourage governments to risk any responses that might be electorally unpopular.

Analysis of Australian government responses to this issue leads to some general conclusions about the capacity of the state to devise coherent policies to deal with long-term problems. Some general difficulties that might be expected in any market economy are compounded by particular features of the Australian political system. The government has accepted as an interim planning target the goal, suggested by the 1988 Toronto conference, of stabilising emissions of greenhouse gases at the 1988 level by the year 2000 and reducing them 20 per cent by the year 2005. The commitment to that target is, however, significantly hedged with qualifications that establish the primacy of economic considerations. The government has explicitly stated that it will only attempt to meet the target if there will be no negative effect on the economy generally or competitiveness in particular. The government has also been advised that meeting these targets will require an integrated package of decisive measures, but the structural and attitudinal barriers to development and implementation of such a strategy are formidable.[2] The 1992 Framework Convention on Climate Change commits the government to limiting emissions, but only in broad general terms, as the moves for the convention to include specific targets were successfully resisted by the USA.

This chapter begins with an analysis of the problem of the greenhouse effect, especially focusing on its implications for industry and the economy. A brief history of the Australian responses and the political debate about government action follows. The general literature in the field of public policy suggests some overall limitations on the capacity of governments to respond to such issues. These limitations are discussed in the particular context of the Australian situation. This approach leads to general conclusions about the relations between business and government in modern Australia. While there is not necessarily a conflict between economic objectives and a coherent response to the greenhouse effect, such a response would undoubtedly affect some current economic activities. Representatives of those vested interests have impeded the development of an overall strategy, their task made easier by the structural and attitudinal barriers mentioned above.

The greenhouse effect

It has been known for more than a hundred years that the climate is related to the presence in the atmosphere of a variety of gases which have the capacity to absorb heat. The name we use for this phenomenon, the greenhouse effect, was coined last century by analogy with the way the glass of a greenhouse traps heat. The greenhouse effect is generally beneficial; without the capacity of the atmosphere to trap heat, this planet would be as hostile to life as the moon. The recent concern arises from the recognition that human actions are changing the composition of the atmosphere, enhancing its ability to retain heat.[3]

The Inter-governmental Panel on Climate Change recently summarised current scientific thinking about the greenhouse effect, taking care to differentiate between what is known, what is calculated with confidence and what is predicted.[4] The observations are that concentrations of the greenhouse gases are increasing and the global temperature is also increasing. The size of the observed increase in temperature this century, about half a degree, is broadly consistent with the results of modelling studies that predict a further increase of about three degrees by about the year 2030. However, the IPCC caution that the observed temperature increase is still within the bounds of historic variations, and so it is likely to be another decade or so before the record will show unequivocally that human actions are changing the climate. The changes to the atmosphere are principally due to the burning of fossil fuels (coal, oil and gas), although the clearing of native vegetation is also a significant factor. The other important factors are the release into the air of chlorofluorocarbons, now being phased out because of their effect on stratospheric ozone, and the production of methane, much of which is a by-product of expanding agricultural production to feed the growing human population.[5]

There is now international pressure to slow down the rate of emission of greenhouse gases. While the particular implications of Australia responding to this problem are discussed below, there are quite general conclusions for industrial economies. Reducing emissions will require a reduction in the rate of burning hydrocarbon fuels. This has economic implications at three levels. First, the extraction and sale of these fuels is a very large industry, so any curtailment of the fuel industries would have a considerable economic impact. Second, other major economic activities rely for their very existence on consumers having unrestricted access to fuel; the manufacture and sale of transport vehicles is an obvious example. The third implication arises from the importance of fuel energy as an input to the production of many goods and services, so curtailment of fuel uses implies some restriction on fuel-intensive industries such as aluminium smelting. Thus an overall strategy to reduce emissions would have an impact on the energy industries (coal, oil, gas, electricity), the energy-intensive areas of production (metals production) and those industries that rely on consumer access to fuel energy (the vehicle industry). For these reasons, there is a widespread belief that responding to the greenhouse effect would have a negative impact on many existing industries, with consequent implications for the economy.

A short history of Australian responses

The crucial step in developing wide public awareness of the issue was an agreement between the government research organisation, CSIRO, and the Commission for the Future (CFF), a government agency established in 1986. CSIRO scientists had been in the forefront of atmospheric research related to carbon dioxide levels and climate change for decades.[6] The commission's task was to monitor developments in science and technology with significant social, political or economic implications and to raise the level of public debate about those issues.[7]

There was an obvious basis for the partnership—CSIRO had the scientific expertise, while the commission had the skills of establishing networks and communicating to a wider public. The cooperative operation was in two phases. In 1987, a conference called Greenhouse

'87 was organised by the CSIRO. It was primarily a meeting of scientific experts to review the state of knowledge about the changing composition of the atmosphere, the possible changes in climate and the wide-ranging possible impacts of those changes. The conference was essentially a scenario exercise, based on the 'most likely' changes in climate, with a range of experts analysing the impacts of these possible changes on the physical, biological and social environment. The conference attracted considerable media interest, mainly concentrated on the worst possible consequences of climate change.[8]

In 1988 the CFF organised Greenhouse '88, an ambitious nation-wide network of conferences in nine cities, linked by video for the opening session. Some eight thousand people were involved altogether, and organisers claimed it to have been the largest ever conference on an environmental issue. The mass media took up the issue, with newspaper supplements and several TV specials. The political pressure on governments made it necessary for them to show interest in the subject. While the response by governments was far from enthusiastic, and while there were still some critics suggesting that the whole issue was based on unfounded fears, the level of community concern made it imperative that governments develop policies responding to the issue.

As in other countries, opinion polls in Australia show that an increasing fraction of the community is concerned about long-term issues. In those nation states in which the government is subject to some form of electoral process, the environment has become a serious issue, to the point of influencing the shape and direction of the elected government. Coghill has compiled the responses of different levels of government in Australia.[9] The response from the national government has been strong on rhetoric. For example, in 1989 the then Minister for the Environment, Senator Graham Richardson, argued that:

> *The most important question we now face is whether we collectively have the foresight and courage to make the necessary changes to ensure we leave our children a better world ... we waste and consume energy at a rate that is truly frightening ... Meeting the challenge will require unprecedented co-operation and vision, nationally and internationally ... There is no quick technological fix. The critical issue is, and will always remain, the need to plan for a more secure and sustainable world. It will require a long-term commitment from all of us as individuals, and a fundamental change in our attitude to the use of resources. Unless we deal with this imperative, we risk undoing in a few decades the material and economic progress which has come from centuries of human endeavour.*[10]

In 1990 the Commonwealth Government announced the establishment of nine working groups to recommend policies for ecologically sustainable development; this became known as the ESD process. The working groups brought together representatives of business, trade unions, conservation bodies and other community organisations, as well as bureaucrats. As the Australian constitution makes no reference to environmental issues, the states and territories retain significant powers in this area. The need to take account of the wishes of the various states led to the nine ESD working groups being dominated by large numbers of state and Commonwealth bureaucrats; for example, the working group on energy use had eighteen members, nine of whom were public servants.[11]

Most states were seeking to protect their economic interests, as exemplified most vividly by the Queensland Government's statement in 1989 that the resource industries are of such economic importance that they should be exempted from any attempt to reduce emissions.[12] The government of Victoria adopted the so-called Toronto goal of 20 per cent reduction in emissions of carbon dioxide by 2005 as an interim target for planning purposes and has been able to persuade its electricity authority to embrace the principle of demand management. As a consequence, the SECV has played a leading role in developing strategies for management of electricity demand, including a move from their traditional hostility to co-generation schemes. The provision of a fair rate for electricity supplied to the state grid was a crucial factor making a proposed co-generation scheme for Melbourne hospitals an economic proposition.[13] Late in 1991 the South Australian Government released its Greenhouse Strategy, also adopting the Toronto target. The government of Western Australia has a commitment to plant 100 million trees by 2000, and Queensland has issued guidelines for coastal development incorporating expected rises in sea level. For obvious political reasons, however, the states have been reluctant to concede policy authority in this area to the Commonwealth Government; for example, the states have resisted the idea of a national plan for coastal management.

Greenhouse: The political debate

When the final reports of the nine working groups on ESD were completed, the three chairs of the working groups commented on the remarkable extent of common ground achieved. They stated their 'clear impression of growing community support for the goals of ecologically sustainable development' and called for the momentum established by the ESD process to be maintained.[14] The recommendations of the ESD working groups then disappeared for twelve months into the bureaucratic morass of some thirty-seven interdepartmental and intergovernmental committees, before being brought back as a National Greenhouse Response Strategy and an ESD strategy for the approval of heads of government in December 1992.

During 1992 there was also a determined campaign to force the Commonwealth Government to back down from its commitment to emission targets. A report by the Industry Commission claimed that there would be significant costs to our economy from meeting the Toronto target, although it conceded that it was unable to quantify the associated benefits from such an approach.[15] The report paid particular attention to the suggestion of a so-called carbon tax, which would be a levy on different fuels in proportion to the atmospheric carbon dioxide released by their use. This proposal was countered by claims that such a levy would be economically crippling. The attempt to put a figure on the costs of emission reduction was based on economic modelling. While the fundamental shortcomings of this approach have been set out in detail elsewhere,[16] it is sufficient to say here that the models used rely on the ability to predict the future values of a range of economic parameters that cannot be known with any precision. The models are also unable to account for non-economic factors affecting energy use; this is a fatal deficiency, because most individual use of energy is dominated by social considerations rather than being the behaviour of economically rational consumers seeking to maximise their marginal utility.

In 1991 a group with clear vested interests in the resource industries commissioned a study by a consulting organisation called 'London Economics'. While the title of the subsequent report gave the impression that it considered the impacts of global warming control policies on Australian industry in general, in fact the study considered only a small group of resource sectors: coal, oil and gas, iron and steel, and aluminium. Focusing solely on hydrocarbon fuels and energy-intensive mineral processing, the study reached the predictable conclusion that these areas of economic activity would be affected by strategies to cut emissions of carbon dioxide.[17] The report made no attempt to quantify the effects on other sectors of the economy. However, other studies suggest that reduced exports of black coal could actually improve the prospects of other export industries such as wool, beef and most grains.[18]

This is a crucial point. Because responding to the greenhouse effect would benefit some industries and damage others, it would have a redistributive effect. It is only to be expected that the large industries that would be harmed are more prominent in the public debate than the much smaller industries that would benefit. Thus the debate has often been cast in terms that suggest that responding would cause overall damage to the economy. Modelling studies do not show this, although they do suggest that there would be negative effects on some existing large industries.

More extreme arguments attacking greenhouse controls have been advanced by fringe bodies such as the Institute of Public Affairs (IPA) and the Tasman Institute. The IPA began a public campaign in 1991, suggesting that there was no scientific consensus on issues such as the greenhouse effect or ozone depletion. The campaign was based on the work of a small number of scientists who differ from the views of most of their professional peers, including one who advanced the astonishing argument that depletion of the ozone layer would strengthen bones and thus have a net health benefit!

The Tasman Institute has promoted a similar argument, using the sort of analysis that has given the entire discipline of economics a bad name. For example, Moran has argued that we should not worry about global warming, even if the models of climate change arising from carbon dioxide levels are correct, because 'carbon free nuclear power' will gradually take over as fossil fuels become more expensive.[19] It is difficult to take seriously an argument so remote from technical, social and political reality that it can conclude that change to 'carbon free nuclear power' will be driven by market forces if a carbon tax is applied to fossil fuels.

Essentially these arguments are simply a statement of an ideological position that governments should not interfere in the market, a position based on the belief that the market is the most efficient means of allocating resources.[20] This ignores well-documented problems familiar to most economists such as inertia, lack of information and the control of markets by large players.

Perhaps predictably, the mass media have supported the case being advanced by these 'economic rationalists'. This is especially true of the Murdoch press, which has been consistently more hostile to environmental issues than other media in Australia.[21] Television features have stressed the uncertainty of climate change forecasts, highlighting the opinions of the small group of dissident scientists and the special pleading of the resource industries.

Finally, the National Greenhouse Steering Committee, comprising officials from all levels of government, produced a draft Greenhouse Response Strategy. It was largely oriented towards investigations, exhortations, negotiation and a pious faith in market forces.[22] The report was released for public comment in 1992, but it received little support. A two-day forum to discuss the report became a fiasco. First, even the environmental groups which had cooperated totally in the ESD process—the World-wide Fund for Nature and the Australian Conservation Foundation—denounced the forum and refused to participate. Then those who did attend, from industry, farming, the union movement and community groups, attacked the report. They said that they had worked hard in the ESD groups to negotiate workable agreements, combining environmental responsibility with conditions to promote economic development, only to have the agreements altered by faceless bureaucrats. The officials had planned to divide the forum into small working groups, but the participants refused to go until their concerns were discussed. There was no basis for moving into small groups to discuss details, as the whole approach was unacceptable. At five o'clock, after a day of battering, the shell-shocked officials announced that the planned second day was cancelled. The level of discontent is illustrated by the fact that the conservative Institution of Engineers, Australia (IEA) issued a press release condemning the report.[23] The IEA were concerned that the bureaucrats had altered the conclusions of the ESD groups, giving the impression that the small groups of officials had decided that they knew better than the rest of the community. A final report was produced and accepted by heads of government in December 1992.[24]

Under the Inter-Governmental Agreement on the Environment, the Australian response to such large-scale issues was negotiated jointly between the Commonwealth, the states and the territories. Since the Commonwealth's formal power to deal with environmental issues is limited to those areas in which it acts in accordance with international treaties, the result of the agreement was that all actions were restricted to the lowest common denominator of the states. That is unlikely to be a recipe for concerted action to address long-term problems.

Formulation of public policy

Lindblom recognised that rational comprehensive policy-making is unusual in a democratic political system; most public policy can be analysed in terms of incrementalism, an approach in which successive small changes are made in response to short-term pressure.[25] Latham argued that what is called public policy is actually the current equilibrium in the power struggle between competing interests, noting that those interests will always try to shift the policy to positions closer to their preferred stances.[26]

Etzioni suggested the model of mixed scanning, in which occasional contextualising decisions form a framework within which successive 'bit decisions' are made by the incremental process.[27] The metaphor he subsequently developed was of society as 'an ocean liner propelled by an undersized engine'; such a vessel would be partly self-propelled but largely at the mercy of the ocean currents, and there would probably be a constant struggle between different groups of passengers about the best use of the limited capacity to determine where the ship is heading. He argued that such a view of the world is a serious impediment to decisive action:

> *Influenced by the competition model of the market, incrementalists reject the notion that institutions can consciously formulate policies that express the collective 'good'. Policies that truly express the collective good can only result from a give-and-take among numerous*

'partisans' (various interest groups and other active groupings). The measure of a good decision is the extent of agreement on it among all those it affects ...[28]

As Walker argues, this approach leads to a fundamental difficulty when applied to environmental issues.[29] There is no prospect even in principle of what Etzioni called agreement 'among all those it affects', since those affected clearly include flora and fauna. This problem can be extended to the equally fundamental problem that a decision might affect future generations more severely than the current human population. Just as there is no prospect even in principle of securing the agreement of flora and fauna on the policy direction to be followed, there is also no prospect of involving future generations in the determination of the best policy response. As Walker also notes, the incrementalist approach typically leads to a compromise solution, but many environmental issues do not admit the possibility of compromise at all. If any development at all is allowed in what was previously wilderness, it is no longer wilderness; if a virgin forest is logged, however selectively and sensitively, it is no longer virgin forest.

Finally, there are structural problems arising from the nature of the modern industrial state, as pointed out by Galbraith[30] in arguing that the nature of the modern state means that politics becomes synonymous with economic management: 'economics is, then, routinely made the final test of public policy'. This focus on economic output as a measure of government achievement leads to the state being, as Galbraith put it,[31] 'an instrument of the industrial system'. The general need for policy not to disrupt the economic system clearly reduces the freedom of the state to take action aimed at alleviating long-term environmental problems in general. As Walker puts it:

> *These factors limit the freedom states have to attend to ecological or other long-term issues. Even when perceived as problems, they will be relegated to second place when the chips are down. Posterity is a poor second to political survival or economic indicators.*[32]

Thus there are quite serious problems in applying the conventional approach to public policy to complex long-term issues. The features of the Australian political system complicate the matter even further.

Features of Australian public policy

The structural problems of federal states such as Australia are well known[33] and so fundamental that notable public figures have called for the abolition of State Governments.[34] The need for agreement between different levels of government is a significant barrier to coherent or decisive policy-making, especially when there are political differences between the parties in power at different levels.

> *Australian federal governments can influence the policy agenda, but they must work hard to obtain co-operation, however grudging, from conflicting levels of government, from a divided public sector, and from policy coalitions and private interests with influence over the outcome of state decisions.*[35]

It is clear that the federal system acts generally as a barrier to rapid change, although there are examples of progressive State Governments being able to innovate in ways that would not have been acceptable nationally. The Wran Government in New South Wales, unable to obtain support from other states or the Commonwealth Government, decided that lead-free motor spirit would be introduced to that state; this effectively forced its use nationally. The governments of New South Wales and Victoria agreed to require energy efficiency labelling of domestic appliances, setting in train a move which has now spread to other states. These counter-examples, however, do not invalidate the general conclusion that the division of power between the states and the Commonwealth usually makes rapid and fundamental change more difficult.

This issue is particularly important in analysing the problem of responding to global climate change. Except for areas sufficiently important for the Australian Government to use its foreign affairs power, such as south-west Tasmania,[36] environmental issues are largely the province of the states. Burning coal to produce electricity accounts for almost half of the national production of carbon dioxide from fossil fuels,[37] but electricity generation and supply is the province of state authorities with considerable autonomy. Although this autonomy of power utilities has only been extensively documented for the particular case of Tasmania,[38] the effect is quite general.[39]

The role of large local authorities should not be overlooked. Brisbane City Council has a budget about two-thirds that of Tasmania and significant powers in such areas as planning and transport; a coherent strategic response to the greenhouse effect for south-east Queensland would thus require collaboration of three levels of government. The political difficulty of achieving such cooperation is considerable; in 1991–92, when the same political party held office at all three levels of government affecting south-east Queensland, it was the first time for more than forty years that such a coincidence of power had occurred. This assisted the Brisbane City Council to undertake structural changes in the area of public transport that had been impeded by political differences, such as combined tickets for travel on buses (local authority) and trains (state authority).

This analysis suggests that there are quite serious limitations to the ability of the Australian state to respond to important problems. While these limits are here applied specifically to the particular case of global climate change, they clearly apply more generally, as has been argued by Davis et al.:

> *The economy is subject to international pressures. Interest groups, distributional coalitions, classes and interests are well organised and able to oppose unacceptable policy choices. There are rival if unequal centres of power, disagreements between levels of government, and a division of responsibility which fragments decision-making. The public sector includes important semi-autonomous organisations which can pursue their own interests and so affect the prospects for central policies. Bureaucracies wield important influence over the formation and implementation of policy.*[40]

This last point is of increasing significance in contemporary Australia: namely, the influence of the bureaucracy in general and the dominant ideology within the senior ranks in particular. The issue of global climate change has coincided with a time in which the bureaucracy is dominated by the ideology of neo-classical economics, often known as economic rationalism. This places an additional constraint on the state's capacity to regulate the activities of the business community, as discussed further below.

Business constraints on policy change

As discussed above, there is a general problem arising from what Walker calls 'the state's close intertwining with corporate interests'.[41] This link between government and business explains a reluctance to intervene in the marketplace, whether to protect consumers or the natural world. This problem is quite a general feature of capitalist economies. Bell argues that the power of business has three broad dimensions.[42] First, individual companies and industry groups seek to exercise power through the normal mechanisms of interest group politics. Just as Greenpeace or Right to Life try to influence the political debate in advancement of their particular views, so do large corporations and industry bodies. In the greenhouse debate, for example, the resource industries have been very active in trying to influence public opinion.

Second, Bell argues, business power can be exercised in more covert ways. It was a common joke in Australian politics during the time of the Hawke Government that the only coherent explanation of transport policy was the close personal relationship between the Prime Minister and Sir Peter Abeles. Recent analysis, even by conservative observers, attributes the decline in fortune of the Abeles empire to the departure of Hawke.[43]

Bell suggests that there is a third important dimension of business power, which

> *stems from the very constitution and organisation of capitalist societies, namely that capitalists own and control much of the economy. This means that many of the important decisions affecting the economy—the level of investment, technological innovation, employment levels and the location of jobs—are not directly under government control. In such systems, governments cannot command business to perform. Therefore, governments remain dependent on business for the provision of a healthy economy and, thus, for the financial resources and electoral success on which governments depend.*[44]

This is an important point. There is a general tendency for broad government policy to support the interests of business, even though specific decisions taken under political pressures might run counter to the interests of particular industries. In general, industries consisting of a small number of very large companies (such as the aluminium industry) are more easily able to speak with a concerted voice than those made up of many small firms, such as the clothing industry. It is also significant that the organised associations of business, such as the Business Council of Australia (BCA), inevitably represent the historical balance of economic and political influence within the business community. Thus the BCA tends to represent established big business, rather than the small business sector or emerging industries. In discussions concerning the greenhouse effect, the BCA has acted as the voice of large companies that might lose most from curtailment of emissions, such as those in the coal and aluminium industries, overlooking the interests of those firms and industrial sectors that could benefit from a government strategy promoting conservation and alternative energy sources. As one particular example, the two representatives of the BCA on the government's ESD Working Party on Energy Use were an oil company executive and a representative of the aluminium industry.[45]

Mercer argues in quite general terms that there has been a consistent failure by Australian governments to regulate industry and commerce.[46] This argument, exemplified by the compliant attitude of regulatory agencies,[47] extends to an explanation of the particular reluctance of governments to intervene for the sake of preventing or moderating environmental problems. It is significant that Australia, as a relatively small economy, has a limited capacity to take action that could restrict the activities of large corporations.[48] The extraction, processing and distribution of fuel minerals in Australia is largely controlled by transnational corporations.[49] Large oil companies have considerable economic power, and even the strongest industrial states have relatively little power to control their actions.[50] Since the sale by the Menzies Government of the Commonwealth Oil Refineries, successive Australian governments have had little influence over the oil industry. Bell cites a particular recent example, the decision to exempt the North-West Shelf development from resource rent tax in response to a direct approach from the then chairman of Shell Australia, effectively threatening to stall the project if the tax were applied.[51] The capacity to respond to the problem of carbon dioxide emissions is fundamentally limited by the fact that oil companies and state electricity authorities together control fuels accounting for about 80 per cent of all the emissions due to burning fuels.[52]

The Australian economic structure is also heavily oriented towards the export of basic commodities such as minerals. The limitations on government action resulting from this orientation[53] reinforce the general argument about the limits on the capacity of governments to intervene in areas seen as important to the overall performance of the economy. Dependence on mineral exports also creates a climate in which governments are apprehensive that 'measures to regain control of Australia's resources could frighten off foreign investors', reinforcing a political culture in which 'environmentally desirable measures are evaluated in the light of their acceptability to business and commerce'.[54]

Bruce Davis suggests that only an unusual conjunction of circumstances leads to intervention such as that by the Australian Government in preventing the construction of the Gordon-below-Franklin dam:

> *it was a combination of public pressure, political leverage by the Democrats and outspoken comment by some Labor and Liberal back-benchers that eventually persuaded the Labor Party votes might be garnered in marginal seats at a federal election if the environmental coalition and especially the Wilderness Society were campaigning.*[55]

A pre-election commitment to intervene was made, despite the constitutional uncertainty about the legality of such an intervention. When the High Court subsequently ruled that intervention could be justified under the external affairs power of the Commonwealth, the decision did not lead to more widespread use of that power. Thus the Commonwealth Government declined to intervene to stop construction of a road through the Queensland wet tropics from the Daintree River to Cape Tribulation. The Commonwealth Government also attempted to enact resource security legislation, despite angry opposition from conservation groups who believed that heritage forest would be destroyed as a result. Where the Commonwealth Government has acted against business interests, as in the Coronation Hill mining proposal, the outcome appears to have been driven by indecision and personal whimsy rather than a commitment to environmental protection.[56]

The emphasis on deregulation and market forces in recent Australian public policy is clear and extends even to such areas as setting up competition for the supply of profitable telecommunications services and selling other efficient government-owned enterprises to the private sector. The dominance of short-term economics in government responses to long-term issues is only partly explained by the mind-set of many of the government's bureaucratic advisers. John Hyde, a former Liberal politician, recently recounted how these policies were introduced to the Liberal Party by a tiny minority of dissident backbench MPs.[57] The spread of this ideology has been facilitated by the intellectual crisis among the traditional Left of Australian politics, formerly a major source of long-term strategies and articulation of moral principle. With the political struggle effectively between short-term economics and short-term expediency, the clear certainty is the ascendancy of short-term considerations over any attempt to impose a long-range perspective. One memorable metaphor from Pusey's study of the senior ranks of the Commonwealth public service encapsulates the attitude towards environmental issues of the economic rationalists in the Australian public service; they are referred to as '(expletive) locusts', in the sense that 'the moment they smell something green it's gone in an instant'.[58]

Against this general trend, there have been a few instances of the Commonwealth Government feeling able to pursue non-commercial objectives; the most notable were its strong role in the renegotiation of the Treaty for the Regulation of Ozone-depleting Substances and the proposed structure for the regulation of mining and exploration in Antarctica. Significantly, these are issues for which there was no short-term economic interest to set against the long-term good (or the political kudos) of adopting a 'green' stance.

Prospects for a long-term view

I have argued elsewhere that the green movement offers the only significant countervailing force to the tyranny of the short term.[59] With the ALP now in many ways devoid of principles by which it can be differentiated from the conservative parties, there is a real prospect of the political agenda of the medium-term future consisting of the struggle between those seeking to promote a green program of sustainable development and the 'Laborials', as Green Independent MHA Bob Brown called the alliance of the ALP and the Liberal Party in the Tasmanian House of Assembly to oppose that program.

In terms of Etzioni's model of public policy, the current struggle is essentially between those who believe that there is a need to move to a new contextualising framework which recognises the need to plan for sustainability and reactionary forces seeking to maintain the dominance of short-term economic considerations over any form of analysis. Some recent discussion has focused on the possibility of 'greening' the labor movement or achieving a fusion between the social goals of the Left and the ecological goals of environmental groups. Dunkley argues that the current problems of industrial society make it unsustainable and that the shortcomings cannot be resolved by orthodox market-oriented solutions; he argues that the only solution is a 'green–red' model

> *which combines the virtues of environmentalism and socialism, which retains much of the decentralism now emerging in both the East and the West and which greatly modifies the machine–chemical economy without entirely abandoning all the industrial or technological aspects of modernity. [These] models ... will need to be more flexible, small-scale, decentralist, conservationist, cultural, traditionalist and spiritual than socialism has hitherto been.*[60]

This is a particular example of a more general argument by Milbrath for climate change as 'the most insistent and persistent teacher' that will spread community acceptance of the need for a fundamental change to the social and political structure, based on a different approach to our relationship with the natural world.[61] There can be little doubt that responding to the problem of global climate change requires social and political change, rather than technological innovation. Several reports, even by bodies as wedded to the existing order as the Australian Institute of Petroleum,[62] have made the point that 'there are many ways in which governments could take positive steps to reduce greenhouse gas emissions while also contributing to overall economic efficiency'. The task was neatly summarised by the Brundtland report:

> *A safe, environmentally sound and economically viable energy pathway that will sustain human progress into the distant future is clearly imperative. It is also possible. But it will require new dimensions of political will and institutional co-operation to achieve it.*[63]

In those terms, the problem of policy change has been cast in extreme terms by those committed to the status quo. It is a common tactic of interest groups to seek to portray their sectional aims as synonymous with the national interest. Given a hypothetical choice between economic prosperity and environmental responsibility, governments are always likely to choose prosperity. The business sectors that could be most affected by strategies to reduce emissions of greenhouse gases have sought to establish that such policies would cause overall damage to the fragile Australian economy. Although there is a significant body of evidence suggesting that the economic benefits of a response strategy would be comparable to the negative effects, those elements of business that would be negatively affected have much more political influence than those which would benefit and have succeeded in capturing government commitment to their position.

As Papadakis and Moore argue in chapter 14 of this book, the simplistic dichotomy between the natural environment and economic progress has largely been supplanted, at the leading edge of the debate, by a more sophisticated view of the world. The debate about Australian responses to the greenhouse effect has, in those terms, been a throwback to the previous era of confrontation. I have argued that this approach has been developed by those industries that would be likely to suffer from a comprehensive response: the industries that depend for their profitability on extravagant use of fossil fuels.

Conclusion

Issues such as global climate change pose a fundamental challenge to our political systems. An intelligent response requires planning on a time-scale of generations, whereas most politicians and bureaucrats are accustomed to much shorter time-scales. Since posterity does not vote, those who wish to protect future interests but who need to retain the confidence of electors can only do so by presenting a coherent vision of the future. In the Australian system, there are few signs of such coherent vision at any level of government.

The consequent probability is that the response to such issues will continue to be a series of discrete incremental measures without any underlying vision of a new sustainable structure towards which we need to move. The problem is likely to remain as long as the thinking of decision-makers is dominated by the priorities of the short term and by narrow economic considerations. A long-term view has emerged only in those instances in which there is no great conflict with more immediate political and economic goals. Adoption of coherent strategies for the long term appears only to be possible when there exists a strong political impetus.

Notes

1 Inter-governmental Panel on Climate Change (IPCC) (1990), *Climate Change: The Scientific Assessment,* Report prepared for the IPCC by Working Group 1, Cambridge University Press, Cambridge.
2 Ecologically Sustainable Development Working Group Chairs (1992), *Greenhouse Report,* AGPS, Canberra.
3 I. Lowe (1989a), *Living in the Greenhouse,* Scribe, Newham, Vic.

4 IPCC (1990).
5 I. Lowe (1989a).
6 See, for example, B. Tucker (ed.) (1981), *Carbon Dioxide and Climate in Australia*, Australian Academy of Science, Canberra.
7 B. O. Jones (1986), *Australia as a Post-industrial Society*, Occasional Paper No. 1, Commission for the Future, Carlton.
8 G. I. Pearman (ed.) (1989), *Greenhouse: Planning for Climate Change*, CSIRO/Brill, Leiden.
9 K. Coghill (ed.) (1989), *Greenhouse: What's to be Done?* Pluto Press, Melbourne, pp. 63–6.
10 G. Richardson (1989), 'Greenhouse—the challenge of change', in K. Coghill, pp. 67–76.
11 Ecologically Sustainable Development Working Groups (1991), *Final Report—Executive Summaries*, AGPS, Canberra.
12 Queensland Government (1989), *Greenhouse Strategy*, Brisbane.
13 A. Rattray (1992), 'Experience from the State Electricity Commission of Victoria's incentives package', paper to Focus for the Future, First National Demand Management Conference, Melbourne.
14 Ecologically Sustainable Development Working Group Chairs (1992).
15 Industry Commission (1991), *Costs and Benefits of Reducing Greenhouse Gas Emissions*, Report No. 15, AGPS, Canberra.
16 I. Lowe (1992), 'Muddled models', *Search* 23, 2–3.
17 London Economics (1991), *The Impacts of Global Warming Control Policies on Australian Industry*, London.
18 Ecologically Sustainable Development Working Groups (1991), *Economic Modelling*, ESD Secretariat, Canberra.
19 A. Moran (1992), 'The notion of global warming has cooled considerably', *Courier-Mail*, 14 January, p. 10.
20 A. Moran and A. Chisholm (1991), *Global Warming—Its Economics and Politics*, Occasional Paper No. 11, Tasman Institute, Melbourne.
21 P. Rees (1991), 'Polluted channels: Environmental news in Australian newspapers', Master of Journalism thesis, University of Queensland.
22 National Greenhouse Strategy Committee (1992), *Draft National Greenhouse Response Strategy*, AGPS, Canberra.
23 Institution of Engineers, Australia (1992), 'Bureaucratic arrogance weakens national greenhouse strategy', Media Statement No. 85/92, Canberra.
24 Commonwealth of Australia (1992), *National Strategy for Ecologically Sustainable Development*, AGPS, Canberra.
25 C. Lindblom (1959), 'The science of muddling through', *J. Public Admin.* 19, 79–99.
26 E. Latham (1952), *The Group Basis of Politics*, Cornell University Press, Ithaca.
27 A. Etzioni (1968), *The Active Society*, Free Press/Macmillan, New York.
28 A. Etzioni (1976), *Social Problems*, Prentice-Hall, Englewood Cliffs.
29 K. J. Walker (ed.) (1992), *Australian Environmental Policy*, University of NSW Press, Kensington, p. 13.
30 J. K. Galbraith (1967), *The New Industrial State*, Penguin, Harmondsworth, p. 358.
31 J. K. Galbraith (1967), p. 297.

32 K. J. Walker (1991), p. 237.
33 F. Groenewegen (1989), 'Federalism', in B. W. Head and A. Patience, *From Fraser to Hawke*, Longman Cheshire, Melbourne.
34 R. J. L. Hawke (1979), *The Resolution of Conflict*, Boyer Lectures, ABC, Sydney.
35 G. Davis, J. Wanna, J. Warhurst and P. Weller (1988), *Public Policy in Australia*, Allen & Unwin, Sydney, p. 205.
36 B. W. Davis (1992), 'Federal–state tensions in Australian environmental management: The World Heritage issue', in K. J. Walker (ed.), *Australian Environmental Policy*, University of NSW Press, Kensington, pp. 215–32.
37 I. Lowe (1989a).
38 P. Thompson (1981), *Power in Tasmania*, Australian Conservation Foundation, Melbourne.
39 I. Lowe (1989b), 'The political role of energy forecasting mythology', in P. Hay, R. Eckersley and G. Holloway (eds), *Environmental Policy in Australia and New Zealand*, University of Tasmania Centre for Environmental Studies, Hobart.
40 G. Davis et al. (1988), p. 204.
41 K. J. Walker (1992).
42 S. Bell, 'The political power of business', in S. Bell and J. Wanna (eds) (1992), *Business–Government Relations in Australia*, Harcourt Brace Jovanovich, Sydney, pp. 46–56; see also chapters 1 and 2 of this volume.
43 R. Gottliebsen (1992), 'Why Murdoch has stuck with Abeles', *Business Review Weekly* 14:29, 42–6.
44 S. Bell (1992), p. 47.
45 Ecologically Sustainable Development Working Group on Energy Use (1991), *Final Report*, AGPS, Canberra.
46 D. Mercer (1991), *A Question of Balance*, Federation Press, Sydney.
47 P. Grabosky & J. Braithwaite (1986), *Of Manners Gentle*, Oxford University Press, Melbourne.
48 G. Crough, E. Wheelwright and E. Wiltshire (eds) (1980), *Australia and World Capitalism*, Penguin, Melbourne.
49 A. Hamilton (1986), *Oil: The Price of Power*, Michael Joseph, London.
50 E. Wheelwright (1991), *Oil and World Politics*, Left Book Club, Sydney.
51 S. Bell (1992), p. 52.
52 I. Lowe (1989a).
53 I. Lowe and J. P. Moran (1985), 'The role of transnational capital in the Australian resources industry—a comparative perspective', in J. Acheson and R. Berry (eds), *Proceedings of the 1984 ACSANZ Conference 'Regionalism and National Identity'*, University of Canterbury, Christchurch, pp. 409–19.
54 K. J. Walker (1992).
55 B. W. Davis (1992).
56 R. Watters (1992), letter to the editor, *Search* 23, 229.
57 J. Hyde (1992), 'Confronting the fruits of policies past', *Weekend Australian*, 18–19 July, p. 22.
58 M. Pusey (1991), *Economic Rationalism in Canberra*, Cambridge University Press, Cambridge, p. 174.
59 I. Lowe (1990), 'Global crisis: Danger and opportunity', in C. Pybus (ed.), *The Rest of the World is Watching*, Pan Macmillan, Sydney, pp. 215–31.

60 G. Dunkley (1992), *The Greening of the Red*, Pluto Press, Sydney, p. 4.
61 L. Milbrath (1989), *Envisioning a Sustainable Society*, State University of New York Press, Albany.
62 Australian Institute of Petroleum (1991), *Global Warming: Alternative Policy Instruments*, Policy Paper 1991/1, Melbourne.
63 World Commission on Environment and Development (1987), *Our Common Future*, Oxford University Press, Oxford, p. 202.

14

Environment, economy and state

Elim Papadakis and Anya Moore

The notion of environmentalism has become an integral part of Western democratic political cultures. It represents, above all, changes in political and social processes, in value priorities and attitudes, and the reshaping of established institutions by ideas about the environment and by the rise of new political and social movements. Green politics has had a major impact on government and on the economy. Established groups, keen to preserve their traditional bases of power, have had to adjust to the entry of new forces on to the political stage. There has been a growth in governmental and non-governmental organisations preoccupied with environmental issues.[1]

The main arguments of this chapter are as follows. In countries like Australia established institutions, particularly agencies of the state, have demonstrated a remarkable capacity to adapt to fundamental challenges to their assumptions about the economy, politics and society. Second, the process of adaptation has involved taking on board substantial elements of the green agenda not purely for cosmetic or tokenistic purposes, but because of a genuine recognition of their validity. Third, it is argued that, contrary to the assumptions of many environmentalists, some of the most far-reaching changes in behaviour towards the environment can be achieved by adopting some of the instruments used by proponents of economic growth, in other words, by appealing to economic rationality. Fourth, despite the rhetoric of many developers, it is likely that preventive measures, statutory intervention and transnational agreements between governments could prove to be the most effective ways of achieving environmental protection as well as economic development. Finally, although many national governments, including the Australian Government, have developed political strategies to channel, contain or manage the potential conflict between environmentalism and development in a way that causes minimal disruption to so-called structural imperatives, like the need for economic growth in capitalist society, and the realities of electoral power struggles between political parties, we argue that these imperatives can be and often are subject to challenge by new social actors and by new ways of thinking about social issues.

A key theme of this chapter is how far Australian governments (particularly the Commonwealth) and the business sector have successfully incorporated green issues. In arguing about incorporation, we draw on the proposition by Scott that the apparent integration of environmentalism into the policy agenda might in fact constitute a 'fundamental shift in the character of conventional politics'.[2] In other words, environmentalism is not simply being accommodated but is gradually transforming politics and society.

As suggested earlier, the impact of environmentalism represents both adjustments in policy and shifts in values and ideology.[3] The strengths of the environmental movement lie in its ability to capture the imagination of the public, to present cogent arguments for why the environment is everyone's concern and must be protected, and to mobilise large numbers of people. In order to sustain this pressure, environmental groups have appealed to morality, drawn on scientific research, staged events to attract the attention of the media, lobbied governments and business, educated the public and (in the case of groups like Greenpeace) engaged in spectacular public protests. As posited by political sociologists, new social movements have developed both conventional and unconventional techniques for political action.[4]

Because environmentalism is not a single-issue movement and represents a significant shift in values and ideology, the way governments and business respond and adapt to it are complex. Any study of this topic is bound to address the apparently irreconcilable and competing goals of the environmental movement and big business. The apparent hiatus between competing goals has been the focus of much government activity and debate. We argue that the dichotomy between the ideologies of big business and environmentalists is partly spurious and that there is plenty of scope for approaches that combine economic growth with strict environmental policies. The Australian Government has placed great emphasis on steering a middle path and on developing strategies incorporating both development and environmentalism. This has not been easy.

This chapter will assess the apparent convergence of different perspectives in relation to actual policy proposals and institutional changes. At one level, the ideological one, the conflict between environmentalists and developers appears to be intense. This, if true, would lend strong support to arguments about new political cleavages and new social conflicts.[5] However, at another level, in terms of institutional adaptation and policies, there appears to have occurred a dramatic shift towards a common understanding both of the problems and the solutions.

These changes might represent the greatest achievement by government, namely, its success in bringing adversaries to the same table and in demonstrating to organisations representing developers or environmentalists that their own survival depends on showing greater understanding for the opposite point of view.

Competing paradigms

To understand the complexity of the debate on environmentalism and the difficulties government faces in providing forums for dialogue between environmental groups and business, it is important to grasp the key ideological differences that figure in the debate. Arguments have also emerged over the questions of economic growth, of the dangers posed by global warming and of the relationship between human beings and the rest of nature. The issue of economic growth has been a major point of contention. The rejection by some prominent environmentalists like David Suzuki (a 'guru' of the no-growth school) of technological progress and of economics has helped to perpetuate the notion of two fundamentally opposed paradigms.[6]

Speculation about environmental disasters is interpreted by business groups as scaremongering tactics. Peter McLaughlin, the executive director of the Business Council of Australia (BCA), a peak body of big business firms, has asked environmentalists to 'refrain from misusing scientific information to "scare politicians", be willing to talk to business groups, and be prepared to point out that consumers, with businesses, were polluters'.[7] This attitude applies especially to the greenhouse effect.

Following Cotgrove, we will refer to those who dramatise the dangers of environmental destruction and who have only limited faith in the capacity of science and technology to address this problem as catastrophists.[8] By contrast, those who have much greater faith in the ability of industrial societies to address the problem of environmental degradation and in their capacity to produce an abundance of material goods are referred to as cornucopians.

The catastrophists have painted a bleak picture of life on earth by using the scenarios presented by scientists. The cornucopians have argued that the catastrophists (including the scientists) have been proved wrong on numerous occasions. Another criticism of the catastrophists (be they scientists or those who dramatise what scientists predict) is that they fail to take into account the capacity of social actors to adapt to change. There is a simple reply to these criticisms: without the warnings by the catastrophists preventive action would not have been taken. It could turn out to be far more dangerous to ignore warnings about the dangers of the greenhouse effect. Predictions by scientists of impending disaster have played a part in stimulating awareness of the fragility of the environment and in the development of green social movements.

A major preoccupation of the cornucopians is to defend the capitalist economy against the assault by the catastrophists. Environmentalism has apparently replaced socialism as the principal threat to capitalism. The 'new abolutism' of environmentalism is apparently 'worse than socialism'; socialism, we are reminded, 'was the emotional sister of fascism'.[9] These arguments suggest a fundamental division between the proponents of environmentalism and development.

Ironically, the cornucopians have adopted similar scare tactics to those of the catastrophists (for instance, by highlighting the more radical proposals of some environmentalists, notably of the 'deep ecologists', those who are preoccupied with the view that non-human forms of life are valuable irrespective of their value to human beings). In attempting to undermine the high moral stance adopted by the catastrophists, the cornucopians have labelled environmentalists like Peter Garrett as hypocrites because their lifestyles and occupations involve high levels of consumption of resources and of emissions of carbon dioxide.

The cornucopians have also accused environmentalists of not caring sufficiently about the poor. A major weakness of environmentalism, at least when it involves the advocacy of negative or zero economic growth (by David Suzuki and Bob Brown, respectively), is its apparent failure to address the aspirations of those who are the most vulnerable during recessions: the poor both in Australia and in developing countries.[10] Economic growth, according to the cornucopians, is also a prerequisite for environmental protection. Without economic growth, countries cannot afford to implement high environmental standards on production processes. Arguments about employment and investment are among the most useful for the cornucopians.

Transforming the institutional order

These conflicts have posed serious challenges to contemporary governments, which have set out to create mechanisms in an attempt to incorporate interest groups into the policy-making process and to defuse conflicts. In Australia the Federal Government has tried to draw contestant groups into the state, to set the policy agenda and to reassert the consensus style of politics espoused by the ALP in a range of arenas, including the environmental arena. One of the major differences between the period since the early 1970s and earlier times has been emergence (on a large scale) of government agencies designed specifically to address environmental issues. A central aspect of this development has been the restructuring of established institutions in order to integrate concern about the environment into the entire policy-making process.

In analysing the incorporation of environmentalism and its influence on the policy process, it is useful to examine trends over time. This allows us to focus on the process of incorporation. The 1960s were an important watershed in at least two respects. New voluntary environmental groups, like the Australian Conservation Foundation, burgeoned. Second, new arguments concerning the importance of institutional change crept on to the political agenda. For instance, in an address to a conference of the Institution of Engineers, Australia in 1971, Sir Garfield Barwick emphasised that conservation was a prerequisite for sustained productivity.[11] Barwick also argued that conservation was a 'paramount partner' of economic growth and development and questioned the one-sided preoccupation with economic growth for its own sake. Although these themes were articulated by élite groups, the prospects for placing the environment on the public policy agenda had appeared bleak in the 1970s.

However, during this period, there were some fundamental changes like the creation of services for national parks at both state and federal levels. In response to pressure by conservation groups, governments formed national agencies like the Australian National Parks and Wildlife Service (ANPWS) in 1975. The ANPWS was to manage parks, to protect, conserve and control wildlife and to carry out research related to these goals. It also had the authority to make recommendations to the government for the establishment and naming of parks and reserves and the protection and conservation of wildlife throughout Australia. One of its earliest recommendations was for the creation of national parks at Kakadu and Katherine Gorge.

The creation of the Australian Heritage Commission (AHC) in 1976 represented another institutional innovation. The AHC was to advise governments and make recommendations for the preservation of the national estate, including the natural environment. One of its roles was to encourage public interest in, and understanding of, issues relevant to the national estate. In other words, it had a strong educative role. The creation of the AHC anticipated concerns about the global importance of environmental protection. The AHC had to consider places that were 'of such outstanding world significance that they need to be conserved, managed and presented as part of the heritage of the world'.[12]

The creation of these agencies represents attempts to incorporate concerns about the environment and establish structures that partly reflect the ideas of environmentalists. These initiatives were complemented by legislative measures like the *Great Barrier Reef Marine Park Act 1975*. Australia also became a signatory to several international conventions, including the United Nations World Heritage Convention in 1974. It also participated in the United Nations Environment Program, which was established in 1972. These were significant precedents for major initiatives in the 1980s. In 1981, under the Fraser Government, Kakadu National Park, the Great Barrier Reef and the Willandra Lakes Region were entered on the World Heritage List. In 1982 the Western Tasmania Wilderness National Parks and the Lord Howe Island Group were also included on the list.

Apart from the creation of agencies like the AHC and the ANPWS, governments had introduced mechanisms for regulating disputes over conservation and development. The most significant and popular instrument was the environmental impact statement (EIS). It had been widely welcomed in the 1960s as a way of identifying the environmental aspects of new projects, although it did not mean that projects would necessarily be halted if they had a deleterious impact on the environment. The *Environment Protection (Impact of Proposals) Act* was passed by the Commonwealth in 1974. According to Dr Moss Cass, the federal Minister for Environment and Conservation, the advantages of the EIS included improvements in the documentation of environmental damage and the potential to increase public awareness of and public involvement in environmental issues.[13]

Woodhead has noted that politicians have been especially interested in the EIS because it has allowed them to gauge the level of public concern over an issue,[14] which provided them with a credible basis for ad hoc decisions as well as opportunities for deferring difficult decisions on projects. Another advantage of the EIS is that it provides governments with an additional source of information since it is undertaken by the proponents of a project rather than a government agency.

However, there are several problems with the EIS process. In preparing their report, developers have to consider financial and temporal constraints: 'The practicabilities of the development approval process prevent other than occasional in-depth studies from being undertaken'.[15] The EIS can therefore be regarded as more of a public relations ploy than a comprehensive scientific investigation. Not surprisingly, environmental impact statements have often been subject to challenges. A major defect in many of these arrangements has been the inconsistency between the different sets of legislation applied in each state and by the Commonwealth, which has made it difficult for firms operating at a national level to plan effectively. There are also other shortcomings that affect all those interested in conservation and development, like the cumbersome manner in which the Commonwealth resorts to the use of constitutional powers over foreign investment, trade, treaties and corporations to override decisions by the states, the inadequacy of mechanisms to enforce environmental protection in most states, the limited opportunities for public involvement in the process and the absence of an 'adequate framework for integrating economic and non-economic considerations in development planning through routine administrative, rather than ad hoc political, processes'.[16] These issues suggest another difficulty, namely to determine where responsibility for integrating economic and environmental values should lie and how to achieve this integration at three levels of government: the local, the state and the national levels.[17]

Transforming the ALP regime

In mapping out the response by governments and government bureaucracies to these challenges, we are interested in how the state reacted to protest movements and to its loss of control over arguments about the environment (for instance, the degree to which society should change from being primarily concerned with the development of natural resources to preserving them for aesthetic, moral and other reasons). The pressure on governments to adopt new strategies for incorporation can better be understood by drawing attention to the scale of the protest actions, their coverage by the mass media and their national and transnational character. These factors are well illustrated by the dispute over the Franklin Dam in Tasmania.

In 1983, for the first time, environmental issues featured prominently in a federal election. Moreover, the question of states' rights, which had been a major concern for environmentalists for decades, assumed a new significance. The Tasmanian Government was confronted by environmentalists who pleaded for federal intervention in environmental policy. The Liberal Government under Malcolm Fraser was unwilling to intervene over this issue and sought to avoid a political confrontation with the Tasmanian Government by offering $500 million for the construction of a coal-fired thermal power station as an alternative to the hydro-electric proposal. When the Tasmanian Government turned down the offer, the ALP announced its opposition to plans for construction of the dam if it were elected.

Although the ALP sided with environmentalists over this issue, it was reluctant to address the question of states' rights. Once in office, the Federal Labor Government offered the Tasmanian Government alternative schemes for creating employment. When they were rejected, the Commonwealth used its powers over external affairs and over corporations to pass the *World Heritage Properties Conservation Act 1983* in order to prevent construction of the dam. The Commonwealth survived a challenge to this legislation in the High Court. The High Court decision was in keeping with a trend towards the expansion of the Commonwealth's power to influence environmental policy. The judgement affirmed the Commonwealth's broad powers to control, 'having regard to environmental considerations, all manufacturing, production or extractive processes conducted by section 51 (xx) corporations for the purpose of trade' and, under the external affairs power, 'to enact a law in pursuance of an international obligation' (namely the World Heritage Convention).[18] Conflicts over other environmental issues have drawn further attention to the problems with clarifying the roles and the powers of the states and the Commonwealth.

Later conflicts over development projects forced the ALP Government (1) to reconsider the appropriateness of many of the instruments used to assess the impact of development on the environment, (2) to assert its constitutional rights in determining environmental policy and (3) to move away from a haphazard crisis-management approach towards a strategy of integration of environmentalism.

In 1984 the ALP was committed to a piecemeal approach. It refused to intervene in the dispute over the Daintree rainforests, arguing that it would only act with the cooperation of the Queensland Government. Yet the State Government refused to participate in the nomination of the forests for World Heritage listing and turned down the offer of $1 million for the development of a management plan for the area. For electoral reasons, the Federal Government was unwilling to provoke a confrontation over states rights at that time.

The crisis-management approach was undermined by three factors. In 1984 the Australian Heritage Commission confirmed that the rainforests fulfilled the main requirements for World Heritage listing. Second, another state, New South Wales, lodged an application for the inclusion of some its rainforests on the World Heritage list. These forests were generally regarded as less valuable than the ones in Queensland. Third, there was overwhelming public support for federal intervention. Finally, following a breakdown in negotiations with the Queensland Government, the Commonwealth nominated the Daintree forests for World Heritage listing and used this as an electoral issue in the 1987 federal election campaign.

The conflicts over the preservation of tropical rainforests (Daintree National Park), the mining of uranium (Kakadu National Park), logging (the Lemonthyme and Southern forests in Tasmania) and the construction of pulp mills (Wesley Vale in Tasmania) all serve to illustrate these points. The ALP Government was divided between proponents of economic growth and of preservation of the environment. More than any previous administration, the government was forced into considering innovations with respect to the process of environmental policy and into considering the electoral implications.

Although it had sided with environmentalists over the Franklin Dam, the ALP found it difficult to keep up with the rise in expectations for a more decisive environmental policy. As pressure increased for a more coherent approach to environmental protection, the ALP adopted a number of tactics to regain control of the agenda. The first was to persuade environmentalists that the ALP was genuinely committed to their cause. The second was to draw attention to the potential overlap between concerns about development and about the environment.

Commitment to and recognition of the importance of environmentalism was reflected in the replacement of Mr Cohen by Senator Richardson in 1987 as Minister for the Environment. The latter was a senior minister from the Prime Minister's faction and a power-broker within the government. Richardson played the role of convert to the environmentalist cause with some conviction. He also attempted a marriage between political opportunism and environmentalist fundamentalism. Richardson never questioned the electoral influence of the environmentalists and saw himself as the champion of environmentalism against the interests of big business in the tough world of pragmatic politics. Until that time, the Environment portfolio was widely regarded as fairly uninfluential. Developers continued to prefer to lobby the economic ministries, the Prime Minister and the Treasurer. This might have been a miscalculation on their part since the environmentalists used the Environment portfolio to great effect.

The commitment to environmentalism by the ALP Government still represented a piecemeal approach, as illustrated by the attempt to address the social and economic issues arising from its decision to list the Daintree forests. As in the Franklin Dam dispute, it undertook to compensate and retrain displaced workers. However, the limitations of Richardson's efforts to handle the environmental movement became more apparent with the broadening of the points for conflict between environmentalists and developers. These limitations were exposed in conflicts over woodchipping in the Lemonthyme and Southern forests of Tasmania and in proposals for mining in the Kakadu Conservation Zone.

Controlling the agenda

These conflicts provoked divisions within the ALP Cabinet, and by the end of the 1980s it had become obvious that a piecemeal approach to tackling environmental problems was unlikely to defuse conflicts. The government developed new strategies, including a more aggressive approach to shaping arguments about development and conservation and establishing new institutional mechanisms for dealing with competing interests over conservation and development.

In the attempt to control ideas and to set the agenda for change, the government exploited the concept of 'sustainable development' (defined by the Brundtland Commission, formed in 1983 by the United Nations, as meeting 'the needs of the present without compromising the ability of future generations to meet their own needs'). Although used by international agencies ever since the 1972 United Nations Stockholm Conference, this concept only became widely adopted in Australia in the late 1980s. The international debate over ecologically sustainable development (ESD) presented the Federal Government with an opportunity to move from a defensive posture to one in which it might control the agenda of arguments about the environment and the economy.

The notion of ESD has, of course, been interpreted in various ways by different political actors. The Federal Government has used this notion in trying to mediate between competing interests by calling for a 'balance' between economic and environmental perspectives. Above all, environmental concerns linked to the notion of an improved quality of life were given much greater prominence than in the past. They have also become an integral part of debates about economic and social policies. Parallel to the attempts to control and influence debates, the government undertook numerous initiatives and created new institutional mechanisms. Despite the focus on environmental protection, the government did not neglect economic goals. The notion of ESD became especially helpful in retaining the traditional emphasis on economic objectives:

> *Ecologically sustainable development provides a conceptual framework for integrating these economic and environmental objectives, so that products, production processes and services can be developed that are both internationally competitive and more environmentally compatible.*[19]

In the 1980s public debate was dominated by arguments about 'rolling back' government activity. In reality, the role of the state in regulating people's lives has become more sophisticated but has nevertheless remained considerable.[20] Among the major regulatory policy initiatives by government in the area of environmental policy, we include the establishment of a Resource Assessment Commission (RAC) in 1989 and the strategy for ecologically sustainable development from 1990 onwards.

The RAC was established to deal with conflicts over development and the environment. Following a time-honoured tradition, the government wanted to defuse or at least distance itself from conflicts by creating an 'independent' body. In its publicity the RAC has emphasised its 'independence', its role in helping the government 'to integrate environmental and economic factors into its decisions about the use of Australia's natural resources' and the importance of identifying environmental, cultural, social, industry, economic and other values involved in the use of resources. Astute commentators have related the establishment of the RAC to prevailing political controversies. The RAC, it was claimed, would be 'a permanent public inquiry mechanism to arbitrate on land-use conflicts, thereby diminishing Senator Richardson's stature as champion of the greenies' and to allow the government 'to set the agenda for environmental debate'.[21]

The RAC was established under pressure from those ministers responsible for Resources, Primary Industries and Energy, and Industry, Technology and Commerce on the grounds that such a body would facilitate policy coordination. They also hoped that the commission would reduce the influence of the Minister for the Environment and circumvent the 'green' department (i.e. the Department of Arts, Sports, Environment, Tourism and Territories, or DASETT), and that bureaucratic agencies concerned with economic development, notably the Industries Assistance Commission and the Australian Science and Technology Council, might have far more say in environmental policy.

However, the RAC has not defused the conflict between environmentalism and development.[22] The RAC was itself confused about its goals. Some members of the RAC argued that it is for the government to assess and decide on the prioritisation of different values. Others wanted to broaden the scope of the RAC to include mediation.[23] There was also tension between the attempt to present different perspectives impartially and the aspirations for the RAC to become a mediator. Any attempt at mediation is bound to involve an expression of certain values.

The RAC not only faced internal contradictions. It was also seen by other government agencies, including senior officials in DASETT, as a direct threat to their role as mediators. Some officials saw the formation of the RAC as an attempt by John Kerin, the Minister for Primary Industries, to 'hijack the environmental debate'. Moreover, the flow of funds to this new agency and other departments has been criticised by DASETT. The RAC was abolished at the end of 1993.

A problem for DASETT is that all economic and coordinating departments, especially the well-funded ones, have also created their own units to deal with environmental issues. The government has also established competing agencies (like the RAC) and created mechanisms (like the ecologically sustainable development working groups) outside the control of DASETT. DASETT has tended to emphasise ecological rather than developmental aspects of policies. However, DASETT has had little choice but to adapt to initiatives like the RAC and the ESD groups.

Partly in response to calls by business groups, DASETT has also taken several initiatives of its own, including proposals for resolving tensions between the Commonwealth and the states through an Intergovernmental Agreement on Environmental Policy and a National Environment Protection Agency (NEPA). The first initiative, announced at a special Premiers Conference in October 1990, emphasised the need for a cooperative national approach to the environment, a better definition of the roles of the respective governments, a reduction in the number of disputes between the Commonwealth and the states and territories and greater certainty for government and business decision-making. The initiative for the formation of a NEPA emphasised the importance of cooperation between states. The successor to Senator Richardson as Minister for the Environment, Ros Kelly, suggested that a NEPA would have to be established in cooperation with the states, that it would be administered by a joint body (like a ministerial council with the Commonwealth minister as chair), that no state would enjoy the power of veto and that decisions by a national EPA would be taken by a majority in order to facilitate decision-making and that state EPAs would enforce 'national standards'.[24]

The establishment of ESD groups represents another effort to defuse some of the conflicts between environmentalism and development and to integrate the warring factions into a deliberative process monitored by government. Federal Government departments like DASETT (retitled DEST in March 1993), Treasury, DPIE and DITAC were well represented in the process.

For environmental groups the ESD process has posed a number of difficulties. If they were to decline involvement, they could be regarded as intransigent and unwilling to engage in rational debate. Some political commentators have used the notion of ESD to try to marginalise environmentalists, to argue that they are not serious about tackling the problems of the environment and of development. Environmentalists were wary of the ESD process. Involvement in negotiations with industry and with government agencies was likely to strengthen the process of institutionalisation of the environmental movement. It would also mean that concessions would have to be made. Initially, Greenpeace, the ACF, the WWF and the Wilderness Society expressed concern about the composition of the ESD industry groups. They felt that economic interests would dominate the groups.

Involvement in the ESD process has forced environmentalists to give greater recognition to market-based strategies for environmental protection. Reflecting the strong involvement by the Treasury in the ESD process, the Commonwealth Government has emphasised that a major cause of the overuse and pollution of natural resources was the failure to attach a market value to them.[25] This fuelled the fears of some environmental groups about involvement in the process, since they detected a bias towards development rather than environment.

A further difficulty has been to get the two sides to agree on the nature of the problems to be addressed. The Commonwealth Government itself had great difficulty in defining the term *ecologically sustainable development*. Various groups have tended to emphasise different aspects of ESD. Finally, each group responded in a predictable manner to the government discussion paper on ESD. The BCA argued for changes at the margin, for an evolutionary approach to environmental problems, whereas the environmental groups posited a fundamental crisis and the need for drastic measures.

The developers

Some developers have welcomed initiatives like the ESD groups and seized the opportunity to regain control over the debate about development and conservation. The approach of the BCA has been to integrate environmentalism and economic development by adopting two strategies: first, to emphasise dialogue between environmentalists and developers and between business and public policy institutions, and second, to draw attention to market mechanisms in solving environmental problems. The BCA has emphasised the 'interdependence' of 'economic development and environmental management'.[26] The emphasis on market mechanisms is supported by government agencies like the Treasury, which, like business, has stressed that the price mechanism is central to environmental protection and that the price of goods should take into account environmental costs.

Further, the BCA has embraced regulatory policies.[27] The BCA appears keen to steer clear of the rhetoric about fundamental conflicts between environmentalism and capitalism. The notion of sustainable development holds great appeal because it apparently represents

> the middle ground between those, quite few in number, whose preference is for economic development while giving little or no weight to environmental implications and those, again quite few in number, whose preference is towards preservation of our natural resources while giving little or no consideration to the economic consequences.[28]

The BCA has extended these proposals to models for institutional design: 'With quite separate environment and economic policy departments each pushing its own agenda it is often difficult to obtain a balanced view of resource use options'.[29]

Despite its pronouncements on integration of regulatory and market approaches, the BCA has far greater faith in markets than in the state. Markets apparently provide the right incentives for environmental protection. The BCA has argued for the removal of 'perverse' incentives like the incorrect pricing of irrigation water, which encourages farmers to use too much of it. Second, wherever possible, property should be owned privately in order 'to create the right incentives for management of environmental assets'.[30] The BCA has recognised that it would be impossible to price all environmental assets (like birds and animals) but has called on government 'to provide a predictable and stable policy environment' for decisions about pollution and exploitation of resources. This call has been echoed by the forest industry, which proposed so-called 'resource security' legislation to guarantee access to forests for economic exploitation.[31] The proposals for this legislation were accompanied by threats that billions of dollars in investment would be lost to Australia and with no guarantee, on the part of the forest industries, that if the legislation were passed, they would actually go ahead with investment.

The call for predictability and stability is, of course, inconsistent with the behaviour of business groups. The consequences of innovation and development are unpredictable and unstable. The BCA, not unreasonably, appears to want government to remain predictable in its approach, while business remains dynamic, aggressive and competitive. However, the BCA appears to be excessively optimistic in assuming that businesses will always behave according to 'an obligation to ensure that its use of the community's natural resources are consistent with the interests of the community at large'.[32]

Business has called on the state to address environmental problems by providing tax incentives (for instance, to mining companies to rehabilitate mine sites and to oil companies to remove offshore petroleum platforms). The state, in other words, is being asked to ensure that environmentalism does not impinge unduly on profit margins. Environmental protection is to be funded by the public purse. Business groups have also argued that legislation on taxes does not reflect 'changes in community attitudes and government policies relating to costs associated with the protection and care of our environment'.[33]

In a partial response to the calls for tax incentives for business, the Federal Government has taken several initiatives. It has extended a scheme for allowing farmers tax deductions for some capital and other outlays on Landcare initiatives. In addition, the August 1992 Budget introduced tax deductibility for cleaning up contaminated sites. Another type of incentive involves sanctions imposed by governments for breaches of environmental laws. Recent legislation, for instance in Victoria, has meant that individuals like company directors could be fined up to $500 000 or face up to five years' imprisonment if guilty of serious breaches of environmental laws.[34] Companies that breach pollution limits set by a government could be fined up to $1 million in most states.

Some developers have accepted the need for such severe penalties. The response by business to environmentalism represents not only an attempt to appear socially responsible but also a belief that development can be combined with environmentalism. The Department of Industry, Technology and Commerce has estimated that by the end of the century Australia could earn $6 billion by developing technology for waste management. Business groups like the ATG Environmental Technology Trust have estimated that this figure could be doubled if it were to include the development of other technologies for sustainable agriculture, energy production and monitoring waste. If this potential were realised, it could make the development of environmental technologies the most lucrative area for economic growth and export dollars.

To counter the catastrophists, some developers have promoted the ideas of Max Singer, a co-founder of the Hudson Institute in the United States. Singer has emphasised the compatibility between environmentalism and development and argued that we need to become 'smarter' in how we manage environmental problems. He has challenged some of the assumptions of developers and conservationists. Contrary to many developers, he has argued that environmental protection measures do not necessarily lead to an overall reduction in employment opportunities (for instance, the loss of jobs in the mining industry might be compensated for by gains in employment for environmental consultants). Contrary to many environmentalists, he has been optimistic about how technology can tackle the problems of industrial pollution. He has also argued that, in countries like the United States, the environment is 'getting better overall'. To take one example, many countries are now attempting to replace trees at a more rapid rate than they are being felled. Wealth, he has suggested, is a precondition for dealing with environmental problems. In addition, predictions about the dire consequences of growth in the world population might be undermined by two factors: (1) the technology is already available for a massive increase in food production and (2) as countries become more prosperous, the rate of population growth generally decreases (and we have already passed the peak rates of population growth).[35]

According to the developers, we should remain optimistic about the capacity of capitalism to address new challenges. However, their optimism might soon appear too revolutionary in the face of a new consensus in favour of environmentalism. Developers have recognised that their survival depends on incorporating aspects of environmentalism. They have proposed a dialogue with environmentalists. They have shown considerable flexibility and adaptability in relation to changes in popular awareness and to changes in knowledge about environmental management.

The environmentalists

Despite these efforts by developers to improve their image and their practices, environmentalists have remained sceptical about the possibilities of reconciling a business culture with environmentalism. In addition, the flexibility of both government and business, reflected in initiatives for ecologically sustainable development, poses a threat to many environmentalists. They could become marginalised and appear intransigent.

Some organisations, like the ACF, are prepared to be flexible. Unlike David Suzuki, the ACF does not regard the notion of sustainable development as a 'swiz'. It has also questioned some of the presuppositions of the catastrophists and demonstrated a capacity to integrate development and environmentalism. The ACF has argued that economic growth does not necessarily conflict with environmental protection by pointing to the deployment of highly efficient technologies for producing energy and resources.[36] There is a correspondence between some of the proposals by the ACF for sustainable development and those by advisers to business like Singer.

Before addressing the similarities, we will focus on the differences. Environmentalists point to the possibilities of more efficient uses of energy and the need for changes in lifestyles. The ACF, unlike business groups, has tended to project into the future on the basis of current trends, to speculate that if historical patterns of economic growth continue, there will be a major escalation in environmental destruction. The ACF is not as optimistic as business about the role of capitalism and technology in solving environmental problems. Rather, it has emphasised a precautionary approach: 'Policies and decisions should err on the side of caution, placing the burden of proof on technological and industrial developments to demonstrate that they are ecologically sustainable'.[37]

Business has attempted to outdo environmentalists in the moral stakes by arguing that a decline in economic growth and development would perpetuate poverty in many nations and would make it more difficult for them to spend money on environmental protection. The ACF has begun to recognise the validity of this argument by accepting the notion of selective economic growth and greater efficiency. However, the ACF has also emphasised the notion of social equity, especially between rich and poor nations. In addition, it has called for changes in lifestyles by rich nations. By contrast, business has remained silent over the question of social equity.

The ACF and WWF have moved towards the position of developers by criticising arguments about economic growth presented by some prominent environmentalists. They argue that the catastrophist approach is misleading, since it claims that economic growth inevitably leads to environmental degradation, to an increase in energy consumption and to the depletion of physical resources. They also point out that there are many ways in which economic activity is independent of the consumption of energy and resources, for example, through recycling of products and through closed-loop production processes. The ACF and WWF have not questioned economic growth per se. They have been preoccupied with the pattern of growth. Changes in the pattern of growth will have to be evaluated in relation to (1) the viability of processes of production and consumption and (2) the potential damage to the environment and the economy.

Like business groups, the ACF has proposed an integration of ecology and economy. Although more cautious than business in its evaluation of the economy's impact on the environment, the ACF, like business groups and government agencies, has questioned the idea that the environmental paradigm is essentially incompatible with the dominant paradigm based on economic growth. The ACF has embraced an alternative approach that represents the attempts by environmentalists and developers to realise their goals in a pragmatic way. Although many tensions persist between the two sides, there is much common ground: both sides have recognised the significance of environmental problems and of price and market mechanisms for ensuring economic growth as well as environmental protection. The convergence between the ACF and business groups has been evident in the promotion by both sides of technological innovation, the recycling of materials, improvements in the quality of products, the establishment of standards for the entire lifecycle of a product (including the disposal stage), greater efficiency in the conversion of raw materials to usable products, energy management services and waste management. Both sides have argued for reform of the taxation system to provide incentives for environmental protection. The ACF and WWF have also proposed a major investigation of how energy or resource usage can be or is being decoupled from economic activity, although both organisations are committed to achieving a balance between economic imperatives and the quality of life in order 'to bring our community into balance with the ecological systems on which it depends'.

Conclusion

Changes in public perceptions have forced business and government to incorporate the environment into most aspects of their policies. The Federal Government has been forced to develop new strategies for dealing with the conflicts between development and environment. It has realised that these conflicts represent clashes over values and over interests. The Cabinet has itself been divided between materialists and post-materialists.[38] Attempts to incorporate the environmentalist challenge have included the adaptation of the Brundtland Commission Report by the ESD working groups, the creation of new agencies to tackle environmental problems and various legislative measures.

The ALP Government has shown immense flexibility in adapting to the fundamental questioning of assumptions about the economy, politics and society by new social movements. In its attempt to incorporate environmentalism, the government has contributed to the transformation of government agencies, which attempted to achieve a new synthesis between apparently conflicting approaches. Our analysis suggests that economic factors still play a key role in policy-making, that established organisations will have difficulty in accommodating environmental protection legislation if it might mean a loss of investment potential and that governments are interested in these issues mainly for electoral reasons. However, the analysis also shows that there is considerable scope for ensuring greater predictability and cohesion in environmental policy and for developing effective policies that reflect the compatibility of economic growth and environmental protection. Both developers and environmentalists have abandoned many of their earlier presuppositions about the relationship between economic growth and environmental degradation.

Notes

1 This chapter is drawn mainly from E. Papadakis (1993), *Politics and the Environment*, Allen & Unwin, Sydney. Without attributing any responsibility to him for defects in our argument, we have profited from the comments of Stephen Bell.
2 A. Scott (1990), *Ideology and the New Social Movements*, Unwin Hyman, London, p. 151.
3 See S. Cotgrove (1982), *Catastrophe or Cornucopia*, John Wiley and Sons, Chichester; A. Touraine (1985), 'An introduction to the study of social movements', *Social Research* 52:4, 749–87; R. Inglehart (1977), *The Silent Revolution*, Princeton University Press, Princeton; R. Inglehart (1990), *Culture Shift in Advanced Industrial Society*, Princeton University Press, Princeton.
4 L. Milbrath and M. Goel (1977), *Political Participation*, 2nd ed., Rand McNally, Chicago; S. H. Barnes and M. Kaase et al. (1979), *Political Action*, Sage, Beverly Hills; J. A. Hannigan (1985), 'Alain Touraine, Manuel Castells and social movement theory', *Sociological Quarterly* 26:4, 435–54; B. Klandermans and S. Tarrow (1988), 'Introduction' in B. Klandermans, H. Kriesi and S. Tarrow (eds), *From Structure to Action*, JAI Press, Greenwich, Conn.
5 R. Dalton and M. Kuechler (eds) (1990), *Challenging the Political Order: New Social and Political Movements in Western Democracies*, Polity Press, Cambridge; Inglehart (1990).
6 'Suzuki: The Habitat interview', *Habitat*, June 1990, pp. 9–12.
7 *Age*, 8 February 1990.
8 Cotgrove (1982).
9 P. McGuinness, *Australian*, 14 July 1990.
10 The failure of writers on environmentalism to consider questions of equity and class is a major focus of S. Bell (1987), 'Socialism and ecology: Will ever the twain meet', *Social Alternatives* 6:3, 5–12.
11 G. Barwick (1974), 'Environmental conservation: A prerequisite for sustained productivity' in R. Dempsey (ed.), *The Politics of Finding Out: Environmental Problems in Australia*, Cheshire, Melbourne.

12 P. Galvin (1990), 'The Australian Heritage Commission: A look ahead', *Canberra Bulletin of Public Administration*, 62, 108–12.
13 Debate in the House of Representatives, cited by G. M. Bates (1983), *Environmental Law in Australia*, Butterworths, Sydney.
14 W. R. Woodhead (1990), 'Shortcomings in decision-making frameworks: Past and present problems', *Canberra Bulletin of Public Administration*, 62, 57–9.
15 Woodhead (1990).
16 R. Buckley (1990), 'Shortcomings in current institutional frameworks for environmental planning and management', *Canberra Bulletin of Public Administration*, 62, 50–6.
17 R. Rickson (1990), 'Environmental awareness, institutional "gaps" and public decision-making', *Canberra Bulletin of Public Administration*, 62, 44–6; C. Hall (1990), 'Local government perspective', *Canberra Bulletin of Public Administration*, 62, 28–36.
18 L. Zines (1985), 'The environment and the constitution' in R. L. Matthews (ed.), *Federalism and the Environment*, Centre for Research on Federal Financial Relations, Canberra, pp. 18–19.
19 Commonwealth of Australia (1990), *Ecologically Sustainable Development: A Commonwealth Discussion Paper*, AGPS, Canberra, p. 1.
20 See A. De Swaan (1988), *In Care of the State: Health, Education and Welfare in Europe and the USA in the Modern Era*, Polity Press, Cambridge. See also chapters 1 and 2 of this book.
21 *Financial Review*, 27 January 1989.
22 See B. Galligan and G. Lynch (1992), *Integrating Conservation and Development: Australia's Resource Assessment Commission and the Testing Case of Coronation Hill*, Federalism Research Centre Discussion Paper No. 14, Australian National University, Canberra.
23 See *RAC News*, March 1990, No. 2; B. Boer, D. Craig, J. Handmer and H. Ross (1991), 'The potential role of mediation in the Resource Assessment Commission inquiry process', Resource Assessment Commission Discussion Paper No. 1, AGPS, Canberra.
24 DASETT (1991), *ASTEC: Environmental Research Seminar. Commonwealth Environment Strategy*, Department of the Arts, Sport, the Environment, Tourism and Territories, Canberra, p. 13. DASETT became DASET in January 1992 when Tourism was detached and DEST in March 1993 when Arts was detached.
25 For a discussion of economic instruments for environmental regulation see M. Johnson (1991), 'Regulating the environment' in B. Head and E. McCoy (eds), *Deregulation or Better Regulation*, Macmillan, Melbourne, pp. 131–40.
26 Business Council of Australia (1990a), *Achieving Sustainable Development: A Discussion Paper by the Business Council of Australia*, July 1990, p. 3.
27 Business Council of Australia (1990b), *Development and the Environment: A Policy Statement of the Business Council of Australia*, April 1990.
28 Business Council of Australia (1990a), p. 1.
29 Business Council of Australia (1990a), p. 24.
30 Business Council of Australia (1990a), p. 16.
31 See N. Economou (1992), 'Resource security legislation and national environment policy', *Current Affairs Bulletin*, 68:12, 17–26.

32 Business Council of Australia (1990a), p. 19.
33 M. Crowe (1990), 'Is the Tax Department an environmental hazard?', *NAB Decisions*, August.
34 *Australian Financial Review*, 8 April 1990.
35 See M. Singer (1990), 'Is there hope?', *Mining Review*, June, 21–7.
36 B. Hare (1991), 'Ecologically sustainable development', *Habitat*, April, 10–12.
37 Hare (1991), p. 12.
38 See E. Papadakis (1993), pp. 15 ff.

15

Women, the state and public policy

Marian Simms

Australia has an extensive network of bureaucratic machinery dealing with women's issues in comparison with the other Anglo democracies. The Australian approach to policy-making contrasts sharply, for example, with the human rights/case-oriented approach of the United States, where many of the initiatives for women's rights have been fought out in the courts. In Australia most of the new institutions and processes dealing with women were set up in the 1970s, and subsequently there were quite extensive borrowings from the US, particularly in terms of the procedures dealing with equal opportunity and affirmative action.

It is a fairly straightforward matter to outline the Australian initiatives (and they are discussed below). It is, however, far more complicated to evaluate them. Certain optimists have tended to see the existence of women's policies as a sign of the significant gains made by the Australian women's movement in its interaction with the state.[1] Some pessimists have argued that the so-called 1972 agenda has not been achieved.[2] The 1972 agenda refers to the list of issues that the newly formed women's movements wished to achieve. They included equal pay, child care, equal opportunity and reproductive rights (such as contraception and abortion). The 1972 agenda was partly about the removal of barriers to women's participation in the public world and partly about opening up choices to women. It is clear, for example, that while in a formal sense women have achieved equal pay (i.e. the same pay for the same work), on average they still do not earn as much as men.

If the 1972 agenda is narrowly interpreted then a claim could be made that it has been achieved. However, those who interpret it in a broader fashion would be more likely to point to the inadequacies of existing legislative and other changes. Susan Ryan, for example, emphasised the achievements of the movement and suggested that it has lost its momentum precisely because it has gained so much ground.[3] Patricia Grimshaw, in contrast, has argued that the movement had not achieved its initial agenda but had run out of steam for other reasons; the movement had become institutionalised in two senses: it had become a wing of government and it had become ossified.[4]

The process of institutionalisation, in the first sense, has often occurred at the state level since, because of the nature of Australian federalism, the states are the major providers of welfare and health services even if the Commonwealth provides the lion's share of the funding. If we examine the list of women's issues, we see that for women, the Federal Government has limited constitutional authority over most of them; refuges, for example, are funded through a joint Commonwealth–state program. Equal pay and wages policy is a matter for the complex conciliation and arbitration machinery. (It should be noted, however, that the Federal Government does have some authority, reflected in the Whitlam Government's decision to reopen the equal pay case in December 1972.) Abortion is largely a state matter, although it has entered the Federal Parliament in respect of the ACT and the funding of abortion under Medibank and Medicare. Child care is a joint Commonwealth–state matter. The delivery of policy on these crucial women's issues is largely a matter for the states. In a glossy 'Progress Report to the People of Western Australia' the then Premier, Peter Dowding, reminded female voters of the range of services available to them, provided by his government.[5] For example, the Women's Information and Referral Exchange (WIRE) had been set up in 1984 'to provide women with information and support to enable them to make key decisions in their lives'.[6]

In general, however, since the middle of the 1970s, State and Commonwealth Governments have been more aware of women's needs than in the past and have enacted changes to improve the situation of women,[7] including increased funding for women's health, refuge and counselling centres. At the Commonwealth level, there were the labour market reforms initiated by the Whitlam Labor Government (1972–75), such as equal pay, and then the Hawke Labor Government's equal opportunity legislation. This package included the *Sex Discrimination Act 1984*, the *Public Service Reform Act 1984*, the *Affirmative Action (Equal Opportunity for Women) Act 1986* and the *Equal Employment Opportunity (Commonwealth Authorities) Act 1987*, which have improved women's rights in relation to job advertising, recruitment, training and service conditions. At both Commonwealth and state levels, bureaucratic machinery exists that undertakes research into women's affairs, advising Cabinet and informing the community of policy developments. However, the legislation enacted and machinery established has related more to the economic position of women as workers than to their political rights or special needs.

The relationship between women's groups, women's strategies and the Australian state is a complicated one. It shares some of the same sets of dilemmas as posed by the connections between the state and other groups and classes, which have demanded change. These problems have been debated extensively, especially the question of leftist attitudes to working with and against the Australian state and the ensuing question of social democracy. As many of the activists in the early years of the so-called second wave of Australian feminism (i.e. the one that commenced in the late 1960s) were themselves active in left parties and unions, we can assumed that they were familiar with many of the debates and dilemmas over the state.[8]

One of the most significant features of the relationship between Australian feminists and the state has been the innovations that have occurred at a practical level. These developments will be described in this chapter. They have also been accompanied by a certain degree of theorising and even more importantly have had crucial implications for debates about future strategies and tactics. These discussions will be divided into a number of sections. First, the role of femocrats will be analysed. Second, the focus will be broadened to the problem of the connections between the women's movement and the state more generally. The women's movement has created a network of institutions that are best seen as being in the twilight zone between the state proper and societal relations. Third, the analysis is further broadened to examine the connection between the political or electoral face of the state, female activists and the development of party policy. The contrast is made with the United States where women's groups have successfully marketed the 'gender gap' concept in order to keep women's issues high on the policy agenda. Finally, the chapter proceeds to consider the development of theory with a capital 'T'. It has moved at two levels in Australia, as the development of 'homegrown' theory has been caught between the importation of international flavours of the month and the attempt to make sense of our own practical developments.

Femocrats

Femocrats are women who have been employed to develop, implement and monitor women's programs in both Federal and State Governments. Femocrats, according to Anna Yeatman, are 'women employed within state bureaucratic positions to work on advancing the position of women in the wider society through the development of equal opportunity and anti-discrimination strategies of change'.[9] Such positions have normally been created by Federal and State Labor Governments, but in some cases Liberal Governments have created (Victoria 1973) or continued (NSW 1988–) women's policy machinery. According to Franzway, Court and Connell, femocrats are 'drawing largely on the WEL [Women's Electoral Lobby] position' because they 'are concerned chiefly with women's rights'.[10] However, Franzway et al. are wrong to assume that because someone has an interest in maintaining or extending the rights of women, they are automatically to be identified with the WEL position. In fact a number of high-profile femocrats, including the first women's adviser at the state level (Penny Ryan in Victoria, 1975), were active in the women's liberation movement rather than WEL at the time of their appointments.

WEL has been one of the great survivors of Australian feminist politics. Since its formation in 1972 it has continued to lobby governments on a range of different issues including equal employment, pay equity, taxation, welfare and child care. Much of its efforts have been devoted to 'holding the line' against attacks on rights and benefits already achieved. This was particularly true during the Fraser years (1975–83) but also became true during the Hawke and Keating Governments (1983–).

Femocrats have been the subject of many debates and have often been in unenviable situations during these struggles. The contradictions of their positions have, ironically enough, been one of the constants in a feminist world, which in other ways has been in a state of constant flux. In the beginning (i.e. the Whitlam years) the 'supergirl' label was employed by the press to refer to women appointed to government positions dealing exclusively with women's issues. The main target was Elizabeth Reid who became the adviser to the Prime Minister (Gough Whitlam) on 'matters relating to the welfare of women'. Press harassment and the general failure to take her position seriously were undoubtedly among the reasons for her resignation in 1975. At the same time, at a state level, Penny Ryan was virtually hounded out of her advisory position to Victorian Liberal Premier Rupert Hamer by the press and anti-feminist women's groups. The press criticism of these so-called 'supergirls' peaked during international Women's Year 1975, when the federally funded Women and Politics Conference came under attack.

Femocrats also were forced to deal with feminist criticism from within the social movement that had produced them. Sara Dowse, who had replaced Reid as the leading spokeswoman on women's issues in 1974 and then resigned during the Fraser years to protest the downgrading of the Office of the Status of Women, suggested that the movement, like guerrilla movements, needed double strategies: small consciousness-raising groups *and* organised lobbying of national, state and local bureaucracies were equally important. Many of the feminist critics of women's advisers (i.e. femocrats) were uneasy about such links with the state and believed the state to be a creature of capitalism and the patriarchy. Sara Dowse, writing in 1982, attempted to respond to these critics. Part of the problem, in her view, was the movement's refusal to accept both the need for and the extent of normal pressure-group-style activities.[11]

Parallel debates have occurred in the United Kingdom. Elizabeth Wilson, underpinning Dowse's argument, maintained that the movement has used both conventional and non-conventional tactics simultaneously. Its problem has been its refusal to come to terms with the reality and significance of its traditional lobbying activities:

> *It is not enough to say that consciousness-raising groups and small campaigning groups and self-help groups have been, at times, inspiring and successful. We need also to look at attempts to create national organisations for national campaigns, such as the National Women's Aid Federation and the National Abortion Campaign. Their successes and failures are never so much as mentioned ... It is surely important to assess the way in which the women's movement has utilised, alongside its 'new' use of small groups as a central organising focus, perfectly traditional campaigning methods. We have marched, lobbied and written to MPs as trade unions and traditional pressure groups have been doing for many years and why not!*[12]

While accepting that their daily lives are full of struggles and contradiction, Anna Yeatman has argued that femocrats constitute an identifiable 'new class' serving their own interests and those of the state:

> *Femocrats are a class of their own in a twofold sense. First, they are women who are committed through their adherence to the ideology of feminism to establishing their own, individualised economic class position. Feminism becomes located as the ideal interest which legitimises these strivings. Second, they are a peculiar class: they neither share the gender-class privileges of men and their superior life chances in the various economic assets markets, nor do they share the gender-class position of most women which hooks them symbolically into dependence in patriarchal (public or private) types of economic support.*[13]

Yeatman's views have widely been seen as challenging but have rarely been directly challenged. Marian Sawer has been a significant defender of the work of femocrats:

Despite the tensions, many femocrats remain involved in the women's movement (when there are enough hours in the day) and have a clear view of the complementary relationship between femocrats and the movement outside: 'The radical demands of the women's movement prepare the ground for the less threatening, but nevertheless important changes to policy and legislation that are pushed through by feminists in the public service'.[14]

The women's movement and the state

Other writers have seen not one 'movement outside' the state but two. Lyndall Ryan, writing in the useful collection, *Playing the State*, has described the relationship between the two wings of the women's movement as follows: 'Women's Liberation as the stormtroopers and Women's Electoral Lobby as the pragmatic face of feminism'.[15] The terms *women's liberation, women's liberationist* and *women's liberation movement* have enjoyed less currency in the 1990s than in the 1970s or even the 1980s. This has led some to argue that the distinction between the two wings is irrelevant and/or was perhaps never really applicable to Australia. Yet the divisions within the broadly defined movement are not just about semantics. They have crucial theoretical underpinnings and implications, in terms of their orientations towards and views of the state.

It has became conventional in the international literature to divide second-wave feminism into distinct subsections.[16] For the United States Jo Freeman has distinguished between the 'younger' and 'older' branches of the modern American women's movement.[17] These branches, in her eyes, had distinct value systems, and the younger branch had an anti-authoritarian and anti-institutional orientation. The older branch, to the contrary, saw institutions as opportunities rather than barriers. It was prepared to work through the state. In Australia the two parts of the women's movement have also had different orientations towards the state.

In Australia in the 1970s it was usual to distinguish between the women's rights and the women's liberationist wings of the movement. Those feminists primarily concerned with women's rights largely accepted 'instrumental activism' as a value system. They wished to extend women's participation in the public world of work, education and opportunities: they wanted women to have a more generous serve of the economic and political pie. This could be achieved by working through the existing system, including the state. For their part the more radical women's liberationists wanted to change the nature of the pie. Not only were they concerned with economic questions but also they mounted a total assault on the dominant institutions and ideology.

They rejected the state and set about forming alternative non-institutional structures. The existing class and occupational structure was rejected and *careerism* was a term widely used to attack those who worked within the system. Women's liberation groups not only attacked the limitations of the traditional pressure-group tactics previously used by civil rights groups but also criticised the instrumentalism and hierarchical structures of existing left-wing organisations (such as trade unions, left parties and certain women's groups).

Thus, women's liberation theorists in the 1970s developed various critiques of existing structures, including the state, trade unions, political parties and the family. At the same time many activists rolled up their sleeves and became involved in practical activities. The significance of the early years of the 'second wave' of feminism in the 1970s was the sheer scope and size of the grass-roots involvement in women's refuges, community child care, rape crisis groups and women's health centres. By 1974 in Melbourne there was the following range of groups: the halfway house group, the women's abortion action coalition, the women's health collective, the rape crisis centre, grapevine and the children's book group. There were other activities as well: the women's theatre group, a music group and an ad hoc collective of women planning a conference around the theme of women and madness (which eventuated in 1975). The names are fairly self-explanatory except for grapevine, which was presented as a 'learning network' to enable women to 'learn from and with each other'. Courses proferred ranged from car mechanics to women's sexuality.

Many groups of this kind were still present in the 1990s. Particularly active were the women's health and refuge groups. By 1991, for example, there were 311 women's refuges in Australia. The important feminist health network, the Women's Health, Information, Resource and Crisis Centres Association (WHIRCCA), founded in 1981, was still active in the 1990s. Volunteer networks have grown up side by side with government-funded women's health centres. These groups or networks have explicit feminist aims. In the ACT, for example, the Women's Health Network consists of activists who wish to maintain the feminist component of women's health policy. The WHIRCCA (NSW) has provided the following summary of its activities:

> *The Women's Health, Information, Resource and Crisis Centres Association is a peer group organisation of community based/oriented non-government women's health services run by and for women.*
>
> *The Women's Health Centres have maintained an interagency network since they were first founded in 1974. In 1981 this network expanded to include the information and resource centres and became known as WHIRCCA.*[18]

The women's health centres, although non-government organisations, are generally funded by government. The same is true for women's refuges. Funding has been a blessing for these groups but it has also had its problems. Concern about the implications of accepting public funding has been a constant theme in debate among activists and observers. The Collingwood health collective disbanded in 1975 rather than accept Commonwealth Government funding on conditions that were unacceptable to it. The Melbourne halfway house collective was often caught in the dilemma between wanting to help survivors of domestic violence and wishing to maintain its autonomy and principles. The terms of government funding had to be negotiated carefully. For example, in the interests of their notions of accountability, governments wanted groups to have all the trappings of formal organisation, secretaries and so on. This contravened the ideal of the collective.

The debates over funding have been partly related to the broader political scene. During the Whitlam years (1972–75), for example, the objections to funding were explicitly linked to a socialist feminist critique of such social democratic governments.[19] During the Fraser years (1975–83) necessity became the mother of invention, and feminists from refuges sponsored demonstrations in the King's Hall of the old Parliament House to ensure continued funding. During the Hawke and Keating years (from 1983) objections had partly given way to an awareness of the problems of institutionalisation that could stem from government funding. Women's experience with Liberal–National Federal Governments had made them aware also that the dominant ideology of economic rationalism would make women's services, along with welfare spending more generally, ready targets for waste-watch enthusiasts.

The politics of the recession have forced the women's movement to become more aware of the economy. To put it another way, the politics of affluence during the first part of the Whitlam years meant that feminists could assume that the state was going to be there for them, and they could pick and choose how best to relate to the state. The state could be ignored à la anarchism—so long as it could be assumed that funding for important projects would be readily available. The dismissal of the Whitlam Government in November 1975 and the subsequent election of the Fraser Government in December 1975 caused extensive consternation within the broadly defined left. In certain quarters the Fraser Government was described as reactionary, hence involvement in the building of broad popular and democratic fronts was justified. Similar debates were to occur in Britain later in the 1970s when the women's movement was to become divided over its attitude towards Margaret Thatcher. Some radical feminists advocated voting for Thatcher on the grounds of her gender.

Marilyn Chalkley has argued that even the onset of recession in the 1980s did not prompt the women's movement to shift its focus from the 'tradition of women lobbying in specific areas, especially the service areas like refuges and rape crisis centres'.[20] Chalkley wrote a short but strongly focused critique of one of the major women's conferences of the 1980s, namely, the National Agenda for Women Conference, which was held in 1986 and funded by the Office of the Status of Women (OSW) and organised by the Women's Electoral Lobby. Chalkley quoted from one academic speaker (Elizabeth Savage) who called for women to widen their agenda 'to consider the broad spectrum of economic and social policy affecting women, and not to concentrate energy in too localised an area'.[21] Sue Brooks, an economist who had just taken over as the head of the OSW, called for the mainstreaming of women's issues. One example she gave 'was the submission the office presented to the Industries Assistance Commission of "Women, Work and the Textile Clothing and Footwear Industries"' following the IAC's draft report on future levels of tariff protection 'as industries are dominated by female workers and employ a significant number of migrant women, any reduction in barrier protection that adversely affects employment will be disproportionately experienced by women'.[22]

Yet an attempt to broaden the concept of women's issues to include economic policy did not result in significant economic gains for women. In fact 1987 was a bad year for women. The May Economic Statement and the September Budget had included new restrictions on family welfare, which were strongly criticised by a range of organisations including WEL and political leaders such as Janine Haines (the leader of the Australian Democrats) and the Liberal Party's Senator Shirley Walters.

Women also learned that the OSW, even with an economist (Sue Brooks) at the top, could not solve women's economic problems nor force policy-makers to factor in women's concerns. Marian Sawer has explained the situation as follows:

> *Despite the increased budgetary and economic expertise brought to OSW by Brooks, its effectiveness in intervening in economic policy-making was limited. Recurring battles took place over the Finance Department options presented to the Expenditure Review Committee for each mini-Budget and Budget, which put at risk all the gains which had been achieved for women. Brooks did not establish the kind of direct line to the Prime Minister enjoyed by her predecessor, Anne Summers. She was not able to use the political process to counter bureaucratic opposition.*[23]

Brooks also had to work in an environment of rivalry with the Women's Bureau, the other major women's office at the Commonwealth level, which had been set up in the 1960s to deal with the integration of female workers and which later under Labor Governments attempted to insert a more feminist dimension into the policy process.

> ... the Women's Bureau viewed itself as more in touch with the interests of working class women than OSW. While OSW was preparing sex discrimination and affirmative action legislation, the Women's Bureau was concerned with issues such as the impact of industry restructuring on women, the needs of outworkers for industrial protection and the arguments for introducing pay equity principles into wage-fixing guidelines. During the Neary period (1983–86), women from the Women's Bureau referred disparagingly to the 'Office of Women of Status'.[24]

There are two faces to women and public policy in Australia in the 1990s. On the one hand, there is the public face of glossy government publications listing the initiatives and the institutions that have been founded by government, often but not always in response to feminist demands. On the other hand, there are the continued actions of women in small groups, often focused on the delivery of services, and the development of networks among the activists in these groups. This second face is not officially part of the state but in many significant ways it is dependent on it.

Women and the electoral arena

Feminists in the Labor Party have tried to replicate American-style gender gap politics in Australia. In 1980 Senator Susan Ryan, ALP spokeswoman on women's affairs, produced a important discussion paper which was redrafted to become *The ALP and Women: Towards Equality* (1982).[25] (Ryan became the first Labor female Cabinet minister when the Hawke Government was elected in March 1983.) She emphasised gender-based economic inequality, which required a gender-based electoral strategy. The ALP also conducted research that demonstrated that good female candidates could be electoral drawcards. Throughout the 1970s female voters had been more likely to support the non-Labor (i.e. conservative parties), and Senator Ryan was able to convince the party that developing policies for modern women and increasing the numbers of female candidates could increase the ALP's share of the female vote and consequently allow it to be elected to the national government. Labor strategists pushed women's issues at the 1983 federal election but this emphasis had practically disappeared by the next election in 1984.

The Labor Government introduced economic rationalist policies of financial deregulation and budget-cutting and had flirted with the idea of introducing a consumption tax. The ALP's support among women declined over this period. One could speculate that the Labor Government's hard-line economic policies and its rejection of social democracy and feminism meant that Australian feminists treated it as their American counterparts had treated the Reaganite Republicans. Certainly the demotion and subsequent resignation of the high-profile feminist Senator Ryan from the government and parliament in late 1987 angered many women.

A number of important lessons emerged for women and public policy in 1987, and some of these lessons were learned during the winter election campaign. Women seemed caught between a Labor Government captured by the philosophy of economic rationalism and a conservative Coalition captured by the family-orientation elements of the New Right. 'Women' featured strongly in the ALP's slick advertising campaign, which was characterised by quite clever negative images of the Coalition alternative. Wendy Woods, an employee of John Singleton's advertising agency (which was doing the Labor campaign for the first time), starred in a key series of television advertisements.[25] Woods took up one of the major themes from Labor's women's policies, namely that the Coalition's policies would hurt women and family; she accused John Howard (the then Leader of the Opposition) of planning to tax 'baby food and school clothes'.[26] In other advertisements Labor had accused the opposition of planning to introduce a consumption tax. Senator Susan Ryan had emphasised in an important speech that voters had a clear choice:

> *You can continue to support our government and ensure that Australian women have a say, a choice and a fair go, or you can jeopardize every gain achieved so far by opting for the economically destructive and socially divisive policies of our opponents.*[27]

Pro-family themes were a central part of the Coalition's policies and speeches. This approach had become traditional for the National Party, particularly under the leadership of Ian Sinclair. What was new in 1987 was the Liberal Party's renewed emphasis on traditional nuclear families and their values. John Howard's *Future Directions* series of advertisements stressed the values of family, stability, tradition etc. It was a 'back to the future' package in a white picket fence. Interestingly enough, however, child care was now firmly on the political (i.e. electoral) agenda as well as the policy agenda. The Liberal Party promised child-care allowances (means tested) but only 'to help *couples* with children' (emphasis added).[28] It was left to the Democrats under Janine Haines to claim that the welfare/family/women's policies of both sides were influenced by the New Right.[29]

Consequently in Australia we never had an electoral gender gap in the northern hemisphere sense, namely, a tendency for a greater percentage of women than men to support the nominally 'left of centre' party. There are several possible explanations. In the first instance the Labor Government under Prime Ministers Hawke (1983-91) and Keating (1991-) have adopted many conservative economic policies similar to those of the Labor Government of Prime Minister Lange in New Zealand. It would be possible to argue that there was no conventional 'left' party in Australia in the 1980s except perhaps for the Australian Democrats. Second, and consequently, more women than men had supported the Australian Democrats, which started life as a centre party but came to be perceived by themselves and by others as more left than the ALP. Third, the Liberal Party had begun to court modern women by the mid 1980s and had moved away from its traditional emphasis on women's role within the family. To be sure, some within the party still looked back to the 1950s model of women in the family, but for the most part traditional 'family values' were increasingly to become the province of its more socially conservative partner, the National Party.

The 1987 election was important not only because some women began to desert the ALP but also because women's issues were seen by both sides of politics as 'important in deciding the outcome of [the] polls', as Liberal leader John Howard noted.[30] It was not the first time that the Liberal Party had discovered the power of the female voter. The significance of the 1987 elections was that the Liberal Party had discovered modern women. *Women: The Next Liberal Government's Policy* said:

> ... the majority of women under 35 are either in paid work or planning to be in paid work. The dual role of homemakers, and outside paid work, can present special problems to women.
>
> In recent times, many women have achieved success in their chosen work. But often success has been achieved because of unusual talent or determination. Good social and political policies should not require that all successful women be heroines or pathfinders.[31]

The topics covered in this document included 'equal opportunities', 'taxation', 'child care and children', 'education, training and retraining', 'dual role', 'older women' and 'women's representation'.[32] On some topics there were echoes of the party's traditional family orientation. For example under 'taxation' it referred to the need to 'positively acknowledge in our tax system the contribution of women at home'.[33] In Australia for many years all taxpayers (including married women) have been taxed as individuals but heads of households have been able to claim a 'dependent spouse rebate'. Conventionally this has meant that husbands have gained taxation benefits from having the services of a wife. Feminist groups have long campaigned against this. Some groups have also called for the tax-deductibility of child care expenses. Anti-feminist groups (and some individuals within the Liberal and National Parties) have called for the introduction of income-splitting between couples to lessen the husband's tax burden and to encourage married women to stay at home.

By 1987 the need for federally funded child care had become accepted by all save the extreme right. The Liberal Party in the 1987 and 1990 elections attempted to 'outbid' the Labor Government on child care. In 1987 it promised to 'maintain Commonwealth funding for childcare services' and to 'encourage the growth of private sector based child care'.[34] Tax reform was to become an even bigger item of the Liberal Party's reform agenda for the 1993 federal election. In November 1991 it produced an enormous and fully documented package of reform called *Fightback!*, which had as its centrepiece the commitment to a broadly based consumption tax, known as the Goods and Services Tax (GST). Australian women have demonstrated a high level of scepticism about a consumption tax.[35]

The above review indicates that women have not met with great success in placing women's issues at the centre of the policy agenda through the use of electoral strategies. They have had limited success, too, in working through the traditional party system. This all contrasts with women's achievements in the arena of bureaucratic initiatives (such as EEO) and in setting up their own institutions. This is not to suggest, as has been discussed earlier, that such initiatives always led to new and significant policy outcomes.

Feminist theory and the state

Changes in feminist practice have led to developments in feminist theory.[36] In the 1970s commentators identified different styles of feminist theory, most notably the radical, the socialist and the liberal varieties. Of the three, the radical was the most recent. Radical feminist theorists have maintained that the primary division in history has been between men and women:

> *For the feminist revolution we shall need an analysis of the dynamics of sex war as comprehensive as the Marx–Engels analysis of class antagonism was for the economic revolution. More comprehensive. For we are dealing with a larger problem, with an oppression that goes back beyond recorded history to the animal kingdom itself.*[37]

Socialist feminists drew on the 'Marx–Engels analysis' and identified modern capitalism as the source of women's oppression. The socialist feminist perspective has become more complex and diffuse in recent years, but it remains the main theoretical alternative to radical feminism. Socialist and radical feminists shared a critique of the oppressive nature of the traditional or 'bourgeois' nuclear family. Liberal feminists believed that the family could be improved.

Radical feminist Shulamith Firestone called liberal feminists 'conservative feminists' because they were concerned with 'the more superficial symptoms of sexism—legal inequalities, employment discrimination and the like'.[38] Socialist feminists were, in turn, critical of the limitations of Firestone's approach. Juliet Mitchell, for instance, argued that the family operated at several levels simultaneously: the economic, the psychological and the ideological.[39]

Radical and socialist feminists also shared a revolutionary critique of society and the state. From the perspective of the 1990s some of their concerns have been called into question. Judith Allen, partly borrowing from the work of the American Catherine Mackinnon, has maintained that feminist theory needs a new direction, for it 'has been a tolerant fellow traveller, along routes dictated by the theoretical needs of others, for quite long enough'.[40] Allen also approvingly cites Rosemary Pringle's rejection of the conventional distinction between liberal, radical and socialist feminisms:

> *The distinction between liberals, radicals and socialists no longer adequately describes the debates that are taking place within feminism. Perhaps a majority of feminists decline any of these labels and would question why anyone would continue to apply them.*[41]

Yet some would argue that the distinction between liberal and other feminisms has continuing validity. This argument is reflected in the debate over femocrats. Certain critics of femocracy have equated it with liberal feminism. They presumably see themselves as having other, superior positions. Clearly Yeatman's emphasis on the particular development of class analysis places her in the socialist feminist tradition.

The pro-femocrat position has certain implicit assumptions about the state. These views remain essentially unexpressed because the pro-femocrat position, by its very nature, does not challenge the right of the state to exist. This position, as we have already seen, draws heavily on the liberal or individualistic strand of feminism. According to the American writer Suzanne Gordon:

> *Feminists in this tradition tend to pursue a doctrine of rights and fairness—'the creation of a level playing field' on which to compete for 'formal equality' with men in the world of work, politics and culture. They propose workplace and public policies that allow women and men unpaid or paid time off to take care of new borns or adopted children, family leave to take care of sick or dying relatives*

or spouses, and more. Flexible work arrangements like job-sharing and part-time and flex-time work schedules.[42]

There are three key elements in this quotation for the purposes of the argument in this chapter. The first is the question of ends; in this case the goal of formal equality. The second is the question of means; in this instance, the creation of a level playing field. The third deals with the question of the best kinds of social policy and will be examined later. The state clearly plays an essential role in social policy reform. In the United States this process has been achieved largely through the legal system and the passage of legislation (e.g. the issue of reproductive rights has been battled through the courts, particularly at the national level). In Australia social policy reform has been advanced through legislation but also through the establishment of a network of special offices, agencies and programs at all three levels of government.

A comparative point to be made here is that American feminists have been much more forthright than their Australian counterparts in claiming links with an individualistic tradition. For most Australian feminists (with the possible exception of some women associated with the Liberal Party and/or business groups) individualism is seen as an inappropriate orientation. One can only speculate as to why there has been such wariness among Australian feminists. One partial explanation might relate to the Australian habit of eschewing theorising, which has been observed by many commentators starting very early in this century.[43] A second possible reason is the contradiction between the capitalist economy and the political/cultural tradition of collectivism (namely, using the resources of the state to promote the economic position of economic groups or sections). This tradition has allowed many Australians, particularly the unions, the Labor Party and academic and other commentators, to argue that somehow Australia is not simply a capitalist society. Consequently, those feminists who defend the femocrat position or who pretend that there are no differences between feminists or believe that sections of the state can be captured, form part of a greater Australian tradition called a social democratic or Benthamite utilitarian tradition.[44]

The third element in the quotation from Suzanne Gordon concerns the issue of the best kind of social policy for women.[45] She introduces a relatively new and important dualism between the liberal strand (i.e., the search for formal equality) and the ethic of caregiving. This, in turn, resonates with the important so-called 'same-difference' debate. Before giving an overview of this important and fairly new debate it is essential to explore the concept of the ethic of caregiving.

Liberal feminists have been accused of confusing caregiving with the exploitation of women. According to this approach liberal feminists 'tend to fear that discussions of caring will derail women's progress in this realm, ushering in a return to the cult of domesticity and women's entrapment in the home and in traditional caring professions'.[46] Gordon then proceeds to analyse the influential *Backlash*, written by Susan Faludi, from the perspective of a caregiving ethos:

> Faludi believes any consideration of 'women's special needs' or qualities will boomerang. 'Special' may sound like superior but it is also a euphemism for handicapped, according to Faludi. 'Most relational scholars', she writers, 'no doubt believed they could bring back the cult of domesticity on their own terms. These academics hoped to push for women's "special rights" without jeopardizing fundamental civil rights and opportunities'.[47]

Iris Young, who has been writing on the 'same-difference' debate since the early 1980s, has distinguished between the 'humanist' and the 'gynocentric' strands of feminism.[48] The humanist approach, briefly, assumes that there are no salient differences between men and women, that they are the 'same' for the purposes of debate. The humanist strand would include liberal feminists and most materialist feminists. I say 'most' here because the commonsense expectation is that materialist feminists would argue that men and women are made, not born. Materialists generally reject essentialist arguments about innate characteristics and argue that the apparent differences (in terms of power, culture and money) can be changed through social action. Yet certain of the 'new' French feminists who would claim to be materialists have argued that women must learn 'to write their own bodies' in order to overcome oppression.[49] This sounds rather like emphasising difference by using it as a starting point yet with no clear idea of the outcome.

The 'gynocentric' strand of feminism would include those sympathetic to the caregiving ethic and others such as eco-feminists and some radical feminists who have argued that the differences between men and women are significant, more deeply embedded and persistent than, say, class differences.

For the purpose of this chapter the significance of the 'same-difference' debate relates to its implications for a theory of the state. The two approaches have distinctive orientations towards the ideal goals of state policy. In the Australian case we could argue that the trend has been for the shift to be from treating men and women as different towards treating them as the same. Clearly femocrats have been an important part of this process. It has been in the USA that 'caregiving' has been articulated by some sections of the women's movement as an important emphasis within social policy. This has been bolstered at the theoretical level by writers such as Carol Gilligan in her important book, *In a Different Voice: Psychological Theory and Women's Development*.[50]

Yet three major problems remain for feminist analyses of the state: the significance of liberal feminism, understanding the nature of gender and gender oppression, and the role of the state in creating gender and gender oppression.

Liberal feminism

Liberal feminism, as noted earlier, was an important strand of feminist thought and practice during the first decade or so after the emergence of the second wave of feminism and was widely accorded commensurate status. Subsequently some of the issues it raised concerning rights and status were relegated to the scrapheap and commentators from the Left and the Right downgraded its position. From the Right, it was alleged that it had achieved its goals and society had now entered a post-feminist phase. From the Left it was stated that the liberal feminist agenda was inadequate and outmoded, and/or that the differences among feminists had become superseded in the face of the challenge from the economic rationalists of the New Right.

One key question emerging from the liberal feminist tradition is 'Why don't women exercise their formal freedoms so as to become female social men?'[51] In other words, why haven't women achieved greater representation in political and governmental arenas, given that they have long achieved political rights as citizens equal with those of men? The issue here relates to the representational face of the state and the role of women as electors, party activists and parliamentary representatives. Debate on this problem/question has led to a 'distinct' body of literature within political science:

> *The growing recognition that inequality between the sexes was both unjust and amenable to change led many feminist scholars to challenge the treatment (or lack thereof) of women as subjects of research in their fields.*[52]

Female legislators have also been the subject of research with a small but interesting stream of literature dealing with the issue of whether women do make a difference to the activity of politics and to the kind of public policies produced. In particular women in certain political arenas (e.g. many states of the USA and the Scandinavian countries) have made an impact both in terms of their numbers and in terms of their policy agendas.[53]

The nature of gender

The second problem concerns the attempts to understand the nature of gender and gender oppression. Different kinds of materialist frameworks have been invoked to form explanations. There now exist several types of materialist frameworks. Differences were noted above between the 'humanist' and the 'gynocentric' tendencies. The latter tendency can be associated with some of the post-modern French varieties of feminist who wish to examine the utility of the category 'woman' critically yet see it as a starting point for examining societal norms critically. The American political theorist Nancy Hartsock has written (and I think persuasively so) about the practical limitations of the post-modern exercise for political action:

> *Those of us who have been marginalised by the transcendental voice of universalising theory need to do something other than ignore power relations as Rorty does or resist them as figures such as Foucault and Lyotard suggest. We need to transform them, and to do so, we need a revised and restructured theory (indebted to Marx among others).*[54]

Other strands have been well analysed by American political economist Joan Smith in an influential paper published in 1983. There were dangers, Smith argued, in

> *neglecting the differences in women's lives and concentrating only on similarities ... By abstracting similar behaviours from their social context in a way that leads to the appearance of a universal patriarchy, it becomes difficult to avoid a concept of 'women's nature' paralleling that created by sociobiologists and others.*[55]

Smith concluded that one simple model of women's nature is not supported by the available evidence. Instead, the feminist enterprise must be part of a broader process of understanding 'what structures, processes or forces have created, sustained and reshaped inequalities'. Inequalities between men and women are but one kind of inequity:

> *Unpaid domestic labour and childbearing and rearing—the roles assigned to women and the roles to which socialist-feminists direct their theoretical and political attention—are one form of social labor that shares important features with a myriad of other activities. Here I have in mind subsistence cropping, informal marketing, informal exchange of services and the multiplicity of other activities that are nonwaged and subordinated to those more conventionally defined as part of the economic system.*[56]

This kind of approach, which emphasises 'difference' but does so within a materialist framework, needs further exploration for its political implications but is not without its problems.

The role of the state

The third problem relates to the role of the state in *creating* gender and gender oppression. Much of the debate among materialist feminists has side-stepped this issue by focusing on the material world and seeing the state as 'outside' or separate from this world. Presumably this is what has led various commentators, such as Catherine MacKinnon, to argue that feminist theory has lacked a theory of the state.[57] This assertion contains two central ideas, namely that feminists have mostly avoided the state arena and that where they have focused on it they have incorporated the traditional (i.e. male), liberal and Marxist views. Others, including the Australian writer Judith Allen, as already noted, have taken the MacKinnon view and ended up by claiming that feminists do not need such a theory.

The two main arguments of this chapter are to the contrary. Not only have feminists through their practices developed orientations towards the Australian state; these orientations also need to be examined, debated and expanded. It is hoped that this chapter constitutes part of this process.

Notes

1 See, for example, M. Sawer (1990), *Sisters in Suits*, Allen & Unwin, Sydney. In 1992 the high-profile feminist Anne Summers was appointed to work in the Prime Minister's office. In various speeches, before and during her period in the PM's office, she has adopted a positive approach. Feminist politician Irina Dunn also gave a positive approach as an introduction to the first conference of the National Foundation of Australian Women. See I. Dunn (1990), 'Forward' in *National Women's Conference—Proceedings*, Canberra.
2 Feminist historian Patricia Grimshaw gave a good summary of the critical approach in an interview on the ABC's *7.30 Report*, 3 April 1991.
3 See S. Ryan, interview on the ABC's *7.30 Report*, 3 April 1991.
4 Grimshaw, ABC interview 1991.
5 P. Dowding (1989), *Progress Report to the People of Western Australia*, Government Printer, Perth.
6 P. Dowding (1989), p. 3.
7 The following section is drawn from M. Simms and D. Stone (1990), *Women in Australian Politics: A Research Report for UNESCO*, copies available from the authors, Political Science Department, Australian National University, Canberra.
8 Activists have included Edna Ryan (Sydney), Merle Thornton (Brisbane) and Zelda D'Aprano (Melbourne). Ryan has been a long-time activist in the Sydney labour movement and has written two influential works on women's employment. Thornton became famous after chaining herself to a public bar in Brisbane while protesting for women's rights to public space and has written some important works of feminist theory, one of which is discussed in this chapter. D'Aprano has also been a labour activist and wrote a critique of the Melbourne left using interesting pseudonyms (e.g. Quartercent). For more detail see M. Sawer and M. Simms (1993), *A Woman's Place: Women in Australian Politics*, 2nd ed., Allen & Unwin, Sydney, chapter 9.
9 A. Yeatman (1990), *Bureaucrats, Technocrats, Femocrats: Essays on the Contemporary Australian State*, Allen & Unwin, Sydney.

10 S. Franzway, D. Court and R. W. Connell (1989), *Staking a Claim: Feminism, Bureaucracy and the State*, Allen & Unwin, Sydney.
11 S. Dowse (1982), 'The women's movement's fandango with the state: Some thoughts on the movement's role in public policy since 1972', *Australian Quarterly*, 54:4, 324–45.
12 E. Wilson (1979), 'Beyond the ghetto: Thoughts on *Beyond the Fragments: Feminism and the Making of Socialism*', *Feminist Review*, 4:1, 28.
13 A. Yeatman (1990), pp. 77–8.
14 M. Sawer (1990), p. 25.
15 L. Ryan (1990), 'Feminism and the federal bureaucracy, 1972–1983' in S. Watson (ed.), *Playing the State: Australian Feminist Interventions*, Sydney, Allen & Unwin, p. 73.
16 This debate is developed more extensively in Sawer and Simms (1993), ch. 9, and the next three paragraphs draw heavily on this chapter.
17 See J. Freeman (1975), *The Politics of Women's Liberation*, David McKay, New York.
18 WHIRCCA (1989), *About: Generalist Women's Health Centres*, roneoed. I am grateful to Dr Gwen Gray for information on the women's health movement of the late 1980s and early 1990s. Information of the earlier period of the late 1970s and early 1980s is drawn from my own experience as a member of a women's refuge group in Melbourne.
19 On funding see R. Pringle and A. Game (1978), 'Women and class in Australia: Feminism and the Labor Government' in G. Duncan (ed.), *Critical Essays in Australian Politics*, Edward Arnold, Melbourne.
20 M. Chalkley (1986), 'Ordering the agenda', *Australian Society*, 5:6, 42.
21 M. Chalkley (1986), p. 42.
22 M. Chalkley (1986), p. 42.
23 M. Sawer (1990), p. 96.
24 M. Sawer (1990), p. 76. Jenni Neary was the director of the bureau.
25 S. Ryan (1982), *The ALP and Women: Towards Equality*, Australian Labor Party, Canberra.
26 For more on the 1987 elections see M. Simms (1988), 'Women' in I. McAllister and J. Warhurst (eds), *Australia Votes*, Longman Cheshire, Melbourne.
27 S. Ryan (1987), *Speech by Senator Susan Ryan on the ALP Women's Policy*, roneoed, p. 1.
28 Liberal Party (1987a), *Women—The Next Liberal Government's Policy*, Liberal Party, Canberra.
29 *Canberra Times*, 2 July 1987.
30 Statement by John Howard, (then) Leader of the Liberal Party, quoted in *Canberra Times*, 10 July 1987.
31 Liberal Party (1987a).
32 Liberal Party (1987a).
33 Liberal Party (1987a).
34 Liberal Party (1987b), *Your Family—The Liberal Approach*, Liberal Party of Australia, Canberra.
35 For an analysis of opinion polls see Sawer and Simms (1993), ch. 2.
36 These issues have been canvassed more extensively in M. Sawer and M. Simms (1993), chs 9 and 10.
37 S. Firestone (1971), *The Dialectic of Sex: The Case for Feminist Revolution*, Bantam Books, New York, p. 82.

38 S. Firestone (1971), p. 5.
39 J. Mitchell (1973), *Women's Estate*, Penguin, Harmondsworth.
40 J. Allen (1990), 'Does feminism need a theory of "the state"?' in S. Watson, *Playing the State*, p. 34.
41 J. Allen (1990), p. 34.
42 S. Gordon (1992), 'Feminism and caregiving: State of the debate', *American Prospect*, 10, 122.
43 See, for example, W. K. Hancock (1961), *Australia*, Jacaranda Press, Brisbane.
44 See H. Collins (1985), 'Political ideology in Australia: The distinctiveness of a Benthamite society' in S. Craubard (ed.), *Australia: The Daedalus Symposium*, Angus & Robertson, Sydney.
45 S. Gordon (1992), p. 122.
46 S. Gordon (1992), p. 123.
47 S. Gordon (1992), p. 123.
48 I. Young (1980), 'Socialist feminism and the limit of dual systems theory', *Socialist Review*, 10:1, 158–69.
49 See R. Tong (1989), *Feminist Thought: A Comprehensive Introduction*, Allen & Unwin, Sydney for an excellent discussion of contemporary French feminism and for an accessible introduction to post-modernism.
50 C. Gilligan (1982), *In a Different Voice: Psychological Theory and Women's Development*, Harvard University Press, Cambridge, Mass. See also the essays in S. Benhabib and D. Cornell (1987), *Feminism as Critiques: On the Politics of Gender*, University of Minnesota Press, Minneapolis.
51 M. Thornton (1984), 'Psychoanalysis and feminist social theory of gender' in M. Simms (ed.), *Australian Women and the Political System*, Longman Cheshire, Melbourne, p. 154. For more on the debate over liberal feminism see Sawer and Simms (1993), ch. 9.
52 H. Silverberg (1990), 'What happened to the feminist revolution in political science? A review essay', *Western Political Quarterly*, 43:4, 887.
53 For good summaries see Centre for the American Woman and Politics (1991), *Studies of Women in Office*, Rutgers University, New Jersey.
54 N. Hartsock (1990), 'Foucault on power: A theory for women?' in L. Nicholson (ed.), *Feminism/Post Modernism*, Routledge, New York, p. 170.
55 J. Smith (1983), 'Feminist analysis of gender: A mystique' in M. Lowe and R. Hubbard, *Women's Nature: Rationalizations of Inequality*, Pergamon Press, New York, p. 89.
56 J. Smith (1983), pp. 103–4.
57 C. MacKinnon (1983), 'Feminism, Marxism, method, and the state: Toward feminist jurisprudence', *Signs*, 8:3, 635–58.

Contributors

Stephen Bell is a lecturer in the Department of Political Science at the University of Tasmania, Hobart. His research interests focus on the politics of economic policy, industry policy, business politics and business–government relations. Recent books include *Business–Government Relations in Australia* (written and edited with John Wanna) (Harcourt Brace) and *Australian Manufacturing and the State: The Politics of Industry Policy in the Post-War Era*, Cambridge University Press.

Lois Bryson is Professor of Sociology at the University of Newcastle. She wrote (with Faith Thompson) Australia's first urban community study, *An Australian Newtown*, and has published widely on poverty, family work, gender, sport, the welfare state and public sector management. Her most recent book is *Welfare and the State: Who Benefits?*

Braham Dabscheck is an associate professor in the School of Industrial Relations at the University of New South Wales. He conducts research into Australian industrial relations, industrial relations theory and wages and incomes policy. He is editor of the *Journal of Industrial Relations*. His most recent books are *Australian Industrial Relations in the 1980s* (Oxford University Press, Melbourne 1989) and a jointly edited work entitled *Contemporary Australian Industrial Relations: Readings* (Longman Cheshire, Melbourne 1992).

Rolf Gerritsen is a foundation staff member of the Graduate Program in Public Policy at the ANU where he is also Director of Studies, Foreign Affairs and Trade. His research interests are in the areas of economic policy, agriculture and resources, and Aboriginal policy.

Peter Groenewegen is Professor of Economics at the University of Sydney and held an ARC Senior Research Fellowship in 1991–93. He has written extensively on public sector economics issues, including an Australian text, *Public Finance in Australia: Theory and Practice*, now in its third edition.

Brian Head was an associate professor of Politics at Griffith University (1986–90) before taking up a senior policy position in the Queensland Cabinet Office. He has edited several books on state and economy, the politics of development, deregulation and the Whitlam, Fraser and Hawke Governments, and has published widely on intergovernmental aspects of social and economic policy and public administration.

Ian Lowe is an associate professor in the Division of Science and Technology at Griffith University. His research interests are in the broad area of policy decisions affecting science and technology, especially in the fields of energy and environment. Recent publications include *Living in the Greenhouse* (Scribe Books 1989) and the print version of the 1991 Boyer Lectures, *Changing Australia* (ABC) with Fay Gale.

Trevor Matthews is an associate professor in the Department of Government and Public Administration at the University of Sydney. His recent publications have dealt with organised business in Australia, Australia's trade policy and élite attitudes to Australian foreign policy. He is co-author of *The Japanese Connection: Australian Leaders' Attitudes towards Japan and the Australia–Japan Relationship*. His current research is on the Japanese and South Korean experience with strategic trade policy.

Anya Moore has worked as a senior officer in the Australian Public Service and is now a planning and project officer at the University of New England, Armidale.

Elim Papadakis is Professor of Sociology and Head of Department at the University of New England. His research interests include political sociology, environmental movements, the welfare state and political behaviour. Among his most recent publications is *Politics and the Environment: The Australian Experience* (Allen & Unwin 1993).

Belinda Probert is a visiting fellow in the Department of Sociology at La Trobe University. From 1990 to 1992 she was Senior Research Fellow at CIRCIT. Her recent research has focused on work, employment and labour market trends. Her recent major publications include *Working Life: Arguments about Work in Australian Society* (McPhee Gribble/

Penguin) and a co-edited volume entitled *Pink Collar Blues: Work, Gender and Technology* (Melbourne University Press).

Marian Simms is a senior lecturer in political science at the Australian National University. Her most recent book is the second edition of *A Woman's Place: Women and Politics in Australia* (co-written with Marian Sawer). She has published widely on women and politics and political parties. In 1993 she was the president of the Australasian Political Studies Association.

John Wanna is a senior lecturer in politics and public policy in the Division of Commerce and Administration, Griffith University. His research interests focus on budgetary policy, economic policy and business–government relations. His recent books include *Business–Government Relations in Australia* (written and edited with Stephen Bell; Harcourt Brace) as well as co-writing *Public Sector Management in Australia* (Macmillan) and the second edition of *Public Policy in Australia* (Allen & Unwin).

Greg Whitwell is a senior lecturer in economic history and the Associate Dean (Graduate Studies) in the Faculty of Economics and Commerce at the University of Melbourne. His major research interests include the development of economic policy in twentieth-century Australia and Europe. He is the author of *The Treasury Line* (1986), *Making the Market: The Rise of Consumer Society* (1989) and (with Diane Sydenham) *A Shared Harvest: The Australian Wheat Industry 1939–1989* (1991).

Index

Abeles, Sir Peter 209, 325
Aborigines 305
abortion 354, 355
Accord, the: as 'corporatism without business' 15, 194, 195, 207–10; 'labourist' origins 217; and business power 16–18, 217–18, 232, 234, 294; and export potential 92, 240; and the Arbitration Commission 144; Mark VI 155, 157, 277, 286; Mark VIa 157; Mark II, 156; Mark VII, 160–1; Mark VI 155, 157, 277, 286; Mark VIa 157
ACTU 144; centralisation of 16; and the 1974 national wage cases 150, 153; and the Accords 154–61, 277; wage indexation 151; power of 198; and prices and incomes policy (1973) 229; and consensus 232–3; and privatisation 283; and microeconomic reform 286
Adelaide by-election 277
Adsteam 274
Advisory Council for Intergovernmental Relations 176
Affirmative Action (Equal Opportunity for Women) Act 1986 355
aged pensioners/care 295, 304, 308
agency capture 30, 256
agenda setting 276
agricultural/rural sector 197, 276; exports 75; protectionism 76, 85, 285, 287; public policy decisions about 76–7; and the ALP 285; *see also* Cairns Group
Airbus consortium 84

Alcoa 205
Allen, Judith 367, 372
AMA 275
AMP 205
Antarctica 328
anticipatory model 254
ANZ Bank 205
AOTC 283
arbitration 8, 15, 142–62, 200, 257, 269
Arbitration Commission 144, 308
Arts, Sports, Environment, Tourism and Territories, Department of 344
Asia Pacific Economic Cooperation 87–9, 233
Associated Chamber of Commerce of Australia 198
Associated Chambers of Manufactures of Australia 198, 200, 203, 204
ATG Environmental Technology Trust 348
Atkinson, Michael 58, 60, 251, 256, 260, 265
attention cycle (of issues) 276
Auditor-General 184
Australia Reconstructed 214
Australian Bankers Association 198, 203
Australian Chamber of Commerce 202, 203, 204
Australian Chamber of Commerce and Industry 202, 204, 218, 274, 275
Australian Chamber of Manufactures 202, 205, 206
Australian Conservation Foundation 321, 338, 345, 349

Australian Council of Employers Federation 198, 203
Australian Council of Local Government Associations 203
Australian Democrats 241
Australian Finance Council 203
Australian Heritage Commission 338
Australian Institute of Petroleum 329
ALP: and welfare 9; and decentralisation and federalism 112, 133; and 'money power' 137; and the Accord 144, 155, 207–10, 240; and environment movement 338
Australian Manufacturing Council 80, 242
Australian Mining Industry Council 198, 202, 203
Australian National Parks and Wildlife Service 338, 339
Australian Retailers' Association 203
Australian Science and Technology Council 344
Australian Sugar Refiners' Industry Association 203
Australian Taxation Office 297
Australian Woolgrowers and Graziers' Council 203
Austria 9
AUSTUDY 300
automobile industry 78, 237, 275, 284, 286

Bagguley, P. 100
balance of payments 13, 130, 156, 212, 226, 236, 237, 239
'banana republic', Australia as 13, 98, 212, 272, 278
Bank of England 130
Barwick, Sir Garfield 338
Beer, Samuel 196
Bell Resources 274
Bell, Stephen 325–36, 327
Better Cities Program 183
BHP 80, 92, 99, 203, 205, 284
Bjelke-Petersen, Sir Joh 154
Block, Fred 33, 46–8, 54
Bluestone, Barry 109
Bridgen, J. B. 128
Brigden Report 9, 11

Brisbane City Council 324
Britain: as an early industrialising society 7; size of the public sector 20; fiscal policy 48; as a 'weak' state 62, 254, 262, 263; under Thatcher 35, 79; imperialism 104; Treasury 123, 127, 261; Poor Law reformers 296; as welfare state 310; women's policy 358
British Petroleum 205
Broadcasting Tribunal 282
Brooks, Sue 362
Brown, Bob 328, 337
Brundtland Commission 329, 343, 350
BTR Nylex 205
Buchanan, James 34
Building a Competitive Australia 239
Burawoy, Michael 111
Bureau of Industry Economics 241
bureaucratisation 40
Bush, President 86
business: lack of unity 16–17, 18, 198–207; radical pluralism theory 31–3; political power of 32, 325–36, 327; public choice theory 34; and the Accords 217–18; investment 232; and the environment 335ff
Business Council of Australia 156, 197, 198, 202, 204, 205, 206, 208, 211, 212, 214–15, 274, 287, 326, 336, 346–8
Business Roundtable 205
Butlin, Noel 7, 137
Button, Senator John 272, 284

Cabinet 4, 169, 356
Cairns Group 87–9
Caltex 205
Cambridge economists 129
Cameron, David 209
Campbell Committee 235
Canada 62, 79, 80, 82, 86, 251, 260, 294, 310
capital: structural power/privileged position of 32, 33, 43, 46–7; common interests of 44; global mobility of 53, 66

capitalism: booms and slumps 120
Car Plan 284, 287
carbon tax 320
Cass, Bettina 296
Cass, Dr Moss 338
Castells, Manuel 99, 102, 103, 105–7, 113
Castles, Francis 9, 66, 286, 291, 309, 310
Cawson, Alan 55
Central America 115
centralisation 254
Chalkley, Marilyn 362
Chifley Government 201, 202
Chifley, J. B. 137
Child Support Scheme 296, 302
Clark, Colin 129
class: conflict 45, contradictions 45
classical political economy 2
coalition analysis 124
Cobb, John 115
Coghill, Ken 318
Cohen, Barry 342
Cold War 67
Coleman, William D. 58, 60, 251, 256, 260, 265
Coles Myer 205
Colonial Mutual 205
colonial governments 8
colonial socialism 137, 261, 270
Commission for the Future 317
commodification/de-commodification 52
commodities, exports 75–6, 104
Commonwealth Bank 131, 132–3, 205, 282
Commonwealth Bank Act 133
Commonwealth Conciliation and Arbitration Commission 131, 210
Commonwealth Employment Service 297
Commonwealth Government, functions of 5–6
Commonwealth Grants Commission 176
Commonwealth Oil Refineries 327
communications technologies 106
community care 304–5
community services obligations 271

comparative wage justice principle 146
Conciliation and Arbitration Commission 131, 142
Confederation of Australian Industry 202–4
Confederation of British Industry 203
Connorism 104
Constitution 144, 169, 175, 180, 181, 182
Coombs, Dr H. C. ('Nugget') 128, 133, 136
Copland, Douglas 128
Coronation Hill 328
corporatism 55–60, 194–218
Cotgrove, S. 336
Council of Australian Governments 189, 190
CRA 205
Crawford, J. G. 129
Crisp, L. F. 137
CSIRO 317
CSR 203
Curtin Government 201
Czechoslovakia 169

Daintree National Park 341
Daintree–Cape Tribulation road 327
Daly, Herman 115
Davis, Bruce 327
Davis, G. et al. 325
Dawkins, J. 174, 178
Deakinite settlement 269
decisional analysis of power 28
Dedman, J. J. 126
de-labourisation 105
depression: of 1890s 8; of 1930s 8, 39, 131
deregulation 36, 90, 103, 273, 276, 284–5; financial 13, 20, 108, 234–5
disability allowances 295, 297, 300
disjointed incrementalism 26, 27, 60, 272, 281, 322–3
distributional conflict 229
dollar depreciation 239
domestic defence policies 9, 257, 272, 286
Domhoff, G. W. 64

Dowding, Peter 355
Downsian median voter models 275
Dowse, Sarah 357
Drucker, Peter 76
Dunkley, G. 329
Dunleavy, Patrick 263
Dutch disease 77
Dyson, Kenneth 254–5, 260–4

East Asian economies 11, 78, 105, 254, 265
ecologically sustainable development (ESD) 319, 321, 343, 345–6
econocrats 274
economic activity, theories of 2, 66
Economic Advisory Council 129
economic defence arrangements 261
economic development, Australia 7–8, 15
economic ideas, power of 123, 128
economic indicators 239
economic liberalism: critique of the state 19, 67; basic propositions explained 37–9; and welfare policy 50; prospects for 113; and economic policy 226; and Hawke/Keating Governments 233, 241; and electoral pressures 236; and industry policy 273; and neo-classical economics 325
economic policy defined 3; distortions 240
economic politicisation 52
economic rationalism *see* economic liberalism
Economic Record 129
economics ministers 241
education 273
Elders IXL 205
élite theory 63–4
elitism/privileged groups 29, 30, 51, 57, 61
Employment Contracts Act (New Zealand) 216
Employment, Education and Training, Department of 241
Encel, Sol 1
encompassing organisation thesis 197

enterprise bargaining 156, 158–9, 210–18, 291
environmental impact statement 339
Environmental Protection Act 1974 339
Equal Employment Opportunity (Commonwealth Authorities) Act 356
equal opportunity 354
equal pay 354, 355
ESD party on energy use 326
ESSO 205
Etzioni, A. 322, 328
European Community 67, 82, 85, 86, 87; Common Agricultural Policy (CAP) 87, 88, 115
Evans, Gareth 89
export culture 79
Export Enhancement Program 85
exports 12, 37; of primary commodities 75, 278; dumping of 76, 278; of wheat 85, 231; of automobiles 275; *see also* voluntary export restraints, Cairns Group *and* APEC

factory work 102
Fadden, Arthur 122
Faludi, Suzan 369
family allowance 295, 297
family income supplement 298–9, 308
Federal Chamber of Automotive Industries 203
Federal Government *see* Commonwealth Government
federalism: federal/state conflict 5–6, 340, 344; political economy of 169–90; new federalism 170, 306; fiscal federalism 170–5, 182, 190; vertical fiscal imbalance 178–80; tied grants 182–4; fiscal equalisation 184–6; and interest groups 199–200; and microeconomic reform 280–1, 283
Federation 5
feminism *see* women's movement
femocrats 356
feudalism 111

Fightback 182
finance and property sector 237, 276, 284
Finance, Department of 184, 190, 226, 241
Financial and Economic Advisory Committee 128, 138
Financial Assistance Grant 181
Firestone, Shulamith 367
fiscal/budgetary policy 9, 120, 121–3, 134–5, 226, 231
fiscal crisis of the state 48–50
flexible accumulation 110
Flinders by-election 153
Ford Australia 205, 237
Ford, Henry 102
Fordism/post-Fordism 101–3, 105–6, 108–13
foreign control/ownership 78–9
foreign debt 90, 156, 212, 234, 236, 239
foreign investment/capital 9, 13, 104, 340
Framework Convention on Climate Change 316
France 62, 114, 255, 262, 265
Frankfurt School 41
Franklin Dam 340, 342
Fraser Government: and wages policies 145, 151, 207, 229; federalism 170, 176; macro-economic policy 228, 229; tariff policy 279; World Heritage listings 339; Franklin Dam 340; and feminism 357, 361
free market policies *see* economic liberalism
free trade 37
Freeman, Jo 359
French regulation school 101
Friedman, Milton 2, 3

Galbraith, John Kenneth 294, 323
Garnaut Report 235
Garrett, Peter 337
GATT 78, 83, 84; Uruguay Round 86, 87, 88, 234
General Motors 112, 146, 205
George, V. 296
Germany 59, 105, 181, 255

Gerschenkron, Alexander 261, 264
Gilligan, Carol 369
global cities 106, 108, 109
global economy 103, 104, 105, 112, 114; globalisation of Australian economy 12–13, 75–93, 98, 104
global warming 336; *see also* greenhouse effect
Goods and Services Tax (GST) 276, 277, 366
Gordon, Suzanne 367, 368
Gordon-below-Franklin dam 327
Gramsci, A. 41, 45
Grant, Wyn 21
Grants Commission 184, 186, 190
Great Barrier Reef Marine Park Act 1975 339
greenhouse effect 315–17; Australian responses to 317–22
Greenpeace 325, 345
Greiner Government 282, 287
Grimshaw, Patricia 354
Gruen, Fred 76

Habermas, Jurgen 52
Haines, Janine 362, 364
Hall, Peter 123, 124–6, 128
Hamer, Rupert 357
Harrison, Bennet 109
Hartsock, Nancy 371
Harvester judgement 8, 147
Harvey, David 110
Hawke, Bob 154, 169, 209, 231–2, 297
Hawke/Keating Governments: tariff policy 13, 263; wages policies 159, 161, 211; federalism 170, 178, 181, 189; 'corporatist'-style policymaking 197, 202; macroeconomic policy 241; microeconomic reform 272, 275, 284; and the welfare state 306; and feminism 357, 361, 365
Health, Housing and Community Service, Department of 306
heavy engineering industry 284
hegemonic stability theory 83
Higgins, Henry Bournes 142–3, 147
High Court of Australia 4, 175, 180, 189, 327
Hilmer, F. G. 212

Home and Community Care Program 304–6, 307
Housing Industry Association 218, 275
Howard, John 364, 365
Howe, Brian 295, 308
H. R. Nicholls Society 211
Hudson Institute 348
Hughes, Helen 11
Hume, David 38
Hyde, John 328

ideology of consumption 110
immigration 8, 257, 271
imperialism 104
import substitution 230
incomes/wages policy 55, 56, 229
India 85
industrial disputes 156
Industrial Relations Act 1988 159
Industrial Relations Commission 208, 211, 286, 308
industrial restructuring: and globalisation 98, 107; company-led adjustment 99–100, 214, 251–6; state-led adjustment 256–66; tripartite-negotiated adjustment 256–66, 279
industrial tribunals 142–3
Industries Assistance Commission 258, 260, 344, 362
industry assistance *see* tariff protection
Industry Commission 87, 187, 233, 235, 241, 272, 320
industry plans/planning 232, 240
industry self-regulation 58
Industry Statement (1988) 272
Industry, Technology and Regional Development, Department of 240, 241, 347
inflation 120, 154, 158, 231, 234; *see also* stagflation
informational mode of development 106
Institute of Public Affairs 320
Institution of Engineers Australia 322
institutional analysis 16
Insurance Council of Australia 204

interest groups: in classical pluralist theory 26–7; in corporate pluralism theory 29, 55, 56; public choice approach 36–7; functionalist approach 51; parentela pluralism 59; pluralistic stagnation 195–7
interest rates 226, 231, 234
Intergovernmental Agreement on the Environment 322, 344
Intergovernmental Panel on Climate Change 316
Interstate Commission 276
investment 274, 237–8
Iron and Steel Industry Association 203

Japan: as a 'small' welfare state 20; as a 'strong state' 60, 62, 63, 255, 262, 265; and protectionism 67, 78, 80, 250; and unfair trade practices 84, 85, 86, and APEC 89; size of the public sector 294
Jay, W. R. C. 184
Jessop, Bob 54, 62
Jobsback policy 218
Jordan, Grant 29

Kakadu 338, 339, 341
Karmel, Peter 1
Katherine Gorge 338
Katzenstein, Peter 9
Keating, Paul 13, 14, 115, 272; *see also* Hawke–Keating Governments
Kelly, Ros 345
Kelty, Bill 159
Kerin, John 344
Keynesian theories/policy: and macroeconomics 15, 38, 41, 282; and protectionism 19, 102, 119; and employment 123; 'bastard' Keynesianism 228
Kirby, Sir Richard 148
Kitay, Jim 161
Korea 76, 85, 89
Krasner, Stephen 61, 254
Kuhnian analysis 123
Kuttner, Robert 114, 115

Labor governments: welfare policy 9, 306; and the Accord 15; and corporatism 55; foreign economic policy since 1983 77, 87–9; and business interests 201–2, 232, 362, 363; use of economic indicators 239; and economic liberalism 19, 249; and the media 242; and trade 273; and microeconomic reform 276, 286, 310; and the Franklin Dam 340–2

labour market policies: training levy 273; Jobs, Education and Training 296; family income supplement 298–9; Job Search allowance 299, 301, 307; Newstart allowance 300, 307; childcare 302; Superannuation Guarantee Charge 303

labour market segmentation of 109, 110; sweated labour 110

labour movement/reformism 41; *see also* trade unions

laissez-faire 7, 10, 39, 52, 257

Lancaster 100

Landcare 347

Latham, Earl 322

Liberal Party 275, 276, 279, 366; Country Party coalition 138, 202

Lindblom, Charles 26, 27, 31, 41, 322

Lipietz, Alain 102, 111, 114

Loan Council 131, 170, 174, 187, 190

logging 341

London 105, 108, 110, 130

London Economics 320

Lord Howe Island Group 339

Los Angeles 108

Lowe, Brian 306

Lukes, Stephen 28

Maddern, Justice Barry 160

Manufacturing Industry, Department of 279

manufacturing industry: in the 1970s and 1980s, 33, 75–93, 271; exports 75; pre 1970s 78; elaborately transformed manufactures 80, 81; restructuring of 99, 275, 284; 'deindustrialisation' 104; and tariffs 240, 274; and state power 250ff; industry policy 272

Marsh, David 18
Martin Committee 235
Marxist theories: of state 6–7, 41–53; revisions 53–5
mass production 105
McColl Royal Commission 276
McEwen, Sir John 229, 257, 263
McKinnon, Catherine 367, 372
McKinsey & Co. 212
McLaughlin, Peter 336
McQueen, Humphrey 104
Medibank/Medicare 174, 355
Melbourne 109
Menzies–McEwen Governments 78, 138, 228, 263, 327
mercantilism (new) in the US 82–6
Mercer, D. 326
Metal Trades case (1967) 147–9, 153
Metal Trades Industry Association 157, 198, 202–4, 206, 208, 215
Metal Trades Margins case (1963) 149
Mexico 86
microeconomics: reform 6, 11, 14, 263, 210; and federalism 6, 177, 189, 226; public interest variable 274; private interest variable 275; partisan coalition element 280, 284–5; microeconomic incrementalism 284
Milbrath, Lester 329
Miliband, Ralph 42–4
Mills, C. Wright 64
Mills, R. C. 128, 137
MIM 205
mining and resources boom (early 1980s) 152
mining sector 237, 341
Mitchell, D. 310
Mitchell, Juliet 367
Mitchell, Timothy 62
Mitsubishi 205
mixed scanning, as decision-making 322
Mobil 205
monetary policy 9, 120, 231, 233
Moore, Sir John 146
Moran, Alan 321
most favoured nation policy 86
multiskilling 100
Murdoch press 321
Musgrave, R. A. 180

National Australia Bank 205
National Debt Summit 206
National Economic Summit 154, 204, 208
National Environment Protection Agency 344
National Farmers' Federation 197, 202, 204, 205–6, 212, 278, 285
National Greenhouse Response Strategy 319, 321
National Greenhouse Steering Committee 321
National Grid Management Council 189
National Housing Survey 307
National Mutual 205
National Rail Corporation 188
National Road Transport Commission 188
national wage cases: of 1983, 144; of 1974 150, 210
nationalism 104, 114
new international division of labour 83, 105
new left poltical movements 294
New Right 37, 204, 209, 211–12, 214, 364, 370; *see also* economic liberalism
New South Wales Bar Association 280
New South Wales Chamber of Manufactures 205
New South Wales Liberal Government 280, 282
New York 105, 108, 110
New Zealand 20, 90, 216, 281, 310
Newton, Max 1
Niemeyer, Sir Otto 130
Nissan 205
Nordlinger, Eric 259
North American Free Trade Agreement 86
North Broken Hill 205
North West Shelf project 327
Norway 9

O'Connor, James 48–50
OECD 9, 75, 80, 93
Offe, Claus 6–7, 18, 50–3, 198
Office for the Status of Women 357, 362

oil industry 75, 85, 146
oligopoly 2
Olson, Mancur 36, 37, 196
One Nation 91, 159–60, 239
OPEC 75
Optus 283
OTC 205

Pacific Dunlop 205
Papadakis, Elim 309
Papua New Guinea 80
Parbo, Sir Arvi 237
partisan mutual adjustment 27, 266
Phonogram Officers case (1982) 146
Pitchford, John 90–1
Plowman, David 201, 214
pluralism 27–33, 58
Polanyi, Karl 8
policy communities 29–31, 59
policy networks 58–60
political business cycle 35
political power, forms of 28, 32
Poor Law Report (1834) 296
Porter, Michael 78
Poulantzas, Nicos 42, 44–6, 53
premiers' conferences 169, 177, 186, 188, 190, 234
pressure groups *see* interest groups
price and wages controls 120
Prime Minister and Cabinet, Department of 241
Pringle, Rosemary 367
private interest government 4
privatisation 36, 282–3; in UK 48; and State Governments 283
productivity and profitability 146
protectionism 8–9, 16, 76–93, 241, 250, 257, 269; reduction of 13, 37; in the 1960s 60; post-Cold War 67; agricultural 76, 77; in US 82–6; in Japan 85, 250–1; in Korea 85; protectionist consensus 229
Public Service Reform Act 1984 355
public administration theory 40
public choice theory 26, 33–40
public–private boundaries 4, 55, 62
public sector employment 294
public sector outlays 294
Pusey, Michael 7, 10, 11, 261, 328

Qantas 205
Queensland 154, 319, 324
Quintex 274

Rattigan, Alf 263
Reagan, Ronald 99, 103
recession 234, 236
Reddaway, W. B. 129
regime of accumulation 102
Reich, Robert 107, 112, 114
Reid, Elizabeth 357
Rennison Goldfields 205
rent seeking 36
reproductive rights 354
Reserve Bank 131, 241
Resource Assessment Commission 343–4
resource security legislation 347
Richardson, J. J. 29
Richardson, Senator Graham 318, 342
Right to Life 325
Rose, Richard 31
Rowley, Charles 34
Ryan, Lyndall 359
Ryan, Penny 357
Ryan, Susan 354, 363, 364

Santos 205
Sassen, Saskia 105, 106–7, 108, 109, 110
Saudi Arabia 85
Savage, Elizabeth 362
Sawer, Marian 358
Schedvin, Boris 133, 134, 138
Schmitter, P. C. 58
Schultz, Julianne 99, 100
Schumpeter, Joseph 64
Scott, M. 101
Scullin Government 133
Seamen's Union 280
service sector 12, 100, 105, 109
Sex Discrimination Act 1984 355
Shell Australia 205, 327
sickness benefits 295, 300
Simon-style rationalism 272, 281, 288
Sinclair, Ian 364
Singer, Max 348
Singleton, Gwynneth 207
Singleton, John 364

Skidelsky, Robert 127
Skocpol, Theda 61–2
Smith, Adam 2, 38
Smith, Joan 371
Social Security Review (1986–89) 296, 306, 307
Social Security, Department of 297–8, 299, 308
socialisation of investment 120
sole parent pensions 297, 300, 308
Soviet Union 169
stagflation 195
State Governments 131, 132, 138, 174, 185–6, 188, 240; and microeconomic reform 272; and privatisation 283
state, the: historical dimensions 2; restructuring of 2; definitions 3–4; liberal democratic states 4; judicial apparatus 4; state and government 4; fragmentation 5; conflicts between States and Commonwealth 5–6; Marxist analysis 6; Britain 7; the US 7; Australia 8; statist development 10; interventionism 10–11, 19, 25, 39, 51, 67; autonomy 17, 45, 227; declining role 19–21; anti-statism 20; growth 20; partisan state-led adjustment 21; statist traditions 21; liberal theories 26; as active and independent 28; as multiple constitutent groups 29; 'weak' states 58, 62, 226; 'strong' states 62, 63, 226; coalition model 63; nation state 115; state capacity 226–7; influence on economy 227; and war 228; protective state 228; agencies 240, 241; intrusiveness 253; statist–laissez-faire amalgam 262; and women's movement 359–63
state-centred theory 26, 60–3, 124, 226, 254
steel industry 100, 284
Steel Plan, the 284
stock market crash (1987) 231
strategic managerialism 214
Streeck, Wolfgang 29, 58, 59, 209

structural efficiency principle 156–60
superannuation 156, 158, 159, 160, 210, 306
Superannuation Guarantee Charge 303
Suzuki, David 336, 337, 349
Sweden 9, 105, 123, 294
Switzerland 9, 294
Sydney 108, 109

TAFE 178
Tariff Board 77, 131, 200, 258, 260, 263
tariffs: Queensland 6; Western Australia 6; South Australia 6; Victoria 6; New South Wales 200; the Brigden Report (1929) 9, 11; effects of business 16–17, 114, 200; anti-protectionism 263; in car industry 237, 241, 284; in manufacturing industry 240, 272, 274, 278; in agricultural industry 285; of sugar 285, 286; *see also* tariff reductions
tariff reductions 236, 241, 273, 286; by Whitlam Government 13; by Hawke–Keating Governments 13–14, 235; 25% cut 229
Tasman Institute 320
Tasmania 324
taxation 38, 39; uniform taxation agreement (1942) 127, 178, 180, 207, 364
Taylorism 101–3
technoglobalism 92–3
technology transfer 79, 83
Telecom 205
telecommunication sector 92, 283
textiles, clothing and footwear industries 78, 79, 89
Thatcher Government 33, 35, 99, 103, 263, 361
Theodore, E. G. 133
Third World 99, 110
Titmus, Richard 293
Tobacco Growers Council 206
Tokyo 105, 112
Toohey, Brian 304

Toronto greenhouse conference (1988) 315
total wage, the 147
tourism 12
Toyota 205, 286
trade: in commodities 11–12; liberalisation 13; Australia's declining terms of 12, 75–7, 156, 212, 242–3, 270; blocs 67, 81, 86; competition 67; new trade theory 84; unfair practices 84; managed 115; post-war protectionism 257–8; strategic trade theory 273; Labor policy 273
Trade Practices Act 211
trade unions 103; strength of 111, 197, 201, 282; 'strategic unionism' 214; and enterprise bargaining 214–15
Training Guarantee Levy 210
transnational corporations 78–80, 83, 92, 104
Transport and Communications, Department of 241
Transport Ministerial Council 188
transport workers 152
Treasury 1, 121, 122, 131, 132, 133, 174, 186, 190, 226, 231, 233, 234, 235, 240, 241, 260
Treaty for the Regulation of Ozone Depleting Substances 328
Truman, David 29
TTNT 209
Turkey 294

unemployment: and state's role 121, 230, 234, 239; Keynesian theory of 123, 126; and wages policy 150, 153, 154, 158; and the superannuation guarantee levy 160; and the Accords 232; benefits 295, 299
United Australia Party 138
United Nations 339
United States: business–state relations 4, 32, 261; pork barrel public policy approach 39; fiscal policy 48; as a 'weak' state 62, 254, 262; democracy in 64; trade policy in 67, 85, 86, 354; dominant world

economy 83; industry policies 252; environmental policy 348
United States trade policy 67, 85, 86, 354
Useem, Michael 198
user pays principle 38

Vernon Committee 12
Vernon, James 12
Veterans Affairs, Department of 308
Vogel, David 31, 32, 33, 47
voluntary export restraints 85

wage-fixing policy: national wage cases 145; over-award payments 147–8; community standard 153, 309; cost of living adjustments 153; wages and incomes policy 154; superannuation–wages–tax trade-off 156; enterprise bargaining 156, 158–9, 208; structural effecency principle 156–60; under Accord 207; second-tier increases 208
wage indexation 150–4, 156, 207
wage reduction/restraint 152, 207, 216
Walker, K. J. 323, 325
Walker, Ronald 128
Walters, Shirley 362
waterfront reform 280, 281
Waterside Workers' Federation 280
Weberian analysis 48, 53, 64
welfare state/welfare policy: in late nineteenth-century Australia 8; as 'social protection' 9, 257; 'welfare efficiency' strategies 15, 39, 274; and fraud 297; social expenditures and fiscal pressures 48–9, 293; Marxist and liberal theories of 50; welfare dependants 52–3; and Fordism 115; 'wage-earners welfare state' 271, 294, 309; the poor in Britain 292; demands on 293; welfare rights of minority groups 294; restructuring policy 298–311
Wesley Vale 341
Westminster systems of government 3, 4, 260
Westpac Bank 205, 208
Wheelwright, Ted 104
White Paper (1945) 121, 126, 127

White Australia policy 8
White, Bob 208
Whitlam Government: and 25 per cent tariff cut 13, 229; 'buying back the farm' 104; and 1974 national wage case 150; and fiscal federalism 170, 174; and regional policy 176; and business 202; and public sector reform 282; and universal welfare policy 307; and women's policy 355, 357, 361
Wiesenthal, H. 198
Wilderness Society 345
Wilson, Elizabeth 358
Wilson, Roland 128
Winkler, J. T. 56
Wollongong 100
Women's Bureau 363
Women's Electoral Lobby 357, 362
Women's Health, Information, Resources and Crisis Centres Association 360
Women's Information and Referral Exchange 355
women's health and refuge groups 311, 360
women's movement 354, 356, 359, 370
Women's Health Network 360
Woodhead, W. R. 339
Woods, Wendy 364
Woodside Petroleum 205
Wool Council of Australia 285
World War II 9, 102, 105, 121, 126, 132, 135, 137, 150
workforce flexibility 100
work value determinations 149, 152, 153
working class 8, 17, 49, 50, 53
World Heritage List 339
World Heritage Properties Conservation Act 1983 340
World-Wide Fund for Nature 321, 345, 349
Wran Government 324

Yeatman, Anna 357, 367
Young, Iris 369
Yugoslavia 169

Zysman, John 251